CAREERS IN ART

AN ILLUSTRATED GUIDE

CAREERS IN ART

AN ILLUSTRATED GUIDE

Gerald F. Brommer
Joseph A. Gatto

Davis Publications, Inc.
Worcester, Massachusetts

Copyright 1984
Davis Publications, Inc.
Worcester, Massachusetts U.S.A.

Printed in the United States of
America

Library of Congress Catalog Card
Number: 83-73179

ISBN: 0-87192-149-9

Graphic Design:
Penny Darras-Maxwell

10   9   8   7   6   5   4   3   2

Preface

The reasons for publishing a book on art careers are many and varied. Basically young people should realize the tremendous importance of art in the twentieth Century, and the broad range of career opportunities available to them. Most people have little idea of the number and scope of art-related careers that are developing around us.

I was recently taken on a tour of part of the Lawrence Livermore Laboratories in California, where engineers and scientists are studying nuclear energy and lasers. When I commented on the excellent graphics and display techniques found in many public areas, I was prompted to ask how many career artists worked in this science-oriented facility. I was overwhelmed by the answer! Over one hundred twenty-five artists of various types are fully employed at Lawrence Livermore. Most of them are graphic designers who visualize and transfer to paper the complex findings of researchers.

Such statistics should be shared with students, teachers, parents and guidance counselors! If art career opportunities are available, how should students prepare for them? What courses should they take? Where should they go to college and how can they get more information? What kinds of people are best suited for these careers?

Most art training in schools seems directed toward fine arts careers. Actually, fine art is only an infinitesimally small part of the total art picture. Art is also design, architecture, landscaping, theater, librarianship, publishing, writing, fashion, illustration, television, film, teaching, research, development and furniture building.

Hundreds of careers require people trained in art and knowledgeable about other areas as well. American art classes are full of such people and we want them to know about stimulating, fulfilling careers that will satisfy their interest in art.

The charts in the back of the book list hundreds of colleges that offer courses which prepare college students for careers in art. Clearly, these schools will graduate huge numbers of artists and craftspeople every year, all looking for career starts in an already saturated job market. These circumstances are no different from those in any other field of work. It is wrong to think that all you need is talent, and the jobs are yours! But it is also wrong to think that because the competition is so great, you should forget about art careers completely. If art is important to you, look through this book. Learn what careers are available and what is happening in the working world of art.

To those who think the arts may lose their importance in a society preoccupied with technological advancement, this book offers reassurance. No matter how technocratic America becomes, its citizens will always need the personal touch of fine art in impersonal surroundings. Business and industry, education, religion, entertainment and science need artists to design marketable products and attractive, functional buildings, to illustrate ideas and teach new techniques. The pattern of growth in art career opportunities will parallel the growth of technology, and there is little doubt that the number of art-related careers, rather than decreasing, will increase in the next decade.

Naturally, an education in art does more than improve your chances of getting a job. An art education is valuable for its own sake. It broadens your cultural horizons, changes the way you look at the world. But those who wish to pursue a career in the arts will probably have to heed the advice of Ralph Putzker of the Art Department at San Francisco State University. "Be prepared for any evantuality," he says, "and be prepared to change your mind. Stay loose. Stay unstuck!"

G.F.B.

How To Use The Book

This book provides important information for anyone interested in an art career. The table of contents lists the careers that are treated in detail; more are summarized briefly at the end of each section. Check the detailed index for a complete listing of all the careers to be found in the book.

Each section includes information on the career area, what typical jobs are like, what personal qualities are necessary for success in the career, what alternate careers may be of interest, what steps toward your career goal can be taken while you are still in high school, and which colleges offer necessary programs. Armed with such information, students should find it easier to decide on suitable career areas.

Special sections titled "Art Career Profiles" are interspersed throughout the book. These describe the activities of typical artists and examine projects and cooperative programs in various career areas. They help to explain selected careers in personal, specific terms.

The illustrations provide a glimpse into the studios of artists at work. They allow you into the environments of many of America's top creative artists.

The book is written for several audiences. *Students* will find information on how to prepare themselves for college and careers, and will be exposed to hundreds of career choices. They will find names and addresses of colleges to attend and places to write for more detailed information.

Teachers will find sources of career information. Career descriptions will help them advise their students, and will provide some insights into possible course additions which would prepare students for college and careers.

Curriculum specialists will learn the requirements students need to fulfill for college and careers. This information may help them set curriculum goals for their departments, and decide upon possible course additions.

Guidance counselors will find an assortment of art careers, and a list of schools from which to obtain catalogs and course information. Suggestions as to the personal qualities necessary for success in certain career areas are also included.

Parents will find hundreds of careers listed which will help them help their children make informed career decisions. They can learn about various kinds of art careers, can see artists in action and can note what types of environments their children might encounter as artists.

Anyone using this book will find the last section, "Additional Information and Resources," extremely helpful. Not only does it list a number of books that provide detailed information about specific careers, but it also gives students and professionals addresses to write to, names of magazines of interest to artists and craftspeople and an exhaustive profile of American and Canadian college art programs.

Contents

Sculptor Claes Oldenberg combines fine and commercial art by using a utilitarian product (an electrical plug) as the subject of a work of fine art (sculpture). *Giant Three Way Plug* is of corten steel and bronze. Photograph: Roxanne Everett

THIS IS AN exciting time to pursue a visual art career. The jobs available are diverse, and artists now receive more recognition for their efforts than ever before. Department stores, grocery stores, buses, theaters, airports and highways need artists. Advertising, packaging, printing and industrial design careers are opening up. Schools at all levels need art teachers to motivate and prepare the next generation of artists. Practically every business, industry and school in the world requires the skill and imagination of an artist, and artists can justly consider themselves part of a profession that has served humankind for its entire existence.

The history of the visual arts is the history of creative men and women whose careers were spent creating visual images and designing products to enrich people's lives. Such noble goals are idealistic and theoretical. In the twentieth century, the practical application of such idealism can be found in the hundreds of art-related careers described on the following pages.

Art is not only to be found in galleries and museums, but on the shelves of stores and on television screens around the world. Art no longer emerges from cloistered painting and sculpture studios, but bursts from manufacturing companies, film studios and industrial complexes, corporations and computers. It is not only produced by painters, printmakers and sculptors, but by talented industrial designers, color consultants, fashion experts, photographers, computer programmers and craftspeople of all types.

Although the number of art career opportunities seems tremendous, there are thousands of art majors graduating every year from colleges and art schools, and the competition for available jobs is very keen. Career openings in your specialized area of interest may not be readily available. Many artists begin their careers by combining jobs or working at art jobs on a free-lance or part-time basis.

Carrying a portfolio from one possible employer to another can often be very discouraging. But perseverance often pays off, and the element of chance can put you in the right place at the right time. If your future career in art matters to you, then the "hustle," preparation and positive attitude that is necessary will be well worth the effort.

This chair, designed by Charles Gibilterra, was built according to his specifications in a manufacturer's shop. The designer has created a chair that is both attractive and functional. This design is a commercial art product. Photograph: Richard di Liberto

Fine Art/Commercial Art

Fifty years ago, artists were often imagined to be poverty-stricken, radical thinkers who lived in Bohemian disarray. Parents were extremely reluctant to allow their sons or daughters to take up artistic careers. Art as a hobby was fine, but as a career? Never!

Today, creative visual artists are among the most respected professionals in business, industry and culture. Career artists help set standards of taste, shape the look and design of the world and make a living doing it.

Fine art includes painting, sculpture, printmaking and some of the more sophisticated crafts. Most fine artists create for aesthetic reasons: as social comment, for decoration, to enhance lives and environments. Their art is an expression of their personal feelings about a subject or idea.

Commercial art is generally created by artists at the direction of others: supervisors, art directors and the like. Commercial artists might work for a television station, an advertising design studio, a toy manufacturer. Commercial artists may have skills, knowledge and training identical to that of fine artists, but their methods of earning a living are different. Commercial artists receive a salary for their work and creative ideas. Fine artists usually work on their own time and try to sell their work through galleries or agents. Both ways of making a living contribute to the development of contemporary art. Both fine and commercial artists make definite and positive contributions to society.

Art as a career has been maligned in the past, but today talent and creativity are recognized as abilities that meet special and specific needs in our society. Fine automobile design is as necessary as fine sculpture. Excellence in interior design improves the environment as much as does beautiful painting. Fine and commercial artists work together in many ways, and their talents are needed in an ever-expanding, technical world that requires artistic work of all types.

Because the skills involved are similar, many fine artists do some commercial designing, and commercial artists often produce paintings and prints on their own time.

Some commercial artists free-lance their talent: they are self-employed and do not have permanent contracts with their clients. They work in their own studios or homes and prepare art work of various types for their clients. They are not salaried, but are paid separately for each job. Other commercial artists work for studios or advertising agencies which do work for several clients or corporations, and still others work within a single corporate structure, designing for their company employer.

A painting such as *Christina's World* is the personal expression of the artist, Andrew Wyeth. Although he sold the work, that was not the motivating force that caused him to paint it. Such painting activity is considered fine art. Collection, The Museum of Modern Art, New York. Tempera on gesso panel, 32 1/4" × 47 3/4", 1948. Purchase.

Personal Traits Important to Career Artists

There are very few young people who know what careers they want to pursue. A student should never close doors that might lead to something significant, but if she or he has good grades in art and a sustained interest in art-related extracurricular activities, a career in art might be worth considering.

Contrary to popular belief, artists do not have terrible temperaments. They do not necessarily spend their lives dreaming, starving or fighting for causes. Art students who ask themselves the following questions about their personalities may discover how suited they are to a career in the arts.

SELF-DISCIPLINE: Can you meet deadlines? Can you set your own goals and achieve them satisfactorily? Can you motivate yourself to work even when you do not really want to?

SEEING: Are you aware of both good and poor design in the objects around you? Does bad design infuriate you? Are you aware of changes in the light during the day? Are you excited by certain colors or shapes, or combinations of art elements? Are you constantly trying to get your friends to see all the things that they seem to be missing?

WORKING: Do you like to work with your hands? Are you always trying to rebuild something to make it work better or look better? Can you work at a project for a long time without tiring of it? Do you think about your art work even while you are not working on it? Are you willing to tear up unsatisfactory work and start over again?

CREATIVITY: Do you come up with new ideas in other areas besides art? Are you looking for refreshing experiences? Can you appreciate art work that is not familiar to you, or that you may not like at first glance? Do you like to experiment with new materials or techniques in your art classes? Are you always looking for new and better ways to express yourself?

WORKING WITH OTHERS: Can you accept criticism of your work, and learn from it? Do you enjoy talking about your own work and that of others? Can you work with others on group projects and benefit from this co-operative effort? Can you praise the work of others as well as criticize it? Do you enjoy other people?

Answering such questions can help students understand themselves a little better. The questions are not a test; the answers need not all be affirmative. Answering them simply helps students assess their art career potential.

High School Classes in Preparation For an Art Career

The number of art classes available to high school students usually depends on the size of the school. Small schools may have only one art teacher; larger schools may have several. Some large city school systems include a school that specializes in the fine arts, providing a curriculum as rich as that of many colleges.

To make the most of their time in high school, serious art students should keep a few basic principles and priorities in mind.

Drawing instruction is absolutely basic and essential. Drawing skill is a prerequisite for further art courses, for entry into art school and for careers in art. An artist who cannot draw is about as useful as an author who cannot read or write.

Painting is second most important. Information about value, color, texture and composition should be included in any painting course. Careers in illustration, graphic design and other areas of visual communication require painting experience.

Sculpture, often called three-dimensional design, teaches artists to use a variety of techniques and materials to develop forms in space. Architects, model builders and industrial designers especially need this type of background.

Art history gives artists a sense of the tradition of which they are a part. Art appreciation classes can inspire and motivate art students.

These four basic areas provide a firm foundation on which to build a career in the arts. Some schools may offer specialized courses in industrial and graphic design, fabric design, printmaking, magazine illustration, photography, ceramics and the like. Students should not feel they have to specialize immediately, however. It is best to try many different courses outside the basic four, and gradually narrow the scope of interest.

Young artists often resent being required to take subjects other than art, and wish to schedule as many art classes as possible. They should remember, however, that art schools and colleges require a certain number of academic credits for admission. Experience in many subjects makes an artist a more complete human being, and the best career opportunities usually open up to artists with broad, general backgrounds and a variety of interests.

Extracurricular school activities can also add valuable experience, knowledge and skills to a young artist's background. Working on a yearbook, magazine or newspaper will hone a student's artistic skills; helping with the design and construction of stage sets, posters and banners give the future career artist a chance to work on practical problems.

Serious art students should be involved in as many art activities as possible. They should investigate the possibility of taking advanced classes at local colleges and universities, and should talk with art teachers and guidance counselors about their interests and goals.

The Portfolio: A Visual Record of Your Abilities

When you apply to an art school or college, the people in charge need several documents: a record of your grades and activities while in high school, several letters of recommendation from your art teachers, from the guidance counselor and from respected people in your community, and your portfolio.

A portfolio is a continuing record of your artistic development. If you are considering a career in art, you will probably work on two or three portfolios in the next ten years, updating them as your style and techniques change. You will use your first portfolio, filled with examples of your best work, when you apply to art schools; you'll need others when you look for your first job or investigate new career opportunities. Whether or not the art school you apply to requires a portfolio from you, it is a good idea to have one, and keep it up to date. Think of it as a way to chart your progress as an artist. Although you may not need a portfolio now, it is never too early to learn how to assess and arrange your work.

Remember that your portfolio reveals your artistic abilities. Consider the following recommendations when you put together your first one.

Show a variety of work. Include drawings, paintings, some graphic designs if you have them, examples of printmaking, photographs of sculpture and other three-dimensional projects and selections from your sketchbook. Emphasize your strongest area or the area that most attracts you. Demonstrate your interest in many different techniques and media.

Admissions officers want to see how good you are at what you do, how creative and innovative your ideas are. The care you take in your work and your pride in what you do are revealed in the way you present your materials. Show only your best work in each area, and be sure it demonstrates your efficient completion of a number of different tasks.

At this stage you are not expected to be proficient in every technique, but you should show competence in many, and your art teacher may help you select your best examples. Admissions personnel look most carefully at your drawing ability (pencil, charcoal, pen and ink and wash drawings), but they also note your ability to work with composition and color in your painting examples (watercolor, acrylics, tempera). Three-dimensional works, mural designs, oil or acrylic paintings and ceramics can be included as slides or photographs if they are too large or awkward to transport. Prints (woodcuts, serigraphs, intaglios, collagraphs) and graphic design pro-

Senior students from Southern California show their portfolios to admissions counselors from various art schools in the area. Portfolio Day at Otis Art Institute of the Parsons School of Design in Los Angeles brings large numbers of talented art students together to work with college representatives. Photograph: Joseph Gatto

jects are also suitable. Sketches, neatly mounted, or a sketchbook will reveal how you solve visual problems. Do not include copies of famous art and omit class projects which are trite and overdone.

Your portfolio should contain a good cross section of your ideas and work, but there is no magic number of works that will impress college officials or that will guarantee you a place in art school. Portfolios usually contain from ten to thirty pieces. Select only your best examples, and do not try to impress people with quantity. Admissions personnel are busy and will resent going through endless repetitious examples. Also, do not show off by presenting work you think you will be able to do someday. Show the best you are able to do *now*!

Package your portfolio in something substantial and easy to open. The large black folders that tie at the top and sides are appropriate; envelope-style containers or canvas carriers work well too. Use a zippered case if you like, or make your own from fiberboard or heavy cardboard. Whatever type you use, be sure your portfolio is neat inside and outside, and keeps work from falling out. Use a size appropriate to the work you are presenting.

Assemble your work neatly. Mount smaller items on boards of similar size. Photographs should be mounted on boards or presented in a notebook. Drawings and paintings should be matted. Your art teacher can help you prepare such materials. Be sure your mats are clean, square and crisp. Do not use fancy or colored mats, unconventional layouts, fancy folds or other gimmicks.

Admissions personnel are impressed only by the quality of your work. Present it simply; it will speak for itself.

Before submitting your selections, stand them around your room or the art room at school and make sure each is neat, substantially mounted and labeled with your name and address. Your portfolio should also have your name, address and zip code lettered clearly on it. Have your art teacher, guidance counselor, parents or friends look it over to see what kind of impression the total package makes.

If you wish to explain your graphic design projects with a written statement, or if you are asked to include written statements with your portfolio, be sure to check your grammar, spelling and punctuation—and be brief. Simple errors can make you appear careless; have an English teacher check your writing for you. You should also include a neatly typed résumé.

If a portfolio must be mailed to an admissions department, it should be self-explanatory, because you will not be present to answer questions about the work. Inside the front cover, tape an inventory list, numbering and briefly describing each piece. Place all drawings together, and group other items in logical categories such as painting, illustration, design projects, and so on. A cardboard container for shipping the portfolio can be purchased from moving companies or shippers, or you can make one yourself. Be sure that corrugated cardboard is at least doubled for sufficient protection.

If you send portfolio applications to several schools,

you may wish to do so by using a slide presentation. Be sure to use a good 35mm camera and the correct film. If shooting outdoors, use daylight film; if indoors, a tungsten film. Never use flash because colors will not remain true. If you have doubts, check on film and lighting with someone at your local camera shop. Shoot until you are satisfied with the slides. Unsatisfactory slide color and presentation can ruin your chances of acceptance. If you are not experienced at taking such photographs, ask your local camera shop owner for help in finding someone who could take them for you. Check with your high school photography teacher or ask a college photography major or college newspaper photographer to help for a reasonable price.

Every year, the National Association of Schools of Art sponsors *Education and Careers in the Arts and Portfolio Day* at a central location. Representatives from many art schools attend to talk to prospective students and review their work. Check with the schools you are interested in to see if they participate in such programs. If they do, your single, well-prepared portfolio can be seen by several admissions officers in a single day. (See addresses for NASA schools in the chart at the back of the book or write to NASA directly—see address in listing of helpful addresses.) Other schools may offer similar opportunities.

Your portfolio is the single most important indication of your artistic abilities. Admissions officers will give it the most weight when considering your application. Present yourself and your work in the best possible light. Start early. Take your time. Make it as outstanding as you possibly can.

High School Work Experience

You can help prepare yourself for an art career by working part-time or during the summer while you are in high school. Any work experience is valuable; jobs that broaden your background in art are a positive step toward your career.

Help local theater groups design, produce and paint sets and background scenery. A store may let you paint signs or make posters. Some commercial design studios hire young people to run errands and do clean-up work. Newspapers can often use paste-up artists. Expand your knowledge of publications by working on school newspaper and yearbook production. Help in the developing and printing rooms of photography labs.

Schools, churches and park recreation departments often conduct summer programs for children, and require help with their art projects. If you or your parents have friends in art-related businesses, they may be able to help you get work there or your art teacher may help.

Regardless of the type of work you do in such jobs, it is important to keep your eyes and ears open and learn as much as possible. What you learn will help you develop your own career, and determine the direction you wish to pursue. In art-related work, the experience you gain is often more valuable than the money you earn.

The competition for such jobs may be considerable, however. Remember that if you must seek other types of work, unrelated to art, you may gain valuable knowledge of other fields. If you find yourself in a work situation that you consider less than ideal, try to turn the work to your own artistic advantage. Use your imagination. You may find that you've gotten more out of your job than you ever expected to.

Choosing a College Or Art School

Art schools provide the maximum amount of art teaching in a minimum amount of time because the student concentrates primarily on art. In three years of study, for example, a student could obtain 3000 hours of art instruction. The number of years a student spends in art school depends on his or her major field and on the degree of concentration offered by the school.

College and university art departments offer four-year programs for the baccalaureate degree in art subjects. In four years of such a program, however, you may be involved in only 1000 or so class hours of art, because a variety of subjects must be taken to satisfy degree requirements.

Art schools are not for everyone. If you enjoy all of your school subjects and a number of extracurricular activities and sports, you will probably be happiest in the art department of a college or university. If you spend most of your time drawing, painting, working on school publications, designing stage scenery and the like, you are probably a candidate for art school.

Art schools and college art departments are often known for areas in which they have particularly strong programs. It is generally believed that if you are interested in some phase of commercial art you should attend an art school, but if architecture or a career in fine art is your goal, you should attend a college or university. This is a generalization, however, not a universal fact. A look through a school's course listing will give you some indication of its strengths and weaknesses.

What should you look for in an art school or college? Here are a few things to keep in mind:

CURRICULUM: Examine the course offerings of the schools you are considering. Do they offer sufficient courses in your major area of interest, and enough supplemental courses to provide a broad base in other areas? If you have not decided on a major yet, does the school offer a strong fundamental program? Are business courses available to help you develop a successful career? Is a degree offered upon graduation? Is an advanced degree program offered in your area of interest?

LOCATION: Most artists and art activities in the commercial art field are found in large urban complexes, because that is where most of the art jobs are located. If you expect to study under the best practicing commercial artists, you will have to go to them. You will note such concentrations in the charts at the back of the book. Suburban and smaller community schools may lack the most visible of the commercial artists, but some do have outstanding programs and teachers. If an urban setting does not appeal to you, you need not abandon your art career plans. Send for the catalogs of schools that interest you, wherever they are, and read them carefully.

SIZE: Schools that offer a wide range of art experiences and have faculties large enough to provide multiple insights into art are considered by many to be the best schools. Generally, the larger the school, the greater the variety of professional teaching. However, larger schools can prove intimidating to first-year students and some have inflexible curricula and requirements. Consider your own personality and what you want from a school when you weigh alternatives.

STAFF AND ALUMNI: Are well-known artists on the staff? Have respected artists graduated from the department? Check on how graduates have done in their careers. Each school usually has a list of prominent graduates and the kinds of contributions they have made to society through their work. Check to see if those in your area of interest have been successful. Guidance staff can help with such information.

CAMPUS: If typical campus social life appeals to you, you should probably attend a college or university rather than an art school. Art schools are often located in a downtown area without a campus, and students do not spend as much time socializing. Instead, they usually work late into the night to complete projects for the next day's classes.

ACCREDITATION: Whether a school is accredited or not is up to the administration of each institution and does not necessarily reflect on its excellence. Accredited schools have undergone examinations by their peers and are judged to have excellent curricula, job placement programs, faculties, student bodies, faculty-student ratios and relationships, and administrations. Although your eventual career is not determined by your school's accreditation, but by your ability, grad-

uates of accredited schools are generally considered well-equipped for their chosen careers.

The school you choose can determine the depth of your training and the success of your career. Make your choice with care. Do not hurry. Get as much information as you can, and visit the school if possible. Seek advice from practical commercial artists or your art teachers.

Entering The Job Market

At the moment you may not be seriously concerned about starting your career. It may seem like a distant occurrence. Remember, however, that competition for most art career positions is fierce. It is never to early to learn how to introduce yourself to the art world.

If you intend to make a living producing fine art paintings, sculptures, ceramics, crafts, prints or photographs you will need to contact galleries, agents and other possible outlets for your work. It takes time to establish your name, build up a following of interested buyers and make gallery contacts.

Perhaps your college will have a placement service that will make the intitial contacts for you; you may have friends in the arts who will help make your job-seeking easier. No matter who you are or what position you seek, you and all artists must make contact with studios, schools, galleries, television studios, offices and personnel managers. Here are a few things to think about when you take your initial steps.

INITIAL CONTACT: Phone or write ahead of time to arrange a date and time for a meeting to discuss possible employment, positions or gallery representation.

RÉSUMÉ: This is an essential document for anyone seeking a job. It contains vital information about you, your work and experience, your abilities and interests. Your résumé may be the first glimpse a potential employer or representative has of you; be sure it is neat and well organized. Have it professionally typed or printed and copied on high quality paper. Some things to include are:

NAME: Full name, with no nicknames.

ADDRESS: Full address, zip code, phone number and area code. If you will have a temporary address, include that as well.

BASIC INFORMATION: Keep it short. Summarize your course of study, special areas of interest, what type of work you are looking for.

EDUCATION: List in reverse chronological order the schools you attended and any well-known artists and teachers with whom you may have studied. Include any honors, scholarships, awards or fellowships you were awarded, and extracurricular activities in which you took part. Mention any offices you held in any organizations.

EXPERIENCE: List (also in reverse chronological order) the jobs held during school, summers, nightwork, etc. List your employers' names and addresses. Mention special skills and hobbies that have to do with art. These will help your employer understand your areas of expertise.

PROFESSIONAL ASSOCIATIONS: If you have joined any organizations at the student or professional level, list them.

PERSONAL INFORMATION: Where you were born, and when. Include any other personal information you feel is vital. Be concise, not confessional.

Keep your résumé brief and businesslike. Do not mention your current philosophy of art. Avoid overstatement and melodrama, irrelevant information and intensely personal notes. Be sure all grammar and spelling are correct.

CONTACT LIST: Make a long list of potential employers. Obtain names from your yellow pages, art directors clubs, art magazines and from your friends. Let as many people as possible know you are looking for work; even the most unlikely acquaintances may know of a useful contact.

WAYS TO ARRANGE INTERVIEWS: Arrange your interviews: by phoning to set up a meeting (follow the phone call with a letter to confirm the arrangements); by writing letters to potential employers, asking for an interview (include your résumé with such letters); by checking "help wanted" ads in newspapers and art magazines; or by going to employment agencies to see what is available. Regardless of your approach, your initial and follow-up letters must be well thought out and neatly, correctly presented.

PORTFOLIO: Your teachers and advisors at art school will be able to help you prepare an appropriate portfolio for your job hunting. Emphasize your strongest abilities and demonstrate the breadth of your interest and professional preparation.

INTERVIEW: What has been discussed above prepares you for the most important part of your job search: the interview. When you meet a potential employer, what you say and how you say it will be closely noted. Be on time. Speak clearly and distinctly, and explain your résumé and portfolio briefly and concisely. Stay on the subject. Allow the interviewer to ask questions about yourself and your work. Be businesslike. Make good and efficient use of your time and the interviewer's. Be sure you are dressed properly; leave your jogging shoes at home.

THINGS TO BE READY TO ANSWER: In your interview, especially for your first job, be prepared to answer questions about your grades at art school, your extracurricular interests, other jobs you have had, what type of work you are looking for, what sort of entry level pay scale you are considering, what sort of references you have and other similar topics. Most of these items are included in your résumé, but employers often like to hear you answer in your own words.

Interviews do not usually end with the employer offering a job. It is a good business habit to follow an interview with a letter to all those who have interviewed you, thanking them for their time, their interest in you and their helpful suggestions and advice. Be sure to get names and addresses before you leave their offices.

When intitial job offers arrive, weigh them carefully to see how they fit into your plans and answer your financial needs. Your first job will be your apprenticeship. You will be learning the business, and learning how to get along with other people: your peers, your art director or supervisor, clients and others. Maintain a positive attitude and learn as much as possible. This experience will help you establish a foundation in your art career.

Most commercial artists go through this job-seeking process several times in their careers. Each time your treatment of the items discussed above will become more sophisticated.

Huge structures require fine details on a human scale. The plantings of a landscape architect and the sculpture of Alexander Calder provide human–sized elements that make the Lincoln Center's entrance inviting. Photograph: New York State Department of Commerce

IF PEOPLE TAKE time to look around them, the extraordinary contributions of environmental planners will become apparent. Buildings of all types are planned, designed and built under the direction of architects, and the spaces in and around them are designed, decorated, furnished, planted and paved according to the designs of other artists.

Urban structures begin with the concepts and sketches of architects and the renderings of architectural delineators. These preliminaries are followed by the work of building contractors, engineers, interior designers, space planners, landscape architects, furniture designers, architectural graphics specialists and color consultants.

Large buildings and exotic designs are impressive because of their size and visual impact, but just as important are the fine details of color, texture, materials and lighting that make up the immediate environment. The careers explored in the following pages pertain to that environment.

The architectural firm of Marcel Breuer and Associates employs hundreds of architects, detailers, drafters, designers and engineers when they develop plans for such huge projects as this IBM headquarters building in Boca Raton, Florida. Photograph: Joseph W. Molitor

Architecture

The definition of architecture has not changed much since Roman times, when it was often described as "convenience, strength and beauty." In his book *Form and Structure of Twentieth Century Architecture,* Talbot Faulkner Hamlin describes the elements of architecture as "use, construction, and aesthetic effect." The words have changed but the definitions are synonymous.

Use means the function of the structure. Architects must insure that the building will do what it was designed and built to do. Houses should shelter families. Office buildings must be comfortable, well-organized places to work. Entertainment centers must handle large numbers of people attending presentations of various types. Manufacturing plant design differs from the design of schools or libraries. Successful architecture provides the best possible use of space for those who will use it.

Construction means assembling the physical parts of the building—windows, walls, foundations, ventilation—which are made of concrete, steel, aluminum and glass. The stability and enduring quality of the structure is of paramount importance. "Use" indicates how people occupy a space; "construction" refers to the structure itself, not human occupation of it. These two elements are always planned in harmony, and both are essential to successful architecture.

Aesthetic effect means the ultimate appearance of the building. Will it be pleasing to look at? Will it fit into its surroundings? Will it be desirable in the community? Will it reflect contemporary tastes? Aesthetic concerns should be inseparably tied to use and construction. Ugly buildings may be functional and well built, but they blight the environment they occupy.

Successful architecture is an art. It must be functional, well constructed and beautiful to look at. This triple emphasis makes it a difficult art. Imagination, training and experience are required of any architect. Producing efficient, beautiful architecture is a challenging occupation.

The characteristics of architectural design place a building in a certain time. The mammoth concrete and brick structures of Rome, the cathedrals of thirteenth century Europe, the graceful temples of China and Japan, American Art Nouveau buildings from the turn of this century, the airline terminals, high-rise structures and stadiums of the present all reflect certain needs. Contemporary architecture satisfies demands for fuel efficiency while catering to the current infatuation with new building materials and techniques. Some dramatic designs reflect a company's desire to establish a specific corporate identity. Others are intended to blend gracefully into their surroundings.

Architecture is the finished product, whether a small house or a gigantic high rise. It is not drawings, sketches or ideas, although these help shape the final product. A sculptor's sketch is not a sculpture, nor is a tune in a musician's head a composition. Architecture is the physical culmination of individual or collective ideas, dreams, plans and sketches. Often hundreds of people are involved, and all must have the same goal: to create a beautiful structure that will be a home or workplace, and a building that works!

Architect

The role of architect has changed drastically in the past several decades. The position used to consist of designing buildings and supervising their construction, but due to today's complex technologies, a popular concern with total environment and legal restrictions, architects must be master coordinators as well. Architectural specialization is now the norm: the building of huge structures requires a team of artists, engineers, contractors, manufacturers' representatives and machinery operators. The chief architect must coordinate the contributions of specialists to produce a structure that is no longer the work of a single person.

There are architects who coordinate mammoth projects; some design single family homes, condominiums, schools and churches; others specialize in remodeling existing structures. All these are complicated projects, no matter what their size.

An architect must be a creative artist, a practical scientist and an astute businessperson all at the same time. A specialized education and vast experience are necessary. It all begins in high school—and the process of learning and changing really never ends.

What architects do
The basic job of an architect is to design and construct buildings, but the task is far more complicated than that.

Before the first sketch is made, the architect must interview the client to find out what uses are to be made of the space. The architect estimates costs, establishes budgets and studies local building codes. Then initial ideas can be put on paper. In large projects, an architectural delineator (See next career description) visualizes the concepts of client and architect, and other artists provide sketches of floor plans.

The exterior appearance of the structure—an office building, for example—should reflect the client's ideas and the corporate image as well as conform to community plans. The use of interior space is the heart of an architect's plan, however. Work spaces, traffic flow, stairways, storage, heating and air conditioning, plumbing, lighting and ventilation must be planned in large buildings. For a house, the architect needs to consider similar functions on a more limited scale. The architect must see that space is used efficiently, not wasted.

The architect then must choose the materials to be used, from concrete to doorknobs. The job requires a variety of on-site experiences, a constantly updated knowledge of what new products and materials have been developed, and an insight into what clients expect.

Detailed drawings are prepared to show how the building is put together: what devices are used for mechanical joinings; what welding is necessary; what type of steel is needed and how joints are prepared and joined. Every square foot of the building must be drawn and identified by its dimensions and the materials to be used.

Large architectural firms often undertake the design and construction of entire downtown or suburban areas that may consist of several buildings and the surrounding parking facilities, roads and landscaping. Such a total urban environmental package is called a system, and also involves planning air quality, public transportation, tunnels and accompanying graphic signs and symbols. Many career artists are part of such environmental design teams.

For every large architectural firm specializing in environmental design there are hundreds of smaller offices dealing with houses, stores, churches, apartments, small office buildings, theaters, markets and remodeling. The types of careers available in such smaller offices are similar to those in large firms, but physical size and total budget differ.

The job of architect is constantly changing. As an architect you express your ideas and the ideas of others in a solid structure. When you erect a building, you interweave part of yourself into the fabric of the community.

What qualities are helpful for an architect?
The ability to draw is the prime requisite, and a love of mechanical drawing is a must! An architect must have vision, imagination and the ability to work with materials of various types in constructing models and three-dimensional forms. An enjoyment of mathematics is necessary to a life that is constantly full of dimensions, proportions and figures. Technical abilities are useful, and an analytical mind is an asset.

If you remember details of things you have seen, work well under pressure, enjoy research and can work on complex projects until they are completed, architecture may be in your future. Organization, determination, the ability to work with other people and coordinate their efforts and a sense of design are important to an architect.

What other careers require similar qualities?
Many of the environmental planning careers on the next few pages require the ability to draw, plan, visualize and coordinate the efforts of others. A city planner, landscape architect, space designer, facility planner, architecture teacher and commercial interior designer have such abilities in common.

Careers that involve drafting ability (industrial de-

Architects must carefully check blueprints and drawings to make sure all details are accurate and that builders are following specifications.
Photograph: Joseph Gatto

signer, drafter, model builder, environmental planner) and several areas of industrial design require similar qualities.

The ability to read blueprints and maintain a working knowledge of building materials is also required for estimators—specialists in pricing and delivering specifications for large construction projects.

What can be done now?

As noted above, architects must be able to draw and work with mathematics. Therefore drawing classes and mechanical drawing (drafting) classes are essential for high school students considering a career in architecture. Include as many art classes as your schedule will permit, and be sure to take an art history class.

Geometry, trigonometry and solid geometry are the most pertinent mathematics courses to take. English, physics and chemistry courses will also help you. Take all the history and humanities classes you can, and take French if foreign languages are available. Most older architectural sources are written in French.

Part-time work will help prepare you for a future in architecture. Work in a drafting office or with any industrial, manufacturing or construction firm. Any job related to architecture is a good source of experience. Try plumbing, electrical installation, building materials, real estate or construction work.

Helpful magazines you may wish to borrow from libraries include: *Architectural Record, Progressive Architecture, Architectural Forum, Architectural Digest, Industrial Design, Interiors, Interior Design, Designers West, Better Homes and Gardens, American Home* and *House and Garden*.

Which colleges offer necessary programs?

Most states require architects to be licensed. A license can be obtained when an architect has an earned architectural degree and three years of on-job experience. Most college architecture students enroll in a five year program of study at private or state universities with schools of architecture. Because these schools are generally fully enrolled, you should apply to several. Courses at the college level will begin with freehand drawing, architectural design, drafting, mathematics and general studies. Later courses include principles of design and construction, design projects, blueprints, lettering, study of materials, mechanics, construction costs, writing specifications, urban planning and environmental design.

ART CAREER PROFILE

Architect Lorenzo Tedesco works on drawings of a house. These will be made into blueprints for contractors, builders, plumbers and electricians to use. Photograph: Joseph Gatto

It is difficult to generalize about the architectural profession. Architects practice as individuals, in small firms, or as companies with hundreds of employees. They design structures and public spaces, furniture, graphics and interiors. They research, teach, administer public programs and write environmental legislation.

Lorenzo Tedesco was born in Florence, Italy, and studied drawing and painting as well as architecture. He established his own firm in 1971; prior to that time he worked with various large Los Angeles architectural offices. His 25th Avenue Apartments in Venice, California received the AIA Design Award in 1976.

He enjoys private practice, and works with one or two associates on a variety of projects: small commercial buildings, interior space planning, medical clinics. The bulk of his work has been in housing for the private sector, designing individual houses, apartments and condo-miniums. For Tedesco this has been gratifying because his clients are the users of his structures, and the relationship is very direct and personal. Each client, each project is different. Developing optimum solutions depends on the architect's (and client's) ability to understand and maximize the unique qualities of each site and program. When interviewed, Lorenzo Tedesco had several comments for young people considering architecture as a career. "While going to architecture school at the University of Southern California, I was fortunate in being able to work part-time for Victor Gruen and Associates. As a junior drafter I was working on real projects, which was very important in terms of finding out what the architectural profession was really like. The office was growing rapidly, and the many talented people on staff made it a stimulating and enjoyable place to be.

"After graduation I made a conscious career decision that still seems valid to me: to try to work in small firms where it is possible to be involved in projects from beginning to end.

"The process of designing buildings is lengthy and fairly complex. It often begins with casual conversation and vague objectives, but ultimately proceeds through steps which are all quite critical: development of a precise program, schematic studies of alternate solutions, cost evaluation, design development, working drawings, specifications, contract documents, filing for permits, bidding, negotiating contracts and finally construction supervision. And these are just the major steps in the process.

"In architectural school there is a tendency to focus on theory. Professors become surrogate clients, but their interests are often very different from the concerns of clients in the real world. What you learn in practice is to listen carefully, understand your client's objectives and to work with different kinds of people.

"After being in several small offices and gaining experience on a variety of projects, I was fortunate in joining a strong and growing firm. I was soon able to function as a project architect and eventually carry through some fairly large jobs, with minimal guidance from senior partners. This was probably the best possible preparation for establishing an independent practice.

"The best advice I could offer young students who are interested in architectural careers is to try to develop total technical competence. Doing a job from

Lorenzo Tedesco, Architect

Each architect has a unique style. Lorenzo Tedesco's use of space and materials in this residence gives it a fresh, clean look. Photograph: Rick Strauss.

In this Venice, California apartment building, the architect makes use of a variety of exterior materials and structural shapes to produce a distinctive living environment on a narrow strip of land. Photograph: Richard Fish

beginning to end may not always be the way one would choose to work, but an architect who has those skills has the best chance of survival and success. Well-rounded experience provides aspiring architects the skills to work with and guide other career professionals, and also enhances the possibility of attracting and serving clients.

"Some important changes have occurred in the profession. The need to conserve fuels is having an enormous impact. We are learning to appreciate older buildings, the richness and diversity of cultural heritage. We are also realizing that no society can afford to build everything anew! As the population grows and urban density increases, as new technology provides the means to alter the environment with incredible speed, the need for sound thinking and good design has never been greater. This is why architecture is so fascinating and challenging. The constraints and complexities that make it difficult are precisely the elements that make it exciting."

Architectural Delineator

Among the first members of the architectural team to be called on are the architectural delineators. Delineators put the client's ideas and the architect's practical suggestions into visual form.

A church building committee might need a drawing of the finished structure to help raise money for the project. The board of directors of a corporation may use an architectural delineation to convince stockholders that a new office complex is called for. Tract developers need drawings or paintings of finished houses to give prospective buyers an idea of how their new homes will look.

Making an idea visible is the work of an architectural delineator. It may be a sketched proposal or a tightly-composed rendering that is detailed and accurate. The artist's personal style will often be evident in the finished product.

What architectural delineators do

After listening to the ideas of the client and the architect, and collecting information from other members of the architectural team, the delineator will first make some quick sketches, often with charcoal or pencil. The suggestions of both client and architect will be incorporated in the final painting. The delineator then makes a large painting of the proposed structure or an entire project. This is usually done in transparent watercolor on illustration board.

Depending on the purpose or use of the delineator's work it may be sketchy or realistic. Trees, automobiles and people are added to the drawing to suggest scale and show how the building will look when completed and opened for use. Sometimes surrounding structures are included so that the total environmental effect is evident.

The delineator's job may end when the presentation is accepted and the client and architect are happy with the work. At times, however, the job includes working with printers or billboard companies to make reproductions of the painting for use in brochures, posters or on advertising billboards.

Some architectural delineators are employed full-time by architectural firms with sufficient projects to keep the artists busy. Others work on a free-lance basis, providing paintings for several firms and offices as projects develop and their services are required. Many delineators teach painting in art schools or colleges or hold other art positions—as illustrators, continuity artists for motion picture companies or graphic designers, for example—and free-lance when needed.

It takes long experience to be able to draw buildings so that the construction materials are easily identified.

Bricks, wood, aluminum, glass, stone, slate, concrete and stucco surfaces have characteristic looks that must be recognizable. Interior materials and textures must also be simulated. Knowledge of proper color coordination is essential.

Architectural delineators can often put their own ideas into a presentation, as long as the basic goals of client and architect are met. Their art can cause excitement over a building project even before the foundation is dug.

What qualities are helpful for an architectural delineator?

The ability to draw and paint is essential. Delineators must be able to turn the verbal expressions of others into a drawing or painting. Such a skill requires imagination, careful attention to details and a strong senese of proportion and perspective. A flair for the dramatic often helps the delineator make a strong presentation of an idea. Sometimes accurate detail is required; at other times more informal techniques are called for.

Experience working in watercolor, gouache and acrylics is usually required, although pen and ink and even pencil are sometimes used in finished presentations.

Delineators must be able to work with other people in the early planning of a building, and must subordinate their own ideas to satisfy the clients. They might be asked to do the work several times, until all parties are satisfied with the result. They must meet deadlines, and therefore must be motivated enough to finish the job on time.

What other careers require similar qualities?

The special skill of the architectural delineator is the visual representation of ideas. This ability is also required in careers such as landscape architect, theme park designer, industrial and interior designer, parade float designer, film continuity sketcher, illustrator, set designer, special effects designer, fine arts painter and painting teacher.

What can be done now?

Because drawing, painting and perspective are important in a delineator's job, you should take as many drawing and watercolor classes as possible. Mechanical drawing and drafting would be very helpful, especially in presenting three-dimensional objects. Model building

A realistic presentation of two proposed structures for the city of Houston, shown in their urban setting. Emphasis on detail and superb handling of media are evident in this rendering. Photograph: Houston Chamber of Commerce

and three-dimensional design classes will provide experience in working with structure and form.

Your sketchbooks should include drawings of buildings, building details and interiors. Practice on foliage, trees, grass and a variety of construction materials.

Part-time work or summer jobs that allow you to be directly involved with architectural delineation are almost never available, but any job in an architectural firm would be very useful. Jobs in landscaping or building construction or cleaning would be helpful. Any art-related work would provide equally valuable experiences.

Supplementary watercolor and drawing classes for high school students at art schools and colleges help students develop the ability to make ideas visible and to work confidently in a variety of media.

Helpful magazines to look through include *Architectural Record, Progressive Architecture, Architectural Forum, Interiors, Interior Design* and *Designers West*. Many of these contain excellent examples of the work of architectural delineators.

Which colleges offer necessary programs?

The first architectural delineators (1945) came from motion picture studios and had backgrounds in continuity drawing and set design. They made the drawings from which builders constructed sets and special effects materials. Even today there are no special schools or courses of study for architectural delineation. A general preparation for painting with an emphasis on the urban environment would be helpful. Transparent and opaque watercolor techniques should be stressed as should three-dimensional design, rendering, color and drawing. A class in architectural rendering is essential, if available at your college.

Look for schools with strong architectural programs; they will provide necessary, specific classes in construction language, materials rendering and delineation. Check the chart at the back of the book.

It is not essential to have a strong architectural background to be a delineator, but if you are interested in pursuing it as a career, your early success will be enhanced by such training.

City Planner/Environmental Designer

While architects are involved with the design and construction of houses, megastructures and industrial and commercial complexes or systems, there are architecturally trained people who work on an even larger scale. Nearly every American city has a city planner. Because this job involves buildings and the urban environment, the city planner is usually an architect. The city planner's office, however, contains experts from many other fields: urban geographers, urban environmentalists, demographics experts, drafters, model builders, hydrologists and engineers. Their joint concern is the maintenance and improvement of the urban environment.

Many communities, after years of discussion and compromise, have developed master plans to control and direct the growth and development of the city. The city planner is usually in charge of such programs and is responsible for implementing them. City planners' offices are crowded with blueprints of completed projects and proposals for changes, revisions and additions. Decisions on new streets, street closures and variances, parks, bike paths, new tracts, marinas and harbors are made by city planners. The look and feel of the community is in their hands.

What city planners do

Because city planners work for city governments, they are directly involved with other government agencies and must consult and advise other city officials. They work with their own staffs to monitor the visual appearance of the city and insure the balanced development of commercial, residential, industrial and recreational elements. Although architects and corporations propose the construction of a high rise structure, the city planner decides whether it will enhance the community or be detrimental to it.

Are pocket parks needed? Is vertical space too congested for another high rise? Is traffic flow being considered when new structures are proposed? Are industrial areas encroaching on established residential neighborhoods? Should a stream be developed as a visual attraction or contained in a culvert? Such questions come regularly to the desks of city planners, and their decisions affect the beauty, function and ultimate welfare of the community.

Typical projects for city planners include harbor redevelopment, planning for a municipal sports complex, revitalization of the urban core area, development of shopping malls and planning for industrial parks. Land use and zoning restrictions also come under the city planner's interest and control.

What qualities are helpful for a city planner?

A city planner must be able to work with people at several levels: with other city officials, with architects, individuals and corporations seeking permits to change the city and with members of the staff. The ability to communicate verbally as well as visually is therefore essential.

Architectural training is necessary because the city planner is concerned with the construction of buildings. But he or she must also have knowledge of pollution control, demographics, drainage and community devel-

Before and after photographs of Baltimore's Inner Harbor show the dramatic impact of construction planned and carried out from 1958 to 1982. Long-range city planning keeps all urban elements under control and makes development more aesthetically pleasing. Photograph: M.E. Warren

opment. The interests of residents must be taken into account, and the city's master plan must be followed.

A city planner works behind the scenes and does not often receive credit for how a city looks or how well it functions. He or she must be willing to work hard in such obscurity and be interested in the successes and ideas of subordinates in the office.

A city planner must be able to read blueprints, work with mathematical formulas and draw. He or she must understand something about geography, geology and hydrology. For a person with such interests city planning is an excellent career choice.

What other careers require similar qualities?
Architectural background, the ability to work with a wide variety of people and the skill to handle and supervise large projects indicates that the successful city planner could also be a successful architect.

Because of the vast experiential background needed for the job, city planners often become consultants to large corporations in areas such as real estate development, environmental planning, corporate expansion and planning, airline terminal development and operations, harbor and marina development and supervision, and the establishment of military installations, industrial complexes and parks.

Of course, all careers involving architecture are open to a person who qualifies as a city planner.

What can be done now?
If your early career goal is to be a city planner, you should begin to broaden your interests as well as focus on ar-

chitectural preparation. Take drawing and mechanical drawing courses as well as other art and art history classes. Sociology, geography and history are important, as are English classes that stress communication.

Photography, with an emphasis on the city as subject, is an excellent hobby that will help you understand urban development. Public speaking and debate groups will help you develop the ability to express yourself clearly and think on your feet.

Part-time and summer work on social programs, with underprivileged children, in the park department or in any area of architecture will help you prepare for your career. Working with landscape contractors or gardeners would also be useful.

Make an appointment to talk with a local city planner. Ask him or her how you can best prepare for a career as a city planner. Perhaps you can get a part-time job in a city planner's office—even if it is only sweeping floors, dusting the drafting tables or running errands.

Look through magazines in the library. There are no magazines especially for city planners, but because the areas of interest are so wide and varied, any and all architectural magazines will help you understand the demands and rewards of such a career.

Which colleges offer necessary programs?
A strong architectural background is essential to a city planner. Colleges and universities with outstanding architecture departments will best prepare a student interested in city planning. Check the charts at the back of the book. Schools in larger urban areas will probably offer direct contact with urban problems and solutions.

Colleges that have good programs in geography with an emphasis on urban geography are natural choices for future city planners. Check catalogs for special courses such as city planning, urban development, the sociology of urban areas and the like. All will help prepare students for a multifaceted career in city planning or urban environmental design.

Landscape Architect

Landscape architects specialize in the planning of outdoor areas and the use of the natural environment. Plants, flowers, trees, shrubs, rocks, ponds and lakes are their design elements. They redesign natural settings to provide comfortable and visually appealing spaces around buildings, along highways and in parks or playgrounds.

Landscape architects work on a wide range of projects. They landscape residences of all sizes, luxury estates, commercial and industrial jobs, housing projects, irrigation and slope planting.

In many such areas, landscape architects no longer simply devise landscaping, but help shape the total environment: buildings, traffic flow and signs. In this respect, they work closely with architects and environmental designers.

What landscape architects do

It is simple to say that landscape architects design landscapes. But because many building projects have become so large, and because landscaping for such projects is so extensive, entire teams of experts are necessary to carry out some of the projects. The landscape architect must coordinate the efforts of many people before beautiful, natural-looking surroundings can be produced.

Landscape architects meet with clients, architects or builders at an early point in the planning to discuss drainage, land contours and the use of existing trees and natural landforms. They prepare site plans and construct models to illustrate potential land use, drainage and elevations. They work with architects to establish a plan for placement of buildings, traffic flow and the use of trees, plants and lawns. This plan will attempt to maximize the use of such factors as view, wind direction for cooling and ventilation, and sun for natural light and solar power.

With help from staff, landscape architects select appropriate plants for every part of their design. Ideas are shown to clients in elevation drawings, schematic renderings and blueprint plans (See Landscape Drafter).

When the buildings are completed, the implementation of the overall design is carried out under the direction of the landscape architect. Grading, soil preparation, drainage, irrigation or watering systems, plant selection and lawn seeding are his or her responsibilities.

Most landscape architects run their own offices and sell their services to clients such as building contractors, architectural firms, government agencies, individual homeowners or developers. Others work in large architectural firms and are in charge of a specialized area of landscape design and construction. About 30 percent of all landscape architects work for governmental agencies responsible for city planning, highway beautification, recreational areas, golf courses and national, state and regional parks. Most of the work is found in urban areas.

What qualities are helpful for a landscape architect?

Landscape architects must be able to work with people—clients, architects or the head of an architectural team above them, as well as drafters, landscapers, earth movers and soil experts on their own teams. They must be open to suggestions and able to compromise, yet influential enough to be valuable to the total effort. Clear and accurate communication is essential.

The ability to visualize a completed project even before the first shovelful of dirt is turned is extremely valuable. It follows that it is necessary to be able to sketch and draw that idea to communicate it to others.

Because the job encompasses many aspects of design and touches on architecture, geology, hydrology and botany, it is necessary to have a wide range of interests. The career calls for the ability to read blueprints, building codes and specifications, and to be knowledgeable about climate, weather patterns, plant durability, ecology and irrigation systems, as well as to have an architectural background.

What other careers require similar qualities?

The career of any member of the landscape architectural team would be suited to a person interested in this career. Landscape drafter, grading supervisor, land contour designer and landscape installer are all related and all work toward a similar goal—providing a natural environment for buildings and roadways. Golf course designers, city planners and urban environmentalists must have similar qualifications.

Small landscaping contractors require similar expertise but usually confine themselves to working on individual houses, apartments or small projects. They are responsible for every phase of the planning and implementation of ideas, and are involved in planting and the maintenance of the program.

Landscape architects use trees, shrubs and flowers to contrast with the vertical and horizontal lines of structures. Such careful planting makes cities more enjoyable places to live. Photograph: Joseph Gatto

What can be done now?

All the suggestions given for architecture or city planning can be repeated here. Art classes and mechanical drawing classes are essential. Ecology, botany and geography courses are all recommended. The ability to sketch and plan is strengthened by constant work in a sketchbook.

Photography, with emphasis on structures, sites, landscapes and natural forms and plant life is a useful hobby.

Part-time work in any architecture-related job is ideal, as is work with a landscape contractor or gardener. It is helpful to work in a tree or plant nursery or a national or state park. Working in your own yard can give you excellent experience in planning, designing and arranging natural elements.

Studying books on Japanese gardens will whet your appetite for further study of landscaping as a career.

Magazines that will provide ideas in this area include all the architectural magazines (See Architect) and also: *Better Homes and Gardens, House and Garden, American Home* and *Sunset.*

Which colleges offer necessary programs?

Colleges with strong architectural schools will offer some emphasis in landscape architecture. The American Society of Landscape Architects (ASLA) has accredited the programs of about fifty schools. The skills required for drafting, model building, cost estimating, traffic flow, environmental planning, blueprint preparation and reading and the like are available there. Check ASLA schools in the charts at the back of the book.

Some agricultural schools have landscaping programs, and their catalogs will detail the courses and training available.

Besides a general background in architecture, courses in surveying, landscape construction, plant materials and design and the study of weather patterns are necessary for the landscape architect.

Landscape contractors may often work without formal architectural training, but the expertise needed for larger landscaping projects requires college study, years of experience and a state-approved license.

The cooperation required in many of to-day's large architectural projects is exemplified in the Portland, Oregon mall project. The project represented a number of design and architectural problems. No single person could possibly have provided expert solutions to all the problems, so many designers, specialists, consulting firms and architectural firms were called on to give advice, design products and construct elements for the mall.

The design team responsible for the Portland Mall concept consisted of two large firms: the Portland office of Skidmore, Owings and Merrill (a nationwide architectural firm), and the San Francisco office of CHNMB & Associates (formerly Lawrence Halprin and Associates). Skidmore, Owings and Merrill had responsibility for the coordination of architectural and engineering design of the mall. CHNMB & Associates took on the task of designing fountains and street furnish-

Efficiently designed trip–planning kiosks occupy eight locations on the mall. A rider can punch in a particular route number and see locations and times of bus stops on the selected route. The kiosks also include ticket vending machines and free telephones linked directly to a Tri–Met information line.

Replicas of the ornate, four–armed Benson drinking fountains of Portland's past are placed throughout the mall. Originally, twenty such fountains were given to the city by timber magnate Simon Benson.

Architectural Design

Many sculptures are placed on the brick sidewalks of the mall. These interlocking forms in Indiana limestone are by Don Wilson, a Portland artist and teacher. They were designed to be climbed and sat upon.

ings such as benches, light fixtures, kiosks and signage. The two firms collaborated on a number of activities, including the location and placement of street furnishings.

Also involved in the project were structural engineering consultants, environmental communication and marketing systems designers, scheduling consultants, lighting and design consultants and the City of Portland Traffic Engineering Department and Tri-Met staff (Portland bus station). This small army of designers, engineers, consultants and construction workers represented artistic talent from three different states and four urban areas.

Many blocks of downtown Portland are incorporated in the mall project. Goals of the project included removal of automobile traffic, coordinated surface transportation, revitalization of buildings, stores and facades, new medium-rise construction, widening of pedestrian walkways and provision for seating and visual enjoyment. Most important was a strong desire to link the modernized mall with the past by using custom-designed street furniture and carefully planned landscaping elements.

A mammoth cooperative effort has given the central business district of Portland a face-lift and a second start.

Other Careers In Architecture

Only about ten percent of people trained in architecture actually become full-time architects. The training of the other ninety percent is not wasted, however, because most of the graduates work at careers closely related to architecture. Many architects find that they enjoy drafting, teaching or model building. Some use their expertise to fuel careers as consultants, planners, advisors and teachers. Here are some other careers related to architecture.

Architectural Critic/Writer (See also Reporting and Writing About Art)

A combination of interests in writing and architecture may lead to a career as architectural critic or writer. Such people write for professional journals and specialized magazines (*Architectural Forum,* for example) and large newspapers, and express their own ideas and opinions of the practicality and aesthetics of new buildings and projects. They must be familiar with the vocabulary of architecture and must have experience to back up their opinions and writings. This background can only be obtained by studying to be an architect or by having worked at the profession for some time. A strong emphasis in the history of architecture is also essential for making value judgments and understanding the continuity of the field.

Architectural Drafter

Architectural drafters prepare finished, accurate working plans and detailed drawings of architectural and structural features of any type of building. From rough sketches they make the detailed drawings that builders and engineers use in constructing buildings. Their detailed drawings are used in the preparation of blueprints.

Drafters must be able to read blueprints and specifications, work with dimensions and proportions and have a knowledge of construction techniques and terms. Architectural drafters require an education similar to that of architects.

Architectural Graphics Artist

Although job specifications for graphic artists are found in the Graphic Arts section, it is important to note this specialized career area. Architectural graphic artists design the signs, symbols, traffic indicators, lettering and numbering for buildings and systems so that entire projects have unified graphics plans. Sometimes these projects may include other graphic materials, such as presentation brochures, stationery, marquees and shopping bags. These designers are trained as graphic artists and work either as part of an architectural firm or on a free-lance or consulting basis to architects or building contractors.

Environmental Designer (See also City Planner)

This area of architecture involves working with total environments or systems. Huge developments may involve many buildings, streets, tunnels, parking facilities, bridges, malls, parks and other urban features. Besides being architects, environmental designers must be familiar with population trends, air pollution control, zoning restrictions, mass transportation, ethnic populations, water supplies, geology, taxes, local politics and the cultural and physical makeup of entire cities. Environmental designers often act as consultants to several building projects at the same time.

Architects often become environmental designers when they realize their interest in the total environmental situation of their project, rather than the structure alone.

Landscape Drafter

Landscape drafting is a specialized career similar to architectural drafting, except that it requires work with natural landscape features, trees and plants. Landscape drafters prepare scale drawings and tracing from rough sketches or from figures and data provided by the landscape architect. They prepare site plans, drainage and grade plans, lighting and paving plans and traffic flow patterns. They also complete plans and drawings for irrigation and watering systems, plantings and details of garden structures and elevations.

A knowledge of plant and land forms is necessary, but most important is the ability to draw, measure and finalize the sketches and concepts of landscape architects and environmental planners. Most landscape drafters are trained as landscape architects, but prefer to specialize in this one area of the profession.

Model Builder (See also Model Builder, Other Careers in Film and Television)

Model builders are found in various industrial design offices and studios as well as in architectural firms. They build three-dimensional models which simulate completed buildings, complexes or portions of cities. When huge redevelopment projects are being considered, model builders are called on to construct miniatures of the project so that laymen, engineers, city planners, environmental designers and government officials can easily understand the problems and advantages of the project.

Often model builders are called on to use wood, aluminum, plastics and plaster to indicate how a structure will be related to its environment, or what impact a building will have on its natural or urban site. As with architectural delineation, models are often used to sell construction projects to a community or to prospective financial backers.

Architectural departments at universities and colleges offer courses in model building that have specific applications to architectural planning, environmental design and the effective use of building sites.

Marine Architect

Marine architects design and supervise the construction of ships, barges, dredges, submarines, tugs and other floating constructions. They are also responsible for their remodeling and repair. Marine architects must be able to read blueprints and to study and understand design proposals. Knowledge of size, weight, cargo capacity, displacement, draft, crew, passenger necessities, speed and engines is essential. Marine architects usually work with a team to carry out projects from concept to finished work.

If you are fascinated with ships and sailing, and are also interested in architecture as a career, this combination might be very satisfying for you.

Mural Artist

Mural artists are usually free-lance fine artists or graphic designers who have a special flair for designing large wall spaces in foyers, hallways, elevator reception areas and other large public spaces. Such decoration is usually symbolic of the corporation or corporations that occupy the building.

Artists who become expert in mural design often have a background in interior design, graphic arts or painting. A sound knowledge of color coordination, graphic symbolism and architectural graphics is very helpful to mural artists.

Many state and local governments have set aside a certain percentage (usually one percent) of the total new construction budget to provide art for public places. When a building is nearing completion, a competition is often held to find mural artists for such buildings. Any artist working with any media is eligible to submit ideas for consideration.

Playground Designer

Playground designers work with landscape architects and recreation and park departments to design and supervise the construction of playgrounds for children. Unique and exciting forms are designed to provide young children with places to climb, slide, crawl, jump and run.

Playground designers are concerned first of all with safety, and then with the use, feel and look of the forms they use. Appearance and appeal of the forms are important, but so is consideration of the playground's visual impact on the surrounding community.

Playground designers are usually trained in industrial design, and have special interest in children's activities and in working on human-scale projects.

Teachers of Architecture

Colleges and universities with architectural departments need teachers to inspire and instruct future architects. Such teachers come from the ranks of practicing architects who would rather instruct college students than run a business of their own. They must be thoroughly knowledgeable in the field of architecture and able to communicate ideas to others. They teach the skills they have learned and the history of the profession, and inspire their students to be successful. Theirs is the responsibility for the next generation of architects, and through them the next generation of buildings.

Theme Park Designer

Theme parks (Disneyland, Six Flags over Texas and Disney World, for example) have become popular family entertainment attractions during the last quarter of the twentieth century. Because they are constructed on empty land and occupy huge areas of open space, the entire projects must start from scratch. Theme park design teams begin with soil studies and feasibility and environmental impact reports. They then hold meetings to plan areas for size, function and traffic flow. The architectural plans are created and drawn up, and individual rides, games, displays, shops, arcades and other entertainment features must be devised, designed and built.

A large variety of artists from various career areas are involved in these processes. The coordination of the whole project is the responsibility of the architect in charge—the theme park designer.

Students in an interior design class construct room models and build scale model furniture to learn about color, space design, traffic flow and materials selection. Photograph: New York School of Interior Design

Interior and Display Design

Even before the architect has finished supervising the construction of a building, new tenants are contacting interior designers and facility planners to begin the exciting process of designing its interior. Owners of new homes, condominiums and offices often seek professional help in space design and the selection and arrangement of furniture and accessories. Owners of department stores, shopping malls, boutiques and other shops require professional advice on formats, traffic flow patterns, colors, lighting, textures, displays, fixtures and accessories that will draw customers and make shopping an enjoyable experience.

The interior design field includes careers directly involved with interior planning and design as well as related areas such as the design and manufacture of wallpaper and custom wall coverings, fabrics, furniture, floor coverings, lighting fixtures and other items and materials. Most of the people employed in these industries have training and background in interior design.

There are specialists in limited categories such as interior rendering, dining table arrangement, antiques, kitchens, color consulting, commercial offices, decorative hardware and so on; there are also designers who work with individual clients, advising and assisting them with every phase of their projects.

As far back as cultural history goes, people have tried to make their interior environments comfortable and beautiful by hanging blankets or scratching or painting designs on walls. As houses became more permanent, these decorations became more sophisticated. Trade with other areas of the world brought exchanges of decorative elements. When times or people were prosperous, decorations were lavish; simpler living conditions dictated a dependence on solid, utilitarian items.

Interiors reflect the lives and interests of their occupants, and the converse is also true: people are influenced by their surroundings. Interior designers understand this and work very closely with clients to create functional, beautiful environments.

Two major elements that all interior designers must consider and establish are design sense and knowledge of materials.

The design sense, or style, of the designer is based on training and experience, and is developed and cultivated by constant study, reading, travel and exposure to the work of others. The designer must be sensitive to the requirements and tastes of each new client and must understand the client's intentions, but should also be able to exert a subtle, personal influence on the entire project. A designer is often hired by clients because they like his or her approach to design.

The designer must also have wide knowledge of the materials with which he or she works. Furniture, carpets, wall coverings, accessories, lighting fixtures and art work all must be chosen and coordinated with care. The designer either has such items custom-made or selects them from stores, wholesale dealers, showrooms or directly from manufacturers.

Successful designers coordinate style and materials effectively, and produce interiors that please both the client and themselves.

There are two professional American societies that guide interior planning in this country. They are the National Society of Interior Designers (NSID) and the American Society of Interior Designers (ASID) (see addresses at the back of the book). Each society provides a definition of its own functions, which can be summarized thus: interior designers plan, supervise and coordinate the design, execution and furnishing of interior space to satisfy a client's needs and desires.

Training for a career in interior design or related fields is best obtained at an art school with a strong interior design department. Because of the specialized character of the profession, courses in college will have to be specially constructed to meet these requirements. Such a curriculum might include course titles such as these: Architectural Rendering and Techniques, Business Contracts, Color and Design, Contemporary Design Analysis, Cost Estimation, Drafting, Drawing, Environmental Design, Exhibition Design, Facility Planning, Lighting, Materials and Textiles, Merchandise, Model Construction, Perspective and Elevation, Textiles and Type and Signage.

This list indicates the range of available classes in a three year program leading to a degree. All the careers in the following section are based on a fundamental art school background of similar courses.

Residential and Commercial Interior Designers

A building, whether residential or commercial, may have outstanding architectural merit and structural integrity, but people live and work inside, not outside. This is the realm of interior designers, who coordinate the efforts of manufacturers, consultants, dealers and clients. Residential designers work with individual clients, creating interiors for single rooms or entire homes, apartments or condominiums. Commercial or contract designers work on larger projects with individual clients, corporation boards or hotel or department store management teams. Residential designers and commercial designers supply similar services, but the size of their budgets and the scale of their projects differ profoundly.

Professional interior designers are qualified by education and experience to solve problems related to the function and quality of an interior environment. They are competent in areas of fundamental design, space planning, color coordination and selection of visual art. They learn to understand the needs of clients through conversation, discussion and analysis, and are able to design efficient, pleasant interiors.

Working arrangements for interior designers vary. Some have their own studios and free-lance for a variety of clients. Some join design firms as assistants or associate designers; others are employed by retail or office furniture outlets to advise their clients. Architectural firms employ interior designers to work on their design teams, and hotel and department store chains, restaurants and large corporations may employ them to work on new or remodeled buildings they own or operate.

What interior designers do
Designing interiors is more complicated than rearranging furniture or painting the walls a new color. Some jobs may simply involve selecting some new furniture and redecorating a few walls in a single room, but others may involve planning and coordinating all the interior arrangements of a gigantic building complex or department store.

Interior designers work with project evaluation, space planning, layout, work flow and comprehensive design. They select furniture, fabrics, wall and floor coverings, accessories, art and decorative elements. They may specialize in residential or commercial accounts. Some work only with new structures while others enjoy redesigning existing spaces. They must consider the personal characteristics of clients and design interiors to suit them.

They often use architects' blueprints to make detailed or perspective drawings or renderings of room arrangements. They are sometimes asked to design a room using several unique pieces of furniture as focal points.

Interior designers present their concepts to clients using scaled floor plans, color and material charts, photographs or drawings of furnishings, material samples and color renderings or sketches. After discussions, questions and possible changes, the final presentation includes cost estimates for all items in the project as well as estimates for labor, materials, custom work and consultations.

When the presentation designs and specifications are accepted by the clients, the designers purchase the furnishings or have them custom made, and supervise their installation. They hire and coordinate the work of all the craftspeople and consultants, until the last doorknob and light switch are in place.

At follow-up meetings with clients, designers evaluate the effectiveness of their designs, sometimes making necessary changes. Satisfied clients are the best advertisements for successful interior designers.

Every design firm, large or small, must deal with mounds of paperwork: specifications, orders, estimates, costs, catalogs and administrative details. Working hours are irregular and are spent drawing plans, making models, shopping and meeting with clients, subcontractors or craftspeople. As much time is spent outside the studio as in it.

What qualities are helpful for an interior designer?
Interior designers must be able to see the design possibilities in an empty room. They must have a strong sense of design, nurtured by experience and study, and knowledge of methods and materials gained through a design-oriented curriculum in art school. They must have a sense of color, form or scale. They should possess patience and an imaginative and creative approach to problem solving.

They should be able to get along well with clients, business associates and dealers, and should be person-

Interior designer Linda Umgelter coordinated the structural elements (wood, stainless steel, glass and plaster) with lighting, display fixtures and plants to achieve the attractive interior of one of Goldwater's Arizona department stores. Photograph: Chaix and Johnson Architects

agencies and large corporations that have many offices, manufacturing facilities or business outlets.

Manufacturers of boats, automobiles, buses, trains and airplanes often employ interior designers to design and supervise the manufacture of furniture, interior features, food service systems and accessories. Industrial designers and interior designers work closely in these areas. Writers for design trade magazines and popular home magazines also come from the ranks of interior designers.

What can be done now?

If you are interested in interior design as a possible career, you should be taking art classes of all types. Drawing, painting, art history and design classes are extremely valuable. Typing and business courses are excellent electives and English, history, public speaking and psychology courses are also useful.

Part-time work in an interior design studio or designer's shop would be ideal. While such jobs are likely to be taken by college students, you can gain valuable experience by working in almost any department store home furnishing section. Your practical skills and knowledge can be strengthened by working for a carpenter, cabinet maker, lamp maker, upholsterer, ceramist or furniture maker.

Magazines that can provide you with good interior design direction include: *Architectural Digest, Interiors, Interior Design, Home Furnishings Daily* (a trade newspaper), *House Beautiful, Better Homes and Gardens, House and Garden, Home* and *American Home.*

Which colleges offer necessary programs?

It is almost impossible to begin a successful career in interior design without a formal education from an accredited school. Associate membership in the American Society of Interior Designers (ASID) calls for a minimum of graduation from an accredited school with a degree or major in interior design or graduation and diploma from a three year professional school. After a two year apprenticeship under a professional designer, one may apply for membership in the ASID.

Schools that have student chapters of ASID are desirable, and those that are accredited with FIDER (Foundation for Interior Design Education Research) are recommended. See the charts at the back of the book.

able, yet sure of their own instincts. They should fully understand the meaning of service as it relates to their careers. More of a designer's time is involved with people than with a drawing board, so communication skills should be well developed.

Interior designers must be businesslike and well organized if they are to handle the multitude of details involved in their work.

What other careers require similar qualities?

People with interior design backgrounds are found in many career areas that serve the industry. They could not do their jobs without the help of these services, occupations and crafts. Such related careers might include: lighting specialist, wallpaper and wall covering designer, fabric designer, floor covering specialist and designer of accessories, decorative hardware, kitchen and bathroom fixtures and the like.

Related services include interior rendering, drafting detailers, color styling, interior architectural delineators, interior decorators, furniture and interior sketch artists and interior illustrators.

Designers who can handle large projects are capable of being interior project coordinators for government

Facility Planner

Facility planning, a relatively new career area, has gained importance as building costs have increased and space has become more valuable. In simplest terms, facility planners determine how to use a client's space to obtain the greatest benefit at the least cost. They work with architects in the early planning stages, developing design programs which specify the kind and amount of space required. Architects base their arrangements of the interior spaces on these design specifications.

Facility planners may work for architectural firms, or large interior design offices or consulting firms which have clients in both the architectural and interior design fields. They are extremely valuable to both professions since they are experts in analyzing and using space in built environments.

Governmental agencies, hospitals, prisons, schools, shopping malls, utilities and various businesses call on facility planners for advice and recommendations. Some large firms may have facility planners on organizational teams within the corporate structure.

Facility planners come from several backgrounds. Some come from interior design or architectural programs, others from the fields of business, economics, public administration or urban planning. Many planners who work in both areas of planning and analysis have an undergraduate degree in one field and a graduate degree in another.

What facility planners do

Facility planners analyze and recommend. They develop long-range plans for space utilization for large corporations or government agencies. Such plans project the number of employees needed for fifteen or twenty year periods, and planners calculate the space necessary to maintain efficiency and comfort until that time. The anticipated cost of building or leasing space to meet future needs may also be included.

A large, complex structure poses a variety of space utilization problems, because each of its components is of equal importance. Facility planners must consider such problems before presenting their recommendations to architectural teams. Photograph: Omni International, Atlanta

Facility planners also lay out space within offices. They make up space standards for certain jobs so that all employees with similar jobs have similar amounts of space. They analyze their client's needs and plan how walls and furniture should be placed to maximize available space.

There are two areas of facility planning which are sometimes combined in one job, sometimes separated into two. These are *facility analysis* and *space planning*.

Facility analysts gather and analyze data. They may develop questionnaires or conduct interviews to find out which departments in a company are growing, what special equipment is needed and what special spaces (libraries, conference rooms, vaults) are required. After interviewing department heads and working with combined statistics, the analysts recommend future space requirements and other departmental needs. They may suggest certain physical changes in the office arrangement which prevent problems caused by congestion, understaffing, traffic flow and space limitations.

Space planners work with floor plans as well as with actual spaces. They plot current locations of walls and furniture, light sources and traffic use, measuring square footage and determining which tasks are done where. Space planners use this information to suggest more efficient use of existing space. They may recommend more efficient furniture or the removal of walls. They draft, make models, draw sketches and prepare graphics for their reports and presentations.

What qualities are helpful for a facility planner?

Facility planners must be able to analyze situations and make decisions and recommendations. They must be good at mathematics and adept at drafting and sketching. They must read blueprints and prepare graphic reports for clients, architects and interior designers.

They are constantly in contact with people in all phases of work, so they must be able to speak easily and clearly to individuals and groups.

Facility planning is ideal for a person who is interested in both interior design and business, and who likes to research and solve problems.

What other career areas require similar qualities?

Because facility planning touches on both architecture and interior design, these fields would also be of interest to a student planning such a career. For someone interested in space planning, other careers might include space consultant, city planner, office furniture and systems designer or any career that deals primarily with making work space more efficient. Space efficiency is an important consideration in the design of house trailers, recreational vehicles and airplanes, and also in the planning and design of stage sets.

A person more interested in facility analysis may also find these careers interesting: an analytical position on an architectural team, consultant to corporations and government agencies, graphic artist specializing in reports, charts, data and visual presentations, and graphic artist designing company reports, summaries and yearly reports to stockholders.

What can be done now?

High school students should take all the art classes available to them, with an emphasis on drawing and drafting. They should also take mathematics courses to strengthen their ability to work with figures, solve problems and make analytical judgements. Public speaking classes, debate teams and English classes help develop communication skills.

Try to obtain part-time work in any drafting capacity. Any jobs listed in the sections on architect or interior designer would provide valuable experience.

There are no specialized magazines that deal directly with facility planning, but architectural, interior design and industrial design magazines would be of interest.

Which colleges offer necessary programs?

Facility planners come from both architectural and interior design backgrounds, so study or a degree in either discipline is excellent. Schools with large departments in either area will offer the courses needed to pursue such a career. Space planners require an emphasis on design theory, drafting and graphics, while facility analysts need courses in research design, statistics, economics and writing. For the most complete training, take as many courses as possible in both areas.

Schools accredited by FIDER (Foundation for Interior Design Education Research) should receive special consideration. Refer to the charts at the back of the book.

Exhibit and Display Designers

Exhibits and display designs are a form of visual merchandising. The services of exhibit designers are sought by museums, galleries, showrooms, trade shows, manufacturers' representatives and department stores. Some of these specialists may be employed on the permanent staffs of large museums of companies; others may freelance or work for consulting or architectural firms.

The skills offered by exhibit and display designers are in increasing demand. Displays are used to attract customers for possible sales, and the designer is an integral part of the merchandising team, as important as the graphic artist who prepares advertisements for newspapers and magazines. The way goods are placed on view in a store can be the key to successful sales promotions.

What exhibit and display designers do

Designers who plan and construct exhibits and displays work with a wide variety of products and materials. They develop visual presentations for the permanent collections, temporary exhibits and traveling exhibitions of museums and galleries of all types. Exhibit designers decide which paintings should hang together, how they should be hung and which receive prime positions. They are also responsible for designing and constructing stands, platforms, display cases, lighted boxes and security systems for the effective exhibition of three-dimensional objects.

Exhibit designers in merchandise marts must use display techniques, props, color, lighting, fabrics and mannequins to attract and hold the attention of buyers.

Museum and gallery display techniques include the design, construction and arrangement of stands, stages, panels, cases and effective lighting, such as in this display of student work at the Cleveland Institute of Art. Photograph: Dennis Buck

Because the selling companies are often competing for very large orders, the initial impact of their displays is extremely important.

Displays in department stores, specialty shops and boutiques rely just as heavily on immediate visual impact; it is vital to their survival in the marketplace. Display designers work closely with fashion consultants, owners and managers to select and display clothing.

Exhibitors at trade shows and state, county and world's fairs are in constant need of designers that can show their manufactured goods, agricultural products, wares, crafts and natural resources to the best possible advantage.

Large department stores often employ directors to supervise and instruct the staffs of specialists who build and maintain interior and window displays. These directors have mechanical drafting ability, carpentry skills, good color sense and some knowledge of the history of art, furnishings and decoration. They keep abreast of all new trends in textiles, furnishings and fine arts. The window display designers who work under them are usually free-lance artists who contract to do a series of windows in different stores.

Exhibit and display designers make sketches and scale models to present to their clients. They are experts at using lights for dramatic effect, building three-dimensional display units, employing type and graphic symbols and using space effectively to unify an entire exhibit.

What qualities are helpful for an exhibit and display designer?

An exhibit and display designer must have a wide range of interests, because an effective exhibit draws on many resources. A visual merchandiser might have to be familiar with photography, painting, basic design, merchandising, fashion design, advertising design, graphic design, space planning and interior design.

An exhibit designer must be able to draw so that he or she can sketch ideas for clients, and must be able to construct models of displays. Because designers are constantly working with clients, store personnel and advertisers, they must work well with others and be able to communicate their ideas.

These designers often work under strict deadlines, and should be able to structure their own time accordingly.

What other career areas require similar qualities?

A person graduating from college with a knowledge of exhibit and display design is also equipped for careers with museum display teams in galleries, theme parks, convention centers, and for consulting companies and others who require visual merchandising. Other related areas of interest include model building, commercial and industrial graphics, display lighting, theatrical lighting, gallery management and advertising design.

What can be done now?

High school art classes are useful for careers in exhibit and display design. Drawing, painting, three-dimensional design and crafts are very helpful. Designing and constructing stage sets teaches students to work with lights and build from models. Working as an artist on a yearbook staff provides vital experience in graphics, layout, meeting deadlines and working closely with others.

Go to museums to study display techniques; look carefully at displays in department stores, shops and shopping malls. Study them at close range to see how they are designed and constructed, how the products are displayed and how lighting is used.

Part-time work in a store's display department would be an ideal introduction to this career area. Any job that requires building will help you understand construction techniques. Express interest in designing window displays for small shops and businesses, the local newspaper or library.

You can also learn much about exhibit techniques by looking through mail order catalogs that display objects in effective surroundings and arrangements. Notice how the photographer takes advantage of display techniques and lighting.

Which colleges offer necessary programs?

Art schools with strong interior design departments are recommended (see the chart at the back of the book). They provide special emphasis in design areas fundamental to a career in exhibit and display design. Some schools offer majors in exhibition design or sales display (check catalogs for this information).

Art schools that stress industrial design often offer some classes in display and exhibition techniques, since they are used in industry, trade fairs and merchandise marts. Fashion-oriented schools provide classes and experience in displays that feature clothing, models, mannequins and accessories.

Museum schools provide direction in arranging displays featuring paintings, sculpture, crafts and multimedia presentations.

ART CAREER PROFILE

The work illustrated on these pages is a small part of the total project designed by EPR (Environmental Planning and Research, Inc.) of San Francisco, for two floors leased by GATX Leasing Corporation at Four Embarcadero Center.

A four-person team assigned to the project included a Project Director, Project Manager, Senior Designer and Interior Designer. They, in turn, used additional staff to work on details of the total project.

The illustrations tell the story. The development of only one small area is shown here; this type of work was done for every room and space on the two floors of the project.

Lisa Bottom, project interior designer, seen at work on this project in her office. Photograph: MATRIX

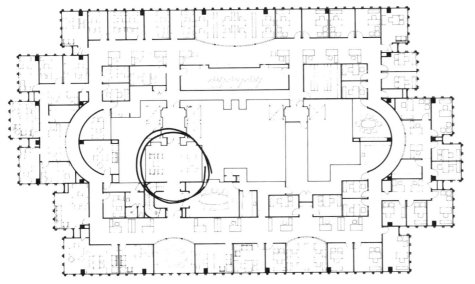

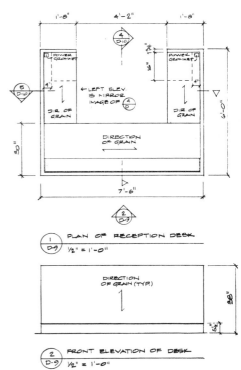

The floor plan and facility planning diagram for one floor of the project. The circled section is the reception area, shown in the following developmental stages.

Elevation drawings for reception desk on left in the rendering. Most furniture in the project is custom made according to the interior designer's recommendations, sketches and drawings.

Environmental Planning and Research

Interior designer's rendering of the design and decoration concept for the reception area. Furniture, colors, fabrics and lighting are suggested. Photograph: MATRIX

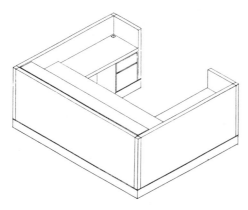

ISOMETRIC - FRONT VIEW OF RECEPTION DESK
1/2" = 1'-0"

Isometric front view of reception desk. This and the elevation drawing will help in the actual construction of the furniture.

Photograph of the finished project. Compare all the preliminary stages with the actual result. Photograph: ESTO Photographics, Inc., New York

Wall hangings, desert plants, lighting, custom flooring, mirrors and furniture create a unique mood for this Palm Springs dining room, designed and photographed by Steve Chase Associates.

Other Careers In Interior Design

Antique Specialist
Antique specialists deal in the single area of interior design that has to do with furnishings and accessories of previous eras. They purchase, restore, refinish and sell items to the public or to interior designers. They may also act as consultants or appraisers.

Contractor's Assistant (Contract Designer)
A contractor's assistant works on the planning team for builders and contractors who plan and decorate model homes, apartment complexes, office suites, condominiums or custom-built houses. The assistant coordinates the work of many suppliers to design and furnish rooms that will help sell homes and offices to prospective buyers.

Design Assistant
Design assistants help designers and design associates in the entire operation of their programs. They oversee workshops and stockrooms and supervise business operations. They must have interior design skills, a knowledge of construction and the ability to manage an office.

Design Consultant
Design consultants are specialists in one or more areas of interior design such as lighting, color, draperies, window treatments, kitchens or baths. They free-lance from their own offices, or are employed by furniture or department stores, manufacturing firms, architects, design studios or supply houses. They offer suggestions and make decisions in their areas of expertise.

Detailer
Detailers make finished drawings from the rough sketches of designers. Their drawings must include notes on dimensions, materials to be used, finishes desired and other information to make them clear and complete.

Facility Analyst (See Facility Planner)

Floor Covering Designer
Rugs, carpets, runners and mats of all kinds are designed by floor covering designers, who often work for the manufacturers of the products. They have a knowledge of the use and application of various materials as well as the production processes, so they can design items and supervise production. Some artists design and supervise the weaving and production of custom-made articles for individual clients.

Floral Designer
Floral designers use wire, pins, tapes, foam and a variety of tools to design living, dried, or artificial displays of flowers. Materials are trimmed and arranged in bouquets, wreaths, sprays, displays and terrariums. Designers must have a knowledge of color, flowers and design. They often work with interior designers to create custom displays for residential or commercial spaces.

Interior Decorator
Interior decorators are often free-lancers who decorate existing rooms and spaces, usually in homes or offices, with objects and materials that can be purchased in stores. They show their clients color combinations, fabric and paint swatches, wall coverings, carpet samples, furniture catalogs and accessories, and suggest decorations and arrangements. They usually work for a fee and a commission on sales and contracted work. They study art appreciation, art and furniture history and color theory and design.

Interior Renderer (See also Architectural Delineator)
Interior renderers prepare three-dimensional drawings and watermedia paintings that illustrate how a proposed and furnished interior will look. They use blueprints and the working drawings of architects as the basis for their work. They are usually free-lance artists who do their work for architects, interior designers or clients who wish to show building contractors what they require. Large architectural and interior design firms have several interior renderers on their staffs.

Manufacturer's Representative (Showroom Manager)
Manufacturer's representatives work for large companies that specialize in the production of home furnishings and decorator materials. They sell their products to buyers from stores, designers and their clients, architects, builders and contractors. This is done at the factory or at central merchandise marts where the representatives coordinate displays, recommendations and sales activities.

Museum Position: Curator of Decorative Arts
(See Museums)

Parade Float Designer

Parade floats are large mobile display units designed to communicate an instant visual message. Float designers work for their clients within certain space, cost and material limitations, and make color renderings of the anticipated floats. They employ a variety of materials in the floats: flowers, cloth, plastic, paper, wood and metal. If possible they also work with the builders who carry out the designs. Such work is seasonal, unless the builder has contracts from float clients around the country.

Photo Stylist

Photo stylists arrange products and accessories to be photographed for national advertisements, publicity or promotional brochures. They may plan entire room settings or simple product vignettes for manufacturers, advertising or public relations agencies. They hire photographers to take the required final pictures for their clients.

Publications (Home Furnishings) (See also Editorial Design)

Some people combine backgrounds in interior design with their writing abilities and become home furnishing writers or editors for trade or consumer magazines or newspapers. Others write advertising copy for their clients.

Publications require feature columnists, reporters, illustrators, department editors and editors-in-chief. Writers report on current styles and trends, new products and materials and outstanding interior design projects, renovations or adaptations. They may attempt to predict future trends. Trade publications include: *Home Furnishings Daily, Interior Decorator News, Interiors, Interior Design* and *Contract.* Consumer magazines include: *Better Homes and Gardens, House Beautiful, House and Home* and *American Home.* Some general magazines have decorating departments or features on interior design.

Set Designer, Theater and Stage (See Scenic Designer)

Space Planner (See Facility Planner)

Staff Designer

Staff designers are employed by large companies, hotel chains and franchise operations to plan and coordinate the interiors, furniture and accessories in their buildings. This type of work is often handled by consulting firms, but if the company is large enough and the demand is constant, a staff designer will be included in the design team.

Teacher (See also Art Education)

Art schools, fashion institutes, colleges and universities whose art departments offer courses in interior design, hire teachers with design experience. In such departments, designers with strong backgrounds, good reputations and successful studios can give students valuable insight into the career fields they have chosen. The best programs are endorsed and accredited by national design associations with rigid requirements, such as Foundation for Interior Design Education Research (FIDER) and American Society of Interior Designers (ASID).

Wall Covering Designer

Wall coverings include wallpaper, grass cloth, photo murals, laminates, printed patterns and custom applications such as murals, fabrics, printed papers, tapestries, metallics, weavings and wood. Some wall covering designers work with interior designers, planners and clients to custom-design and produce the coverings for interior spaces. Others design for companies which manufacture wall covering products for the interior design industry or retail sale.

Window Display Designer

Window display designers work on the staffs of large department stores or other large retail outlets. Very often they are free-lance artists who contract to do a series of windows in different stores or the shops located in a large shopping mall.

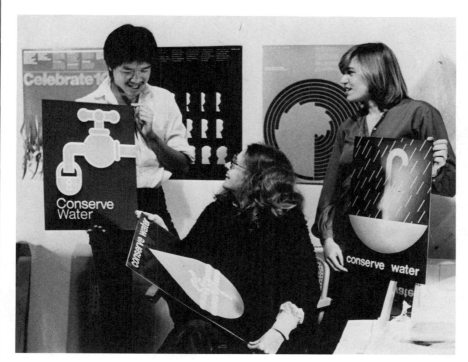

Graphic design students at California College of Arts and Crafts compare the award-winning posters they prepared for a competition sponsored by the East Bay Municipal Utilities District. Such posters contain all the elements of good graphic design. Photograph: California College of Arts and Crafts Public Information Office

ART CAREERS IN the commercial world often overlap, and extend into areas such as television, film, education, publications, theater, interior design and architecture. For the sake of organization, however, three major areas of business-related art will be considered in this section: graphic design, industrial design and fashion design. It is the function of all artists in these fields to create designs that communicate with specific audiences and are attractive and functional enough to sell products and make profits.

An advertising agency art director checks over the art work of cartoon illustrator Rowland B. Wilson. Close cooperation and communication are necessary to put together a successful ad. Photograph: Hill, Holiday, and Conners Agency

Graphic Design

Graphic design started in fifteenth century Germany with the invention of the printing press. The first craftsmen-printers, responsible for arranging type and illustrations on printed pages, were also the first graphic designers. Graphic design did not really become an art form, however, until the late nineteenth century, when the Englishman William Morris insisted that art and design should be combined to make mass-produced goods more attractive. Teachers at the Bauhaus, a German school of design established in 1919, believed in basing the graphic design of manufactured goods, packaging and advertising on fine art design principles. Bauhaus concepts are still the basis for contemporary graphic design. In the past fifty years, graphic design techniques have improved with the development of new media (acrylics, epoxies, alkyds), new techniques (airbrush, photography, montage, dye transfers), new materials (plastics, mylars, acrylics sheets, dry-transfer lettering) and new equipment (overhead projectors, duplicating machines, computers, lasers, thermal and electrostatic photocopiers, laser scanners).

Today technological advances are changing the entire field of graphic design. New products and processes perfect and speed up the design and production of graphic images. In spite of increased mechanization, however, graphic designers still must have fundamental training in art, design and composition.

Art Director/Advertising Design

Creative directors (also called Senior Art Directors or Executive Art Directors) head large design teams. They attained these positions after working successfully at lower levels in a particular agency. As directors, they are responsible for entire advertising campaigns, and work with art directors, artists, marketing staff and clients. They are the creative mainsprings of the agencies, conceiving the ideas, developing the budgets and strategies, exploring them with their staffs and convincing clients of their effectiveness. They do the creative thinking.

Taking direction from creative directors on most advertising design teams are the group supervisors, who guide the development of the advertising programs. They must have a thorough knowledge of their own personnel, their free-lance suppliers, other agencies and their clients. They must know a great deal more about advertising then anyone else on the team. They deal with graphic designers, art directors, illustrators, budget directors, typographers, photographers and clients. They deal largely in concepts and ideas, and delegate the supervision responsibilities to art directors and the actual work to graphic designers and the rest of the staff, or to free-lance suppliers and contract artists.

Art directors, who work under this supervisory staff, are involved with the working processes in design studios and advertising agencies. They work with their supervisors and other staff members to put together total packages for presentation to clients. In small offices, they may do all the work themselves, sometimes with the aid of apprentices. In large offices, they are responsible for conceiving and developing ideas, making sure agency standards are met and overseeing the development of programs within the studios. If necessary, directors in large offices buy photographs, illustrations, type, lettering and other art work from art services or free-lance artists.

Art directors develop attention-getting devices to attract the audience to the copywriters' verbal messages, which are the core of the advertisements. Formerly, art directors were given copy and expected to create decorations for what had been written. Today's art directors are businesspeople. They often deal directly with clients, and supervise every phase of the advertising project to its completion. They are a combination of graphic designer, journalist and businessperson, and must be talented artists vitally interested in advertising and communication.

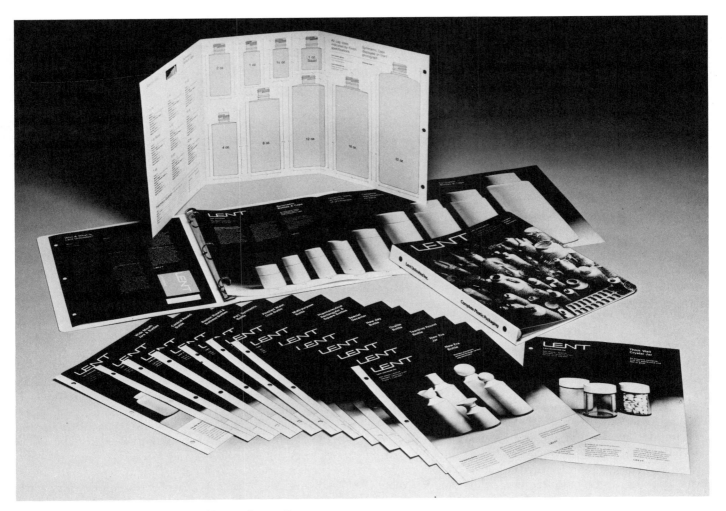

A typical design program was developed by art director Ramon Munoz for Lent Unlimited, Inc. It consists of a three ring folder and multiple fold-out inserts which graphically explain, describe and illustrate the plastic packaging which Lent designs and manufactures. Photograph: Ramon Munoz

What art directors do

After meeting with group supervisors, creative directors and clients, art directors take over the advertising projects and make all the creative decisions. The size of the agencies where they work determines how much of the work they do themselves as they develop the ad concept according to the client's wishes. They select and arrange the elements of the ad (color, white space, illustrations, photographs, body type, display type and the like) and prepare rough sketches of the ideas. If the client or supervisor requests changes, they are made at this early stage. Following these discussions, the art directors make comprehensive layouts which show all the elements in their correct positions. Art is drawn carefully and large type elements are lettered in so that the page looks very much like the finished work.

After approval of the comprehensive by the client and supervisors, the directors obtain the finished art and type from agency designers or free-lance artists, photographers, letterers, illustrators, typesetters or photo compositors. They oversee the assemblage of these elements, which is done by paste-up and production artists (See Layout and Paste-up Artist). The comprehensive is the show piece. The paste-up is photographed by those who make the printing plates. Art directors consult printers on final color, placement, paper stock, inks and approval of the final proof sheet. The ad is then ready to print.

In small agencies, art directors will complete all these tasks themselves, or may send them out to free-lance specialists. In medium sized or larger agencies, art directors will have graphic designers carry out these tasks under their supervision. In some cases, a free-lance graphic designer may function as an art director, taking on all the aspects of an advertising promotion, annual report project or corporate identity program, working directly with clients, purchasing agents and printers.

What qualities are helpful for an art director?
Art directors deal with clients, group supervisors, graphic designers, paste-up and free-lance artists and many specialists from other agencies. They must communicate accurately, so that all parts of the program are carried out smoothly. They must work well with people, and should have first-hand experience in advertising business.

Art directors are directly responsible for all aspects of their projects and must be able to do the work themselves, if necessary. They must be adept at sketching, preparing visual roughs, paste-ups, dummies, photography and illustration. They must have excellent design backgrounds, be extremely neat and be able to meet deadlines imposed by others and by themselves.

Complete understanding of current trends in design research, type and illustration is a must for a good art director, and a fertile imagination that can visualize and develop ideas is even more desirable.

What other careers require similar qualities?
Most areas of graphic design would be enjoyable to a person who had art direction as a goal. Experienced art directors become group supervisors and creative directors, or may start their own design agencies. Free-lancing in various areas of graphic design is also a possible career option.

Other careers that involve creative planning and working with people include: corporate art director, graphic designer, promotion designer, specialized industrial designer, type designer, television title designer and the like.

Magazine and book publication, photography, teaching, museum graphics, signage, architectural graphics and some phases of environmental planning also require qualities akin to those of an art director.

What can be done now?
Take high school drawing and painting classes, and all the design courses available. Art history and art appreciation are important, and as the best art directors have varied interest, you should take history, psychology, business and science courses. Written communication is the number one concern of art directors, so take all the English classes you can.

Work on yearbook or newspaper staffs as photographer, designer, cartoonist or paste-up artist is very useful.

Part-time work in any capacity at an advertising agency will give you great experience. Any job is valuable, as long as you learn while doing it, so watch what others are doing around you, and ask questions. Jobs in the printing industry (no matter how large or small the business) will help you understand the practical aspects of graphic design. Work in a sign painting studio will improve your lettering ability. Even a job in a department store will make you aware of retailing and the impact of advertising on that industry. It will also help you become familiar with the types of clients for whom you someday may work as a designer.

Magazines that contain excellent examples of graphic design and the work of art directors include: *CA (Communication Arts)*, *Print*, *Art Direction*, *Graphis* (from Switzerland) and *Design* (from England). Also check on *Art Directors Annual*, *Penrose Annual* (from England), and *Graphis Annual* (from Switzerland).

Which colleges offer necessary programs?
Graphic design is a combination of art, advertising, graphic arts (printing & typography) and photography. Prepare yourself as much as possible in all these areas if you plan to be an art director. Depending on which school you plan to attend, necessary courses for art directors come under several different curricular headings: Graphic Design, Advertising Design, Commercial Art, or Advertising or Editorial Art. Typical graphic design courses may include: Airbrush painting, advertising techniques, art appreciation, business of art, cartooning, color and composition, computer graphics, design, drawing, figure drawing, graphic design, illustration, keys and mechanicals, layout design, lettering, merchandising art, painting, perspective, photographic processes, portfolio, production techniques, retail advertising, typography and visual communication.

Though some types of art direction jobs are available in almost every town and city in the country, schools in large cities will be able to provide you with visits to important studios and agencies, and arrange seminars and meetings with well known art directors who work nearby. Check the charts at the back of the book for schools offering necessary graphic design courses and programs.

Corporate Art Director

The need for graphic material in large corporations has increased tremendously in recent years. These corporations regularly require magazine and newspaper advertising, promotional materials, television ads, corporate and annual reports and countless in-house publications, brochures and pamphlets. Such corporations also require help in office design and the purchase of art. These functions were formerly contracted out to advertising agencies, graphic design studios, free-lance artists and interior designers. Today's emphasis on graphic products and corporate identity has induced many corporations to employ their own art directors or staff to design and maintain control over their products, packaging and promotion. Some non-profit institutions (religious, cultural, educational, hospital) also employ full-time artists to produce or supervise all phases of their graphic design programs and visual presentations.

Corporate designers are also responsible for visual material that company representatives use in their sales promotions and seminars, such as slides, videotapes, charts, graphs and photographic enlargements.

What corporation art directors do

The first job of most corporate art directors is to pinpoint the character of their companies. The art directors design company logos, which will appear on all graphic material, according to the company's projected growth. This corporate identity may determine the decor of main and branch offices and the color scheme of stationery, packaging and advertising materials. In some corporations, these jobs will be done from beginning to end by the art director, who must thus have practical experience in all phases of graphic design. In others, some or all of the work may be delegated to staff artists or outside agencies and supervised by the art director.

Corporate art directors are responsible for the public image of their companies. They are part of company teams, and will be consulted about art and design decisions. They attend staff meetings and make suggestions on design-related subjects.

They work with salespeople, production workers, management personnel, distributors and boards of directors. They must know their products, the sales pro-

Corporate art director Dick Loyd, Director of Art Services for Coca Cola of Los Angeles, helps some members of his staff develop a promotional program layout. Photograph: Gerald Brommer

One of the country's first corporate art directors was Bud Roberts (left) of the Shell Oil Company. He is seen here with designer Hal Power, discussing art and photos to be used in an advertising promotion. Photograph: Shell Oil Company, and Graphics Today

Commercial Art and Design

gram and their market. They are concerned with the image, the growth and the productivity of the company or organization, and are vital links in the corporate structure.

What qualities are helpful for a corporate art director?

Corporate art directors must be self-disciplined and must adhere to schedules and tight deadlines. They should get along well with vendors and salespeople, and understand management objectives. They take responsibility for projects from beginning to completion. They are familiar with all phases of graphic design and the technical and aesthetic aspects of photography. Above all they must have mature judgment, sound design sense, versatility and the willingness to work as team members.

Art directors work in a structured atmosphere. Dealing with suppliers, display houses, typographers, printers, graphic artists, administrators, photographers, salespeople and others is tremendously challenging.

What other careers require similar qualities?

The careers of other art directors and group supervisors are similar in nature but are not as all-inclusive (See Art Director, and Editorial Art Director). Corporate art directors may feel comfortable working as art directors in publishing houses, for magazine or newspaper editors, for some government agencies or library systems. Since a broad range of interests and abilities is required, such people probably would not be satisfied with single-duty careers, such as layout designer or package designer.

Free-lance work in a variety of areas (graphic design, interior design, publishing, corporate identity systems or architectural graphics) would provide a range of experiences that would parallel the work of corporation art directors.

What can be done now?

Because corporate art directors are involved in all areas of graphic design, early preparation should include art classes, English, public speaking, drafting, history, photography and special interest areas.

Part-time work that would help you prepare for a job as a corporate art director is the same as for other graphic designers (See Graphic Designer). Work in any manufacturing plant or other company will provide corporation experience on a practical level (working with people, observing production methods, packaging operations, shipping and the like).

Magazines that are concerned with graphic design include *CA* (*Communication Arts*), *Print*, *Art Direction*, *Graphis*, *Design* and *Design Drafting and ReproGraphics*.

Which colleges offer necessary programs?

Colleges and art schools offering graphic design courses will provide the necessary background. Courses in package design, corporation identity, publication graphics, photography, typography and advertising techniques are essential. Check the charts at the back of the book and search through catalogs from various schools.

Future corporate art directors should take a variety of courses, followed by several years of practical experience in a number of graphic design positions.

Graphic Designer

Graphic designers are the architects of the printed page. They combine the resources of many specialists (illustrators, photographers, typographers and copywriters) to create a visual presentation intended to attract attention. In a sense they are generalists with art skills who understand the psychology of marketing.

In advertising, graphic designers work with copywriters to produce ads, brochures and package designs. In publishing, they work with editors to produce layouts, covers, books and magazines. In manfacturing companies, they design products, packages and promotional materials. In corporations, they are responsible for brochures, stationery, logos and other visible representations of the corporate image. Graphic designers in consulting firms deal with any and all of the above situations.

Graphic designers work closely with related professionals such as architects, audio-visual programmers, computer graphics artists, environmental designers, copywriters, exhibit designers, newspaper staff and product and package designers. The study of graphic design might easily lead to careers in such related areas.

Graphic designers must have a broad experiential background to cope with the equally broad range of assignments that might be given to them. If you like to solve problems, make drawings and paintings, work with people, relate to media and do a variety of things in art, perhaps a career as a graphic designer is desirable for you.

Gretchen Goldie, a graphic designer for Bright and Associates, Inc., created this stationery system for photographer Chad Slattery. He asked for something unique and memorable, something that said "photography." Examples courtesy Gretchen Goldie

What Graphic Designers Do

The essence of graphic design is visual communication. Graphic designers are visual problem solvers who take the ideas of business people and translate them into something the public can grasp. Their designs—whether for products, packages, or advertising—must be exciting, imaginative and compelling, and must reach the intended market.

There are no clear-cut distinctions between the capabilities of art directors and graphic designers, and their functions overlap in many instances. In small agencies, they may be the same people, capable of doing all the required work. In large agencies, graphic designers are given their assignments by art directors who are responsible for several concurrent projects and the functioning of many graphic artists.

Commercial Art and Design

Art directors explain the client's needs to graphic designers, and offer suggestions and guidance. After research and analysis of the design problem, designers work on pencil sketches called roughs, which will give clients and art directors several possible solutions, or arrangements, from which to choose. When these visual roughs are modified and the most effective one is approved, the designers work up detailed drawings in color and include major type blocks, display type and carefully drawn and detailed sketches of all art work, arranged and laid out to exact specifications and size. This comprehensive layout is shown to the art director and client for further modification and approval.

When the comprehensives are approved, graphic designers begin working with their resources (copywriters, typographers, computer artists, illustrators, photographers or other artists or specialists) to get all the elements of the program finished on time. When all the necessary elements are collected, they are turned over to paste-up artists (See Layout and Paste-up Artist) who prepare the materials for photocopying and final plate making. Press proofs from the printer will show the designers, art directors and clients how the finished products or ads will look. Success or failure of the graphic production will be determined by public reaction.

Graduates with graphic design majors begin their careers by working in studios, creating layouts, logos, drawings, paste-ups, photostats, sketches and some finished art work under the direction of more experienced designers.

Some graphic designers become specialists in certain products (trademarks, books, magazines, television or packaging) while others enjoy the challenges of variety and work with all types of clients. Some enjoy doing most or some of the tasks involved with the production process, while others enjoy supervising such jobs, delegating them to staff members.

What qualities are helpful for a graphic designer?
People involved in graphic design are generally visually aware of what is around them, enjoy solving problems and like to work with people. They must be able to sketch almost anything, devise layouts, enjoy doing research, and have a good sense of design and color.

Most graphic designers try to avoid being influenced by fads, wanting instead to be distinctive and imaginative. They are committed to professionalism, ethics and quality in their work. They must be able to work under deadlines and must be self-disciplined, especially if they free-lance. They must be able to organize their work, their products and their studios to be efficient and productive.

A curiosity about developments in all areas of graphic design and a broad range of personal interests outside the art field enrich client/artist relationships.

What other careers require similar qualities?
Careers across the board in the graphic and industrial design fields require similar qualities. Being able to organize the efforts of many people to solve a single problem is also required in areas of urban planning, architecture, environmental design and in film and television industries.

Graphic designers would fit easily into careers in the design and production of books and magazines. Museums, department stores, franchise operations, public relations firms and many corporations need people with graphic design qualifications.

What can be done now?
Take drawing, basic design, drafting, painting, photography, crafts, printmaking and graphic design classes in high school if possible. Keep your projects organized so they can be put into portfolios. Work on the yearbook staff if you have the opportunity, and design posters for school or club activities.

Part-time work for a design firm or free-lance designer will provide excellent experience in the field, but such jobs are difficult to find. Look at the other graphic design careers for other work that would be helpful, and also for magazines that will help you understand the graphic design field.

Which colleges offer necessary programs?
Several types of schools offer programs helpful to graphic design students. Art and design courses at community colleges will help sharpen the skills necessary for further education and future careers. Some continuing education programs at colleges or universities will provide design backgrounds for further training. Trade schools will help develop your skills in the production aspect of graphic design: layouts, paste-ups, beginning and advanced photography and design.

Four year art schools and colleges that offer accredited degrees in graphic design are listed in the charts at the back of the book. Some of those schools offer a fine arts approach; others stress the advertising aspect of graphic design. By checking through school catalogs, you will be able to determine which approach seems best for you and your interests. Discuss this with your art teachers and counselors. A visit to the schools and a look at student production can also help you determine if their direction and teaching coincides with your own feelings about art and graphic design.

Graphic designer Harold Burch at work in his studio, surrounded by examples of his own design projects. Photographs courtesy Harold Burch

Harold Burch is a graduate of Art Center College of Design in Pasadena. For a brief period after graduation he headed Harold Burch Design as a free-lance designer/photographer, where his clients included A&M Records, MCA Records, Capitol Records, and Greg Zajack Photograhy. Since 1979 he has been affiliated with Ken White Design in Los Angeles, as Creative Director. His list of clients is impressive and includes NASA, Knudsen Corporation, Max Factor, Disney Epcot Center, Jet Propulsion Laboratory and Pioneer Stereo, among many others.

Harold Burch is accomplished in both fine and commercial art. His drawing, painting and photography are known widely on the west coast. His design work has appeared in *Graphis, Typography II* and *AGIA II*. When helping secondary students select careers in the visual arts, Burch feels that varied approaches to

communication must be used. He agreed to develop the concept of a brochure for the California Wine Council, and retrace his steps for students to show them what is involved in bringing an idea to fruition. You can follow the planning and organization necessary to implement the visual concepts of a top designer.

Let us assume you are asked to design a brochure for the wine industry. Where do you start? Research is the first step in all design problems. You must ask yourself *who* will read this graphic product. The general consumer? The amateur chef? The wine connoisseur? How sophisticated are their tastes? To be effective, you must talk to your audience on their terms.

The next question is *where* the brochure will be used. Will it be mailed out? Will it be sold in a store? If so, what kind of store? Will it be handed out at

conventions or in schools? Will it be available in supermarkets?

The next step is to determine *what* you want to say. If your research had told you that the general consumer is your audience, then you may want to educate them about the different varieties of wine, or methods of making wine. If your audience is the amateur chef, you may wish to stress cooking with wine or serving the proper wine with different meals.

How do you wish to say it? This is where you formulate your idea and determine in what fashion it is to be presented. The *how* is the culmination of your research. In the case of the brochure for the California Wine Council, we have found there is a series of cooking classes being offered in the California wine country. This is perfect for our brochure, since the blending of food and wine is a natural. This is where we decide the major direction of our effort. *We will talk to amateur chefs about the benefits of cooking with wine.* Now we have a direction to pursue. From this point on, every decision will be based on this idea.

In the execution of this idea the *format, word* and *image* are used to convey the client's message. The designer must be flexible. Sometimes the words are the most important element and the images and format follow. But the images can be most important or the format can be the principle element and the words and images supportive.

Let's look at the *format*. Sometimes the form a project takes is predetermined (like a twenty-page brochure). If not, it is the designer's job to determine the format. Should it be a brochure, a poster, an

Harold Burch, Graphic Designer

index file or small pamphlet? Since most amateur chefs do not have the space in their kitchens to hang posters, and an index file or small pamphlet just isn't big enough to present the amount of materials we have, a brochure seems the best solution. And we will make the brochure slightly undersized for easy reference.

Then come the *words*. At this point we hire a copywriter to determine the direction and copy strategy for the brochure. The general direction is the combination of food and wine. A good way to do this might be to develop recipes combining the two. Because of increasing interest in foreign foods, we will present recipes from various countries. We can pick a region from each of these countries, talk about their wineries, and choose a major chef from that region to share one of his or her recipes. Once the copy is written it will be given to the client for approval and revisions.

For the *images*, we will need pictures for visual interest to show the results of the recipes. Will illustration or photography complement the text? We should have "product shots" of the finished recipes, a picture of the region from which the recipe originates, the chef, and possible additional location pictures. We are concerned with the mood of the landscape pictures, and the accuracy of the food pictures, so we decide to use photography instead of sketches or illustrations. For the best results, two photographers will be used. One will shoot the location shots, the detail shots and the chefs at work. The other will shoot the product shots of the recipes and any additional studio still lifes. We will art direct the food shots in the studio, and make creative decisions concerning composition, lighting and effect. This can

take anywhere from four to ten hours per shot and will require a food sytlist to cook the food and prepare it aesthetically.

By this time we will have determined the number of pages, the design of each page, chosen the typefaces and decided on any small graphic devices we might use (borders, rules, etc.). A comprehensive (an indication of how the printed brochure will look) must be approved by the client, and we can then order the type, select the photographs and start the final production of the project. This involves placing the type and photographs in position on boards, which are turned over to

the printer with detailed instructions. Before printing the job, he will show us proofs of each photograph. We check them for color balance, making sure everything, especially the food, is the color it should be.

The final step in our job is to visit the printer to make sure the job is coming out to our satisfaction and expectations. This is the last chance to make any final adjustments. From development of ideas to final printing, graphic designers are solving problems and making decisions that affect the appearance and effectiveness of the ultimate product.

As art director, Harold Burch devised the concept and arranged for the model, the set, the accessories, the lighting and the photographer for this photograph for a record album jacket. The client was MCA Records, the photographer was Greg Zajack.

The logo is clean, neat and efficient. The interlocking arrows suggest movement both outward and back again.

Problem
To redesign the graphic look of the Southern California Rapid Transit District in the Los Angeles area.

Designers
Saul Bass, Herb Yager & Associates, who have also designed corporate identity programs for United Airlines, American Telephone and Telegraph, Celanese, Lawry's Foods and Warner Communications.

Concept
Overhaul the entire visual image of the system, from corporate logo to the complete line of equipment. "The bus is such a pervasive object in our environment," Bass said, "that cleaning them up and making them more attractive helps eliminate visual pollution."

The concept was intended to produce a unified system of graphic design from top to bottom.

Solutions
Over a three year period, completely redesign all aspects of the Rapid Transit District equipment and design: colors, symbols, type, street information boards and the buses themselves.

Orders were initially placed for 1200 new buses (about half the district's fleet) to replace many of the older vehicles. The design of these new buses helped determine the use and applilcation of color and signage for the entire system.

The fifteen-year-old color scheme of yellow, ochre and silver was replaced by new and brighter hues. The new color scheme features a white top, black above the tinted windows, white below them, and yellow, orange and red stripes along the sides from front to back. "The whole concept, including the colors and symbol, presents a strong visual signal," according to Bass. "The stripes, for example, will give the buses a sense of motion. They are also the unofficial colors of Southern California—yellow, orange and red."

Graphic Design

The new RTD equipment makes use of fresh new colors and design concepts.

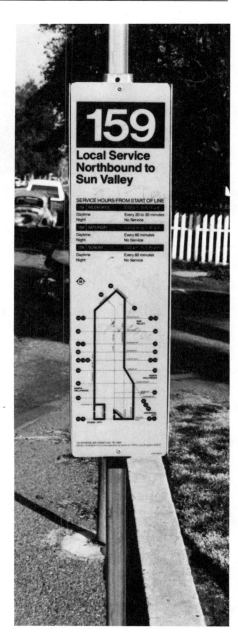

The new four-sided information signs replace flat green boards.

The old symbol or logo was a boomerang shaped symbol, a sort of flying half circle, enclosing the slanted letters RTD. The designers thought this was a "dated graphic idiom," commonly used on automobiles and appliances in the 1950's, and was not a contemporary graphic device. The new symbol is a cluster of multi-directional arrows in red, with the letters RTD upright beside it. The use of arrows in the symbol is an expression of the breadth of the RTD system, and signifies movement and direction.

Bass hopes that the new buses, new colors and new logo will be a "visible expression of the commitment to excellence of the Los Angeles region's primary public transit system."

Another part of the Bass/Yager design program was the development of four-sided bus information signs which were placed at 30,000 bus stops in several counties. Diagrams, schedules and information are graphically displayed in an attractive format that helps the bus users understand the system and makes the buses more accessible. Their yellow color with black lettering is easily readable, attracts immediate attention, and is instantly recognizable. It is also a fine piece of graphic design.

Further graphic design changes and additions were made on information brochures, route maps, schedules and driver identification badges.

Such a completely new visual identification program was conceived and designed to complement and enhance a renaissance in public transit in Los Angeles. Clarity and simplicity are essential in such instances, and graphic designers are the artists who develop programs to solve such wide-ranging problems.

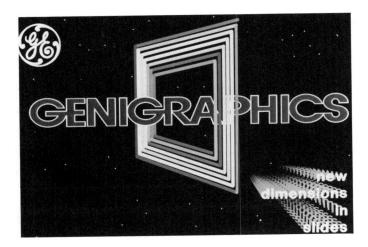

Computer Graphics Designer

No other art career area integrates artistic ability and contemporary technology as completely as the computer graphics field. Because computer capabilities and programs are constantly changing, their practical use is also in constant flux. But the creative and design abilities of artists remain almost constant. Regardless of the type of program or the desired result, the designer must have a solid foundation in design principles and visual problem solving.

The use of computer graphics is revolutionizing the graphics design field. While there will always be a need for the personal and creative approach to solving visual problems, there is also a need for speed, accuracy and the ability to update visual information. In such cases, computer graphics is the logical answer. There is no need for pens, brushes, X-acto knives, rulers or paste pots. Instead, the designer may use an electrical stylus and electrical tablet to draw any image in any color or intensity desired. Some systems use keyboards that can be programmed to design, recall and place images and letters on the screen. Many artists are beginning to work with sophisticated electronic equipment to create graphic images for their clients.

Engineers and industrial designers are also using computers to draw and analyze tools and products. They can put an image into the computer, revolve it, turn it and project it three-dimensionally. With printouts available at every stage, the time saved in drawing alone can be tremendous.

What computer graphics designers do
Computer systems require different inputs and programs and produce different results, but all designers look for a computer which makes or calls up designs quickly, which can make countless alterations in the visual material, and which is adaptable. Some systems rely on hard copy printouts; others are capable of producing slides for visual presentations. The needs of the designer and client will dictate the system to be used.

Some systems permit the graphic artist to create original art or modify existing pictures, charts or diagrams with a broad selection of colors, saturations, line weights, shapes and intensities. Art can be broadcast live, transferred to videotape or stored in the computer's memory for later use. It can also be run through a printer to produce hard copy.

Artists may use electronic pens (styluses) to communicate with some systems. Slight pressure activates the commands and images can be drawn on video screens. Multiple type fonts and colors are available. Previously drawn shapes that are needed often can be recalled from the memory system. All work can be revised, parts can be erased and replaced and all can be reduced or enlarged instantly. The electronic palette in some systems does all routine work, allowing the artists to see the finished product in a variety of color combinations and sizes. It is like having an electronic scratch pad.

Other systems excel at producing graphs, designs and various types of art from computer consoles. Artists use the generating system to translate ideas and rough sketches into slides for video presentation. Computers can store thousands of symbols, many colors and type styles and layout formats, which can be combined in any way necessary. These elements (type, for example) can be stretched, squashed, flattened or thinned down in any color and to any size with the touch of several keys. The full color image on the screen can be altered to fit required changes and then can be stored for future changes or use, put on tape, duplicated or made into slides. The graphic artist controls all these operations.

There are many other systems, programs and methods for creating graphic images and speeding up the graphic design process. For possible applications to the editorial design field, see Editorial Design.

What qualities are helpful for a computer graphics designer?
They must have solid foundations in graphic design and the desire and ability to work with computers. Since this field of design is new and rapidly changing, its career

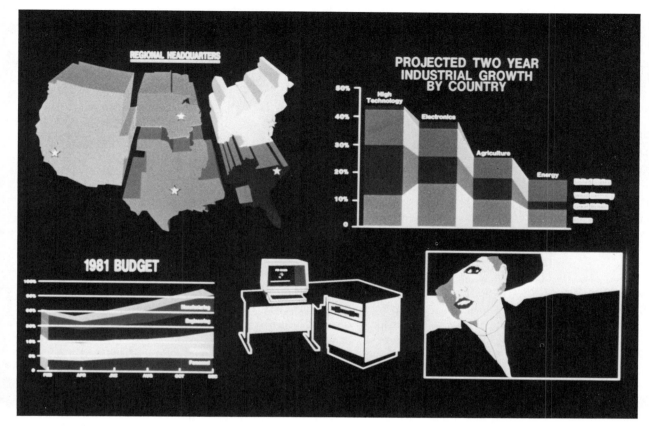

DICOMED's D38 Design Station is part of the DICOMEDIA II
Slidesystem. Photograph: DICOMED Corporation, and *ReproGraphics*

possibilities are many and varied. Artists interested in experimentation, expansion of graphic design ideas and research in programming and visual production are likely candidates. Such careers require patience, curiosity and insight into both design and computer programming.

What other careers require similar qualities?
All areas of computer programming, design and use, as well as industrial design with computer technology (See Industrial Design) would be possible alternative careers. This area of design is so new, however, that there will be many career opportunities in the future that are not presently in existence.

What can be done now?
Prepare as you would for any graphics design career: by taking all art classes possible. Include English, science, mathematics, history and computer science in your schedule. See other areas of the Graphic Design section for further activities and emphases.

Join computer clubs at school or in your community and try to attend or teach at computer camps in the summer. Take a summer job in a computer shop or the electronics department of a discount or department store.

Specific computer systems will change as technology changes. The latest equipment will be found in large design studios and advertising agencies, as well as government projects and laboratories. Artists working with such computers will learn on the job.

Visit museums of science and industry to become familiar with computer possibilities. Magazines such as *Computer Graphics World, Design Drafting and ReproGraphics, Byte, Compute*! and *Interface Age* will keep you up-to-date on new equipment and various phases of graphic design.

Which colleges offer necessary programs?
Any schools with strong graphic design emphases will offer the necessary background and training. Check the charts at the back of the book. Some schools have computer graphics in their curriculums, and you should check their catalogs for such courses.

Layout And Paste-up Artists

Layout refers to the sketched arrangement of pictures, headings, copy and captions in an ad, a magazine article or a book. Layout artists get all the copy and pictures from designers or art directors and fit them into given spaces (a single or double page spread, for example). They must know about typography, photo sizing and cropping and how readers look at printed pages.

Paste-up is the assembly of all the pieces in a design job, and the final preparation for photography and plate-making. The finished product is often called a "mechanical" because it is part of the mechanical process of reproduction and printing. Paste-up artists use the plans of layout artists as their guides, and neatly and accurately paste the photo-ready type, headings, line art and photostats (photograph indications) exactly in place, so they are camera-ready for the photographer and engraver. (See Editorial Design.)

Paste-up and layout jobs are excellent training positions for graphic designers, art directors and photoengraving specialists. The first jobs held by most graphic design graduates are in agencies where they work on layout and paste-up.

What layout artists do

Layout artists begin their work by gathering all available materials for a page or an ad: typed copy, photographs, art work, logo, graphic design roughs and whatever else is required. They study the material and determine the client's intention. They confer with the designer and select heading, body and caption type to suit that purpose, and order the type to be set.

Layouts are usually done with pencils and charcoal or pastels on layout pads. Headlines are sketched in the exact size and proportions they are to have in final print. Body copy is indicated by a series of parallel lines. The size of this block of type is determined by the layout artist, who knows how to fit copy to a required space. Pictures (photographs and illustrations) are also fitted to size and space requirements and are sent to the photo lab to be enlarged or reduced to fit the designs. Layout artists must know and follow the elements and principles of design when preparing these layouts.

Good layout artists develop crisp, simple styles which can easily be read by graphic designers, clients and paste-up artists. The work must be clean and directions must be easy to follow, since layouts are the blueprints for the finished work.

One of Coca Cola's graphic designers shows the final paste-up, including acetate overlays and directions, that is required to produce the printed door knob advertisement shown at right. Photograph: Gerald Brommer

What paste-up artists do

There are two types of paste-ups: one the printer simply uses as a guide; the other is the camera-ready work used to shoot the final film for the photoengraver. In the first, the artist pastes galley proofs (initial copies of the set type) into trial positions to check the size and location of copy. From these paste-ups the printer makes page proofs, used for the final editing and correcting of text and captions. This is often the first job that a young artist gets in an agency.

Camera-ready paste-ups must be done accurately and neatly because they will be reproduced exactly. The paste-up artist works on illustration board and draws the necessary guides and boundaries in blue pencil, then carefully traces the layout on the board. Because photographs and halftone illustrations will be photographed separately, at this time their spaces are indicated exactly on the board with solid blocks. These areas are either inked precisely with black ink or blocked in rubylith, solid red plastic sheeting. Final photographs and art will be shot through these "windows" which will appear clear on the photographic negatives (See Editorial Design). All ruled lines and black areas are inked in by the artists.

When all type proofs, photostats and prints are gathered, the artists are ready for final paste-up. Following the traced outlines, the items are cut to fit and are adhered in place with rubber cement, glue sticks, wax or other methods. Type must be straight and accurately positioned; it is generally put in place with a pair of

64

tweezers. When type, lines and "windows" are in place, and photographs and artwork are correctly sized, the paste-up is camera-ready. The rest of the reproduction process is up to the photoengravers and printers.

The graphic designer or art director in charge of each project will be watching carefully to see that the entire job is done to the client's specifications and satisfaction.

What qualities are helpful for layout and paste-up artists?

Layout artists must have a background in design, composition and typography. They should be aware of current trends in type, layout styles and techniques and must try to satisfy the particular needs of each client. They use simple mechanical devices to determine photograph and illustration proportions quickly, and should be able to specify type to fit required spaces. Layout artists must be familiar with many layout styles and be able to adapt their ideas to fit the purpose of each job. Good design sense and the ability to draw are essential.

Paste-up artists must be neat and painstakingly accurate above all. They must be able to work under deadlines and to give clear directions to photographers and engravers. They work with a variety of tools (T-squares, triangles, ruling pens, X-acto knives, compasses and the like) and must be familiar with new tools and materials peculiar to their work. Their positions in agencies require that they take direction from others (layout artists, graphic designers and art directors, for example). Following such directions is crucial to the outcome of the projects and the ultimate satisfaction of the clients.

What other careers require similar qualities?

The ability of layout artists to organize pages and form well-designed page units is required in magazine and book publishing and editorial design (See Editorial Design). Newspaper layout work is generally not as creative, but provides excellent experience. Publishers and printing companies that specialize in school yearbooks or annual reports will often offer layout services to their customers, and employ such artists.

The skills of paste-up artists (neatness, accuracy and the ability to meet deadlines) are requisite for many art careers, and most graphic designers begin their careers in such jobs. Similar qualities are needed for drafters, industrial designers, animation artists, publication staff artists and positions in the printing trades.

What can be done now?

Your classes in high school should include drawing, drafting, composition and design, printmaking and photography. Take other art classes if available and if they fit your schedule. Work on a yearbook or newspaper staff is extremely useful, especially if layout and art positions are open.

Part-time work in a print shop or in any kind of art studio would be beneficial and would help you understand the entire production process.

Looking through well-designed magazines and books is an enjoyable way to learn. It makes you aware of a variety of layout styles and of the need for excellence in design, execution and production. There are many excellent magazines which will give you a feel for layout. *CA* (*Communication Arts*), *Print* and *Art Direction* are oriented toward graphic design. Good design can also be seen in the ads and layout of *Life, Omni, Architectural Digest, Museum, Portfolio* and most of the interior design magazines. Check your school library or the public library for others, and watch for outstanding advertisements, billboards, and television spots. Also study the brochures published by auto manufacturers, banks, furniture manufacturers and clothing manufacturers. You should establish a resource file of excellent examples for future use.

Which colleges offer necessary programs?

Art schools and college art departments that have graphic design emphases will offer the necessary courses for a background in layout and paste-up.

Many community colleges offer courses that will be beneficial, and trade schools often place special emphasis on courses that prepare students for production and paste-up jobs.

No degrees are essential for this work, but if the job is to be a step on to a higher position, other courses and a degree will be needed. Your schooling will make you familiar with the general processes involved in producing paste-ups and layouts; the specific requirements of each studio or agency you work for may differ. You will learn these requirements on the job.

Check the charts at the back of the book for schools that offer strong programs in graphic design.

Type designer Ed Benguiat puts the finishing touches on his pencil outlines for a new typeface that emphasizes subtle curves and a variety of visual weights. Photograph: Type Face Corporation

Letterer, Calligrapher, Type Designer

Almost every piece of commercial art makes use of words; some advertisements and design programs use words alone. Successful graphic designers must have complete knowledge of lettering, letterforms and typography. Though they may never have to produce finished hand lettering, they must be able to draw accurate letters in their layouts and sketches. When finished hand lettering is needed, designers call in specialists: letterers and calligraphers. For type and typesetting needs, the work is turned over to typographers who use letter systems designed by type designers.

Early type designs were based on handwriting. Following the invention of the printing press, German and Italian print types were the basis for succeeding styles of lettering. Type styles went through centuries of gradual development to suit the growing needs of the printing industry. Thanks to lasers and other electronic equipment, type styles today are in the thousands, with new designs being created almost daily.

In this age of computerization and electronics, it is interesting that there has been a recent resurgence of interest in hand lettering, and art schools report heavy enrollment in calligraphy classes.

What letterers do

Letterers are skilled in hand lettering with pens, brushes, ink and paint. In spite of the thousands of type faces available electronically, designers often require a unique style of lettering, and therefore the expertise of letterers. The design teams in large agencies usually include one artist who is especially adept at lettering by hand.

All letters are made up of definite, separate parts: vertical, horizontal, round, half round and slanted strokes. These strokes have been used in various combinations for centuries, and successful letterers must know the history of lettering. Graphic designers know that it requires great skill to work at lettering, and they call on experts when such skills are needed. They also realize that distinctive lettering, rather than packaged type, may be more appealing to their clients.

Letterers make final art in ink or paint to fit the designed pages. They may ink letters in one-stroke techniques or they may first sketch their letters to determine size and style, then draw them carefully with pencil before final inking. They use T-squares, triangles and rulers along with pens and ink to produce the finished letters. Their work must be neat and exact and meet the design requirements for style, since it will then be photographed for platemaking.

Letterers must master both individual letters and script (connected letters). They may need to letter or script the words or lines several times and then select the best examples to paste-up on the finished art.

What calligraphers do

The word calligraphy is Greek for "beautiful writing." Calligraphers can be a bit more inventive and creative than letterers; they need not work from prescribed styles, and their job is to embellish, to decorate, not simply to letter. They use a variety of special pens, and must constantly practice to keep their work fluid and under control.

Calligraphers generally work at their own pace and in their own studios. There are few calligraphers who work full time; more often they work at other jobs and take on calligraphy assignments as time permits. Advertising agencies, special events promoters and civic and cultural agencies often request their services.

Some large cities and counties employ calligraphers in their graphic design departments, where they are responsible for the decorative lettering on special awards, plaques and documents.

What type designers do

All the type you have ever seen in print was designed by type designers. For hundreds of years, there were only a limited number of type styles, because type was cast in metal and the use of many styles would have been extremely clumsy and costly. Today, thousands of type faces are designed to be reproduced by photo composition processes and computer composition terminals. The printing industry is beginning to use digital offset plate exposure systems (bypassing film) and various laser technologies which will expand the possible use of type styles.

Type designers work for a variety of companies that produce type in several forms, from stick-down letter sheets to computer tapes. Designers work with the traditional elements of letters, but make innovations and distinctive departures and additions. To the layman, these differences might hardly be noticeable, but to graphic designers who must use letters that work with an ad format or illustration theme, such unique characteristics are essential. Some companies have type designed and patented to be used only by their firms in advertising and brochures.

Type designers must be able to carry their concepts out in all letters of the alphabet, in both upper and lower case. All the elements of such new alphabets must work well together. The designers sketch, design and draw the letters carefully, finally inking them exactly as they wish them to be. They are all done in a single large size, and then are photographically reproduced in a variety of sizes. With certain computer capabilities, a single letter can be expanded, condensed or slanted at various angles at a moment's notice, and custom letters are thereby immediately available to designers and art directors.

What qualities are helpful in these professions?

Neatness, exactness and a sense of proportion are essential to all artists working with lettering. All such artists must work within certain size restrictions, and must be able to work in great detail, on small surfaces and with a limited range of art materials. Often they must redo their work in order to get an exact fit or to make sure all letters are well composed, spaced and drawn. Patience and perseverance are necessary in such circumstances.

What other careers require similar qualities?

People who like to work with type will feel at home in several areas of the printing trade: as a typographer, typesetter or computer operator, for instance. Careers in various publishing industries require expertise in working with type, type styles, sizing, specifications, reproduction and printing.

The qualities of patience, care, neatness and exactness are required in several other art fields, including graphic design, industrial design, architectural drafting, drafting, airbrush work, sign painting, architectural graphics and in media-related design positions.

What can be done now?

Include drafting, drawing, design and printmaking among your high school classes. If print shop is available, it should be taken also. Lettering or special calligraphy classes are often available from the extension divisions of colleges. Check with your local art schools.

Work on school publications (yearbook and newspaper) is a natural outlet for your interest in type. Part-time jobs in printing shops provide practical work with type, typesetting, sizing, styles and the actual printing process. All such experience is excellent preparation for future jobs in graphic design.

Magazines and periodicals that can offer career suggestions and ideas include: *Print, CA (Communication Arts), Design,* and *U&lc.* You can get an idea of type styles by picking up a catalog of stick-down type from your local art supply store. Your library will probably have books on lettering and calligraphy.

If you are interested in decorative lettering, there are calligraphy societies that exhibit their work annually in many cities. Check with your art teacher or art supply dealer to locate one in your area.

Which schools offer necessary programs?

All colleges and art schools with good graphic design departments will have courses in lettering and type design (Check the charts at the back of the book). A look at catalogs will tell you if such courses are available at the schools you are considering. Some community colleges and trade schools also offer courses in lettering and calligraphy. Expert calligraphers often teach classes at adult evening schools, privately or at extension divisions for some universities and colleges. Owners of art supply stores will know if such classes are available.

Using felt markers, a graphic designer makes as many as fifteen idea "roughs" that are submitted to the client.

When the client approves one of the comprehensives, the finished art work is prepared.

Outdoor Advertising Designer

Billboards got their name a half century ago when bills (posters) were posted to wooden "boards." Today, sophisticated outdoor advertisements are developed by large companies employing many artists. Displays take the form of prepasted poster sections affixed to standardized panels, printed or silk screened sheets that are pasted to existing display panels, or hand painted sections assembled on the display site. Some displays have electronically controlled moving parts, some are painted on location and others use plastic panels lit from the inside.

Many types of artists create these outdoor advertisements, and by following a single project from start to finish (a billboard advertising Springfield peaches), it will be easy to see how they must work together.

What qualities are helpful for an outdoor advertising designer?

Graphic designers who work for outdoor advertisers must be able to sketch, make layouts and put comprehensives together. They must know photography, painting, illustration and type design, and above all must be aware of advertising psychology and marketing techniques. They always work with clients and other artists in preparing their designs, and must therefore be able to work well with people.

Photographers and painters must be skilled in their fields. Indeed, many are exhibiting artists who work for outdoor advertisers on a daily or free-lance basis and who photograph and paint on their own time. They must be skilled in the use of color and proportion.

Color photographs, lettering and necessary art are pasted up to create the accurately scaled "mechanical." The mechanical is photographed onto two glass plates, one for the left and one for the right portion of the design.

The design is projected full size (this one is 14 by 48 feet) onto white paper placed on a wall covered with grounded copper or steel screening. The pattern maker traces the image with a 500-volt electric pencil, whose arc creates thousands of tiny perforations in the paper.

This process produces a "pounce pattern:" a super-sized tracing made by the electric pencil. This full-sized pattern is placed on white primed sections of plywood. Workers then use "pounce bags," made of porous cloth and filled with charcoal dust, to daub and rub each line of the pattern. These dotted lines are then "heavied up" to serve as a guide to painters.

The painters mix their colors to match the color photographs.

The gigantic painting process starts. Even with special motorized scaffolds and large brushes, it takes five or six days to finish the painting.

When finished, the painted sections are taken out of the studio and placed in an outdoor display unit.

All photographs courtesy Foster–Kleiser, Inc.

What other careers require similar qualities?

Graphic designers in other fields require similar backgrounds and training. Some contemporary artists who work in very large realistic styles had their training in outdoor advertising studios. Some sign painters and muralists have similar interests in large visual presentations.

What can be done now?

Drawing, painting and design classes should be taken in high school. You should work on posters for every possible activity in school. Some schools have service clubs which make posters, signs and ads for school activities, and you should be active in such organizations. Help design and paint stage sets for plays and musicals, and generally become involved in visual presentations of all kinds.

Part-time work in an outdoor advertising company would be ideal, but other useful work experience might be found in a printing shop, sign painting studio, department or hardware store, graphic design agency or newspaper ad department. Any job which puts you in contact with graphic designers is beneficial.

Take photographs of attractive displays and begin a collection of such resource materials. This will sharpen your eyes, make you more aware of excellence in design and provide you with ideas for posters and design projects.

Which colleges offer necessary programs?

Most outdoor advertising designers have graduated from schools with excellent graphic design or advertising design departments (check the lists at the back of the book). Special college training is not necessary for skilled positions in the studio, but on-the-job training is desirable. Trade schools in large cities offer courses that will help in some of the skilled positions. Painters will need either fine arts or illustration background and training.

Record Jacket Designer

The visual graphics on hundreds of record jackets immediately attract the attention of anyone who walks into a record shop. Their combined impact is overwhelming. That some graphic designers spend their time designing only record jackets is an indication of the specialization now found in the graphic design field. There are design studios located in the record production centers of the country that work only on this type of project.

Several types of clients employ these specialists. Large record companies who have recording artists under contract employ their own graphic designers. Successful recording artists and groups may wish to produce their own albums with an independent recording studio, and will then engage graphic design studios or free-lance designers to produce the jackets.

As in other graphic design projects, the artists involved in designing record jackets must work with other artists, illustrators, copywriters, typographers, letterers, photographers and printing establishments to produce the cover. They may do most of the work themselves or they may employ other agencies and artists to do some of it.

What record jacket designers do

The initial approaches to designing record jackets vary according to the company, the recording artist and the designer. Some musicians have their own ideas about the jackets, while others leave such matters in the hands of

Commercial Art and Design

Graphic artist Charlie White, a top designer of record jackets, uses his airbrush to obtain the effects for which he is well known. Notice the size of the art is twice the size of the eventual jacket. Photograph: Joseph Gatto

their agents, the recording companies or the graphic designers.

After the initial contact is made, however, the idea is developed much like other graphic assignments. When the title is determined, the designer listens to the record, talks with the recording artist or group if possible, watches a performance or carries out other research if necessary.

The graphic designers prepare rough idea sketches that present several possible approaches to the album cover, according to the client's wishes and the album's mood. When one of them is approved, a detailed color sketch(called a comprehensive drawing) is prepared. This will indicate color, type of art, display and body type and exact format.

The designers then arrange for all the elements to be produced. Photographers, illustrators, letterers, typographers, copywriters and printers are contracted, if necessary. The illustrators and photographers are vitally important, since the album cover must compete for attention with hundreds of other jackets in the record shops.

Factors influencing the visual design may include the mood of the album, the historical content, the activities of the composer or author, the performance style of the group, the style of music or message, the personalities involved or the wishes of the producer or musicians.

Once the elements are gathered together (art work, body type, photographs, heading and display type) the design is prepared for the cameras and for final platemaking and printing.

Purchasers are attracted to a record by its cover. The jacket designer must recognize the importance of his designs, and be familiar with the audience of the performer. The jacket must have dignity, uniqueness or visual punch and must work in harmony with the contents to form a unified package.

What qualities are helpful for a record jacket designer?

All those involved in the design of record jackets must have an interest in the content of the albums. They must be able to create meaningful designs and illustrations. They must work well with a variety of people: recording artists, symphony directors, design agency personnel, talent agents and visual artists of various types.

They must be able to meet deadlines—sticking to an album production schedule is crucial to the success of the record. Jacket designers must be able to listen to the ideas

of others, combine them with their own knowledge of color and design and create jackets that visually suggest the contents of the records and the desires of their clients.

The size and shape of record covers is somewhat restrictive, and designers must be satisfied to work within these limitations. They must be familiar with all phases of graphic design, from illustration to typography and production.

What other careers require similar qualities?

Careers in book and magazine publishing and illustration are closely akin to record jacket design (See Editorial Design). All deal with editorial content, interpretive illustration, appropriate graphic design and typography.

Illustrators who provide art for records can also work well for advertisers, magazine editors and book jacket designers. Designers and illustrators who can work within prescribed limitations can also design brochures, annual reports, posters and television graphics. The ability to sense moods and design accordingly would be helpful in most television and film graphics and in film animation and background preparation (See Film and Television).

What can be done now?

Drawing, design and painting classes should be taken in high school. Other necessary courses include art history, history, music history, literature, English and business. You should work on student publications and be involved in making posters and signs as much as you can.

Collect well-designed record jackets and examples of fine illustration. Study illustration techniques and try them out in your painting classes. Visit local art schools and see what design majors are producing. Study carefully the graphic effects on television and in film.

Look through magazines such as: CA (*Communication Arts*), *Art Direction, Print* and the like. Be constantly aware of appropriate art in books, magazines, brochures, advertisements and record jackets.

Which colleges offer necessary programs?

Schools with excellent graphic design departments will provide the necessary training. Look through catalogs for classes in: graphic design, illustration, lettering and perhaps a specialized class in record jacket design. Most successful jacket designers have strong backgrounds in illustration and editorial photography. Check the list in the back of the book for schools offering such background.

Schools in cities where records are produced may have access to special resources (artists, designers, field trips, part-time work, seminars, meetings and guest lecturers) of the industry.

Other Careers In Graphic Design

Advertising Agency Fashion Art Director (See Other Careers in the Fashion Industry)

Advertising Agency Television Art Director (See Other Careers in Film and Television)

Airbrush Artist
Airbrush artists are expert at painting with airbrushes (small art tools which spray fine mists of color) and can represent smooth, shiny surfaces and transparent materials. They are often illustrators who may be hired to produce designs for record or book jackets or advertising programs (See Record Jacket Designer and Other Careers in Editorial Design). They are either free-lance or studio artists and are often fine artists who are hired because of their special skills or styles of working. Some airbrush artists specialize in photo retouching (See Other Careers in Photography).

Architectural Graphics Artist (See Other Careers in Architecture)

Art School Design Teacher (See Art Education)

Bank Note Designer
These artists engrave plates for the printing of special government securities such as stamps, bonds and paper currency. They are familiar with engraving techniques and printing processes, and are able to adapt preliminary idea drawings for use on engraving plates. They work in great detail, and must be capable of using line effectively.

Ben-Day Artist
Ben-day artists work in large design studios, publishing houses and printing establishments where they apply ben-day tints (shadings in the form of dots of different intensities) to drawings or zinc plates. Stick-down patterns are used in their work, which is closely involved with the printing industry. Ben-days are also used by architects, cartoonists, technical illustrators and many graphic designers in preparing art work for photo reproduction.

Block Engraver
Using special tools, wood engravers incise lines into hardwood blocks which are used to print book illustrations, advertisements, greeting cards and finely detailed art work. They often reproduce black and white photographs in line and texture.

Book Jacket Designer (See Other Careers in Editorial Design)

Compositor (See also Typographer, below)
Compositors set type for ads and body copy. They use machines, computers or hand methods to assemble proofs in galleys. They determine type size, style and compositional sequence, and follow copywriters' scripts and directions. They also proofread for errors, make corrections and work closely with graphic designers, layout and paste-up artists to make type fit required spaces.

Creative Director (See Art Director)

Engrosser (See also Calligrapher, Letterer)
Engrossers use pen and ink to letter formal documents such as diplomas, testimonials, charts, citations and appointments. These artists are usually called calligraphers, and are generally free-lance artists, or their lettering tasks are part of a larger job.

Executive Art Director (See Art Director)

Graphic Arts Technician
These artists work with art directors and graphic designers to prepare camera-ready work for photographing and plate-making. They operate machines that type master copies (stencils, tracings, direct plates and photo-offsets), and use offset duplicating machines and various cameras. They are usually employed in large design studios.

Greeting Card Designer (See Other Careers in Editorial Design)

Group Supervisor (See Art Director)

Illustrator (See Editorial Illustrator)

Municipal Graphic Designer
These artists design signs and symbols for cities. Their work appears in public places such as parks, municipal buildings, city vehicles, subway systems and bus stations. They must have a working command of color, type, graphic design and symbols in order to make travel directions and locations clear and easy to understand. Awareness of contemporary building materials and various painting media is essential.

Muralist (See Other Careers in Architecture)

Paste-Up Camera Artist
These artists work with graphic designers in preparing copy, photographs, art and decoration for final plate-making. They size and adjust visual material, photographs and copy, then photograph and print the work, and mount illustrations and copy on paper, following the layout artist's designs. They crop illustrations and photographs, size the type blocks and prepare spot color applications and backgrounds. They also prepare type headings for layouts. They work in the darkroom, developing all types of photographs. They often work in design agencies or as free-lance artists, but are most often employed by book and magazine publishers.

Photographer See Photography)

Poster Artist (See Sign Painter, below)

Promotion Designer
Promotion designers work in design agencies or within corporation design departments. They devise and carry out promotional programs and campaigns for selling special products, but are not involved in consumer sales campaigns. They work with art directors, but are responsible for the total development of the programs, including concept, writing copy, illustration, layout, paste-up, and camera-ready completion. Although they work with other staff or free-lance photographers, illustrators and letterers, they often do much of the preparation work themselves.

Retail Store Art Director
The retail store art director, who works for large department or chain stores, plans the ads that a store places in various publications. He or she designs the store's posters and counter signs. (See Showcard Artist, below). Retail art directors must coordinate the elements of graphic design, type, color illustration and photography in order to present a unified store image.

Senior Art Director (See Art Director)

Showcard Artist
Showcard artists paint, print or write small signs or showcards for use in stores. They use brushes, markers or simple printing machines to make signs that usually stand on counters, in displays or in decorated windows. They must have knowledge of type styles and the spacing of letters, and be able to letter freely, quickly and easily. Such signs are not permanent and are replaced regularly.

These artists are usually employed by large stores or mechandising chains, and often work in display departments.

Sign Painter
Sign painters design, draw, lay out and paint letters and designs on a variety of surfaces. They use drawing and measuring tools to insure accuracy. The medium they use depends on the location of the finished work and the quality of the surface. They must have knowledge of letter styles, type, color and design. Many fancy lettering styles cannot be found in typical type books, and must be custom-designed by sign painters.

Silk Screen Artist
There are numerous jobs connected with commercial silk processes and graphic production. Silk screen companies do production work for many types of clients, and there are silk screen divisions in some manufacturing companies and design agencies.

The commercial silk screen process is used to make posters, ads and greeting cards and to decorate a wide variety of materials.

Silk screen workers prepare the frames, design the art and type, cut the stencils and print the work by hand or by machine. Inspectors and supervisors oversee the work. Artists with special skills and interests are especially valuable in this industry.

Sketch Artist
Advertising agencies employ sketch artists to draw and render the pictures on print ad comprehensives and TV storyboards. Sketch artists can draw almost anything in any medium. Their work does not often appear in print because it is only made for comprehensives and layouts; illustrators make the final art. They often work within agencies, but are also free-lance artists. Working and drawing eight hours a day in this job is the best possible training for an aspiring illustrator.

Title designer (See Other Careers in Film and Television)

Typographer (See also Compositor, above)
Typography combines aesthetic decisions with technical processes and is an important part of graphic design. Typographers understand type styles and their application to design and expression. They calculate space, determine type size and prepare type to fit assigned layouts. They are expert in preparing type for printing and in the use of machines and computers.

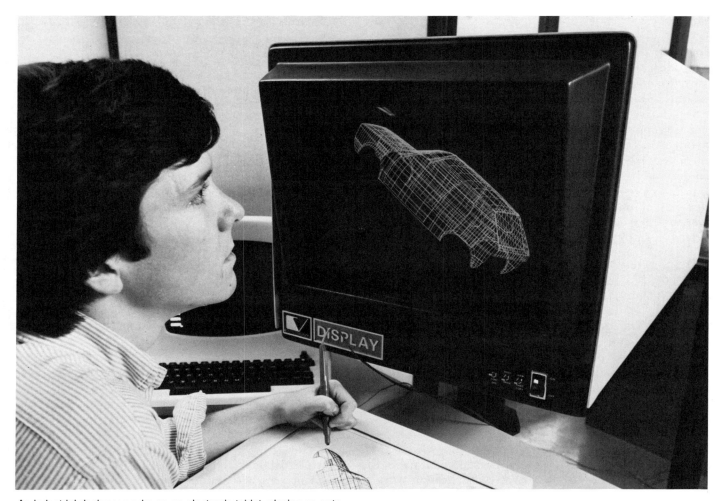

An industrial designer works on an electronic tablet, placing an automobile design on the video screen. The image can now be turned, rotated and analyzed from any angle the designer desires. Photograph: University of Detroit and *Drafting and Repro Digest*

Industrial Design

Industrial designers shape products. From concept to final packaging, they are responsible for the quality, aesthetic appeal and function of items consumers purchase and use. Designers determine the characteristic "look" of a line of automobiles or the quality one "feels" when picking up a telephone or ballpoint pen. Their skill and expertise have certain effects upon our well-being, life-style and physical environment.

Like architecture, industrial design requires broad training. Designers must be part engineer, architect, drafter, sculptor, graphic designer and salesperson. They are more than artists; their skills must combine artistic talent with manufacturing know-how. Some designers are generalists, and work on a variety of products, packages and applications; others are specialists, exploring a single area such as plastics, small appliances or lighting. Still others advise corporation designers on product development.

Industrial designers are especially skilled in working with three-dimensional form. They have a knowledge of natural and synthetic materials and technological progress, and an awareness of function and aesthetic form. They work with products, packages for those products, and with the tools and processes by which the products are made. They design for the general consumer, for business, industry and transportation.

Industrial design became a specialized field in the 1920's, when consumer products were first mass-produced. Suddenly merchandise was created for a mass market rather than a specific customer, and consistency of design, safety in use and corporate identification became important considerations.

Louis Sullivan, an American architect, coined the phrase in the 1890's that was also to become the credo for industrial designers: "form follows function." This means that the form of an object is determined by how it will be used. A chair is something on which we sit (that is its function), but it is also something that we must look at (that is its form). First it must be useful and comfortable; second, it must have a fine appearance, enhanced by the designer's use of texture, color, style and decoration. Industrial designers are experts on the way people and products work together.

Industrial designers may work in any of several career situations: design consulting firms, free-lance studios, on the design staffs of manufacturing companies, in educational institutions, government agencies or research firms and for the armed forces. In all of these situations they must understand the basic principles of engineering and speak the language of engineers. If the product has mechanical parts, engineers will create them, but industrial designers determine how they will look and how easily and safely they will handle. They also work with architects on facility planning of commercial buildings.

To obtain the broad background necessary for a successful industrial design career, college training is almost essential. A series of basic art classes (drawing, painting, sculpture and the like) may be followed by courses in basic engineering, materials, manufacturing methods, model making and drafting. Many schools offer major emphases or degrees in Industrial Design, and their curriculums may include courses such as: airbrush techniques, display design, drafting, drawing, experimental design, furniture design, industrial design, interior design, lettering, model making, package design, product design, rendering, sculpture, shop practice, transportation design and welding.

In addition to these, there may be specifically detailed classes in automotive design, lighting design or other subjects related to manufacturing. Other studies often include basic architecture, graphics, photography, social science, marketing, human engineering (how the body works), creative writing, ecology, business and communications.

Employers generally look for people who have some grounding in architecture or engineering, for example, rather than artists who have specialized in a single area. A broad base of interest and studies helps make an industrial designer more versatile in his or her approach to practical design problems.

Computer technology is becoming increasingly important to industrial designers and engineers. Electronic manipulation, on a video screen, of geometric shapes and complicated drawings simplifies the analysis of a part or product. Stored information can be used to design special tools to produce required parts of a newly designed product. Established products can be redesigned by computer systems and made more efficient, easier to handle and better looking.

Package Designer

Package designing combines the three-dimensional skills of an industrial designer with the two-dimensional expertise and design sense of a graphic designer. Bottles, tubes, boxes and protective overwraps are the creations of package designers. They are also responsible for the graphic symbols, words, color and design of labels.

Some packaging is simply utilitarian, providing safe storage and shipping, and easy handling. Other packages are designed to attract the attention of consumers. Package design can also help project a specific corporate image.

Whatever the packaging problem or intention, package designers who free-lance, work in design offices or on corporation design staffs attempt to enclose products in packages that will protect and enhance them.

What package designers do

The final results of package design give little indication of the planning, effort and creative expression that went into them. Package designers begin their problem solving processes, after meeting with clients and art directors, by sketching many possible solutions. These ideas are evaluated and modified, and the three or four best sketches are culled and presented for approval.

Sometimes one sketch is immediately approved. Often, however, several are singled out and developed into three-dimensional models complete with color, lettering and graphic applications.

Color renderings of the anticipated packages illustrate their possible appearance in advertising media. Photographs of the models indicate the package's visual im-

pact. Package designers develop multi-media presentations to demonstrate the effectiveness of their ideas.

These ideas are either approved by the clients, art directors or corporate boards, or are sent back for further modification. When the package designs are finally approved, they are sent to manufacturers to be produced.

What qualities are helpful for a package designer?

Package designers are proficient at three-dimensional design and must make accurate models of packages, containers and wrappers of all sorts. They must be visual problem solvers who work mostly with form and space.

They must be able to work well with art directors, clients, manufacturers and salespeople, and must also enjoy working alone on projects until they are completed.

They must be able to sketch, draw and paint and have strong backgrounds in color and design. They should be able to evaluate their own work and accept the suggestions and ideas of others. Package design is only one part of a total project which includes product development, advertising, graphics and the like. A package designer must be a good team member, working toward team accomplishment, not individual glory.

IBM's designers often win prizes in industrial and package design competitions. This large box is designed to hold many packages that hold other packages that hold electronic typewriter ribbons and erasing tapes. Photograph: Joseph Gatto

What other careers require similar qualities?

Package designers would also feel comfortable working in graphic design studios or advertising agencies. The ability to work as part of a design team is vital to any graphic or industrial design situation.

Skill with three-dimensional materials and at model building is necessary for careers in sculpture, stage design, architectural graphics, television set design, display design and model building.

What can be done now?

High school art classes should include drawing, painting, three-dimensional design, sculpture, drafting and graphic design. Other classes may include business, psychology, mathematics, English, creative writing, home economics and consumerism. Model building is an excellent hobby directly associated with package design.

Collect good examples of creative packaging, containers and bottles of all types. Study packaging in department stores and observe its use on television and in magazine advertisements. Fine examples of package design can be seen in some science and industry museums or at trade fairs.

Part-time work in any graphic design situation would be helpful (sign painting, department store display, label design and production, graphic design agency), or in a grocery store where containers are handled and sold.

Magazines that provide insights into good packaging include: *ID (Industrial Design), Packaging Design, Craft Horizons, Print, CA (Communication Arts), Package Engineering, Packaging Review* (England) and *Modo* (Italy).

Which colleges offer necessary programs?

Art schools and colleges with good industrial design programs will offer excellent courses in package design. Many graphic design curriculums also include such courses. A strong background in three-dimensional design, graphic design and product design and development are necessary. Check the charts at the back of the book.

Degrees in industrial design are not essential, but thorough preparation will broaden your career opportunities in package design. Some trade schools may provide practical courses in model building, product photography and graphic design that can be the basis for further study or the start of a career.

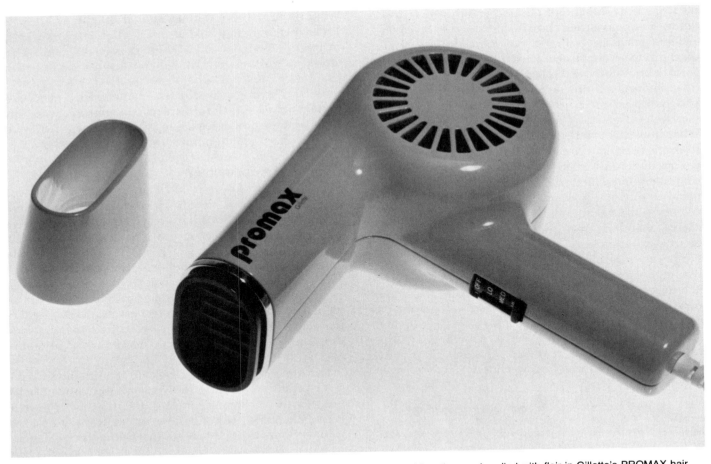

Form and function are handled with flair in Gillette's PROMAX hair dryer, designed by Dale Fahnstrom and Robert Peterson. Photograph: Robert Peterson Designs

Product Designer

Product designers can be found in every manufacturing industry that makes consumer products. Such artists are hired to create new products by combining their artistic talent, design sense, understanding of consumer needs and broad market perspectives with knowledge of various materials and manufacturing processes.

They must know what competing manufacturers are producing and be aware of style trends. They research product performance, work with samplemakers to develop prototypes and estimate sales impact on the potential consumer market.

Product designers must be able to convince creative directors, sales managers and boards of directors that their new designs are competitive and worth putting into production.

Product stylists, often incorrectly called product designers, are designers who refine and revise existing designs to adapt to changing market requirements or the facilities of their manufacturing companies.

What product designers do

Product designs of every type do not just pop into the heads of designers as they lean back in their swivel chairs, staring at blank drafting tables. Successful variations and innovations in product design are the result of months of creative thinking and sketching, research and analysis, samplemaking and testing. They are usually cooperative creative efforts accomplished by design staffs.

When a newly designed product is first proposed, a research specialist studies the client's design problem, talking with sales representatives, sales managers, consumers and engineers. Product designers begin to make sketches of their own and competitors' products, because the new design must look better, work better, and, if possible, cost less than the competition's. A selection of rough drawings that present several solutions will be cut down to two or three possibilities. These are converted into clay studies to assess the three-dimensional effect and to study the aesthetic qualities of the forms. Adjustments, revisions and changes are based on the designers' and clients' personal wishes.

Finished drawings or watercolor renderings are made from the clay models. The final design is chosen for its appearance, utility and market potential.

Using detailed rendering and input from engineers, the product designer helps a samplemaker develop a presentation model. This full-scale model is constructed of the proposed materials and is an actual working product, a one-of-a-kind sample. When the working presentation model is finished and approved, drafters develop working drawings for the actual tooling and production in the factory.

Product designers supervise all phases of product development, insuring that the ultimate, finished products reflect their ideas and meet their standards for quality, function and appearance.

What qualities are helpful for a product designer?

Product designers enjoy doing research and spending long periods of time on single projects. They are aware of current trends in styles and technology, and keep up-to-date on the development of new materials and applications of old ones. They are acutely aware of current public tastes in designed objects.

They watch the way people use things (how they are handled or how people sit in them and so on) and are able to apply their findings to the design of better products. They are able to draw, have strong color and design backgrounds and talent and can communicate their ideas verbally as well as visually. They are capable of working with other members of design and production teams, as well as administrative personnel, engineers and sales people.

What other careers require similar qualities?

Industrial designers have a range of skills so wide that many careers closely parallel theirs. Package designers, graphic designers, interior designers and environmental planners need similar qualifications. The work of design photographers, model makers, samplemakers and sales representatives is closely related to product development. Product designers may also feel comfortable in supervisory positions in most manufacturing companies or in wholesale or contract showrooms. They might also free-lance in any number of design related positions, and could function as corporate art directors.

What can be done now?

Take drawing, painting and art history classes in high school, along with drafting and three-dimensional design or sculpture. Product photography and model making are excellent and productive hobbies.

Part-time work in any drafting office is valuable. Jobs in any manufacturing company, carpenter shop or design studio will give you useful background experience. A position as store clerk allows one to handle products and become familiar with public reaction to products, designs and consumer psychology.

Magazines that may provide some career guidance to future product designers include: *ID* (Industrial Design), *Package Engineering, Modo* (Italy), *Interiors, Product Design and Development* and *Technical Photography.*

Study current product design by spending hours in department stores and shopping malls, looking at the products designers have created.

Which colleges offer necessary programs?

Schools with industrial design programs will feature courses in general product design. Check the charts at the back of the book. Some schools emphasize certain types of products in their course offerings (furniture design, automotive styling or ceramic design, for example) depending on their dominant local industries. Check catalogs for specialties that might fit your specific interests.

Though degrees are not required in the design departments of many manufacturing plants, they have come to stand for the most complete professional education. A degree assures the employer that you have solid design training and background. Portfolios, however, remain the prime selling point when you are looking for a job.

Designer Larry Wood first draws some ideas based on staff market research. The marketing division approves one idea for next year's toy line.

Toy Designer

How is a scale model car like one of Mattel's Hot Wheels designed? What do artists and industrial and graphic designers do on such a project? The accompanying photographs give you a glimpse of what a toy designing career would be like.

What qualities are helpful for a toy designer?

Toy designers perform all the functions of other industrial designers, but work on a smaller scale. They must like to work in miniature, therefore, and must be aware of changes in children's interests and in industry trends.

They work with researchers, other designers, engineers, model builders and production staff to see the product through. They are part of a team, and so must be cooperative, versatile and interested in group accomplishment.

What other careers require similar qualities?

All industrial design careers require similar qualities. The specific interests and goals involved may vary, but the step-by-step processes (research, sketching, designing, model building and production) are similar.

Many toy designers begin as industrial designers and later move into toy designing. Larry Wood worked in the design department at Ford and later for Lockheed Aircraft before joining Mattel and starting a career in toy design.

What can be done now?

Take drawing, painting, design and drafting classes in high school and supplement them with areas of special interest such as auto shop, wood shop or home economics. Model building and photography are useful hobbies.

The design staff works from Don Prudhomme's Pepsi Challenger. They measure it carefully. It is photographed from all angles, even the engine and interior details.

Part-time work in toy stores or toy departments will give you practical experience in handling, working and selling all kinds of toys. Study the toys that seem most popular, and keep notes on them and their design.

Collect fine toys, toy catalogs and advertisements from children's magazines. Keep an organized file that will allow you to study developing trends and excellent designs.

Which colleges offer necessary programs?

There are several schools that offer toy design courses in their curricula, but such special courses are not necessary, if you get a solid background in industrial design. Most toy designers come from other career areas, and almost all have industrial design backgrounds. Those backgrounds taught them to analyze products, develop concepts, make models and working drawings and supervise complete developmental processes.

Check the charts at the back of the book for schools which emphasize industrial design.

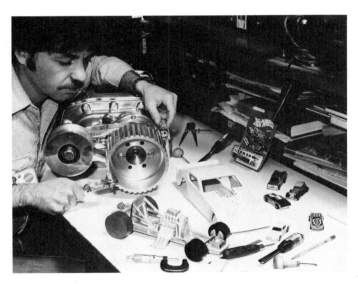

Drafters make detailed view drawings of the angles and contours of the car. These, the photographs and some actual parts are handed over to the model builders, who build models four times the size of the actual toy. The wood models are mechanically reduced to final size and tooling is designed to make the finished product.

The final product will be in the coming year's toy line. The design staff will also design the toy's package and write the instructions that go with it. Photographs courtesy Larry Wood

A unique prototype table of marble, stainless steel and glass. Designed by Charles Gibilterra. Photograph: Richard di Liberto

Furniture Designer

What makes a favorite chair so comfortable? Why do some interior designers and decorators request items only from certain furniture companies? Why do museums collect furniture? Such questions can be answered better after studying the styles, expertise and products of top furniture designers, who work for large manufacturers, as consultants in industrial design studios, or as free-lance designers who offer their services to many manufacturers.

All furniture designers keep meticulous files full of magazine articles on current trends, advertisements of top product lines, trade bulletins, company brochures, sharp ads and well-designed items of all types. These files, a personal design library, are indispensable. From them come most of the designer's ideas for furniture.

Some furniture manufacturers come to the free-lance designer with requests for chair or desk designs; at other times, the designer may come up with a new idea and make a presentation to a potential client. The more experience a free-lance designer has and the more he or she works with certain clients, the easier it is to anticipate their needs and make pertinent suggestions for new products.

What furniture designers do

A major furniture manufacturer comes to a free-lance designer and asks for thoughts and ideas on a new conference chair, for example. They want it upholstered, with a wooden frame. The designer goes into the files and pulls all available resource material on wood and upholstered chairs, all ideas on conference chairs, and any other possible files on wood, upholstery, office furniture and the like. Ideas are important. The more ideas the designer has to draw from, the better are his or her chances of coming up with a satisfactory solution.

All sorts of possible ideas and solutions are tacked above the drafting table: pictures, sketches, ads and notes. Any and every possible solution is sketched out, with the goal of a comfortable wood and upholstered conference chair constantly in mind. Notes are made on the sketches and eventually the best thoughts are tacked to a large board. Knowing the client's line of existing furniture helps the designer select several drawings of functional, appropriate chairs.

After choosing the best sketches, the designer builds models and makes renderings and drawings that show construction details of the proposed forms. These models and renderings are shown to the client in a presentation, and after an exchange of ideas between designer and client, the most successful ideas are made into working drawings for the prototype. The working drawings, based on the designer's knowledge of manufacturing techniques and engineering design, are sent to the manufacturer, whose staff builds a prototype in their shop. From this accepted prototype, final working drawings are made. Contracts are then drawn up for royalty payments to the designer, or the company may pay a flat fee for the idea and the drawings.

Designers also come up with original ideas in the course of their work and may know of a client that might be interested. The designer makes drawings, builds models and prepares a unique presentation with which he or she will try to sell the client the idea. If it does sell, the above procedure is carried through again.

What qualities are helpful for a furniture designer?

Free-lance designers must have the self-discipline to work alone and meet self-imposed deadlines. Any furniture designer must be organized, and ought to keep a complete and up-to-date filing system. Free-lance designers must also have a business background and a working knowledge of tax structures, contract complexities and general business trends if they are to work closely with corporations.

They must attend lectures and seminars to stay abreast of current trends in furniture design, interior design and architecture. They should read widely and absorb ideas from visual sources like television, books, magazines, ads, shows, lectures and museums.

Furniture designers must communicate verbally as well as visually and must be sensitive to client wishes and suggestions. They should have an interest in all types of

product design, not only furniture. They must draw well, be excellent drafters, and be as much at home in interior design as in industrial design.

What other careers require similar qualities?

There is an obvious relationship between interior design and furniture design, and many furniture designers come from backgrounds of architecture or interior design. Any product design specialist requires exactly the same skills as a furniture designer: drawing ability, visualizing, drafting, rendering and model building. The only differences are what products and applications are of special interest to the designer.

Related fields include: furniture illustration, architectural rendering, showroom management, furniture production supervision and furniture drafting.

What can be done now?

Take all the high school art classes you can, especially drawing, drafting, painting and three-dimensional design or sculpture. Wood shop can help you understand furniture construction, and model building of any type is an excellent and useful hobby.

Part-time work in any drafting capacity is an asset, as is work in furniture or cabinet shops. Working for an interior designer can provide you with valuable contacts and teach you to put furniture to its most effective use.

Magazines that contain articles on furniture and advertisements of major manufacturing companies include: *Contract, Interiors, Architectural Digest, Interior Design* and *Design West.* You can begin your own filing system, using examples from such magazine sources. Write to those companies whose work interests you, and ask for catalogs and brochures about their products.

Which colleges offer necessary programs?

Manufacturers of traditional furniture generally draw their designers from schools on the East Coast, mostly those near the major furniture manufacturing centers (such as in New England and the Southeastern United States). West Coast schools generally stress a more creative approach with an emphasis on industrial design. Check catalogs for specific classes in furniture design. Check the charts at the back of the book for the strengths of such schools.

Areas of emphasis may include: industrial engineering, product design, manufacturing technology, economics, wood sciences, furniture drafting and product illustration. Trade schools offer courses that provide practical training in wood and metal furniture construction. In the Southeast, where major furniture construction is concentrated, these courses are directly related to nearby industries.

The keyboard, screen, printer and disc drive of a personal computer system present an integrated appearance which the designer attained by using similar materials, colors, logos and design forms. Photograph: International Business Machines Corporation

Communications Designer

The tremendous advances in communications technology have been accompanied by an equally impressive increase in data processing machines, computer hardware and sophisticated video and information processing equipment. Computers and their accessories must be designed to compete in the burgeoning communications market.

Designers of these products either work for major corporations in this expanding field or for consulting firms which design or consult on products for these and other manufacturing companies.

Information processing systems and communications equipment may already seem outstandingly efficient, but intense competition and the increasing complexity of technology will force designs to change accordingly. When these communications systems are in general use, the need for safe, efficient designs will become especially important. Young industrial designers will find great stimulation in what lies ahead in this career area, both in private and government sectors.

What communications designers do

Designing a computer terminal cabinet is similar to designing any other product. From sketches and drawings, models are built; when the plans are approved and the working drawings made, the units are constructed in prototypes and finally manufactured and put on the market.

The working components of communications systems (designed by industrial designers and engineers) must be housed in attractive, efficient cabinets that suggest a corporate identity. Often many products make up the line the company has on the market, and each must be coordinated in design, format, color and logo to make an integrated and recognizable family of products.

Communication designers work with advanced technology. They design new components for equipment still on the drawing board. The products they design will need frequent revision. Their contacts are engineers, programmers, technologists and scientists who are inventing and revising communication systems.

Typical communication products include: telephones,

typewriters, printers and telecommunication systems; television, radio, stereo and audio systems; satellite and space communication systems; computer hardware systems; radar, sonar and other detection systems; video games and recreational systems and all the accessories that go with each.

Specialty careers in the communications design area include: industrial designer, drafter, stylist, designer, package designer, industrial illustrator, product photographer, model maker, graphic designer and technical illustrator. Check the index for details on these career opportunities.

What qualities are helpful for a communications designer?
These designers are interested in electronics, enjoy working with scientists and electronic engineers, and speak their language. They must also communicate verbally with other designers, production staff and salespeople.

They are aware of changes and innovations in the communications field and are ready to adapt to new concepts, materials and needs. They enjoy the intense competition that such a career field engenders, and are stimulated by ever-changing requirements and product development.

They must have strong industrial design backgrounds, especially in product and package design. They think clearly in three-dimensional formats and are adept at drafting and model building.

What other careers require similar qualities?
The ability to function as designer in a highly competitive field is required of industrial designers in the automotive, airline and transportation fields. Excellent verbal communication and adaptability are required in all areas of industrial and graphic design. Almost any area of industrial design would probably be enjoyable to a communication designer. The ability to work as part of a team, rather than as an individual star, is required in all design firms and in many consulting organizations.

What can be done now?
Art classes in high school should include drawing, painting, art history, three-dimensional design (sculpture) and drafting. Courses in computer science would give you practical experience in handling existing equipment. Expand your communication skills by taking English and public speaking courses.

Visit stores where communication products are sold (telephone stores, computer centers, television and radio shops) to see existing products and pick up brochures for reference and future design ideas. Trade shows, conventions and demonstrations are held regularly in large urban centers. Arrange to attend some of them; notice the newly designed products and pick up brochures and ideas.

Study good design wherever it is found—not only in communications equipment. Magazines that are helpful include various computer magazines, such as *Byte, Computer Graphics World, Interface age, Compute!*, and also *ID (Industrial Design), Product Design and Development* and *Technical Photography.*

Which colleges offer necessary programs?
An excellent background in industrial design with an emphasis on product design is necessary for communications designers. Check the charts at the back of the book for such schools in your area. Some schools offer courses in communications design. Check specific school catalogs for exact course titles and offerings.

Automobile Design

Automobiles are the result of years of research, planning and development. It may take 24 months before a single model moves through styling, engineering, manufacturing, assembly, and testing stages and into the dealers' showrooms.

Marketing researchers first gather information from consumers, salespeople, mechanics, production workers and designers. What do they like or dislike in current models? What would they change? What materials are most popular?

This information is passed on to product planning specialists, who propose changes based on these findings and their own ideas. This "paper program" is evaluated on the basis of projected engine requirements, safety standards and costs. Stylists, whose primary concern is design and appearance, make preliminary sketches of interior and exterior ideas. After management approves the overall plan, the stylists complete the details of the design.

What automobile stylists do
Stylists prepare hundreds of sketches of new and alternative ideas for an automobile and its parts. Each idea complements the other; the design must be unified and coordinated.

Design ideas gradually develop from these sketches into an acceptable styling theme. The most promising of these designs are built into full-size clay models over a wooden framework: three-dimensional representations of the stylists' drawings. These are finished to a glossy smoothness and a plaster mold is made from which fiberglass models are produced. These models, fitted with glass and wheels and perfectly painted and trimmed, look exactly like production models. The most promising model is selected by company executives and design specialists, and further development continues.

Designers who specialize in textiles, colors, fashions and plastics build the seats, steering wheel, door handles and other interior parts. They make full-scale renderings from which full-size models (called *trim bucks*) are made in wood. Actual fabrics and paints are used on the bucks to show their final appearance. The design of the automobile is now set, although production is still many months away.

What design engineers do

While stylists work on the appearance of the car, design engineers design the nearly 13,000 parts that go into it. Not all of them must be newly designed, but many are modified according to recent technology, or are re-shaped.

These parts require hundreds of sketches, final renderings and detailed drawings by drafters so that tools can be made to produce the parts. Industrial design engineers must design every bolt, belt, housing and clamp to make all the parts fit and work together. Computers have taken over much of this design work; they now assemble data and produce detailed drawings.

After all elements are checked by computer for stress, durability and function, experimental parts are hand-made in the company shop. These are also tested, and prototypes are constructed and tested before final production plans are put into operation.

In an industry as huge as this, industrial designers, stylists and design specialists must work together to produce a single product. Their hope is that it is better designed, more reliable and less expensive than the competition's model.

What qualities are helpful for an automotive designer?

Automotive stylists and industrial designers must be able to work as part of an extensive team, and must work well with people. Their imaginations must be flexible enough to work around such restrictions as space, cost and projected use. They must turn data and information into visible ideas, and must be able to communicate those ideas.

Familiarity with the uses and characteristics of many materials and a good foundation in color and design are essential to automotive designers. Although they sketch and render in two dimensions, they must be able to work in three dimensions, complete models and refine shapes in clay and wood.

Idea drawings such as these are often the starting points for designs of the future. Several aspects of such ideas may appear in production models several years down the line. Photograph: General Motors Corporation

A GM industrial designer works on details of the "Aero X" experimental concept car. Photograph: General Motors Corporation

Reduced scale models, sculpted in clay, help GM designers check overall design concepts. When put through wind tunnel tests, the car's aerodynamic qualities can be fully noted and modified if necessary. Photograph: General Motors Corporation

Commercial Art and Design

Using a light pen on a cathode ray tube, this Ford designer sketches a windshield wiper system. A complete three-dimensional study is possible, and modifications can be made on the spot, before models are built. Photograph: Ford Motor Company

Full scale trim bucks, made of wood in GM's design shops, allow full testing for size, comfort, utility, design and appearance. Photograph: General Motors Corporation

Full size clay models of cars are fashioned, finished and painted to allow stylists to check and modify exterior design and appearance. This clay model is of a proposed GM electric car. Photograph: General Motors Corporation

What other careers require similar qualities?

Industrial design work in any large manufacturing plant is similar to the work of automotive designers. All such situations require teamwork, good verbal communication and familiarity with a variety of materials and processes. Drawing and rendering ability are common to all industrial design careers.

Experienced automobile designers make excellent industrial design consultants because of the wide range of materials and products with which they have worked. Design of carpets, fabrics, seating and equipment or control panels are all related careers in other industries.

What can be done now?

Include drawing, painting, design, drafting and art history classes in your high school schedule. Automotive shop classes will give you a chance to work on body design and styling. Physics and computer classes will familiarize you with the mechanical aspects of automobile construction. Model airplane and auto building are excellent hobbies.

Part-time work in any graphic or industrial design studio would be ideal. Work in a garage or an automobile parts and accessories shop will give you abundant practical experience.

Collect brochures from auto dealers and pictures from magazine ads which show excellent styling and design features, and save them for future reference. Drawing and photographing cars can be an excellent way to learn about their forms and functions. Restyle and redesign parts of your own car: you'll acquire practical experience in body and interior design.

Magazines that may help you determine your career direction in automobile design might include: *Road and Track, Motor Trend* and many other car magazines; and also *Product Design and Development* and *Modo* (Italy).

Which colleges offer necessary programs?

Some art schools place special emphasis on automotive design, and offer many classes that will be of direct help. Automobile companies generally select their designers and stylists from such schools. Be sure to get a good industrial design background as well. Check each catalog to see if your needs will be met. Check schools in the Detroit, Chicago and Fort Wayne areas, and Art Center College of Design in Pasadena. Check the lists for industrial design programs in the charts at the back of the book.

Cheryl Hughes, of John Fluke Mfg. Co., Inc., sketches graphic design ideas.

Cheryl Hughes, an industrial designer at John Fluke Mfg. Co. Inc., is generally responsible for the company's product development and package design. She was asked to undertake the redesign of the company's demonstration van from both graphic design and space planning standpoints. Although it was not part of her regular responsibilities, her general design background qualified her to work on this innovative project.

Fluke's large truck/trailer system houses and displays company products and is used as a show room, presentation and demonstration area, and sales and promotion department. The designer was asked to update the van, make it visually more attractive, replan the interior and give it an air of sophistication more suited to manufacturers of high quality, precision instrumentation.

Such planning and design is the result of research, talks with salespeople and company executives and a thorough knowledge of the corporation, its products, its image and its goals. Industrial designers are the backbone of such a design program.

Industrial Designer

A redesigned exterior of Fluke equipment is painted light pewter and dark umber, highlighted with bold red lettering. The simplified, straightforward design suggests the company's reputation for precision and reliability.

This uncluttered interior still lacks a simple signage system, but already has a more open, less interfering background for viewing highly technical instruments. Sliding doors eliminate interference at the left, and brochures are kept in convenient racks next to the instruments they describe. Traffic flows unimpeded through the simple and clean arrangement.

Other Careers In Industrial Design

Airline Interior Designer (Stylist)
The interiors of an airline's planes are custom-designed to project a specific corporate image. Seating, overhead storage, food service systems, colors, interior walls, windows, carpets and decorations are unique to each airline. They are designed by artists and industrial designers working for the major airlines, or for design firms the airlines consult. Special factors considered by designers are traffic flow, efficiency, time-movement studies (to determine how long it takes to do certain tasks), pleasant appearance and comfort. Often, outside artists are contracted to carry out parts of the total design package under supervision of the project designer.

Automobile design detailer
Detailers work with drafters and designers to produce full-size or scale detail drawings of complete automobile bodies or chassis parts. Detailers include specifications and designers' notes so that complete mock-ups can be made in the planning stages of development, or so that machinery can be made to make parts for production models.

Automotive Design Layout Artists
These specialists work with automobile design detailers and drafters and prepare the final working drawings of all automobile parts, components and systems. Using specifications, sketches, notes and other design data, they draft the master drawings in mylar or other materials.

Automobile Interior Designer
These specialists design the components of automobile interiors using metal, plastics, color and fabrics. Project supervisors work with them as they design and coordinate headliners, seats, carpets, dashboards, steering wheels, door panels, sun visors and the like.

Cartographer
Cartography is the art of making maps, a career that combines a knowledge of geography with an interest in lettering and art. Maps such as topographic sheets or air pilot charts require technical accuracy; vacation area maps or illustrated diagrammatic presentations have less stringent requirements.

Cartographers usually have educational backgrounds in geography, geology and map making. They use technical pens and tools to measure and draw the areas being mapped. Technical maps allow little creative interpretation, but illustration and personal style are encouraged in the making of non-technical maps.

Drafter (Automobile design)
Automobile design drafters execute working drawings of automobile parts, assemblies and systems. They make rough sketches and work with mathematical proportions and ratios. They read blueprints and work out detailed specifications for automobiles, vans, trucks and their components. They work closely with stylists and engineers in solving design problems and making ideas workable. Automobile drafting provides an excellent foundation for artists who are interested in automotive styling or engineering.

Drafter
Drafters prepare clear, complete and accurate working plans and detail drawings from the rough or detailed sketches and notes of engineers and designers. They make final sketches and finished drawings for model builders and production people. They prepare charts and graphs from statistical data. They coordinate visual information from engineers, designers, clients and project directors and prepare the working drawings which determine the final form of the product.

Furniture Reproducer
Furniture reproducers generally work in large manufacturing companies, preparing working drawings and templates of antique or custom furniture from which to make authentic furniture reproductions. They sketch from the original pieces or use drawing instruments to make exact copies. They work closely with production staff to insure authenticity of design.

Glass Blower (Glass Technologist)
These craftspeople develop specifications, make sketches and blow and shape glass for test tubes, retorts and flasks. They also design and blow components for condensers, vacuum pumps, barometers and thermometers. At times they sketch and blow glass to a client's specifications.

Heavy Equipment Designer
The massive equipment used to move earth, mine coal, drill wells, launch missiles and create energy from wind and water are all conceived, drawn and presented by equipment designers. This specialized area of industrial design involves as much technology as design, and is more concerned with production capability than with aesthetic appearance. These industrial designers, who have a special interest in heavy production, work for companies which produce the equipment.

Industrial Illustrator (See Technical Illustrator)

Inlayer
Inlayers use leather, metal, ceramic, cloth, paper, plastic or wood to make decorative patterns in the surfaces of furniture. They often work in custom furniture plants cooperating with furniture and interior designers.

Lighting Designer
Lighting design is an offshoot of interior design, but the design and production of lighting systems and fixtures is the realm of industrial design specialists. Lamp shops are full of the products of the designers who work for large manufacturers of mass-produced products. Custom design and installations are often required for offices, libraries, galleries, museums, theaters, arenas and some condominiums and homes. Lighting designers work with many materials to create the special products and effects that clients desire. They determine the lighting need and also design lighting fixtures to fill the need.

Model Maker
Model makers either work in the industrial design departments of manufacturers or design firms, or are free-lance designers who build models for many clients. They work from the directions and drawings of designers and stylists to form three-dimensional models in wood, metal, plastic, paper and glass. The models may be full-sized or scaled down sizes of proposed products; they must be detailed and accurate, because they will be used to build prototypes, tools and production models. A background in sculpture, jewelry making, machine shop, photography and design is highly recommended.

Ornamental Metalwork Designer
Using various joining techniques, ornamental metalwork designers plan and create grills, latticework, statuary, railings, lighting fixtures and the like. They often design tools and templates for shaping and finishing such products. They must be familiar with mechanical, welding and brazing techniques, and must have some background in drawing and design; detailed sketches and drawings are essential in making high quality products. They often supervise the metalworkers who construct custom-made products from their drawings.

Product Photographer (See Photography)

Safety Clothing and Equipment Designers
This career combines elements of both fashion and industrial design. These designers develop practical clothing and equipment to protect workers from a variety of industrial hazards. They draft plans for the equipment and make patterns for the clothing.

Senior Designer or Design Director (See Art Director)

Sports Equipment Design
With the increased leisure time available to many people has come a surge in recreational and sporting equipment usage. The designers of this equipment must be familiar with the uses of the things they design. Most work for large manufacturing companies which make ski equipment, squash racquets, frisbees, roller skates, and other types of equipment for professional and amateur athletes.

These designers often modify and adapt previous ideas, but are also involved in designing new equipment.

Stencil Maker
Stencil makers work for carpet manufacturers, and lay out and cut patterns and stencils used in printing multicolored designs on rugs. They use opaque projectors, stencil knives, pencils, brushes, ink and paint in their work. They make pencil copies of symmetrical designs on tracing paper and indicate sizes and color specifications. They prepare proof copies for design directors and inspect the production pieces for accuracy and correct colors.

Tool Designer (Tool and Equipment Design Specialist)
These industrial specialists design a variety of cutting and drilling tools and related dies, jigs, templates and fixtures, either for production work or for experimental use in all types of metal work. They use geometric and algebraic formulas and standard engineering tool data to design tools and machines. They must have backgrounds in mechanical drawing and engineering, and in working with metals. They draw preliminary sketches and concepts, prepare layouts and make detailed drawings for submission to machine builders and die makers.

Transportation Designer
The design process for other forms of transportation is similar to that of automotive design, and includes the designing of railroad rolling stock, buses, trucks, airplanes (personal and commerical), recreational vehicles, motorcycles and the like. Certain technologies are standard for each kind of production, and the respective designers must know the use and function of equipment.

Designers work with engineers, model makers and drafters in preparing sketches, renderings, models, mock-ups and presentation models for their companies. They are expert at research, idea testing and data compilation, as well as drawing and developing concepts.

Students at the Art Institute of Chicago get first hand experience working with fabrics to design and create their clothing projects. Photograph: Art Institute of Chicago

Fashion Design

Every year Americans spend over 100 billion dollars on clothing, accessories and jewelry. The apparel/textile/fiber complex is this country's leading single employer.

The American fashion industry's primary centers are New York City, Dallas and Los Angeles, but the fashion world is found in every urban center in the country in the form of advertising agencies, merchandising outlets and custom designers. Rapid world-wide communication and the increasing mobility of the population have made fashions almost universal. Fashions designed in Paris, New York, London or Los Angeles can be found soon afterward in stores across America.

Such universal style is a recent occurrence. In the past, fashions and national characteristics dictated by the textiles, dyes and other materials indigenous to the country or available through trade. As cultures began to have more contact with one another, fashions changed accordingly, and often. Theater and film costume designers must have a thorough knowledge of fashion history to be able to dress actors accurately for period plays, films or television productions. A study of historical clothing design is required of all fashion design majors because it forms the basis for all contemporary design.

The fashion industry requires steady concept and style changes from imaginative, stimulated designers. Many of the ideas for such changes come from young artists new to the field. Design modifications might be based on ethnic dress, trends in art, sporting events or international influence. Designers translate concepts into designs for modern, wearable clothing, and must learn to observe and incorporate elements of these ideas into their work.

Mass production of clothing begins when a high-fashion designer shows his or her collection for the season to buyers, private customers, merchandising staff and fashion editors. They decide what the trends for the season will be, when copies, "knock-offs," "copy-downs" and adaptations can appear, and which designs will serve as a starting point for their lines. Advertising campaigns in magazines and trade papers precede actual production and test the mass market. When the time is right, and orders are coming in, production begins.

Design and production are followed by sales. Fashion merchandising is the vital link in the system. If the clothing is advertised and sells very well, the whole process is considered successful and can continue to operate.

The world of fashion includes a broad spectrum of designers, products and services. Although we are most conscious of the designers themselves, they are supported by a small army of fashion illustrators, photographers and models; textile, jewelry and accessory designers; men's, women's and children's specialists; textile and patternmaking technologists; advertising, display and exhibit designers; apparel production managers, fashion buyers and merchandisers, show room managers, advertising and communications specialists, fashion editors and writers. These specialists are further supplemented by factory workers, machine operators, weavers, seamstresses, silkscreen printers, cutters and tailors.

After the fashions are designed, tested and manufactured, they are turned over to fashion merchandisers who advertise and sell them to the public. Jobs in fashion retailing exist across the country in boutiques, department stores and mail order and catalog showrooms. Retail executives need a working knowledge of all facets of the fashion world.

College courses in fashion design and illustration programs may include: accessory design, advertising and communication, color psychology, costume design for theater film, design sketching, draping, fashion design, fashion illustration, fashion merchandising, millinery design, pattern drafting (patternmaking), surface design, tailoring and sewing techniques, textile design, window display and workroom procedures.

Michael Novarese works on drawings for his own line of designer clothes. His drawing table is full of ideas, sketches and finished drawings. Photograph: Joseph Gatto

Fashion Designer

Fashion is a reflection of its time. Contemporary consumers come from a wide range of backgrounds and lifestyles, and fashion designers must consider this diversity when they create their designs. Apparel designers must constantly be asking such questions as: Who is my customer? How does he or she want to look? What materials and costs are to be considered? Designers keep extensive research files containing photographs, magazine pages, tear sheets and drawings of thousands of apparel designs. They devour *Women's Wear Daily*, the trade paper which reports on current trends as well as what is coming from the drawing boards of major designers. They consult buyers and merchandising experts on developing trends, and combine this research with their own ideas in an attempt to come up with something new and different that people will want to buy.

Some fashion designers have their own studios and staffs; some are free-lance designers, selling their ideas and sketches; some work with limited lines of apparel and others work for manufacturers who produce apparel for the mass market. Regardless of the type of clothing being designed, the process is quite similar. It is the inspirations behind designs that differ.

What fashion designers do

All fashions begin as sketches. These may be original drawings done by a famous dressmaker, the ideas of an aspiring designer or copy sketches that will be "knock-offs" of more expensive designs. The ideas—for single pieces, matching items, ensembles and the like—are worked out in detail on paper.

When the sketches are approved by clients or company owners, fabric samples are made by skilled craftspeople who cut and sew directly from the drawings. When these samples are available, a price, based on the approximate number manufactured, the materials used and the estimated time involved in manufacture, can be estimated. The samples are previewed by selected buyers and merchandisers from large store systems, or by the buyers who make up the company's or studio's clientele.

Commercial Art and Design

Prospective buyers suggest changes in the samples according to their knowledge of their own buying public. If necessary, the changes are made, tentative delivery dates are scheduled and tentative orders taken.

The apparel line is thus pared down to its best-selling items, and they are put into planning. Production starts when confirmed orders are in hand.

Patternmakers measure each part of the sample and develop patterns for the item in one basic size: 34 for women and 36 for men. From this basic piece all the other sizes are measured and adapted. The finished patterns go from cutters, who may cut up to three hundred pieces of cloth at a time, to sewers, who finish the work.

Finished pieces are distributed around the country to stores who placed orders. Merchandisers and retailers take over the consumer research, advertising and selling of the goods, and complete the fashion cycle.

Free-lance designers and designers who operate their own fashion studios or boutiques follow similar procedures, but work with limited staffs on a smaller scale. Their creations are often original in concept and design, and might only be produced singly or in very limited quantity. Such individually designed pieces are generally very expensive.

What qualities are helpful for a fashion designer?

Designers of apparel must have creative imaginations and must always be changing their ideas and concepts in order to produce fresh, exciting fashions. They enjoy research into past designs and are avid observers of contemporary trends, fads and ethnic influences. They enjoy intense competition and are able to work under restrictive deadlines.

Fashion designers are very interested in colors, textures, fabrics, materials and accessories, and are adept at drawing and quick sketching in many media.

Designers must work well with their staffs. If they are free-lance designers, they must also work with buyers, clients, and media representatives. They must be articulate, able to discuss and describe their own creations and to speak about and for the fashion world.

Free-lance designers must have a great deal of self-discipline and must bear the responsibility for the successes or failures of their designs. The day-to-day functions of their staffs and other design, production and presentation personnel are also overseen by the free-lance designer.

What other careers require similar qualities?

All elements of the fashion cycle require people with similar personal qualities: intense interests in fabrics, colors and textures, and in creating clothing that satisfies current tastes.

Designers of sports specialty clothing and equipment work under similar competitive conditions. (See Other Careers in the Fashion Industry.) Interior designers have a similar interest in colors, textures, and materials (See Interior Designer). Teachers of home economics (clothing, food, interior design) must have related backgrounds, training and interest.

Costume designers in theater, film and television require the same training, but generally have a stronger interest in period fashions (See Costume Designer).

What can be done now?

Take all the high school art courses you can: drawing, painting, sculpture, design, printmaking and art history. Home economics, English, and world and American history all have direct bearing on fashion design. Working with your school or community theater group may give you a chance to design costumes, fashions and period clothing, and to work with fabrics and colors.

Part-time work in department stores, specialty shops or boutiques would allow you to work with clothing, customers, merchandising managers and display designers and would give you valuable insight.

Magazines and trade papers will keep you up-to-date on fashion ideas and products. Look into such publications as: *WWD* (*Women's Wear Daily*), *Harpers Bazaar, W, Mademoiselle, Town and Country, Vogue* and others.

Which colleges offer necessary programs?

Most schools with well-rounded art programs offer courses in fashion design, and some have very strong emphases in the field. Check the chart at the back of the book. Schools near apparel production centers will have visits by experts, tours of plants and part-time work programs as part of their curriculum.

The centers of women's fashion design are New York City, Los Angeles, Chicago, Miami, Boston, Philadelphia, Dallas, St. Louis and Cleveland. The men's fashion industry is represented in New York City, Boston, Baltimore, Cleveland, Rochester, Southern California and Eastern Pennsylvania. Check schools in these locations.

Although a college degree is not essential to becoming an excellent fashion designer, it assures employers of your substantial background and training, and will ready you for the competitive design regimen that faces every newcomer to the field.

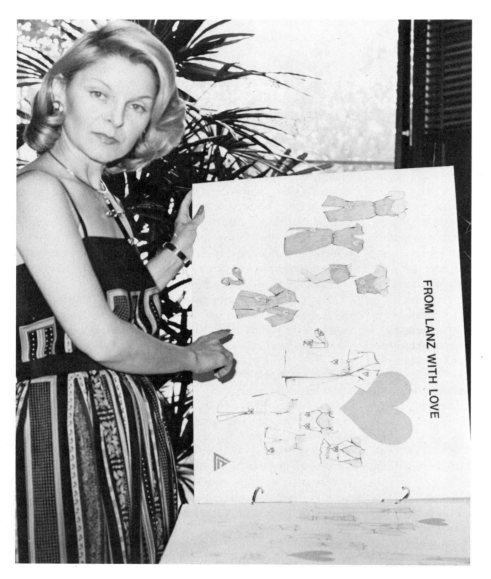

Lynn Cartwright displays a line concept she designed for *Lanz*. When approved, the designing of each piece in the line begins. All photographs: Joseph Gatto

Lynn Cartwright is a fashion designer prominent in the West Coast active sportswear industry. She designed the apparel for the U.S. Gymnastics Federation's 1984 Olympic team, and is a design consultant for major apparel manufacturers like Ocean Pacific, Nike, Asics Tiger Corp., Catalina, Lanz and Russell Athletic Sportswear. Prior to being a consultant (or free-lance) designer, she was a full-time designer and owner/designer of Skippy of California, maker of children's and teens' sportswear and dresses.

As a designer, Cartwright is responsible for providing manufacturers with their product lines. Generally, there are two to four lines, or seasons, that the manufacturer offers yearly: Spring and/or Summer, Fall and/or Holiday, or Cruise. The designer works approximately one year in advance of the introduction of the line on the market. Designers thus must educate themselves as to the colors, fabrics and designs that will be on the market when the line breaks one year later. In order to do this, Cartwright subscribes to a number of European and American design and color reporting services. Her design research trips abroad also keep her aware of fashion changes. Europe, she says, is the foremost overall fashion leader, although the United States takes the lead in active sportswear design.

Lynn Cartwright's career now spans approximately eighteen years. Reflecting upon those years, she recalls significant experiences that have contributed to her growth as a professional.

"To succeed one must establish definite goals, I believe. I knew I wanted to be a designer, but I wasn't quite sure what that meant. I did know that being a fashion designer meant living either in New York or Los Angeles, the fashion centers.

Lynn Cartwright, Fashion Designer

After twenty Minnesota winters, California seemed the place to go for a fashion design career.

"I arrived in Los Angeles armed with enthusiasm and aspirations, but no experience. It was frustrating to be turned down for jobs, and I soon realized that most people in the industry must start from the bottom and work up.

"I found that a liberal arts education was not enough, so I enrolled in a design trade school program. The practicalities of life required that I work while attending school. The jobs that I got (one as a fashion illustrator, one as an assistant buyer for a large department store) gave me valuable experience and a taste of what the fashion world was like.

"By the time I left the trade school I had acquired solid, local experience and felt ready to enter the garment industry. I started as a patternmaker, working under a designer. I was so grateful to get that job, I would gladly have paid *them* for letting me work!

"Knowledge of garment construction is important to any fashion designer. From that first job I gained a sense of the technical requirements of designing, and learned of the psychological realities of working at a career. Suddenly I had to relate to people of all ages and personalities, from widely varying social, racial and economic backgrounds. This was quite an eye-opening experience. Part of being a fashion designer is being a good administrator of the people who work with you and under you. These early experiences taught me how to relate to the kinds of people who would someday become my support system.

"I worked as a patternmaker and assistant designer for four years, learning business procedures, terminology and the job's demands. Finally, I declared myself ready to venture off on my own as a manufacturer. I set up a small business manufacturing children's clothing. Because I had very little money to start with, I found myself doing everything! I designed and made patterns and markers,

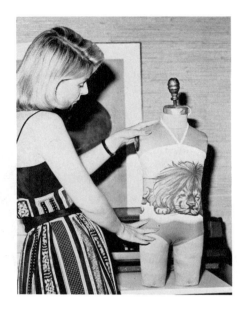

Working on a swimsuit for *Catalina,* the designer checks the production model against her original design concept.

cut garments, sold to department and speciality stores, administered, shipped and did the books. And I broke even!

"My experience handling every facet of fashion design convinced me to concentrate on what I do best: designing. I accepted a job with Catalina Swimwear, and spent a fruitful ten years there, polishing my professional skills.

"But working for a large corporation has its limitations. I went as far as I could as an in-house designer, and yet wanted more, so I left Catalina and began consulting for other companies.

"Now I reflect upon what a wealth of experience I got working for some of the top apparel firms in the United States. I have benefited greatly from working with the successful people who influenced my career and my life.

"The rewards of a fashion design career are many. Along with the rewards of making use of one's creativity, there are financial and social rewards. You feel a profound sense of reward, for example, when you see your garments being enjoyed and worn on the street, in the gymnasium or at the beach. You feel you are contributing to society as a whole."

Lynn Cartwright's designs for *Catalina* sportswear, like these from a trade catalog, have appeared in magazine advertisements across the country.

Fashion Illustrator

Drawing the latest styles and trends for fashion advertisements is one of the most popular and practical careers open to the young artist specializing in illustration or fashion design. A quick look through any major newspaper will show that most fashion illustrators are employed on the advertising staffs of department and chain stores. Others work for textile companies, pattern houses, garment manufacturers and fashion designers such as Halston or Calvin Klein. Some work for newspapers, magazines and advertising agencies that handle fashion accounts. Still others operate as free-lance illustrators, called on for seasonal work or special promotional programs.

The heart of fashion illustration is drawing the human figure—especially the elongated, slender fashion figure. Illustrators must be able to show how fabrics fall on the body, whether they cling or stand free, and whether they move with or against the body. Some artists specialize in children's, women's, or men's apparel and are called on when required. The ability to draw figures in motion is essential.

Fashion illustrators reproduce textures and patterns—the roughness of tweed, the translucency of chiffon—simply, so they can be recognizably printed in newspapers.

They must be familiar with current hair styles, cosmetic trends, shoes and jewelry, as well as seasonal sports, school activities and ethnic influences.

In smaller shops, store systems or agencies, fashion illustrators may also be required to draw other products for newspaper ads.

College courses that prepare young illustrators for these career positions may include: drawing, life drawing, fashion drawing, painting, photography, anatomy, fashion advertising, illustration, graphic design, color and art history.

What fashion illustrators do

Typical fashion illustration assignments follow similar patterns, regardless of the agency or working situation of the artist.

The advertising art director supplies a rough sketch layout of the proposed ad, so the illustrator will know how the page will look where each illustration is to go. The garment to be illustrated is modeled, accessories are added and the illustrator has the model move and stand in various poses. When the pose is decided upon, the illustrator sketches in line and value to suggest the feeling of the clothes and the necessary detail. These sketches are made into finished drawings that will be reproduced in

An example of Stephen Bieck's fashion illustration, complete with registration marks and notations. Photograph: Joseph Gatto

the ad. Materials, fabrics and accessories are drawn in detail. Color is used in some ads, but most newspaper illustrations are line or line and value drawings.

Illustrators use their design background to arrange the elements on the page and to get the most benefit from the space available. Most stores require a certain atmosphere in all their illustrations. When this atmosphere is changed by store management, illustrators must be able to change their techniques and media accordingly.

The finished drawings must meet newspaper and advertising deadlines and must attract the attention of potential customers. Illustrators do not design clothes; they present finished products to the public in an attractive way.

What qualities are helpful for a fashion illustrator?

In addition to a talent for drawing and painting, illustrators must possess taste, flair and an understanding of current fashion trends. They must be responsive to the ideas of art directors and designers, and be able to combine their own ideas with those of their clients and art directors. They must work well with other graphic artists and advertisers.

A thorough background in fashions, the history of fashion, graphic design and composition is essential.

Fashion designers must enjoy constant drawing and sketching, and understand that the purpose of their illustration is to attract customers and sell goods.

What other careers require similar qualities?

An intense interest in fashion can also be applied to careers in fashion design and merchandising. Teaching figure drawing or fashion illustration may also interest illustrators. Product illustration requires the same ability to draw well and quickly.

Fashion illustrators might also be interested in magazine and book illustration or in fine art painting. Some phases of graphic design (quick sketching or concept illustration, for example) and interior design (drawing and rendering) require similar qualities.

What can be done now?

Students in high school should be taking drawing, painting and sculpture classes. A consuming interest in drawing is the mark of a potential illustrator. Use your sketchbook often. Look closely at the techniques and styles used in fashion advertising in newspapers and magazines. Sketch such designs and work with a variety of materials and techniques.

Visit art schools and watch fashion illustrating classes in action. Take supplementary life drawing classes at local art schools or colleges. There are often scholarship classes for talented high school artists.

Look at magazines for ideas, especially such as: *Vogue, Harpers Bazaar, Glamour, W, Mademoiselle, Town and Country* and the trade paper *WWD*.

Part-time work in boutiques or department stores will help you understand buyers' interests and fashion merchandising.

Which colleges offer necessary programs?

Schools which have fashion design departments (check the charts at the back of the book) will also have majors available in fashion illustration. The basic courses will be similar to those in fashion design, but the emphasis will be on drawing and illustration techniques and skills. Some trade schools also offer courses in basic fashion illustration.

A degree in fashion illustration will show prospective employers that you have substantial training and experience in both fashion design and illustration, and are competent at drawing, design and the mechanical skills necessary for quality illustration.

Other Careers in the Fashion Industry

Accessory Designers

Accessory designers work in many materials to provide accent for basic fashions. They generally work for the companies that manufacture the products, but many are free-lance designers. They sketch, design, and supervise the basic models for such accessories as purses, belts, shoes, pins, necklaces, scarves and stockings. They usually have a strong background in fashion design.

Advertising Agency Fashion Art Director

This fashion art director is a staff member of an advertising agency, responsible for the production of ads for department stores or manufacturers who produce items in the fashion field. He or she must deal with photographers and models, and should have sound knowledge of graphic design and type composition.

Fashion Consultant

Fashion consultants are employed by department stores and specialty shops to offer advice to individual clients and store personnel. They are trained in fashion design, coordination and merchandising. Some consultants are free-lance specialists who work for several stores or individual clients who rely on their expertise and fashion knowledge.

Fabric Designer

Fabric designers can be classified in three groups: weavers, surface designers, and related designers and artists. Most work for manufacturers, designing and supervising the production of finished materials. Some are free-lance artists who design and produce fabrics for sale to manufacturers. College courses for fabric designers include two- and three-dimensional design, painting, printmaking, weaving, fashion and materials and home furnishing classes.

Weavers construct cloth on looms, and often work from their own original patterns. They may work on hand looms, but more often they design patterns to be woven on commercial looms. These fabrics are woven quickly and in large volume.

Surface designers create patterns that are printed on existing fabrics. The printing may be silkscreened or block printed by hand or by machine, depending on the quality and quantity desired by the manufacturer.

Some fabric designers also create wallpaper, linoleum and floor tile patterns. Rugs, decorative upholstery fabrics, writing paper, towels, linens and other patterned surfaces are also designed by these artists.

Fashion Coordinator

Fashion coordinators are employed by department stores and chain stores and work with apparel buyers to give a unified look and tone to the store's lines. They promote the image of the store or system in public and the media by producing fashion shows and arranging for special promotions. They are aided by publicity directors who have strong fashion backgrounds. Some fashion coordinators are responsible for photographic coverage in newspapers and magazines.

Fashion Copywriters

These specialists write an ad copy that appears in magazines, newspapers and on television. They work for advertising agencies, department stores, or specialty shops and malls, and can write effective copy for men's, women's and children's clothing as well as for accessories and related fashion products.

Fashion Display Director

These specialists design window and store displays that draw attention to fashion ideas and featured styles. They work with promotion experts, merchandisers and department managers in selecting apparel and accessories for displays. They are expert at display techniques, lighting, use of mannequins, draping materials and three-dimensional and graphic design. Their displays set a tone in the stores and are often coordinated throughout a store system. They work with other store display artists to coordinate seasonal and topical promotional programs.

Fashion Editor/Writer

The fashion industry and the buying public are kept up-to-date on what is happening in the fashion world by editors and writers who work for fashion magazines or write fashion material for other magazines or newspapers. They travel to show openings, review current trends and styles, work with photographers to develop feature articles and inform their readers of fashion developments and industry happenings. They have strong backgrounds in fashion design and merchandising and are articulate speakers and writers about clothing, accessories and design.

Fashion Merchandising

Although fashion merchandising has little to do with design and art, it is a vital link in the fashion cycle. If goods are not sold, the system breaks down.

Fashion merchandisers are buyers, fashion promoters, coordinators, department managers and salespeople, merchandise managers, personal shoppers, inventory control workers, copywriters, display designers and consumer relations officers. Many of these careers are best served by a fashion design background, while others require a fashion merchandising emphasis in college.

Fashion Photographer (See Photography)

Fashion Production

After the designers have created the ideas and samplemakers have sewn their sample designs, production personnel take over. Patternmakers, cutters, sewers and finishers are involved in the process. Supervisors and managers oversee the operations and quality control experts inspect the fabrics and finished pieces before they are sent to stores and put in the hands of merchandisers.

Fashion Specialists

In addition to display directors and fashion coordinators there are several other specialized fashion careers. Bridal consultants plan and coordinate wedding clothing and accessories. Fashion stylists prepare models for fashion shows and photographic shootings. They work with art directors in planning wardrobes, accessories and makeup.

Patternmaker

Patternmaking technology requires knowledge of the principles on which commercial garment sizing is based. Original design ideas are transformed into muslin and paper patterns in a basic size (34 for women and 36 for men). These patterns are dissected, discussed, reassembled and finally made into a pattern that will serve as a manufacturing standard.

Patternmakers must also get the maximum number of pattern pieces from available yardage.

Related careers include pattern grader, supervisor, production executive and production manager.

Sports Clothing Designer

The vast field of sports clothing has recently become a special interest area for designers. Clothing for skiing, jogging, hiking, surfing and numerous other games and activities must be designed to meet specific requirements and provide any necessary protection. Team sports (both school and professional), bands and drill teams also require specially designed equipment and clothing.

Designing for these special areas requires a thorough knowledge of the sports and a background in materials, fashion design and sports safety.

Part Four | Entertainment and the Media

Students majoring in film must be able to work with all facets of the discipline. Here a film major synchronizes sound and image during an assignment. Photograph: Brooks Institute

A MERICA AND DOZENS of nations around the world have become media-oriented societies. Films and television, books, magazines and theater events entertain and educate the population in countless ways. In order to supply the visual materials for all these media uses, career artists of many backgrounds are employed by the television and film industries and publishing companies of all types.

Production experts are becoming aware of the importance of artists who can visualize, conceptualize, design and produce the ideas, settings and illustrations required to improve their finished products. In spite of new techniques and applications, the necessity for good, clean design remains constant.

Film and Television

Design techniques and production methods in the film and television industries have advanced rapidly in the last half of the twentieth century. Career artists, photographers, art directors and designers have played major roles in this development, and continue to be important partners in its progress.

Los Angeles and New York were the early centers for the film and television industries, primarily because of the dry, clear, sunny weather in Los Angeles and the concentration of actors and related personnel in New York. But television production today does not require the huge sound stages, natural sunlight or accompanying satellite industries film demands, and television career opportunities are now available in most major cities around the country. With the fantastic growth of the cable industry, most television stations need graphic designers, photographers, computer assisted design specialists and a variety of other artists.

More and more artists are becoming involved with setting the tone and developing the designs that tie productions together. Film artists and technicans are now judged by their abilities in areas such as motion graphics, graphic design through time, computer-oriented art and graphics and work in expandable fields of art such as special effects and animation.

College curriculums in film and television career preparation include such courses as: set design, quick sketching and color rendering for television, animation techniques, introduction to video, tape and stage production, production techniques, editing, sound recording, film writing and photographic communication. Preparation for film and television careers requires a unique and specialized art background.

Art Director

Those responsible for coordinating the efforts of artists, graphic and costume designers and scene builders are known as art directors. Because of their practical experience they work with directors and producers to develop successful visual environments in both film and television production. They are responsible for the authenticity of sets, costumes, props and locations.

Art directors in television, film and theater all need similar qualifications. They must have experience in and mastery of script analysis, mood development, set construction and supervision, procuring materials and equipment and complete project development from script to stage and/or production. The career requires all that the theater set designers' jobs require (See Scenic Designer), and knowledge of motion picture history and technique. Some college courses provide background, personal insights and experiences in each of these areas, and some schools have developed extensive curricula in film and television career areas. Check the charts at the back of the book for such listings.

Magazines that may help in understanding the film and television industries include: *Videographs, Millimeter, Emmy* and *Cinéfantistique*, among others. Most cannot be found in regular libraries, but the libraries of art schools probably subscribe to them.

Young artists interested in becoming art directors should learn all possible facets of film, television and theater art and design production. Years of experience in these areas will teach them how to direct successfully the many art activities necessary for topflight productions.

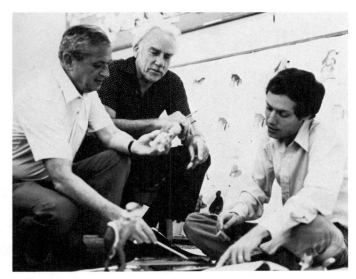

The directors of the film review some animation boards and make suggestions and additions. Photograph © MCMLXXXI Walt Disney Productions

Animators draw the characters' exaggerated poses. Photograph © MCMLXXXI Walt Disney Productions

Film Animation

The media area that makes use of the most artists is film animation. Artists are used at every part of the process from initial concept development to final editing and production. The Walt Disney Studios were responsible for the initial efforts; since then animation has developed into a full-fledged industry. And after years of refinement and development, the basic process remains much the same.

The animation process

The picture sequence from Walt Disney Studios illustrates the process and defines the roles of artists at various stages of production. Once the story is selected and scripted, researchers determine the architecture, settings, locale, costumes and dominating colors and furnishings. Armed with this information, artists begin to work. First they develop storyboards. Each board contains about sixty sketches with parts of the story written on strips below each. It takes three storyboards to outline a short subject, and twenty-five or more for a feature film. This comic strip-like board, reviewed by directors, provides the basic outline of actions, characters, movements and progress of the project.

Top animators sketch and develop the characteristics of the principal figures. When they are approved, the search begins to find people with voices that fit the characters. Those voices are recorded reading the script.

The animation director and the layout artist direct the production of the film. The animation director is responsible for getting the story on the screen, following it from storyboards to premier showing. He or she selects the best angles, orders the art and music and coordinates all the personnel to create the finished work. The layout artist sets the mood, determines the backgrounds and scenes, sketches the concepts for other artists to paint and is responsible for the look and mood of the film.

The director has the songs, music and sound effects recorded, supervises the sketching of characters and oversees the development of backgrounds and selection of colors. He hands the scenes to animators who begin animation.

Of two hundred artists in Disney's animation department, fifty are animators whose expert pencils bring the characters to life. The rest are "breakdown artists" and "in-betweeners." Animators have sketches of the background, tape recordings of the voices and sketches of the characters they are to do. They often use models or themselves to capture facial expressions. They draw the main movements or extreme poses while other artists fill in the dozens of required drawings to complete the movement. It takes twenty-four drawings for each second of film time. When the required drawings are tested and approved, they are ready to be inked and painted on the reverse side of clear plastic sheets, called "cels."

In the meantime, background artists paint the settings that were earlier sketched by the layout artist. Many of these background painters are fine artists, who are well versed in architecture, design and color, and their paintings furnish the environment for the animated action. Background colors must complement each other and the characters must stand out.

In the camera department, the finished and sequenced cels are photographed against the proper background, one at a time. A feature length film will require 110,000 such exposures.

The character drawings are inked and painted onto cels. Photograph © MCMLXXXI Walt Disney Productions

Background artists paint the settings. Photograph © MCMLXXXI Walt Disney Productions

A feature film may call for 800 backgrounds, which must be coordinated to allow the figures to stand out. Photograph © MCMLXXXI Walt Disney Productions

Finally, the director will preview, adjust, edit and complete the film, readying it for screening and production.

Hundreds of artists are involved in the production, and each is expert at his or her job. The degree of cooperation and the effort required are tremendous, yet the finished product must look as though it fell together with the utmost ease.

What qualities are helpful in film animation?

The essential qualities are the ability to draw, a mastery of the processes involved and the ability to work cooperatively to create a unified product. Patience, self-discipline and the ability to work on a single project for extended periods of time are also demanded of animators. Some feature length films require several years to complete. Animators must carry out the directions of others carefully and completely, and must meet all deadlines.

What can be done now?

Take all the drawing and painting classes possible. Extra scholarship drawing and figure drawing classes at art schools are very helpful. Other art classes, cartooning and design instruction, art history, history, English, music and literature courses provide excellent background.

Look at figures and backgrounds in all types of animated features. Draw figures, storyboards, and backgrounds in your sketchbooks. Work your way through cartoon instruction books. Magazines that may help include most comic books that deal with cartoon figures. Work on the school newspaper as staff cartoonist or on the yearbook art staff. Develop your own characters and ideas as you go along.

Which colleges offer necessary programs?

Schools near animation centers (New York, Los Angeles, Chicago, for example) would provide the necessary classes and background. They would also give you the opportunity to visit animation studios or have animation artists visit your classes. Animation instructors should have practical experience in studio work.

Schools can provide the necessary background in drawing and animation procedures, but individual studios will have their own way of doing things and will train young artists to work according to their production needs. Most studios have special training programs for such purposes. Some studios (Disney, Hanna-Barbera, for example) have staff artists on the faculty of local art schools and workshops to give students a head start in training and processes.

The director completes the film by editing and polishing it. Photograph © MCMLXXXI Walt Disney Productions

Television Graphic Artists

Variety is a key word in television production, and it is also a vital ability of television graphic artists. They must be able to do everything from quick sketches to finished art, using any and all media, and they must be familiar with electronic and computer designing techniques. Small television stations may employ one or two artists; large studios will have ten or more artists on the staff.

What television graphic artists do

They usually follow their projects from concept to final taping and screening. During the process they may use several media, have a few trial viewings in the control room and watch their ideas come to life on the screen. Typical jobs are likely to include such projects as:

- Designing and preparing advertising or promotional pieces for the sales department of the station (layout, typesetting, headlines, halftones, negatives, color, screens and final product).
- Designing newspaper and TV ads for the station.
- Designing and preparing news graphics (the visual art behind the newscaster), used to set the mood or establish visual contact with viewers.
- Designing, constructing and painting sets for new shows.
- Making art cards for commercials. These are usually in color, and make use of type along with logos.
- Shooting still photos in color or black and white. Also processing film and making prints.

- Designing station Christmas cards, graphics for station vehicles, logos for minicams, signs for lobbies and all other art work for the station.

A typical project

The sequence of photographs illustrates a typical visual project for television, and shows the use of electronic equipment in preparing the graphics. Graphic artist Gretta Moore of WJXT in Jacksonville, Florida is working with news reporter Angela Estell in developing a news graphic for a series on "Pregnancy After 35."

The reporter is focusing on the process of amniosentesis, a test used to detect possible birth defects. The graphic elements are: the pregnant woman, the fetus and the hypodermic needle.

Each camera image can be electronically tinted any color, although the original art was only black and white. The artist here decided that the background and mother should be brown, and the mother's outline should be a contrasting yellow. The fetus was made pink on black. Clarity and exaggeration are important features of television graphics.

Final airing involved one moving graphic and one stationary one. A crew member slid the needle card left and right until the artist and director were satisfied that the process was properly shown. It was taped and used for a few moments on the program.

Part of the work was done in traditional graphic media (ink, brush, pen and cutouts), but the final products were manipulated by a director and an electronic switcher which determined colors, locations and movement.

Moore and Estell discuss the project to be sure the reporter's ideas will be carried out correctly and effectively.

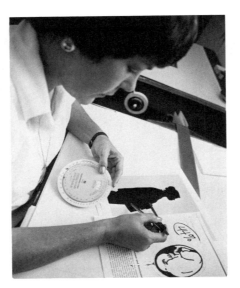

The artist sizes the fetus drawing to fit the abdomen of the silhouetted woman.

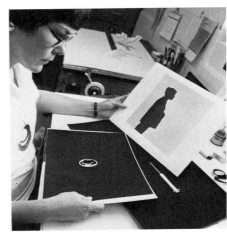

A high contrast stat is made, and the fetus drawing is reduced in size and made into a negative image so it can be superimposed on the silhouette. The needle is made from white paper and mounted on a black card.

Entertainment and the Media

What qualities are helpful for a television graphic artist?

Anyone interested in TV art must be able to conceptualize and deliver finished products fast! There is not time for lengthy thought processes or reworking of ideas. Artists must be confident that they can quickly produce what is needed. Visual statements must be strong to be impressive on the screen.

Because most of the graphic work involves electronics, a constantly changing field, artists must learn on the job and be quick to pick up new ideas and adaptations. The artist with the best foundation in design and design concepts will be the most prepared to do this.

What other careers require similar qualities?

Work in such areas of film production as special effects, title preparation and film graphics calls for similar qualifications. The ability to work quickly and confidently is an asset to any graphic designer, even if electronics are not involved.

The field of television art is relatively new. Art schools therefore are often in need of teachers who have had experience in television graphics.

The ability to carry projects from concept to finished product and to work in all media and types of graphic design are also required of corporate art directors.

Police and court sketch artists must also be able to work quickly and accurately, and often prepare materials for television newscasts.

What can be done now?

Quick sketching is vital to a television graphic artist, so drawing classes are essential, as is sketchbook practice. Draw everything and anything. Get involved in all art classes and art projects at school.

Watch television graphics and look at advertising in magazines to see what techniques are being used. Collect excellent examples of advertising design and look through magazines that may show technical developments in the television industry: *Videography, High Technology* and *Emmy*, for example.

Supplementary classes in drawing and computer programming would be helpful. Part-time work in any design capacity (layout or paste-up, for example) is good training, as is work for technical industries or television sales and service.

Which colleges offer necessary programs?

College courses offered at large art schools will prepare students for careers in television art; check the listings at the back of the book. A sound and fundamental design background is absolutely necessary, and a strong and well-presented portfolio is a must.

At large stations in large market areas, courses in TV art will probably be required for employment. But in smaller market areas, confidence and a superior portfolio of graphic designs and drawings will help get you a job. Practical experience may lead to jobs in larger station environments.

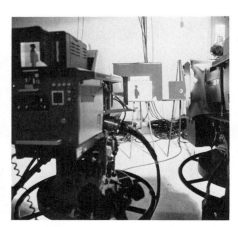

In the studio, two of the camera cards are set on easels and two cameras take separate pictures on videotape.

In the director's studio, the silhouette of the mother was changed electronically to a simple outlined figure. The fetus drawing is now superimposed on this figure in the position and location the artist chooses.

In the final stages, the graphic artist prepares a newspaper ad to attract viewers to the program. Photographs courtesy Gretta Moore

Special effects photography can combine cartoon figures with the movements of live actors. Effects in *Jack and the Beanstalk* are visual rather than actually constructed.
Photograph: Hanna-Barbera Productions

Special Effects Artist

The magicians of film and television productions are the special effects artists, who create the illusions and design and construct the devices that thrill millions of viewers. They turn ocean liners over without losing lives or damaging the vessels, explode gigantic bridges without hurting anyone, build monsters and make huge sandstorms and torrential rains.

They use unconventional tools, machines and materials to create the special effects called for by scripts and directors, yet they also rely on everyday materials to produce some necessary effects and moods.

Special effects artists develop within the film industry. No special training is required, and no degrees are offered in special effects. The background of a special effects artists usually includes extensive training in film: camera work, film direction, production, art direction and set decoration. School training is followed by apprenticeship in the industry and succeeding years of experience. Creative people call on this experience when they consider ways to devise special effects.

What special effects artists do
Special effects artists work closely with producers, directors and art directors to make an unusual situation look realistic. Whether what is called for is an intergalactic war, a flood or a flying automobile, the ingenuity and imagination of special effects artists are challenged by the demands of the film.

The need for most special effects is determined early in a film's production, by consultation with the director. Often, however, there are spontaneous developments of such effects while the film is in production, and last minute changes and adaptations are required. In many films, the success of the story line depends on the convincing use of special effects.

Some effects are the result of a film's specific needs and may not be called for again (as the shark in *Jaws*, for example); other effects can be modified and used again and again (such as the barges that hold camera crews for shooting naval battles between scale model ships).

Special effects artists must adhere to their own budget for their part of the film and often must rely on unconventional means to produce dramatic effects. They work closely with the studio property shops, whose engineers and constructors can build almost anything. Whether the film is set in space or under the surface of the earth, no film challenge is beyond a special effects artist.

What qualities are helpful for a special effects artist?
They must be creative, able to build all types of things and to draw, sketch and paint what others will construct. They must have a thorough knowledge of film techniques and of the history of special film effects. They

must be able to put a director's ideas into visual form, complete with movement, sound and light.

They must be as adept at building sculptural forms as they are at handling camera angles and lighting. They must work well under the pressures of time and a limited budget. They must be able to take directions and delegate responsibility.

What other careers require similar qualities?
The qualities of creativity, film sense and the ability to build and engineer are called for in stage design, set construction and in some areas of kinetic sculpture. Design work in theme parks require artists with similar abilities and skills.

Display artists who design booths at fairs and conventions must also be able to develop concepts, design products and build displays that operate according to certain requirements.

Film art directors, scenic designers and directors come from backgrounds and training similar to that required of special effects artist.

What can be done now?
High school classes in all phases of art should be taken, with special emphasis on sculpture and three-dimensional design. Strengthen your photographic skills by taking classes and joining clubs. Shop classes will teach you the skills required to build and engineer many special effects. Work on the stage crew at school will develop your stage sense and design skills. Darkroom work for the newspaper and yearbook is also helpful.

Part-time jobs in engineering and construction will help you learn and understand building techniques. Film lab work is useful: it teaches you darkroom skills and how to work with light and color. Working with your own movie or videotaping camera is a sure way to gain early experience in experimenting with special effects.

Look at movies built around special effects: science fiction and period films, space-oriented subjects, chase scenes and the like. These will motivate you to learn more about the skills required.

Some books and movie magazines have sections that explore this phase of movie and television production. Write to production companies and ask for materials that may explain some of their dramatic achievements.

Which colleges offer necessary programs?
No schools offer complete programs for special effects artists. Look carefully at course offerings in the catalogs of schools that have extensive film departments. Check the charts at the back of the book.

Stage design and set construction training may lead to special effects positions in the film or television industries.

Other Careers In Film and Television

Advertising Agency Television Art Director
Ad agency television art directors specialize in television commercials. They direct the use of print art, live action, animation and other film techniques. They must be able to plan and draw storyboards (consecutive small drawings illustrating scene change in a film) for presentation within the agency. Once the art director has approval, a production studio or free-lance designer/filmmaker is given the job. The art director keeps track of all advertising production, from filming to final editing and showing.

Background Artist (Film and Television)
Background or scenic artists design and paint the visual environment in which sound stage action is filmed. They paint on huge canvas backdrops and after research can simulate nearly any scene or interior. They work in studios large enough to hold rolls of canvas often more than seventy-five feet wide. They work with directors and sketch the initial concepts that are then painted by a small army of background painters. These designs will vary from elaborate baroque palace rooms to simple park-like settings. Background artist often have been trained to set designers, but gain on-the-job experience while working in the studios.

Camera Person (Film and Television)
There are many types of camera positions in the film and television industries. They all require training in film techniques, production and design.

CAMERA OPERATOR: operates the camera that photographs color stills for cartoon animation. (See Film Animation)

CAMERA TITLE OPERATOR: photographs title cards of various types in television production (program titles, station titles, lettered captions for language translations, etc.).

CAMERA OPERATOR (Film): works both indoors on soundstages and outdoors on location, following the instructions of directors and cinematographers. He or she operates the cameras, adjusts the lenses and loads and unloads the film. Camera assistants are available to help with most jobs.

TELEVISION CAMERA PERSON: television stations have a hierarchy of jobs related to the operation of cameras. Photographers work with videotape as well as film, but their understanding of light, shadow, color and design must be thorough to produce excellent results. In some areas (such as news taping) speed and accuracy are more important than excellence of design. Included are video specialists in areas such as: news, sports, minicam operating, film and tape editing, ENG (electronic news gathering), photography editing and camera work in studio situations (live and taped programs). Background and experience required include: camera operation, set production, lighting, staging and cinematography. Training in video camera work and 16mm photography is essential, but most stations and networks like to train their camera operators within their own systems.

CINEMATOGRAPHER (Film): these camera specialists supervise all camera work on sets and on locations. They check lenses and camera angles, watch lighting conditions and establish the mood in the films. They work closely with directors, and must study scripts to determine the kind of equipment needed (cameras, lenses, lights, reflectors, shades, etc.). They also work closely with special effects artists to establish methods for photographing the effects called for by the directors.

Continuity Artist

Continuity artists take scripts and break them down for shooting. They sketch possible scenes so directors can envision them. Where special effects are involved, they sketch scenes leading into the scene, the special effects themselves and subsequent scenes. An average film involves 1,500 such sketches, all of which help directors, cinematographers and set designers establish the mood and feeling of the film.

Costume Designer (See also Costume Designer, Theater and Stage Design)

Costume designers usually receive training in fashion design and theater costume design. After reading a script, they conduct research and work with the director and wardrobe staff to decide upon all the clothing to be worn in the production. They sketch and render the costume designs from which costume seamstresses cut and sew directly. Many designs are made specifically for certain actors, but when huge numbers are involved they may be generalized or drawn from wardrobe departments. A thorough background in fashion history is required; the authenticity of the film is established by the characters' clothing.

Director of Photography

These specialists plan, direct and coordinate filming and taping for film or television productions. They select cameras, accessories, equipment, film and tape. They instruct camera operators and assistants. They supervise camera angles, equipment, distances and movement, and are responsible for starting and stopping the action in each scene or "take." They review the completed work and assist with editing and adjusting before final prints are made.

Film Editor

The work of film editors starts after shooting is completed. They take all the footage and edit, splice, rearrange and complete the final product. They are responsible for the "feel," pace and continuity of the production. They work with producers, directors, cinematographers, sound technicians and assistants to arrange all the parts of the film cohesively.

Films for Art Education (See also Film and Television)

Films for art education include how-to-do-it films as well as documentary productions on the lives and work of various artists. They also include the various productions that help make young people aware of their environment and instruct them in the fundamentals of design and aesthetics. Films also are made about certain art styles and periods (for art history use and as motivational materials) and may include documentation of museum collections. Such aids make art teaching more meaningful and complete by expanding students' visual vocabularies. All the jobs associated with general filmmaking are required, but the director, producer or company owners should have backgrounds in art. Some companies specialize in art education films; others produce occasional films on art while relying primarily on other subjects. Television programs, designed originally for the general public, are often made available for use in art classes.

Often, former art teachers become involved in the production of method and media films because they understand the problems and needs of classroom teachers. Art historians often assist in or direct the making of documentary films on periods and styles of art or on particular artists, lending authority to the productions.

Makeup Artist

These specialists are responsible for the facial appearances of all actors in a production. They age young people, create monsters and are experts at making beards, mustaches and goatees. They use rubber, plastic and clay to produce miraculous results for both film and television. Often makeup artists work on a single face for hours before the actor goes before the cameras. The skills required are based on a background of theater and sculpture training.

Model Builder

Model builders in the film and television fields are craftspeople who can build anything to scale. They use wood, plastic, cardboard, plaster, clay, glass and natural materials to construct any structure or object a script requires. They work with special effects artists, art directors and cinematographers. Some models may be built to be destroyed; others can be used many times. Model builders have a background in stage and set design and construction, sculpture, special effects, carpentry and metal construction.

Photographer (See Camera Person, above)

Scenic Artist (See Background Artist, above)

Set Designer

Set designers design, select accessories for, decorate and coordinate the sets used in film and television. They work with an extensive staff. After sketching and rendering ideas for sets, they order furniture, draperies, pictures, lamps and rugs that will enhance the scenes in their productions. They work closely with scenic supervisors, scenic artists, property managers, art directors, costume designers, directors and producers in establishing the mood and authenticity of the sets. They must work with lighting and camera locations to get the best results. Their training is in theater arts, set design, stage management and interior design.

Storyboard Illustrator

These illustrators work for large advertising agencies or are hired on a free-lance basis. They take rough sketches from art directors and develop them into finished sequential drawings for presentation to potential TV commercial buyers or industrial clients. These drawings illustrate the action of the commercial (similar to the storyboards used in animated films; See Film Animation). Appropriate dialog is scripted under each drawing in the series. This gives clients an idea of how the tape or film might look before any money is spent on production.

Storyboard illustrators also sequence events in television pilot films to give producers and client advertisers a feel for the project.

The artists must be able to sketch quickly and work rapidly, because multiple drawings must be produced in a short time. Such illustrations develop ways of suggesting detail rather than actually using it in their work.

Television Camera Person (See Camera Person, above)

Television Electronic Designer

These designers explore the possibilities and use of videotape, computers and advanced electronics to make films and commercials. They must have a thorough knowledge of the latest electronic and technological equipment, and must use it imaginatively and creatively in television screening. They may work in design studios, for large television stations or networks or as free-lance designers. They are responsible for many special effects and the electronic graphics used in program introductions, commercials and advertisements.

Title Designer

Title designers are the graphic artists who design the hundreds of titles used at the beginnings of television programs or films. Some are animated, others are photographic, but all contain type, names, titles and graphic effects. Title designers must be at ease with all type styles and graphic processes, and electronic and computer design components. They have a solid background in graphic design, and must be flexible, willing to experiment, creative and able to generate fresh ideas quickly. Many title designs are the products of top national graphic design studios, while others are created in the graphic design studios of small television stations.

The Theater And Stage Design

Drama and theater had their beginnings in Greece in the fifth century before Christ, and their basic elements have remained constant over several thousand years. Architects are concerned with the structure, seating arrangements and physical construction of the performing areas; art directors, directors and stage designers create the sets and scenes that are the environment of the staged action.

Stage productions, whether on Broadway or in a high school gymnasium, are the collaborative efforts of actors, directors, stage managers, stage technicians and the designers of scenes, sets, costumes and props. Musical productions (opera, light opera, musical comedy) involve all of these people plus singers, soloists, dancers, choreographers, musicians and conductors.

Theaters have always included stages or performing areas and auditoriums for the audience. Traditional theater (of ancient Greece, Shakespeare's era or Japanese and Chinese tradition) is performed on a platform surrounded by audience on at least three sides. European and American theater is "illusory" in that the audience, separated from the action by a curtain or proscenium, watches performers on a raised and lighted stage. The actors perform their lines as if the audience were not there.

The design and preparation of this stage is the realm of the scenic designer. His or her intention is to make the elements on the stage seem real and convincing, or to suggest a particular scene which the audience completes.

Purposeful theater successfully combines three elements: audience, place and performer. The single area that directly involves visual artists is *place*. The place is the physical stage on which the actors move and speak and the illusory space provided by the scenic designer.

"Staging" refers to the entire theatrical presentation, including words, performers, setting, costumes, makeup, lighting and properties. All elements must be coordinated to produce the maximum effect, and all are under the control and direction of the director. Theater areas that directly involve career artists are scenic design, stage lighting, scene painting, property design and construction, costume design and makeup. Visual artists in these areas are responsible for the sense of place in the play, the mood, the authenticity of effects, clothing, arrangement of props and overall visual impact of everything on the stage. They coordinate their efforts with directors, stage managers, actors and, sometimes, the play's authors.

If the action of a play is set in 1982 or 1582, all the visual artists involved must research their special areas to make the final product as authentic as possible. This may involve buying or building furniture, securing or designing and sewing clothes, finding rugs, furniture and accessories from that period of time, or building and painting them to match actual items.

The world of the theater is a fascinating place for a visual artist who also has strong interests in theater and drama. Regardless of size or style, theatrical performances rely on visual artists to complete the illusion begun by the author of the play.

Scenic Designer

Stage scenery was designed by craftspeople from the guilds until the Middle Ages, when it was turned over to artists. Each Renaissance and baroque state had its court painters who supervised the construction of sets and stages. From the mid-nineteenth century until today, commercial scene painting studios, stocked wth an ample supply of artists, have taken over the designing and painting of scenic backgrounds and sets. Large permanent theater companies in major cities maintain their own scenic and property shops, where the design and construction of sets is carried out in close cooperation with directors and producers.

The responsibility for creating settings for plays,

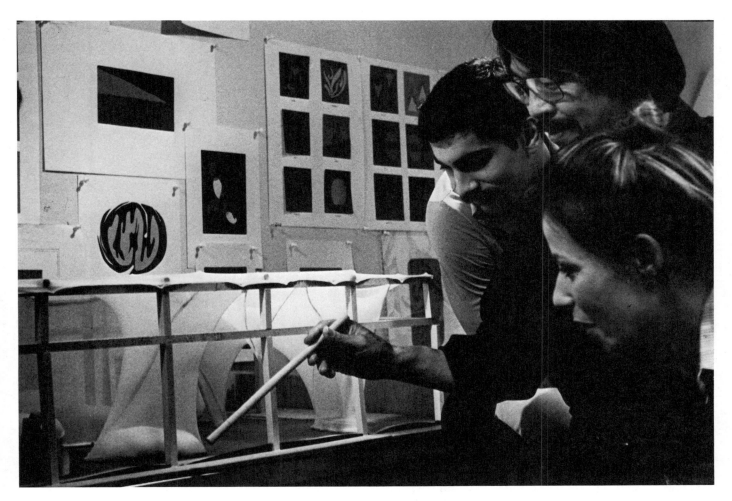

Students majoring in stage design work on a model that allows them to determine circulation and scale. Such models are built for every major American stage production. Photograph: New York School of Interior Design

operas and musicals has traditionally been handled by fine artists, scenic artists, skilled artisans and others unconnected with the theater. But today most scenic designers have had training in theater as well as art, and are extremely qualified for their work.

Carpentry, painting, property and drapery shops used to be separate businesses (and still are in most European theater cities), but since 1950 these activities have been combined in single scenic departments in many major American cities. Some resident theaters (Metropolitan Opera and the Los Angeles Civic Light Opera, for example) maintain their own combined shops.

Stage scenery has run the gamut from highly elaborate Victorian decoration to minimal use of props and sets; from contained areas on a single platform to multi-platformed stages where wings, aprons and rotating sections are employed. Stage lights are sometimes hidden, sometimes exposed. Today's scenic designers take advantage of every possible device, old or new, to bring excitement to their stages.

What scenic designers do

After reading the play, a scenic designer meets with the director to develop an overall plan for the production. Small sketches of stage ideas are made and later expanded into color renderings or scale models, usually one-half inch to one foot. Research on the clothing, furniture, windows, doors, lighting and accessories is necessary to create the feeling suggested by the script. The research and initial ideas are made into final renderings and models which become the basis for set construction in the shops. Dimensions, cross-sections, floor plans and diagrams are included to insure careful adherence to the designer's plans. The designer supervises all construction, painting, assembling, finishing and positioning of the parts and furnishes the working drawings from which everything is made.

Set designers paint huge drops to suit the style and environment of the production, and the concepts of the director. Photograph: Joseph Gatto

Scenic design shops used to work mostly with large flats on which the scenes were painted. Today's staging calls for three-dimensional construction, and scenic shops contain a variety of equipment for such production. Steel has replaced wood in many cases. Metal workers are now as important as carpenters in the shops, because construction must be extremely strong, yet as light in weight as possible. Plastic is cast in any shape and finished to look like wood, metal, fabric or stone. Furniture is made by staff carpenters or bought, and props and accessories are acquired. Gradually the ideas of the scenic designer become reality and the parts are ready to assemble.

Surfaces and textures are as important as the lights that play on them. Plastics of various types have replaced the glue, powdered cork and sawdust textures of the past. New materials are a constant challenge to designers: they encourage experiment and inspire unique ideas.

Once all the components of the stage set have been collected, the set up takes place. Everything is brought to the stage, tested and put in place. Final touch-up painting is done and the stage is ready for the actors.

Traditional stage construction techniques are still widely used, but some scenic designers are experimenting with new ways to use patterned lighting, electronic gear and film-slide devices. Such electronic staging demands new approaches to stage design and technical direction.

Many new playhouses use open stages, arena formations and flexible platform construction. Scenic designers must alter their concepts of staging, sets and scenes if they are to present plays that make full use of these technical innovations.

What qualities are helpful for a scenic designer?
It has been said that a scenic designer should be historian, archaeologist, antiquarian, architect, sculptor, painter, visionary, poet, carpenter, electrician and engineer—and part actor. While this has some truth, more important to scenic designers is the ability to develop and react to ideas, and to be able to concentrate fully on the play at hand.

Scenic designers must love to read, especially plays, because they must get their ideas for sets and props from their reading. They have a deep concern for carrying out the theme of the production but are able to add their personal touches. They must work well with others; they are only one part of the team that produces the finished play.

They must be prepared to work within time and space restrictions, yet produce sets that look natural and effortless.

What other careers require similar qualities?
Any aspect of the theater arts will appeal to artists interested in scenic design. They would enjoy careers in costume design, lighting, set painting and perhaps directing or acting. They would be comfortable in set decoration and painting departments in film and television studios. Interior design (See Interior Design) might be appealing, due to the similar need to work with materials, textures and colors to enhance an environment.

Designing floats (See Other Careers in Interior Design) for large parades is similar to scenic design, except that the stages are moving down the street. Working in property shops, building period furniture and teaching stagecraft in high school and college require the same backgrounds and qualities necessary for scenic designers.

What can be done now?
Take high school classes such as art history and studio (drawing, painting and three-dimensional design in particular). History and literature classes are vitally important, as are courses in drama and stagecraft. Wood and metal shop classes will give you practical experience in construction techniques.

Work on school plays and musical productions doing lighting, set design, set painting and the like.

Attend college, community and professional plays and pay special attention to the design and construction of sets and their connection with the theme of the play.

Work in summer theaters (in prop or scenic departments) is extremely valuable. Read plays and design sets, build models, design costumes and make layouts for them. Magazines such as *Theatre Crafts* and *Opera News* will allow you to read about sets and scenes currently in production.

Which colleges offer necessary programs?
There are several schools that emphasize theater arts in the context of art. Many colleges and universities have excellent theater arts departments which emphasize scenic design, lighting design and art direction as well as acting. Check the charts at the back of the book. Also ask drama teachers, stagecraft teachers and guidance counselors about schools from which you may get catalogs.

A college degree is not essential for success in scenic design, but the background and experience you will gain in such programs is difficult to get anywhere else. Practical experience as well as college training will give you the knowledge and experience you need to start a career in scenic design.

Costume Designer

Costume designers consult directors and scenic and lighting designers from the start of a production. The color, shape and line of all the costumes must be considered in relation to the sets and lighting plan. Some resident companies have their own costume designers and staffs, while in other situations, free-lance designers and costume companies bid on design jobs when a new play is in production.

Costume design requires research into fashions of the past, and a basic knowledge of fashion history is essential. This historical approach to fashion is stressed in schools that feature fashion design, drama or theater arts. Authentic period costumes are the result of such study and background.

Portraits and sculpture of earlier artists often serve as sources of information for costume designers; they must therefore have a working knowledge of art history. Museums are excellent places in which to conduct research for costume design.

A thorough knowledge of fabrics is essential in order to create authentic costumes. If the actual fabric cannot be duplicated today, designers must know how to make a substitute material look like the original fabric called for in the script.

What costume designers do
After the costume designer reads the play, and the director and scenic designer have been consulted, rough sketches are made of all necessary costumes. These are researched, modified and redrawn several times before the approval of the director is sought.

When the director approves the sketches, the costume designer starts searching for fabrics. This may be easy if the play is set in contemporary times, but more difficult if set in the Middle Ages. Cloth swatches, chosen by the designer for their authenticity and color, are stapled to the sketches. When the cast is chosen, sketches are redrawn in accordance with each actor's particular appearance. All accessories (glasses, purses, beads, shoes, gloves, watches and the like) are also the responsibility of the costume designer.

If the costumes are made within the company's own shops, production of pieces can begin immediately. If not, the designs are opened to bidding from outside costume companies. Experienced workers in costume houses or the company's own department make all costumes and their undertrimmings. They are fitted on the actors before muslin patterns are made for the overgarments. Cutters, drapers and fitters work with the actors under the supervision of the costume designer. Patterns are made to fit only the actors in the play, and are fitted directly to them or an exact dress form.

Every fitting is crucial; the second fitting (including shoes, wigs and hats) and the third (complete wardrobe) require the approval of the designer.

About ten days before opening night, a dress parade is held. All the costumes are worn in front of the appropriate sets, so the director and designers can be sure that all parts work together. There are always last minute adjustments in color, use of spray paint and dye, and changes in the colors in lights, no matter how careful the designers have been.

When all costumes are approved, they are turned over to the wardrobe staff, who take full responsibility for them as long as the production runs.

Bolts of material are stored in racks at the Los Angeles Music Center, waiting to be made into clothing for forthcoming productions. Photograph: Joseph Gatto

What qualities are helpful for a costume designer?

Costume designers are under constant pressure to produce designs and create costumes within a rigid time frame. Last minute changes and alterations are common and designers must be able to think clearly in crisis situations.

They must have a thorough knowledge and love of fabrics and fashion history, and must be able to communicate and work well with the people in their shops (cutters, drapers, seamstresses and fitters). They must work closely with scenic designers and directors to unify the production.

Costume designers must have a keen sense of color and a definite sense of taste and style, to know what is appropriate and right for each situation. They must make confident decisions based on the look of the total production.

What other careers require similar qualities?

Careers in various parts of the fashion industry lack a theatrical setting, but require similar qualities. Design consultants and fashion show directors and promoters need similar backgrounds. Other careers in theater costuming may be of interest to costume designers (seamstresses, wardrobe masters, fitters and the like), but they carry less responsibility.

Museum work that includes fashion history and the curatorial duties connected with it would be a natural alternative career.

Teaching fashion history and costume design in college art or fashion departments would make excellent use of the accumulated knowledge of a costume designer.

The ability to sketch and render costumes makes such designers good fashion illustrators or designers. The necessary background and training are similar.

Film and television studios also have costume departments. They employ similar production techniques and require designers with similar qualities, interests and backgrounds.

What can be done now?

All available art classes (especially drawing, painting and art history) should be taken in high school. Home economics classes that include sewing provide practical experience in that craft. Literature, history and English classes are extremely important.

School plays and musical productions often need people to work on costumes and wardrobe. If costume design interests you, this is the best place to get some experience. Attend plays and operas, and pay special attention to the costumes and how they relate to the productions.

Study the fashion sketching techniques in magazine and newspaper ads, and apply them in your sketchbooks. Frequent museums that have good fashion departments and study the characteristics of certain periods and places. Study paintings for the same reasons.

Film and television productions set in specific historical contexts can provide excellent close-up looks at period clothing. Study them. Many books and some historical magaines feature costumes of earlier times. Some art magazines are illustrated with paintings that contain period costumes. There are many sources for growth in awareness and knowledge of costumes and accessories.

Which colleges offer necessary programs?

Costume designers come from two types of backgrounds: fashion and theater. Both offer costume design courses and both backgrounds are important to the theater industry. Check the catalogs of schools that interest you to see if they offer sufficient training in costume design to satisfy your needs. Check through the charts at the back of the book.

Schools with theater arts departments will offer you practical experience in working with actual productions. Schools with fashion design departments will feature more courses in theory of fashion, fashion drawing, illustration, rendering and the designing aspect of costume work.

Consult your drama coach or art teacher to find out which direction may be best for you and then write for catalogs. Best of all, visit the schools to see which meets your career training needs and seems to provide the best working atmosphere.

Other Careers In Stage Design And Related Arts

Art Director
In some large productions (operas or light operas for example) an art director assists the director and producer in supervising all aesthetic aspects of the production. He or she coordinates the work of all designers and production staff to insure authenticity of costumes and sets and a unified visual impact. Art directors have had experience in most phases of design and production work, and use their expertise to advise production heads and designers.

Costume Design Department Workers
Important members of the costume design production team include cutters, patternmakers, seamstresses and fitters, who work under the direction of the costume designer. They do the actual production work and often are skilled in several aspects of the process. In small shops, they may be required to perform several tasks. Work in costume departments is excellent practical training for future costume designers.

Hair Stylist/Designer
Hair stylists are responsible for the arrangements of both natural hair and the wigs needed in various productions. They research colors and styles to be sure their actors look authentic. They work closely with costume designers to achieve the look that the directors require.

Lighting Designer
Lighting designers are very important members of theater design teams. The employment of light in a darkened theater controls the mood and feeling of an entire production. In large theaters lighting designers work with a staff of lighting technicians to develop the quality of light dictated by the production. They can produce daylight, candlelight or moonlight on stage. They use washes, floods and spots to provide general illumination or carefully controlled patterns of light.

Lighting designers work with lights stationed all over the theater. They use colors to create warmth or coolness, and are responsible for spotlighting when it is called for.

Some experimentation is used in working with programmed lighting and computer directed cues, but most lighting programs are manually operated from a complicated schedule drawn up while the production is in development stages. Directors and scenic designers are involved in this scheduling to insure continuity and the correct illumination of props, scenes and costumes.

Makeup Artist
Makeup artists produce magic from their boxes of makeup materials. They read the scripts and, with plastic, clay and colorings, make the actors' appearances match the author's descriptions. They are masters of special effects on the human body—bleeding wounds, for example—but can also strengthen the assets in an actor's face. Their skills are developed in theater training and on-the-job experience. Some courses in makeup are available in theater-oriented curricula.

Opera And Ballet Work
Operas and ballets often involve tremendous numbers of people performing on huge stages. All traditional theater careers are required in such productions, but on a larger scale. Stages are larger, so scenes and props are correspondingly large. For enormous casts, costume design and wardrobe jobs are mammoth undertakings. Many opera and ballet companies have their own design staffs, but others use the same procedure for getting design work done as those employed by theater companies.

Historically, many fine artists (particularly in Russia and France) have become involved in designing opera and ballet scenery and costumes.

Program Designer
Theater programs, posters and media ads are usually contracted out to local graphic designers or free-lance artists. They come to rehearsals, sketch the characters, grasp the feeling of the play and submit ideas for producers and directors to approve. They watch over the entire production of programs and ad material from concept to delivery. Deadlines are vitally important where program design is concerned.

Property Shop Workers
Stage properties add detail to the words, action or music of a production. They help make a stage situation seem more natural and authentic.

Workers in property shops can produce almost anything—or a facsimile of anything. They transform ordinary materials like wood, wire and plastic into gold, marble or precious stones.

They are masters of constructing with wood, steel, plastic, fabrics, muslin, wire, paper, paste and paint. They create textures or smooth surfaces, stairs and windows, lighting fixtures and fireplaces.

Their products must be fireproof, authentic in color, shape and size and real enough to fool the eyes of the audience. They work under the direction of the scenic designer who is responsible for the final appearance of the stage and all that is on it. The property shop provides all the props called for in the script and by the director.

Property shops hoard period furniture, lamps, accessories, paintings and rugs, and their workers know where to get almost anything they don't keep on hand.

Puppet Designers

Puppet designers work with clay, papier-mâché, cloth, plastic and other materials to create puppets of all types. Puppetry is a special type of theater entertainment that requires specialists who design, construct and operate the puppets. Rod, hand, shadow and string puppets also require stage sets and scenery. Many puppeteers design and construct their own puppets and stages, but some seek help from outside design sources.

Scene Painters

Scene painters provide the visual background for a stage production. They are masters of illusion who can make ordinary canvas look like walnut panelling or solid concrete. Their skill is essential to successful stagecraft.

They stretch their canvases on the floor, or hang them as they will finally be placed. They must be able to draw, paint, and render surfaces and textures, and must know how colors will react to colored lighting.

The canvas or other fabric is mounted on wooden frames. These may hang or stand as hinged or propped flats on stage. Scene painters work from small sketches which are enlarged to full size on stage.

Set Construction Worker

While scene painters produce illusions on cloth, set construction workers build three-dimensional designs for the stage. Platforms, walls, stairways, balconies and the like are built by set construction workers and later painted by scene painters. Such construction is often designed to emphasize depth or size, and may be askew or distorted to create the desired effect.

Steel is used as well as wood in today's theater, and construction workers must be able to weld as well as use a hammer and nails. They work directly under the supervision of the scenic designer.

Wardrobe Staff

Wardrobe workers are responsible for the care and availability of costumes. They clean, press and repair every costume in readiness for every performance. In larger productions, there may be elaborate track systems to bring hundreds of costumes to the right place at the right time. Work in a wardrobe department can provide excellent background for future costume designers, cutters, seamstresses or fitters.

Editorial Design and Illustration

In spite of dire predictions in the 1960's that television would soon replace newspapers and magazines, both continue to be dynamic and important means of moving information and ideas. Magazines especially have met the challenge of competition with television by becoming more specialized. Many are not even sold in stores, but can be obtained only by subscription or by joining specific organizations. Art magazines alone have proliferated in the past twenty years. There are now specialized art magazines that appeal only to graphic or industrial designers or to fine art painters, for example.

In America today are over 1,700 daily newspapers, 8,000 magazines and journals and 1,500 television stations. Several hundred book publishers release over 20,000 new titles each year. All of these editorial functions require artists, art directors, illustrators, layout and design artists, photographers and printers. These editorial designers use words, pictures, colors and layouts to make the transmission of information as interesting and attractive as possible.

Editorial cartoonists comment on local, national and international events and circumstances. Artists illustrate news stories with drawings, photographs, maps, diagrams and cartoons. Magazines need cover artists, layout specialists, sketchers, photographers and illustrators as well as technical artists such as typographers, mechanical artists and printing specialists.

Book publishers maintain art staffs or deal with consultants or free-lance designers and illustrators who design the pages and covers of their products.

Both the design and production of printed materials in this country employ large numbers of skilled artists and technicians. From the art director's concepts and ideas to the printshop apprentice's job of cleaning presses and sweeping floors, there are dozens of career opportunities for young artists interested in editorial graphics and publication design.

Science illustrator Mary Butler checks her drawings of items from the Los Angeles County Museum of Natural History. They will appear in a new museum publication. Photograph: Joseph Gatto

The publications branch of the media works with film and television to communicate ideas, relate events as they happen and provide entertainment to peoples around the world. Career artists design and prepare completely the visual content of media communication. The arrangement of all the parts of books, magazines, brochures and newspapers is the responsibility of art directors and graphic designers. The illustration of such publications is the work of various kinds of illustrators or photographers. The actual preparation and printing are technical and production processes of the graphic arts industry. The financing and distribution of the printed product is the responsiblity of the publisher. In such a cooperative venture, none could function fully without the presence and abilities of the others.

Several of the elements of this four-faceted process of communication have been treated in detail in other sections of this book—graphic design, for example. Those dealing with media and verbal and visual communication are covered in this and the next sections. You may refer from one of these sections to the other to get a more complete idea of the breadth of the graphic design career area. In magazine productin alone, the range spreads from layout and graphic design to illustration, a form of fine art.

This diversity calls for equally diverse background and college experience to train the people involved. Graphic designers in art schools and colleges study design techniques and concepts, typography, production techniques, rendering, and publication design. Illustrators take courses in illustration techniques, drawing, anatomy, layout, quick sketching, figure drawing, painting techniques and editorial illustration. Special areas of interest and study might include children's book illustration, fantasy and science fiction illustration, botanical illustration, medical illustration, sports illustration and related courses.

Art directors put all these special talents, interests and abilities together to produce books or magazines that call attention to themselves and hold reader interest by the arrangement of their contents.

Illustrator Bill Robles' drawings appear on television news programs and in magazines and newspapers.

Editorial Art Director

Editorial art directors work for magazines and newspapers, establishing the overall design and composition of the pages. This format, once established and approved by the publication's editor or publisher, becomes standard, at least until another format is developed. A regular format gives the publication a characteristic feel, makes it differ from all other magazines, even those with similar contents. Art editors are therefore responsible for the particular and characteristic appearance of the magazines or papers on which they work.

Each article, feature and special area receives direct attention from art editors. They select the parts of an article that have special impact and point them out to the illustrators or photographers who will furnish illustrations for the assignment. The art directors design every page of the magazine, newspaper or catalog by balancing type, headings, art and photography.

What editorial art directors do

The skills required for editorial art directors and the techniques involved in designing pages are similar to those of other art directors and graphic design executives. They specialize, however, in working on magazine, newspaper and catalog layouts and design. They supervise all art, design, photography and typography done on such publications. They may do some designing and illustrating themselves, depending on the size of the staff and of the publication, but generally their jobs are supervisory and administrative. They know and understand the various aspects of the printing process and are familiar with typography and color separation processes and problems. Color separation is the process of separating full-color images into the four primary printing colors: red, yellow, blue and black. From these separations four negatives, and then four plates, are made. These will be used to print the original image using just four colors.

All the necessary components for each page (typed manuscript, photographs, art and illustrations) are assembled by art directors. Working within an established design format they arrange these components in the most pleasing or suitable way, and make rapid sketches of them. In magazines, these pages are made as visually attractive as possible and often involve the careful design and use of white space. In newspapers, white space (except in advertisements) is filled up with short articles and small items so that the page is filled with type, headings and photographs. These rough sketches are handed to page designers, production artists or assistant art directors who decide on type size and style, display type (headlines) and size, photograph or drawing sizes and other design components such as ruled lines, color blocks or tinted areas. The art director often has some say in these decisions.

Type is then ordered, photographs and art are reduced or enlarged, layouts are made (See Layout Artist) and all materials are pasted up for final shooting prior to platemaking and printing. The editorial art directors follow this process closely, supervising and suggesting at each level of activity until the final products roll off the presses.

In smaller publishing ventures, some or all of these tasks are performed by the art director, or some are free-lanced to artists and graphic designers who work in their own studios.

Because many new special interest magazines are being started monthly in this country, there are more editorial art directors (about 8,000) designing publications today than ever before.

What qualities are helpful for an editorial art director?

Because these editorial specialists must supervise the jobs done by their staff members, it is essential that they work well with people. They must have a thorough understanding of printing processes, mechanical and layout techniques and graphic design. They must also be able to sketch and draw with ease and clarity. They must be able to determine the main points of articles they read, and to develop design ideas from these points.

They must work well under deadlines, and make quick decisions when necessary.

Their design convictions should be strong, but flexible enough to accept changes when the publication will be better for them. Editorial art directors spend much time studying the formats of other publications and keeping up-to-date with current trends in typography, illustration and publication.

What other careers require similar qualities?

Any art career in publishing requires similar qualities and abilities. Graphic designers in advertising fields need similar backgrounds and interests (See Graphic Design).

Careers involving typography, illustration or photography—all elements with which art directors work—might appeal to someone interested in editorial art direction. College teaching in any of these areas might also be of career interest.

Graphic design of specialized publications such as museum brochures and catalogs, annual reports, mail order catalogs or limited edition books and anthologies would require skills called for in editorial design.

Corporate art directors require the same backgrounds

This sequence of photographs illustrates the design process for a catalog page showing a selection of cheeses. The art director sketches a layout on a double page spread. The props (cheeses, grape leaves, and the like) are set up and lighted. The scene is shot with a large format camera. The photo, text type and heading are combined according to the art director's sketch for an effective spread. Photographs: Teri Sandison

and abilities but such a career would involve broader areas of interest and application of skills.

What can be done now?
High school art classes should include drawing, painting, graphic design, printmaking and art history. English, literature and history classes are also essential to an understanding of writing and publishing. Work on student newspapers, yearbooks or other publications is extremely valuable. Take printshop courses if they are available.

Study magazines to see what the art directors have done with layout and design to obtain the characteristic look and feel of each one. Clip or sketch especially effective layouts and notice how they relate to the subject that is presented. No special magazines will teach you how to do layouts, but the better designed ones teach by example.

Part-time work in any publishing area (printing, graphic design studio, newspaper composition, for example) will prove valuable. Any jobs that provide background experience in printing and publishing are extremely worthwhile.

Which colleges offer necessary programs?
Check the charts at the back of the book for schools that offer strong programs in graphic design. A wide selection of courses will expand interest in several design areas and provide students with the range of experiences required for an art director's position.

High supervisory positions, like that of art director, go to artists with a wide range of courses, practical experience and job accomplishments. If your goal is such a position, concentrate on a successful graphic design major (with an emphasis on publications, perhaps), an equally successful graphic design experience and career, and then move toward becoming an editorial art director.

Editorial Illustrator

Illustration closely resembles fine art painting in many ways, but its purpose is less aesthetic and more practical. Editorial illustrators are artists who illustrate books, magazines and newspaper articles and an occasional advertisement.

The individual styles of various artists are extremely important in the field of editorial illustration. One artist's style is appropriate for children's books, while another may be suitable for romantic stories. Some illustrators specialize in certain media and are called on whenever art directors require that specialty. Pen and ink, watercolor, acrylic, black and white, collage and line drawing are examples of such specialties. Other illustrators specialize in certain subjects, such as automobiles, people, animals, landscapes or sports activities.

Some editorial illustrators work on the staffs of large magazines, newspapers or publishing houses, but most are free-lance artists who also illustrate advertisements.

What editorial illustrators do
An illustration job begins at the art director's desk, (See Editorial Art Director) where the most important concepts of a book or article are noted. The art director then calls in a staff or free-lance illustrator to discuss the various possibilities. After some sketch ideas are approved, the illustrator begins work on the assignment. The artist has generally been chosen by the art director because of his or her characteristic style and technique.

Editorial illustrators make paintings or drawings using the most appropriate media (airbrush, acrylic, watercolor, pencil, gouache, pen and ink or woodcuts, for example). They match the proportions of the space called for in the art director's layout, but the work can be done in any size. It will be photographically reduced to fit the page.

When illustrators have finished their work they deliver or send it to the art directors who give final approval or may suggest a change or two. The work is then photographed, and if in color, color separations are made to the correct size, and these are sent to the printer for platemaking and eventual printing in the publication. In book, magazine and newspaper work there are production deadlines to meet, and artists must work within these definite time restrictions.

When free-lance illustrators are not working on an assignment, they are painting and drawing to improve their skills and add important work to their portfolios. They send their work, résumés and follow-up materials to as many art directors as possible. This self-promotion is necessary until their reputations are established.

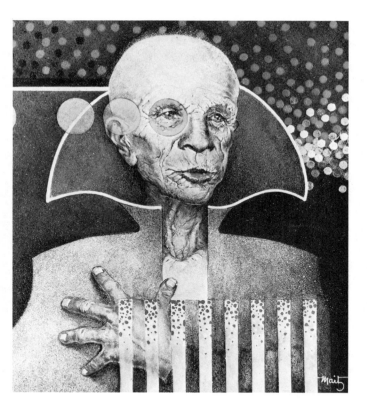

Don Maitz used a mixed media technique to create this science fiction illustration for *Aliens*. Photograph: *Today's Art*

What qualities are helpful for an editorial illustrator?

Editorial illustrators must be able to draw and paint, above all else. They must be able to work rapidly and efficiently and budget their time, especially if working on several jobs at the same time. They must be able to meet deadlines; magazines and newspapers will not wait!

They must be good at creating illustrations that parallel the written word. Good design sense and the ability to see what is needed in each editorial situation are vital characteristics of competent editorial illustrators. They must be flexible, able to change their approaches when tastes begin to change and aware of the work of other illustrators.

The field of editorial illustration is extremely competitive; only a dozen or so artists are at the top of the national ladder at any one time. This often forces many illustrators to seek additional work in advertising, television or other commercial art fields.

What other careers require similar qualities?

The ability to draw and paint, so essential to editorial illustrators, is also necessary in all other fields of illustration: fashion, advertising, product, storyboard, architectural rendering. See the index to locate such information.

Successful careers in illustration usually lead to positions such as art director, art supervisor or other executive or administrative positions. Many illustrators, however, prefer to remain at their drawing boards, producing quality illustrations of various types.

Free-lance illustrators require self-discipline to meet deadline schedules and to set their own working timetables. These qualities are also essential in fine art painters, who must maintain definite schedules to be able to produce paintings for galleries.

Many illustrators have galleries exhibit their paintings. This gives them a second outlet for their creative work and a second source of income. Many of today's successful painters in watercolor, acrylics and oils have spent years working as illustrators and becoming masters of technique and media.

What can be done now?

High school students should take all the drawing, painting and two-dimensional design classes available. Any and all art classes will provide good working experience with a variety of media, but painting and drawing remain most important for illustrators.

Collect examples of excellent illustrations from magazines and file them by subject matter, style or artist. Learn to recognize top illustrators by their styles and work, and notice the subtle changes in their work from year to year.

Study illustrations in children's books and take note of illustrations in other books, periodicals, brochures and posters. Work on newspaper and yearbook staffs will give you practical experience in the planning and production of printed materials.

Magazines that will help you understand illustration career opportunities include: *Art Direction, Print, CA* (*Communication Arts*) and *American Artist*. Check the *Art Directors' Annual* for the work of top illustrators each year.

Check with the Art Directors' Club in your own city to see if you can attend some meetings or go to their exhibitions. Get on their mailing list.

Which colleges offer necessary programs?

Some schools offer majors in illustration and can prepare students for any type of illustration work. Other schools may offer majors in specialized illustration fields, such as editorial or fashion; some may lump illustration and graphic design together and call it commercial art. Almost every art school and most colleges and universities with extensive art departments can prepare students for careers in editorial illustration. Drawing and painting classes make up much of such a course of study. Figure drawing, rapid sketching, painting in all media and printmaking provide the wide range of experience necessary for the illustrator. Check the charts at the back of the book.

Diplomas and degrees are not necessary in landing illustration jobs, although they may assure art directors that you have spent time in the proper art classes. Art directors are most interested in your portfolio, in how well you draw and paint.

Book Designer

Book designers are responsible for the format and final appearance of the books on which they work. Authors, researchers or compilers furnish the manuscripts; book designers arrange everything between the book's covers in an attractive and appealing way. Book designers may work for publishing houses, where they are often involved in mechanical and manufacturing processes. Other designers work free-lance for several publishers. They design the book's pages and perhaps its cover, but leave production to the publishing staffs.

Book designers work mostly with editors. They use their design experience and other skills to help them decide on the type, size, layout, format, use of color and other physical arrangements of the book. Sometimes they are called on to design a book's cover or jacket, but often that task is turned over to illustrators.

Book designing is becoming more technical, as are other careers in graphic design. Computerized typesetting is responsible for part of this change. Some book designers now work at CRT terminals, receiving an author's words through telephone lines. Digital typesetters make some phases of the work of book designers a bit easier, though more technical in nature.

What book designers do

A designer is given a book's manuscript by an editor or art director, who often tells the designer how many pages are wanted, the size and shape of the book and how much money is available for typesetting, paper, printing and binding. Photographs may be supplied by the author, or an art editor may be assigned to secure them. The designer often selects an illustrator to make the book's illustrations cohesive and unified.

A designer first reads through the manuscript and discusses it with the editor. He or she makes thumbnail sketches to show the organization of the contents, chapters, columns of type, headline, pictures, color and the like. From these idea sketches, full-size pencil layouts are drawn, showing all the elements on a two-page (facing) spread. This includes type margins, picture placement, chapter titles, captions and headings. Type style and size are selected by the designer.

After the layouts are approved, the designer furnishes type samples. These show a chapter opening and one typical two-page spread from the text, and will serve as a guide for the rest of the typesetting procedure. The designer then marks the entire manuscript for type, including instructions to the compositor (See Other Careers in Editorial Design), who returns galley proofs to be checked by the author, editor and designer.

The designer then makes up a grid sheet, showing trim size (actual size of the book's pages), margins and placement of type for the two-page spreads. When these are printed, the designer makes a page layout "dummy" of the book, cutting the galleys, putting blocks of type on each page, placing pictures and sizing and cropping photos to fit. This will serve as a guide for the mechanical artists (See Layout Artist) who will paste up the final camera-ready pages for the printer. "Camera-ready" means completely finished, ready to be photographed so that printing plates can be made.

When the pages are made up in film, blueprints are made for the author, editor and designer to check. If the designer is to work on the cover, he or she does so while designing the book.

What qualities are helpful for a book designer?

Book designers must be able to accept the suggestions of editors, art directors and authors, yet be able to inject their own personalities and concepts into the process.

Book designer Penny Darras-Maxwell, designer of this book on art careers, looks over black and white photographs for content and composition before deciding where to place them on the page and what size to make them. Photograph: Robert H. Meservey

This requires sensitivity to other people and to the message and contents of the books.

They enjoy making type, layouts, illustrations and ideas work together effectively. They must understand the entire printing process, and must keep up-to-date on contemporary type styles and processes.

They must accept changes in design and production procedures (such as computer technology) and become proficient in new techniques and methods.

Book designers, especially those who free-lance, often work alone. They must be motivated and disciplined to meet deadlines and production schedules.

What other careers require similar qualities?

Careers in all areas of publishing would be of interest to book designers (See the rest of this section). Estimators, art editors, design directors, design consultants, cover artists and instructors in book design share common goals and qualifications.

Magazine production and yearbook design and production are closely associated with book design careers. Many free-lance book designers also free-lance in other areas of graphic design.

Layout and paste-up artists require similar abilities but take on less responsibility than do book designers.

Corporate designers (See Corporate Art Director) are often involved in projects similar to those of book designers, particularly the production of brochures, pamphlets, annual reports and corporate graphic designs.

What can be done now?

Art classes in high school should include drawing, painting, printmaking and design (graphic design, if available) as well as art history. Because book designers work on all types of books, they benefit greatly from a broad background in a variety of subjects. The wider your background, the more design jobs will be available to you.

Work in any capacity on the yearbook staff at school, especially on the design staff, if possible. Part-time work in a printing establishment will give you a practical working knowledge of printing processes. Any graphic design work is beneficial. Work in a book store or book department will familiarize you with contemporary book design and allow you to see how customers react to different types of books and designs.

Magazines that will provide insights into this career area include: *CA* (*Communication Arts*), *Art Direction* and *U&lc*.

Which colleges offer necessary programs?

Schools with strong graphic design departments will provide excellent background for book design. Schools in areas where many publishing houses are located (Boston, New York, Philadelphia, for example) will have added available resources in the form of field trips, seminars and part-time job opportunities. Check the list at the back of the book, as well as catalogs from various schools. Some offer specialty courses in book design and typography. Check with local museums; some also offer courses in these subjects.

Courses in computer graphics and work with digital typesetters will help you stay abreast of contemporary technology.

College and university training in publications will give you excellent background in technology, type, design and production methods. Graphic design or book design courses at any school will provide the necessary art background. Many trade schools can provide training in areas such as paste-up, layout and bookbinding.

Some book designers use computerized typesetters in their work. This digitized system printed out the stars and type at left. A color sketch of the idea is on the right, below the screen. Type and symbols may be slanted, enlarged, reduced or fattened at the whim of the designer. Photograph: Penny Darras-Maxwell

Using typestyles specified by the designer, book manuscripts are typeset to make galleys, such as these (left) for the book *Jewelry*. The designer plans placement of text and illustrations to make a "dummy." The dummy is a model for the two-page mechanicals (bottom), which are photographed to print the book. Photograph by Jackie Robinson.

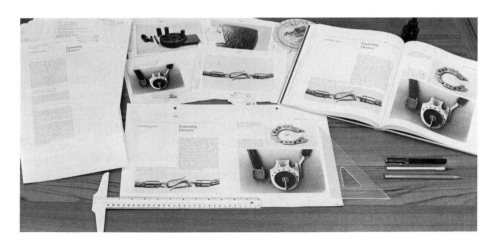

After eight years as a book designer for Little, Brown and Company in Boston, Janis Capone decided it was time to strike out on her own. She had been a free-lance designer on the side for two years, and it was beginning to take up a great deal of her time. "I had five outside jobs going," she says. "My job was getting in the way of my free-lancing!"

Janis Capone seems to have fallen into book design. Her interest in art began in high school, but she "just couldn't take it seriously. I didn't think people could live at their hobby, so it was just a hobby for years and years." She majored in art history at Rollins College, and left after two years because she had taken nearly every art course the college offered. She then considered enrolling in an art school to pursue her interest in geometric design. But for financial reasons she decided to "work for a few years and see if anything else came up."

After a secretarial course which she thought "would give me something I could get a job with," she went job-hunting in Boston, looking for positions in publishing or advertising which would expose her to graphic design. She was eventually hired as a secretary in Little, Brown's trade sales department. Her secretarial training made her a fast worker; when she finished the day's routine tasks she would ask for other work, and so learned a great deal about the publishing industry.

"I liked publishing, but not sales," she admits. "When a secretarial position opened in the production department, I applied for it and got it." Traditionally, secretaries at Little, Brown moved up within their departments, acting as apprentices under more experienced staff members until they were qualified for more responsibility. There was then no such thing as a graphic design major in college; that sort of training was obtained on the job. "No specialized degrees in that area existed when I was in college," says Capone. "Book design was taught in Boston for the first time in the mid-70's. So I guess you could say I got my degree at Little, Brown University."

Capone gradually moved up in the production department, working as assistant to the head designer and then as a designer herself. She designed such hardcover books as Norman Mailer's *Pieces and Pontifications* and Lee Witkin's *Photograph Collector's Guide.* "I enjoy photography books the most," says Capone. "I enjoy choosing photos, and having the author come and discuss the book with me. Usually editors keep their authors under lock and key—and it's like walking on egg shells working with some of these writers' egos—but I do enjoy working with them."

Capone spent more than ten years at Little, Brown, and designed books for eight of those years. But after ten years she felt she'd gone as far as she could.

Janis Capone designs a page layout. The work of creating a dummy might require four to six weeks for a book such as *Jewelry* (photos above), which has more than 500 illustrations to fit into 288 pages. The book's length is specified by the publisher.

Janis Capone, Book Designer

This book cover was made from Janis Capone's mechanical (left) and from sized, color-separated photographs (color proofs in center). The cover is printed as a flat sheet, then attached to boards to make "cases" prior to binding. Photograph by Jackie Robinson.

She got her first free-lancing job, while still at Little, Brown, through a friend, a typesetter, and found it less restrictive than her work at the publishing company. "Free-lancing opened me up to do other things—like covers. I like to design the whole book. And people really started calling while I was still at Little, Brown. That gave me the incentive to leave."

Free-lancing, Capone found, is "a new way of working, that requires a different attitude. There's more decision-making. You have to decide what you want and how to get it. At a company you don't have to worry about all that, but working for yourself you're doing whatever you've set for yourself—with your own motivation and discipline. It's scarier."

Capone makes valuable contacts through membership in Bookbuilders of Boston, an association of publishers and suppliers. Their annual book show keeps her in touch with what other designers are doing, and introduces her to judges.

"The most useful way to make contacts," she asserts, "is just by calling people and showing them your portfolio. Just sit down and call people. Lots of contacts come from references: someone I've worked with will tell someone else. It's a small industry. Sometimes you really wish it was bigger."

On a typical design job, Capone first meets the production art director and the editor in charge. "They show you the job, and you estimate its cost and quote on it.

You have to be available to do the book, of course. If your prices are right and you get the job, you sit down and start designing."

Text design seldom causes great controversy among publishers or authors, but Capone says, "Covers are a problem. The author or the editor will say, 'There's just something wrong with the type . . .' but they can't describe it. They say they want 'friendlier' type, or 'sexier' type, type that is 'approachable by college students.' What is that supposed to mean? Covers are a visual, emotional thing. The book's interiors have to be organized, but jackets seem to stir emotions, and it's hard to get a group of people to agree on anything."

Capone, who hopes to open her own design studio eventually, offers some advice to aspiring book designers. In spite of increasing specialization in colleges and art schools, she feels hands-on experience is still the best way to become a good designer. "One of my favorite expressions is 'Get a Job.' You must start working at book design, take it off the theory shelf and put it into practice. Be patient. Don't expect to do it in a year. Practice. Do the work over and over; experiment. And keep your eyes and ears open.

"It sounds like old advice, but there's always something I don't know. I feel I know less now than I did five years ago, and am less qualified now than then. You never know it all.

"Don't work for a place whose work you don't respect. Find good people to work under. Many people will work for free for a really good designer. Read lots of book show catalogs. Subscribe to *Print* magazine—it shows good work. Keep in touch with who's doing what, and who's good in your area. Stay in touch with the field through seminars and lectures—those are good places to meet people and find work.

"Be willing to do a lot of routine work along the way. It's better to do paste-up with a good designer than to be sitting at home waiting to be offered a top level job as an art director."

The political satire of Jim Borgman is featured on many American newspaper editorial pages. His style is direct, sure and contains strong value contrasts, which make his messages clear. Art Work: Jim Borgman and King Features Syndicate

Cartoonist/Comic Strip Artist

Attitude is the key to the best cartooning. A good cartoonist develops insights into political situations, finds the humor in problems and their possible solutions, delineates the character of people and articulates ideas and goals in an attractive or incisive way.

Cartoonists of all types use exaggeration and a finely honed drawing technique to make their points quickly and clearly. Cartooning includes such areas as gag cartoons, comic strips, cartoon panels, political satire, editorial cartoons, advertising and illustration cartoons and animation (See Film Animation). All media are employed, but most cartoonists rely on brush, pen and ink, wash, crayon and Zip-a-Tone (commercially printed stick down patterns of dots or lines).

Gag and comic strip artists want to entertain; editorial and political cartoonists want to influence public opinion. Some work for small papers or magazines, some for large newspaper chains, and some are syndicated: their work appears in many publications at the same time.

The cartooning field is very competitive. Individual cartoons can be sold to newspapers or magazines, but comic strip artists must have a fresh idea or style to get a syndicated strip published regularly.

There is a broad market, however, for advertising cartooning, the type used in newspapers, magazines and television to sell products and ideas.

What cartoonists do

Ideas are the lifeblood of every cartoon. Local happenings, political trends and events, worldwide situations, the weather, education, sports or other subjects can trigger an idea for a cartoon. Gag cartoonists who cannot always generate ideas will rely on gag writers, to whom they pay a percentage of their income from each published cartoon.

All cartoonists, whether they work on speculation, belong to a newspaper staff or are syndicated, must draw continually. Established artists refine their ideas before sending them to publishers. Cartoonists seeking initial contacts prepare dozens of panels or strips to deliver or send to potential publishers, hoping for acceptance.

Every Wednesday, scores of cartoonists living in New York deliver their work to magazine offices downtown, hoping for a sale or two. These weekly rounds are a ritual that has been in effect in New York for many years. Many cartoonists from across the country send batches of twenty or more "roughs," or sketches, to editors. Some editors accept or reject the cartoons immediately; others keep them longer before deciding.

Editorial cartoonists generally use strongly brushed ink strokes in their work. They add values by shading with a grease pencil or lithographic crayon, and sometimes by adding Zip-a-Tone patterns.

What comic strip artists do

Comic strip artists work on their own, at their own pace. Once they have established a story line (this is often done by the artist, but may be done by a collaborator or partner) and the principal characters are drawn, production begins. A script is prepared and the artist animates its dialog in much the same way as he or she would create a storyboard. The sequence is broken down into strips of several panels each, and linear roughs are made in pencil. When these are considered satisfactory, they are inked with pen or brush. If values are part of the technique, they are added with gray ink washes or patterned Zip-a-Tone. Each strip is given a publication date and a batch of ten or twenty are sent together to the newspaper's comic page editor. If the strip is syndicated, the originating newspaper office sends the copyrighted art work to every paper that buys the material.

Cartoonists breaking into the comic strip field need a good story idea, an engaging main character and a distinctive style. They must prepare at least a two-week sequence for consideration. The art work is done about two to three times larger than the printed product.

What qualities are helpful for a cartoonist?

Editorial cartoonists must be vitally interested in political affairs and able to present complicated issues in simple graphic terms. They work quickly, have fertile imaginations and are able to generate ideas daily. They must be able to meet deadlines consistently. Some ideas come easily, but others come only after a struggle, and the artist must be able to stay at the drawing board until the panel is finished.

Comic strip and gag cartoonists must be able to generate story and gag ideas, or must get such ideas from writers. They must also be able to work quickly in the particular style that makes their drawing distinctive. They work on their own and must have enough self-discipline to create steadily at their own pace. They must stay ahead of schedule and meet production deadlines.

Of course, cartoonists of all types must be able to draw well. They use line expressively, and communicate through their particular linear style. They must also be able to letter well in a style compatible with their art.

What other careers require similar qualities?

All fields of cartooning require the ability to draw well with ink and brush or pen. Some cartooning is done in graphic design studios and advertising agencies, where several staff artists may be cartooning specialists.

Because some forms of cartooning resemble illustration in technique, style and purpose, linear illustration is a possible alternative career area. Children's books, manuals, how-to-do-it sequences and the like all require techniques similar to those used in cartooning.

The ability to draw with line is required in technical, medical and fashion illustration. Some cartoonists are excellent fine art painters and divide their production time between these two areas of interest. Others enjoy teaching cartooning or other art courses in art schools.

Designing humorous greeting cards (See Other Careers in Editorial Design) can be an excellent alternative career for talented cartoonists. Animation work (See Film Animation) in film and television requires skills and abilities that are similar to those required for cartooning, although the ideas and concepts are supplied by others. Drawing caricatures is a natural extension of cartoon techniques.

What can be done now?

Take high school art classes in drawing, design, painting and printmaking. Get involved with making posters, lettering and working on the school newspaper staff, as a cartoonist if possible.

Study the styles of many cartoonists. Collect good examples (newspapers, magazines and greeting cards are good sources) and keep a file of them. Draw constantly, and work to develop a cartoon style of your own. Take special drawing classes, particularly figure drawing classes, at art schools. Some schools even offer special cartooning classes for high school students.

Many magazines contain cartoons that can help you understand style and exaggeration. Look through *The New Yorker*, for example, and check the editorial pages of your newspaper. Check *Writer's Digest* for cartooning tips.

Which colleges offer necessary programs?

Many art schools and colleges offer courses in the concepts and techniques of cartooning. All types of drawing courses are essential, as are classes in preparing mechanicals and art for reproduction. Graphic design classes and lettering are also important.

Check the catalogs of various schools to see if they offer courses in several aspects of cartooning or animation. Schools with well-known cartoonists on their faculties are highly recommended. Again, check catalogs or ask the school registrars.

No degrees or specific backgrounds are required for selling cartoons or strips to publishers, but good school art experience will help prepare you for alternate career opportunities as well as provide competition and personal contacts.

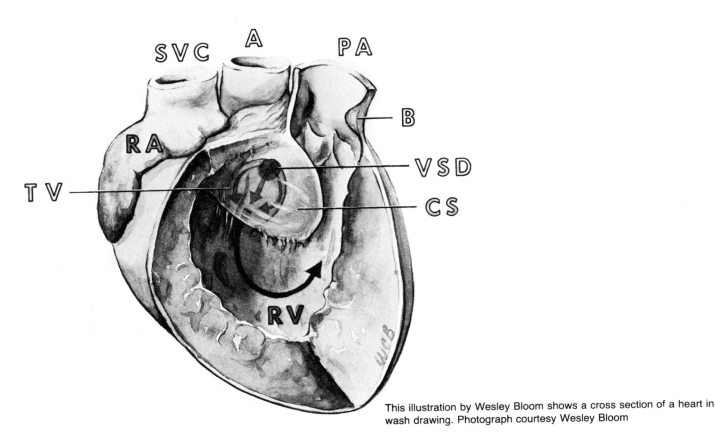

This illustration by Wesley Bloom shows a cross section of a heart in wash drawing. Photograph courtesy Wesley Bloom

Medical Illustrator

While medical illustration is an ancient art form, only in this century have training centers been established where students can acquire the knowledge and skills for such a career. Medical illustrators create graphics of all types to educate the general public, to instruct doctors and to demonstrate a wide variety of biological problems and anatomical situations. They design for publications, films, television and exhibits, using both two- and three-dimensional techniques.

Medical illustrators must be accomplished in a variety of techniques and media, and feel equally at ease in fine arts, graphic design, illustration and basic technical illustration. Strong foundations of medical knowledge insure the authenticity and clarity of their visual interpretations.

Some illustrators specialize in a single medium (pen and ink or airbrush, for example) or focus on a single medical specialty (such as neurosurgery or ophthalmology), but most of them handle a variety of assignments.

Regardless of the specific work involved, the ability to convey information clearly and effectively is possible only when the illustrators are thoroughly familiar with their subject matter, and possess imagination, versatility and technical capability acquired through adequate training.

What medical illustrators do

Most medical illustrators are employed by medical schools and large medical centers which conduct teaching and research programs. Others work in nonprofit institutions, such as dental and veterinary schools, or private, state and federal hospitals. Some are free-lance artists who live near medical centers, medical publishing centers, pharmaceutical manufacturers and advertising agencies, and who illustrate for all types of clients. Some work for publishers of medical journals or medical textbooks, or for companies that sell medical goods, supplies and equipment.

Drawing and illustration may be done by artists working in small studios, or by illustrators who are part of a large media production unit made up of graphic designers, medical photographers, television personnel, education specialists, chart artists and art assistants.

Assignments are given by medical supervisors, research specialists or art directors. The medium chosen depends on the material to be illustrated and the use to which it will be put. Illustrators may be asked to draw with extreme accuracy and realism, or to prepare a simple explanatory diagram. The assignment may require only pen and ink, or the addition of washes or color. It may be

130

for slide presentation or textbook illustration. With adequate training, medical illustrators can handle any and all such visual communication problems.

They may work as members of research teams, both to provide illustrations and to assist with research problems. They may also be asked to write scripts for lecture programs or media presentations. At times they prepare three-dimensional models for instructional purposes, and also can make models of artificial body parts (such as eyes, noses or ears) when cosmetic or functional improvements are required.

Medical illustrators are often asked to prepare charts, graphs, tables and diagrams to illustrate statistical data provided by researchers. They are undoubtedly the visual communicators of the medical profession.

What qualities are helpful for a medical illustrator?

Because extreme care is often required in such illustration work, medical illustrators must be meticulous and accurate in their work. Patience and the ability to work for long periods of time on a single detail are necessary.

Along with this technical ability, illustrators must be able to simplify extremely complex ideas and present schematic diagrams. Technical drawing ability and an intense interest in biology and medicine are essential. Because of the highly technical nature of the work and the medical background required, medical illustrators must feel at home when working with scientific materials and be capable of communicating with medical doctors, researchers and scientists.

What other careers require similar qualities?

Few art careers require the rigid standards and technical expertise needed for medical illustrating. Medical photographers and audio-visual artists in other technical fields require similar qualities, however. Many types of technical illustration (See Technical Illustrator) require patience, care, attention to detail and accurate drawing skills.

Technical textbook illustrators and drafters in various specialties must also be able to work under experts of all types to communicate clearly and accurately their findings and data.

What can be done now?

Take all the studio art classes available, and begin to accumulate technical knowledge by taking biology, physics, chemistry and psychology courses. A general college preparatory program and as much art as possible is usually best.

Look carefully at, and practice drawing, the illustrations in science texts. Study the techniques and media used for them. Attend special high school drawing classes at art schools, especially those in figure drawing from a model.

Part-time work in any graphics situation will help you develop skills and techniques that will be of use in later career positions. Work in hospitals and pharmaceutical manufacturing plants will give you practical experience with the people and subjects you will meet as a medical illustrator.

Which colleges offer necessary programs?

Schools of medical illustration are few in number, and entrance requirements for the several openings each year are stringent. Three or four years of college or art school are part of these requirements, and should include a balanced education in art, pre-med biology and humanities. Most students admitted to schools of medical illustration have majors in art, or have interdisciplinary majors such as art and biology.

A course of study requires two or more years to complete, and may include such classes as: gross human anatomy (dissection and sketching), histology (microscopic anatomy), physiology, human embryology, pathology (nature of disease) and neuroanatomy. Illustration courses may include: graphic techniques, operating room sketching, ophthalmologic illustration, molding and casting, basic medical photography, exhibit design and multimedia presentations.

The following medical schools offer accredited programs. For information and catalogs, write to the Director, The Medical Illustration Department of:

The Medical College of Georgia, Augusta, Georgia 30912

University of Illinois Medical Center, 1914 W. Taylor St., Chicago, Illinois 60612

The Johns Hopkins School of Medicine, 624 N. Broadway, Baltimore, Maryland 21205

University of Michigan, Ann Arbor, Michigan 48109

Ohio State University, 1583 Perry St., Columbus, Ohio 43210

University of Texas Health Science Center, Dallas, Texas 75235

University of California at San Francisco, 1855 Folsom St., San Francisco, California 94103

A technical illustrator at Lockheed Aircraft Corporation works with an engineer in an aircraft cabin. He is making isometric installation illustrations for the company's technical manuals. Photograph: Lockheed Aircraft Corporation, and Industrial Art Methods

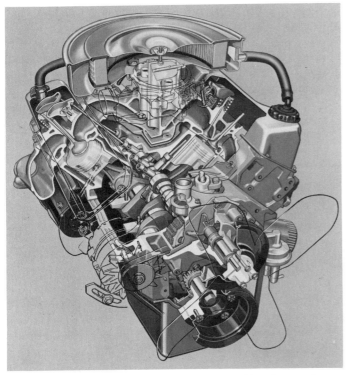

Technical illustrator George De Angelis used an airbrush to render this full color cutaway illustration of a car engine. Phantom lines show the placement of exterior parts. Photograph: Ford Motor Company

Technical Illustrator

The growth of technologies of all types causes an accompanying increase in the demand for technical illustrators. These artists are employed in a broad range of industries, and each area requires artists with special interests and capabilities. Some render finished illustrations of technical products from sets of blueprints. The interior of an automobile engine, or a complex electronic component may be illustrated in detail so that mechanics and technicians can understand the functions and placement of its parts. Some artists draw exploded views of units for catalogs or assembly procedures. Various operation manuals are filled with the work of technical illustrators, presented simply and completely.

Complex machines, now commonplace, could not be built or understood without the drawings of technical illustrators. Electronics plants, airplane and automobile plants, missile factories and government agencies make use of such skilled artists. All types of museums, mapping establishments and technical book companies rely on technical illustrators to visualize their concepts and products.

Technical illustrators are employed by companies involved in space exploration, meteorology, geography, earth sciences, scientific research, medicine (See Medical Illustrator), environmental protection and nuclear energy. They are specialists who work in their fields of expertise and interest, and may be called on to illustrate anything from a nuclear reactor to the eyeball of a rainbow trout.

What technical illustrators do

Technical illustrators either work in the art department of large corporations or agencies, or are free-lance artists whose areas of expertise are well known to industrial firms and corporations which require such illustrations. Some technical illustrators work in art studios which have a reputation for fine work in technical fields.

They discuss the requirements for each assignment with scientists, authors, engineers or art directors. The illustrator must research, study, photograph, sketch and make detailed notes on the objects he or she will illustrate. After rough sketches are approved for concept, content and comprehensiveness, he or she completes the final illustration, usually made to be reproduced in manuals, textbooks or assembly or service instructions.

Technical illustrators work in a variety of media, depending on the desired appearance of the published work. Some use pen, brush, ink or washes for black and white reproduction. Some use airbrush to reproduce the texture of finished products; others use watercolor or acrylic paints. Whatever media is used, extreme attention to detail is absolutely essential.

Technical illustrators use several types of projections and perspectives to produce the clearest possible drawings. The success of the illustration is not in how many people think it is beautiful, but in how useful and explicit it is. For this reason, the illustrator's job is not finished until the reproduction process is completed and the printed illustrations are tested in the shops, or appear in manuals, catalogs, books or brochures.

The computers used in industrial design are also used to produce technical illustrations and printouts. With these computers illustrators enhance, design, show projections and perspectives and reproduce art for demonstrations, illustrations, visual aids and reproductions.

What qualities are helpful for a technical illustrator?

Regardless of the field covered or the products illustrated, careful attention to detail is essential. Technical illustrators must be able to use their chosen media to explain or diagram their subjects simply and clearly. They must have analytical minds, and enjoy devising ways to explain processes with pictures rather than words. They must often think like engineers or scientists. The ability to work with computers is also desirable in most technical illustration positions.

Technical illustrators must be perceptive in their work, and in their contacts with people. They must take directions and revise and adapt their drawings to suit the requirements of each assignment. Technical illustrators are very important members of technical production teams: their work is essential to the sound and successful operation of machinery and electronic devices.

They should have a combination of interests, such as art and biology, engineering, science or botany, for example. A strong capability in drawing is necessary, as is the ability to visualize finished products from spoken concepts, rough sketches or blueprints.

What other careers require similar qualities?

All fields of technical illustration, regardless of special interests, call for artists with similar qualities. Medical illustrators, cartographers, schematic diagrammers and engineers of certain types must have similar abilities and interests.

Industrial designers must often work with concepts and sketches to make the finished drawings from which production models are built (See Other Careers in Industrial Design). In fact, industrial design and technical illustration are closely related in their emphasis on detail, need for clarity, simplicity and completeness.

Drafters in architecture, construction, product design and package design require qualities, interests and abilities similar to those called for in successful technical illustrators.

What can be done now?

Take high school drawing, painting, graphic design and drafting classes. Pursue studies in areas of special interest such as biology, physics, botany or mathematics.

Study technical illustration in books, manuals and assembly instructions to learn techniques and classify methods of illustration. Keep files of good examples and make note of areas that are of particular interest to you. Work in your sketchbook to develop style, technique, concepts and methods of showing perspective. Study industrial design magazines (See Industrial Design) and send away for brochures and pamphlets that contain fine technical illustration.

Part-time work in printing establishments may give you practical exposure to ways in which reproduction is used in technical illustration. Work in graphic design studios will provide background in processes and techniques. Jobs in areas of special interest to you can provide you with valuable background experience.

Which colleges offer necessary programs?

Schools that offer sound programs in general illustration will usually have several courses geared toward technical illustration. They usually concentrate on techniques (airbrush, rendering, perspective, for example) rather than specialized areas of interest (such as medicine, aircraft, geography). Once you start a career in a specific industry, you will receive training on the job in the technology you will be required to illustrate.

Often schools that are near major centers for certain technologies (computers in Texas and California, automobiles in Michigan, aircraft in Washington and California, energy in Tennessee, solar power in Arizona, oil drilling equipment in Oklahoma, for example) will provide special courses to help supply those industries with competent illustrators. Check college catalogs for such local details in course emphasis and scheduling. Check the lists at the back of the book for schools with strong illustration departments.

All high school students are acquainted with their school yearbooks, and many art students work on yearbooks as part of their art background. Yet the work done in a yearbook printing plant remains a deep mystery to most students. The book appears miraculously in the spring, and almost no one realizes the work that went into it.

There are dozens of artists and numerous tasks involved in producing and publishing any book or magazine, and school yearbooks are no exception. The sequences shown here are part of the art and publication process at American Yearbook Company plants. Both black and white and color pages are shown in preparation. Much of the work is done simultaneously, and not necessarily in the order seen here. All photographs courtesy American Yearbook Company.

Manuscripts are composed, designed and typeset by a typographer on this computer, which can set type in any size required.

Halftone black and white photographs, supplied by schools, are enlarged or reduced to fit the designed spaces (left). Each one is identified and all which will be reduced by the same percentage are placed on the copy board. This large format camera (above), seen here shooting halftones, uses huge negatives.

The final paste-up (including photos and type) is compared with the layout sketch to check accuracy of location and placement.

Yearbook Publication

Wherever halftones will appear, rubylith windows are cut and adhered to the boards (far left). Separate negatives are made for halftones, for blocks of type and for ruled lines. When line negatives are prepared (left), the windows are carefully cut out and halftone negatives are stripped in place.

In four-color printing, a laser scanner (far left) makes four separate negatives: yellow, red, blue and black. These "color separations" are used to print tiny dots of the four ink colors to produce full color prints. Four-color negatives (left) are stripped in place for final plate making.

Type and halftones (color or black and white), are now combined in negatives which are contact printed on photosensitive metal plates (far left). The imprinted metal plates are put on the presses and inked. The final printed plates (left) come off the press ready to be folded, gathered, trimmed, bound, covered and delivered.

Other Careers in Editorial Design and Illustration

Airbrush Artist

Airbrush artists are employed by many industries, publishers and branches of graphic and illustration design. Besides doing complete original work (See Record Jacket Designer), airbrush artists touch up photographs, pottery, greeting card designs, household appliances, artificial flowers, toys and art work of all types. Artists must have training in the use of airbrushes in order to operate them effectively.

Architectural Delineator (See Architecture)

Bookbinder (Book Maker)

Some bookbinders custom bind individual hardbound volumes for collectors, but most operate machinery and cut, sew and glue the various parts of books in production situations. They use sewing machines, handpresses and cutters for their work in large publishing or printing firms. Some bookbinders also do custom repair work for libraries and schools.

Book Jacket Designer

These artists are employed by studios specializing in book jacket design, or may be free-lance illustrators who work for various publishing firms. They combine type and illustration or photography to create a book jacket that arouses public interest. They hire illustrators and photographers to provide art work when they require assistance.

Botanical Illustrator

This specialist's area requires a strong interest in plants of all types, as well as illustration techniques. The work of botanical illustrators appears on pages of pamphlets, books and magazines, usually in the form of detailed pencil drawings, pen and ink illustrations, colored pencil work or watercolors.

Caricaturist

Caricaturists are primarily free-lance artists who work for newspapers and magazines, but who may also be involved in advertising, illustration and greeting card design. The necessary skills are similar to those of cartoonists, but caricaturists emphasize facial or body features to create a sometimes comic, but completely recognizable, drawing of a particular person.

Cartographer (See Other Careers in Industrial Design)

Chart Artist

These graphic designers specialize in making charts and diagrams that summarize data and present visual statistics. They work in art agencies or for publishers of books, textbooks, and magazines that use such material. They are often cartographers who are especially interested in and expert at chart making.

Children's Book Illustrator

The styles and techniques these illustrators use are especially attractive in children's books. The work of a children's book illustrator appears in picture books, religious literature, juvenile nonfiction and novels, school textbooks and workbooks. They are usually free-lance artists whose portfolios are well known to publishers of children's books. In the United States, several awards are given each year to illustrators and designers of children's books.

Comprehensive Illustrator (See Sketch Artist, below)

Designer (See Book Designer)

Greeting Card Designer

Greeting cards, no longer used only for birthdays and holidays, are a billion-dollar-a-year industry. Photographers, designers, illustrators and cartoonists are finding more work every year in greeting card design. Some artists work for large companies such as Hallmark; others are free-lance artists who sell their ideas and art to several companies. Most card designers are illustration majors in art school; some are graphic designers. Often illustrators and designers hold one job and free-lance their card ideas and art as a second source of income. There are a large number of art-related jobs in greeting card companies.

Industrial Illustrator

Artists who are excellent renderers and who can work from blueprints and plans can be successful industrial illustrators. They use all necessary media to render finished products and prepare camera-ready art for reproduction. They work from plans, not actual products, and so differ from technical and other illustrators.

Lettering Artist (See Graphic Design)

Lithographic Photographer
These photographic specialists set up and operate the large cameras used to photograph illustrations, other photographs and printed materials (proofs) to be transferred to printing plates. They make negatives or positives in preparation for line and halftone printing requirements.

Mural Artist (See Other Careers in Architecture)

Paste-up Artist (See Graphic Design)

Photo Researcher
Photo researchers work with art directors, book designers and authors to obtain photographs and art for reproduction in various publications. They conduct their research in public and private libraries, museums, private collections, public relations sources and photo and art archives in this country and abroad. They work with free-lance photographers and photo agencies. They are usually on the art staffs of book, magazine and periodical publishers.

Product Illustrator
These artists are generally free-lance illustrators who work with advertising agencies, mail order catalog publishers or industrial clients. They use any required medium to make realistic presentations of manufactured items. Such items might include furniture, automobiles, tools, toys, packaged items or garden equipment.

Science Fiction Illustrator (Fantasy Artist)
Science fiction artists combine basic illustrative skills with the resources of their imaginations. They often use mixed-media techniques to achieve the surrealistic effects they want. They illustrate the pages of books and magazines, and also work in film and television, and design album covers, toys and games.

Sketch Artist (Comprehensive Illustrator)
These artists sketch illustrations for comprehensive layouts that are put together in art departments and agencies (See Graphic Design). Usually they are hired when art department staff are unfamiliar with the subject, or when no one has time to work on the sketch. Illustrators use the sketches (when approved) to generate ideas; they are discarded when the publication is ready for printing.

Storyboard Illustrator (See Other Careers in Film and Television)

Teacher
Students who are interested in learning about illustration and editorial design need teachers to show them appropriate styles and techniques. Art schools and colleges usually hire teachers with practical experience in their subject area.

Typographer (See Graphic Design)

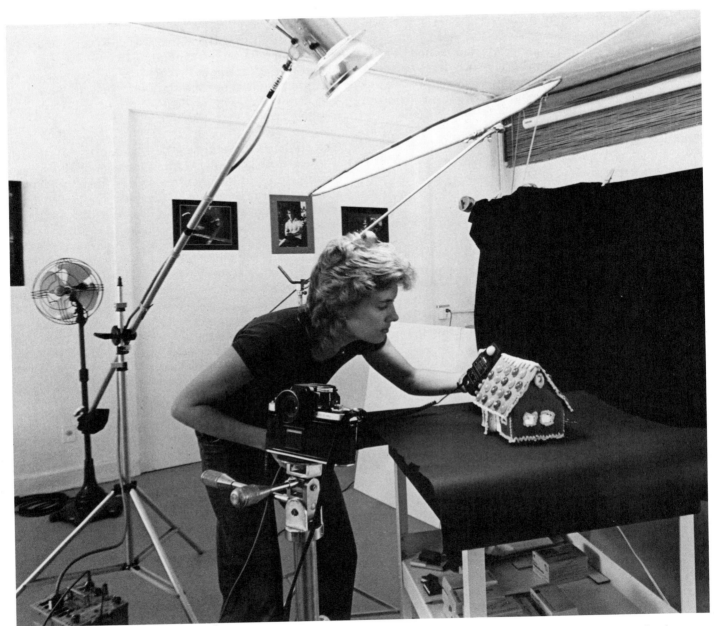

Illustration photographer Alice S. Hall takes a meter reading for a studio photograph of a small, decorated house. She will create a composite illustration which she will complete by airbrushing. Photograph: Alice S. Hall

Photography

Try to imagine a world without photography! No pictures in the newspapers, no illustrated magazines, no movies, no school yearbooks, no medical X-rays and no snapshots of vacation trips or favorite friends. Photography has become an important part of almost every art career area listed and discussed in this book. Photographers are involved in both fine art techniques and commercial applications, and photographic career opportunities are expanding rapidly.

Within the broad spectrum of practical photographic careers, there are many opportunities for the artistically inclined, the business-oriented, technicians, engineers, craftspeople and journalists. There are opportunities to work alone, to establish small businesses, to become free-lance photographers, to work on large teams in major advertising agencies or to become integral parts of public relations firms, service organizations or governmental agencies.

Success in the field of photography depends on the photographer's ability to produce excellent work. Clients do not care where or if photographers went to school, or whether they attained degrees. Excellent photography is their only concern. However, schools which stress photography will be able to train young artists to handle assignments, become technically proficient and to work well with clients.

As in drawing, printmaking, crafts and painting, there are photographers who treat the medium as fine art, while others use it for commercial purposes. Fine art photographers produce their work for themselves, to sell as works of art in galleries and shops. Although the names of fine art photographers—Ansel Adams and Wynn Bullock, for example—are familiar to many people, there are far more photographers working in commercial areas than in fine arts. They work in such practical fields as portrait and architectural photography, but may also photograph more commonplace objects and events: banquets, store windows, food, automobiles, sports events and the like. Their work appears in a vast number of publications and audio-visual materials.

Many photographic experts prefer to work in darkrooms, and may operate laboratories that develop and print the work of others. Custom labs (specializing in black and white or color work) handle expert developing, enlarging, photograph copying and printing, and prepare prints for publication and other forms of reproduction. Such experts work for advertising agencies, publishers, free-lance photographers, fine art photographers and commercial photographers of all types, and have become essential in many areas of advertising and commercial art.

The long list of career opportunities at the end of this chapter attests to the importance of photography.

Those photographers who succeed most rapidly have usually become expert in other areas as well. Expertise in a combination of fields (photography and sports journalism, for example, or photography and meteorology or architecture) make the photographer more valuable; he or she may work for specific markets and command higher fees.

This book uses photography to show you hundreds of examples of artists and their work. Without these photographs, the work of hundreds of photographers in many fields, this book would be words alone. With them, the world and work of artists comes to life.

Photojournalist/Press Photographer

The popular image of a photojournalist is that of a debonair photographer, draped with several expensive cameras, covering exciting events in exotic parts of the world. Although this does happen, the majority of photojournalists work for newspapers and magazines, covering routine events at home and looking for a story that will bring them national publicity.

Almost all photojournalists begin their careers by working for daily or weekly newspapers or syndicated wire services. Several skills are involved: handling spot news such as sports and press conferences, illustrating feature articles on museum discoveries, for example, and recording routine social gatherings and family get-togethers. The challenge to photographers is to turn such routine assignments into interesting images.

Editors want photographers who are knowledgeable in many areas; photographers with abilities in art and design are more sought after than those who have taken only journalism classes. An understanding of the world and of design helps photographers take more meaningful pictures.

A complete portfolio should include excellent examples of photographic work and proof (contact) sheets.

Editors look for images with storytelling impact; by looking at proof sheets that show all the images taken in sequence, editors can easily see how sensitive the photographer is to subject, story, people and context. Art school courses will help students develop portfolios that include the desired range of subjects and themes. Some photographers can develop excellent portfolios on their own, and can obtain fine career positions right out of high school, but such situations are not the general rule.

There are two ways to break into the photojournalism field. One is by showing portfolios to editors and being hired because a position is open. The other is to free-lance for several publications until one hires you. Some photographers prefer to free-lance throughout their careers, selling individual images or photo essays to various publishers.

What photojournalists do

Photojournalists are required to take pictures, develop film and make prints. They must be familiar with all types of equipment and must handle many types of cameras. Their darkroom techniques are essential to publication editors who require certain contrasts and exposures for their special purposes.

Some small newspapers may require photojournalists

Photojournalists must be aware of unplanned pictures which might be more interesting and have more appeal than the assigned photographs. Photograph: Randy McBride and *The Los Angeles Times*

to own their own cameras, but most newspapers and magazines supply the required cameras, lenses and film, and also provide completely equipped darkrooms in which to finish the work.

Newspaper photographers are assigned to cover events on their own, or to accompany reporters and take pictures to illustrate specific articles. Magazine photographers may have longer-range projects that involve travel and more personal approaches to photojournalism. Magazines such as *People, Life, Sports Illustrated, Time, Newsweek* and many movie magazines are built around the work of photojournalists.

Some photographers accompany police units, cover routine arrests and look for stories that may be of interest to readers. All photojournalists keep ongoing portfolios of their best work, with examples of their particular specialties and abilities, to be ready to apply for better and more creative positions when openings occur.

What qualities are helpful for a photojournalist?
It is necessary that photojournalists operate all types of cameras, know how and when to change lenses and be expert at all darkroom procedures. They must be able to do everything from taking the picture to printing the image. They must be able to work under pressure at times and meet deadlines as required. The nature of news demands that photographs be available for the next editions—a day late and it is no longer news.

Photojournalists must be sensitive to the personal situations of their subjects. They strive to capture the essence and importance of the moment. They understand visual design and what elements produce effective images.

What other careers require similar qualities?
Any photographic career will call for similar abilities and qualities. Some graphic designers have a strong interest in photography and can use their skills when working in design agencies. Free-lance photographers and graphic designers must be knowledgeable in similar areas of visual design and photographic techniques.

Some printing and publishing careers call for photographic abilities and expertise. Skills in photography can be combined with other interests (architecture, science, travel, animals, sailing and the like) to create careers that satisfy the artists and help special interest publications, corporations or organizations.

What can be done now?
Courses in high school should include drawing, design, art history and photography, if available. Photography clubs (in school or community) will give you some valuable experience. Some photography clubs and art schools offer special classes for teenage photographers.

Part-time work in camera shops or photographic labs will be extremely helpful. Work on student publications as photographer for a newspaper or yearbook: such work will teach you the basics of photojournalism. Some portrait studios hire students as part-time help. Jobs at printing or publishing companies can be very valuable.

Some magazines that provide excellent introductions to careers in photojournalism include: *Editor and Publisher, Modern Photography, Infinity, Aperture, The Professional Photographer* and *Rangefinder*.

Which colleges offer necessary programs?
All schools with photography departments offer courses that teach the skills necessary for photographic careers. Check the charts at the back of the book. Because photojournalists should have broad experience, other art and design classes should also be taken, as should courses in history, art history, English and creative writing. A portfolio preparation class is a must!

You need not have a degree to land a job; editors hire according to your portfolio, not your schooling. However, a degree assures editors that an applicant has passed required courses and is able to handle all necessary procedures.

Community colleges also offer courses in various phases of photography. Several correspondence schools offer home study courses that are excellent, but students must be highly motivated. Check with: New York Institute of Photography, 880 Third Ave., New York, NY 10022; School of Modern Photography, Little Falls, NJ 07242.

Fashion Photographer

Fashion photography covers a wide range of photographic activities and purposes. In large cities, photographers may take pictures for department store catalogs, or work for garment manufacturers; in a small town, they may take photos for local specialty shops' newspaper ads. Some sort of fashion photography takes place in almost every city in the country.

Fashion photographers must have a complete training in all aspects of photography although they specialize in fashion work.

Free-lance photographers keep a portfolio of their fashion work to show to prospective clients or new ac-

Magazines, newspapers, fashion dailies and weeklies carry examples of today's fashion photography as both illustrations and advertisements. Photograph: Gerald Brommer

counts. They may also have portfolios for their other specialties, such as food, room interiors or sports.

Fashion photographers often study fashion history and go to a modeling school to learn models' tricks for moving. They can then communicate more easily with models and people in the fashion world.

What fashion photographers do

Fashion photographers work in several ways: they may shoot a special photo session for a client, on location or in a studio, or may cover a fashion showing, shooting models in action.

In special photo sessions, the client—manufacturer, store or designer—supplies the apparel; the photographer hires the models. Studio sessions are set against a seamless paper backdrop or with appropriate props, where lighting conditions can be controlled. These photographs may be used for magazine advertisements, catalog illustrations or feature articles in fashion magazines.

Fashion photographers may also be asked to photograph models and clothing at downtown shopping malls, on a yacht, at the races or in a foreign country. On such assignments a project art director may supervise shooting sequences and site selection.

Fashion photographers are also asked to photograph models in action at fashion shows or special live presentations. In such cases, they set their lights and arrange their equipment before the show begins, and shoot rapidly when the action starts. The client will use such pictures in newspaper and magazine news stories, trade publications, or for publicity purposes.

For magazine advertisement layouts, the photographer will usually get suggestions from the art director. These will be rough sketches that indicate to the photographer whether to have the model standing or sitting, moving or still, full length or otherwise.

What qualities are helpful for a fashion photographer?

Fashion photographers are adept at all types of photography, and are capable of using all of their equipment to create the proper mood and result. They must understand the requirements of each job and be able to communicate them to the models. They are experts in both color and black and white photography and darkroom procedures.

They must be able to work under magazine and newspaper deadlines and often put in long hours to finish an assignment. Self-discipline, therefore, is essential.

What can be done now?

High school photographers should be involved in many art classes (drawing, painting and design) and photography classes, if they are available. Photo clubs will give you some practical experience. Work on the yearbook staff as photographer will accustom you to working with people and developing your own picture-taking and darkroom techniques.

Try to get part-time work in camera shops, on school newspapers or local advertising papers. Time spent working in the darkroom is never wasted.

Any magazines that specialize in photography will acquaint you with equipment, cameras and techniques. They include: *Professional Photographer, Studio Photography, Rangefinder, Modern Photography, Studio Light, Camera* and the like.

Which colleges offer necessary programs?

Most art schools and universities offer some form of photographic major (check the charts at the back of the book). Write for catalogs to see if your anticipated area of interest is treated specially. Check the school's facilities: equipment, studio space and materials. Also find out what you can about the photography faculty and their areas of expertise. Fashion photography should be taught by someone with experience in it.

Some excellent correspondence training is available from New York Institute of Photography, 880 Third Ave., New York, NY 10022, and School of Modern Photography, Little Falls, NJ 07424. Such training is limited, however, by your own supplies and equipment.

Entertainment and the Media

Product photographers learn to use backgrounds, light and shadow to present their subjects to their best advantage. Photograph: Georgia Schwender

Product and Food Photographers

Photographers work in a service business. Talent and awareness are essential, good equipment is necessary, attention to detail and reliable techniques are required. The most important task of any photographer, however, is to satisfy the needs and requirements of his or her clients.

Product and food photographers are specialists with similar functions. Both photograph items which clients wish to use to promote products and ideas.

What product photographers do

Product photographers take pictures of products in ways that make them dramatically appealing. They work with agency art directors, clients or corporate art directors to make the photographs clearly understandable to their audiences. The photographers may be employed by magazines or by the product's manufacturer. They often work on location at factories or showrooms, but also bring products to their studios, where the environment can be more carefully controlled.

Product photographers may photograph models, full-sized mockups or actual products (See Industrial Design). They work in both color and black and white. They control lighting, backgrounds, scale, value and mood to suit the products and the needs of clients. Their work may be used to advertise new products or to sell new ideas to possible manufacturers.

Some of the photographs in the Industrial Design section of the book are examples of the work of product photographers, who not only take the pictures, develop the film and make and deliver the prints, but also must make out bills, determine costs and set up production schedules.

What food photographers do

The functions and techniques of food photographers are similar to those of product photographers, but the subject matter is far different. The studios of food photographers generally have functioning kitchens with sinks, stoves, tables, counters and windows. These photographers work with home economists, food editors, cooks and food design specialists who direct the arrangement, cooking and preparation of all food, utensils, tables and accessories. Food photographers soon learn to do these tasks on their own, but magazines usually require that specialists oversee the projects. The photographs present food in attractive, appealing and authentic ways, and enhance the written articles.

The proliferation of specialty food magazines and newspaper food sections has increased the need for photographers who specialize in this type of work.

What qualities are helpful for food and product photographers?

All successful photographers must know how to handle a variety of cameras, lights, reflectors and related equipment. They must be willing to make large financial investments in such equipment, in studio space and in developing and printing materials.

Both types of photographic specialists must be extremely aware of detail, light, color, mood and contrast. Their darkroom techniques must satisfy the specific needs of their clients, and their work must reproduce well.

They must be service-oriented and must work well with people. Sensitivity to their clients and their subject matter is important.

A carefully developed portfolio is essential to attract new clients and increase business. Food and product photographers usually begin work in studios, or as assistants to successful photographers, but most of them plan eventually to control their own studios or work on a freelance basis.

The ability to work under deadlines is essential. Most clients use the photographs for advertising or features in magazines, newspapers or brochures, and all of them have printing deadlines to meet.

What other careers require similar qualities?

Almost every other type of photography career calls for similar qualities. The photographer must be aware of the need to satisfy the clients' requirements. Competition is keen; if the work is not of the necessary quality, there are many other photographers waiting to take over the account.

The ability to work under deadlines is essential to all photographic careers, as well as all graphic design careers.

Many product photographers would be comfortable in corporate photographic situations, where numerous photo applications are required.

What can be done now?

Superior photography, like excellent painting, is based on a knowledge of design. Classes in high school should include drawing, painting, design and art history, along with photography. Classes in chemistry and physics will help you understand developing processes and the science of lenses, filters, light and electronics.

Work on student publications and enroll in camera clubs. Active participation in school events, work with people and practical photographic experience will give you confidence. Part-time work in photography labs, camera stores, on local publications or in design studios will provide excellent experience and practical training.

Some magazines that will prove helpful are *Technical Photography, Studio Photography, Professional Photographer* and *Rangefinder*. Superb examples of product photography can be found in the pages of *Designer's Choice, Industrial Design* and in the advertisements of *Architectural Digest*. Excellent food photography can be found in *Gourmet, Bon Appetit* and *Good Housekeeping*.

Which colleges offer necessary programs?

Every major college, university and art school offers courses of study in photography. Some photography schools (Brooks Institute in Santa Barbara, California, and Hallmark Institute of Photography in Turner Falls, Massachusetts, for example) offer excellent backgrounds in several special areas.

In photography, portfolios and production are far more important than a degree, but employers and clients can be assured of your excellent training and business practices if you are a college graduate. Check the charts at the back of the book for schools with strong departments, or write for more information to Professional Photographers of America, 1090 Executive Way, Des Plains, IL 60018.

Illustration Photographer

Magazine stands and record shops are full of the work of illustration photographers. They operate the same types of cameras and employ the same darkroom techniques as do other career photographers, but their reasons for taking the photographs and their types of assignments differ somewhat.

They are often free-lance photographers, working out of their own studios for a number of accounts and clients. They may also work full-time for large advertising or design agencies, carrying out the assignments given to them by art directors and graphic designers. Their photographs have taken the place of some of the work previously done by illustrators such as painters, printmakers, sketchers and graphic designers.

Illustrative photography illustrates magazine stories or feature articles and brochures, annual reports or advertising pieces for studios and agencies. Many of the illustrations are traditional in concept, executed under the careful supervision of art directors or client representatives. Other assignments may call for innovative approaches to picture taking and experimental darkroom techniques.

What illustration photographers do

Whether working free-lance or for an advertising or graphic design agency, illustration photographers receive their assignments from art directors or other client representatives. At initial meetings, the job's problems are discussed and several solutions are outlined. Art directors usually have definite concepts in mind. Photographers must be able to understand the desired outcome and suggest several possible solutions.

When the problems and possible solutions are defined, the photographers decide on locations, models, lighting, camera angles, necessary equipment and the time needed to complete the job. Cost estimates are presented to the clients, and when all arrangements are satisfactory, the photographers begin to try to solve the visual problems. Some take many pictures, others only a few. Some rely on their darkroom techniques to solve the problems while others use their cameras to greater advantage.

Several possible photographic solutions are brought to the art directors or clients, who work with their graphic

Los Angeles weatherman Dr. George Fischbeck is photographed for a humorous and cleverly planned KABC-TV spot advertisement. Photograph: Eric Myer

designers to determine the images that will create the best layout and the most impact. The photographer's work is finished when the print is selected for publication.

What qualities are helpful for an illustration photographer?

People with broad experiential backgrounds and wide personal interests will be able to handle a greater variety of illustration assignments. Of course, competence in picture taking and darkroom techniques is essential, as is a desire to experiment.

Because illustrations must be carefully planned and expertly composed, a thorough knowledge of design and layout is essential. Illustrative photographers must work well with people and be able to comprehend the requirements of each assignment. They must be willing to follow the instructions of art directors and often must subordinate their own personal ideas to those of clients and art directors.

They must be patient with models and subjects, yet firm in giving directions. They must be businesslike in all their dealings and strive for client satisfaction.

What other careers require similar qualities?

Almost all photographic careers require similar qualities, although their purposes may vary.

Some art directors and graphic designers deal with photography in their work and thus have similar interests and abilities. Photographers who can carry out illustration assignments may also be interested in experimental illustration, science fiction illustration, special film effects, layout, television work and film editing. Magazine or corporate art directors must often have photographic capabilities as well as design expertise.

Teaching various types of photography in college, art schools or high schools combines an interest in people with photographic abilities and knowledge.

What can be done now?

Take high school painting, design, photography classes, and other specialized art classes when they are available. Develop a wide range of interests by getting involved in a variety of courses and extracurricular activities. Join the camera club and work on student publications.

Part-time work in camera shops, print shops, on any type of publication or in a design agency will be extremely helpful in many ways. Study both photographic and painted illustrations for impact, design qualities, mood and composition. Collect the best examples for reference and ideas.

Check the illustrations in magazines such as: *CA (Communication Arts)*, *Print*, *Art Direction* and *Graphic Design*. Photography magazines that offer excellent examples of illustrative photography include: *Modern Photography*, *Technical Photography*, *Studio Light*, *Professional Photographer* and *Camera*.

Which colleges offer necessary programs?

All schools that have photography departments will offer sufficient training in the use of cameras and in proper darkroom techniques. Some will specialize in certain types of photography that may be of specific interest to you. Check their catalogs for specific courses and areas of interest.

Good business practices impress possible clients, so schools that stress art business may be very helpful.

ART CAREER PROFILE

Jason Hailey sets up his shots carefully, using his crew and equipment to their best advantage. All photographs courtesy Jason Hailey

A young man impatiently rang the bell at Jason Hailey's studio in Los Angeles, and a lab assistant asked if he had an appointment. "Not really," he replied, "but it is important that I see Mr. Hailey as soon as possible!"

When Jason Hailey appeared, the young man told him that he was 27 years old and wanted to make it "big" in photography before he was 30. "Tell me what to do to become successful in the next three years," he insisted.

For one of America's premier photographers, the young man's words were rather ironic. Jason Hailey has spent the better part of forty years in photography to achieve his well-earned and respected position as one of the nation's finest photographic artists. He entered the field as a Navy photographer during World War II, working on assignments while in the service. Through hard work and careful preparation, he was eventually able to land assignments with international accounts that include Toyota, Datsun, Jeep, Ferrari, Smith International, Kodak, Xerox, Pioneer Stereo, Schlitz, Pabst, Bigelow, Price Waterhouse, Allis-Chalmers,

Flying Tigers, Westinghouse, Penn Corp. and many more.

Jason Hailey is an illustrative photographer in both print and film. He carries out assignments for magazines, billboards, posters, brochures, annual reports and special projects for architects and designers. He also works on television and documentary films. His television commercials are seen nationwide and his work often takes him all over the country as well as abroad.

Jason Hailey does not confine his abilities exclusively to taking pictures. He also teaches, writes and lectures on professional photography. He has attended, taught and lectured at colleges from coast to coast, where he refined his abilities, talents and skills, and subsequently passed them on to many young people. During a twenty-five year period Hailey earned six degrees, including fellowships in the American Society of Photographers and in the Institute of Incorporated Photographers of Great Britain.

In addition to work done for his many accounts (which he refers to as "service art"), Jason Hailey works on fine art pro-

jects. His *Selective Eye*® photographs have received special recognition for works done without commercial motivation, and have been published and exhibited in many parts of the world. Many of the prints are included in private, corporate and museum collections, such as those of Atlantic Richfield, The Museum of Modern Art and the California Arts Commission.

About eighty percent of Hailey's work is service art (advertisements), ten percent is fine art, and ten percent is film. The distinction between the three does not present any conflict to him. "Advertising is a service art. It is work that serves a useful end, a specific objective—it is photography *about* something. Fine art photography, on the other hand, is more than a picture of something—it is something in itself."

Jason Hailey, Illustrative Photographer

Jason Hailey, in Italy, prepares his equipment to photograph a Ferrari automobile. Above, right, is the photograph as it appeared in the ad.

Hailey's exceptional ability is demonstrated in an advertisement for Ferrari automobiles. He was flown to Italy to photograph the beautifully crafted automobile as soon as it was completed. Shortly after the advertisement appeared in publications, it had to be withdrawn because it was so successful that Ferrari could not supply enough cars. Hailey's superb photograph stimulated readers to buy automobiles with $50,000 price tags.

Jason Hailey offers some suggestions to young people who anticipate careers in photography. "The ad photographer must have an intense interest in merchandising, must be research oriented, must be willing to ask questions, must fully grasp the marketing objectives and must get all the information. When all of the above have been completed, and only then, should the photographer pick up the camera! The photographer is a producer/director, orchestrating from the initial concept to the completed work. Effort, control and a sense of humor are required to reach a high level of proficiency. Reliable equipment is a must. Photography is designing, and good design does not just happen, it is shaped with solid art training!"

Architectural Photographer

The job of architectural photographers is to find and isolate the beauty in structures. Their photographs focus on the strengths and assets of both new and old buildings. They usually work with architects, photographing building interiors and exteriors and models of proposed buildings, communities and cities. Their work is generally used in brochures, films, books, magazines, multi-media presentations and promotions. For this reason, architectural photographers must be well versed in graphic design, architecture and interior design as well as in photography.

By study and constant exposure to good architecture, photographers become aware of excellence in design. They learn to communicate this quality through perceptive, imaginative photography.

What architectural photographers do

After meeting with architects and getting to know their work and the goals they have established, architectural photographers plan their projects. They make use of the weather, clouds, time of day and time of year to emphasize a building's structure, shape, form, texture and mood. They treat buildings as if they were three-dimensional sculptures that must be presented effectively in two dimensions.

Good architectural photographs are not the result of luck, but of careful planning. The photographers study camera angles to determine the best possible location for the camera. Extraneous materials should be eliminated from view, other buildings should be out of sight or diminished and conflicting elements such as signs and automobiles should be hidden.

Once the photos are taken, adjustments in light, shadow and mood can be made in the darkroom. Some photographers like to take many more shots than needed, selecting only the best ones on which to spend darkroom time. Others like to take more time setting up their shots, and so take fewer photographs.

Most architectural photographers work to deadlines. Because their photographs are used in dated publications, photographers must allow for retakes, darkroom work and other unplanned events when setting up their production schedules.

What qualities are helpful for an architectural photographer?

Architectural photographers must be patient, willing to wait for optimum lighting and weather conditions. They must have a special sensitivity to textures, light qualities

Architectural photographer Wayne Thom prepares for his assignment to isolate Seattle's Metropolitan Plaza building in a photograph that will emphasize its structural qualities. At right, the finished photograph shows the Metropolitan Plaza in excellent light. Camera filters emphasize the clouds; distracting signs and buildings have been eliminated. The photograph was taken for the architect. Photograph: Wayne Thom

and color nuances as they plan their projects. They must also be able to set up their shots slowly and thoughtfully, and not rush around shooting indiscriminately.

Architectural photographers have a strong sense of design and an understanding of the basic philosophies and language of architecture. Because they communicate primarily through graphics, they must also be familiar with the workings of that branch of design and art.

They must be able to work to deadlines and set up the schedules required to meet them. They must work well with others and be able to operate their studios according to the needs of architects.

They are primarily interested in visual communication, with buildings as their subject matter and camera and film their medium.

What other careers require similar qualities?

All photographic careers require similar abilities with camera and darkroom equipment and qualities such as patience, awareness, attention to detail and the ability to work with people.

Architectural photographers would be familiar with the work carried out in a large architectural firm. They may enjoy site planning, facility planning, architectural graphics, delineation and other architectural careers.

Because their work is closely associated with publications and promotions, they may feel comfortable working in design studios that emphasize graphic presentations.

What can be done now?

Photography should be taken in high school or at special classes at community colleges, art schools or extension schools. Take art classes such as design, drawing and printmaking to learn about design concepts. Work on school publications; join a camera club—these will give you excellent practical experience. Art history classes that deal with architectural history can provide you with important background and knowledge.

Take pictures of buildings and of architectural details, and arrange your collection of prints or slides in a meaningful, systematic order. Look at magazines that contain excellent photography: *Architectural Digest, Historic Preservation, Architectural Record, Designs West, Interior Design* and *Interiors.* Collect excellent examples of architectural photography to use for current and future reference.

Which colleges offer necessary programs?

There are few schools that have special architectural photography courses, but a general major in photography will give you such experience. The best practical experience is obtained by working for well-known, accomplished architectural photographers or in a large photographic studio where architectural firms are frequent clients.

Practical experience can be obtained by working for real estate offices and local hotels and motels, photographing houses, buildings and rooms.

Architectural photography is very specialized; many product photographers and general photographers will supplement their own programs by taking architectural subjects as needed. Large metropolitan areas have the greatest need for architectural specialists.

Other Careers in Photography

There are countless photography-related careers that are essential to commercial art. Not all such careers are listed here, but if you wish to combine your interest in photography with another art career area read both the photography and other art career sections carefully.

Aerial Photographer (Space Photographer)
These photographers take pictures from aircraft of segments of the earth. They are called on to photograph natural and urban landscapes to help record natural phenomena, develop plans for cities and learn the effects of pollution. Their work also is used for mapping, surveying and related purposes.

Photographers working with satellite cameras are able to show weather conditions, land-use patterns, military operations and ecological changes.

Airbrush Artist (See Graphic Design)

Audiovisual Designer or Artist
Designing and constructing art work for slides, filmstrips, films, overheads, flip charts or other visual presentation materials for school systems is the work of audiovisual artists and designers. Working with photographers and production staff in the development of ideas, sketches and final art work, the designers must have backgrounds in color, design and often in type and lettering. They should also be familiar with film production and sound coordination techniques.

Designing these materials for schools requires an active imagination and the ability to work with people from many disciplines. The production of the final camera-ready art requires a thorough knowledge of many printing techniques and production methods, and the ability to work with certain size or color restrictions. The majority of the finished audiovisual aids will be used in primary or secondary education subject areas.

Audiovisual Photographer (See Audiovisual Designer)

Biological Photographer
Often employed by hospitals or medical laboratories, these photographers take pictures of medical, biological and other phenomena to illustrate scientific publications, records or research. They use still, motion picture and television cameras to record anatomical structures, microscopic specimens, plant and animal tissues and physiological and pathological processes. Such work requires a combination of intense interest in science or medicine as well as strong abilities in photography. (See also Medical Photographer, below.)

Commercial Studios
Commercial studios are generally large operations, employing many specialist photographers and technicians. Such studios are able to take on assignments in architecture, interior design, product development, catalog photography, illustration, advertising and other specialties. The work is often done for advertising agency art directors or their clients. (See Graphic Design and Industrial Design). The wide range of experience available in such commercial studios is excellent training for photographers who may wish to specialize or establish individual reputations.

Corporation Photographer (In-Plant Photographer)
Many companies employ photographers as part of their corporate technical staffs. Depending on the size of the companies, they may hire from one to thirty or forty photographers. (General Motors' Photographic Department has about 1,000 employees.) Manufacturing concerns are typical environments for such in-plant photographers, but so are department stores, large banks, insurance companies, mail order catalog houses, libraries, museums, government agencies and police departments.

Film (Motion Picture) Careers
(See Film and Television)

Film Developer
Working for large film laboratories, film developers operate the machines that develop still or motion picture film. They determine the type of processing required, and use their acquired skills and film developing techniques to produce the best possible results.

Fine Art Photographer
(See Fine Art)

Industrial Photographer (See Product and Food Photographer)

Laboratory Chief (Photographic Laboratory Supervisor)
Using their highly developed laboratory skills, these photographic specialists supervise and coordinate the complete range of activities in photographic laboratories:

developing film, making prints, photocopying, enlarging, reducing, custom printing, airbrushing, retouching and spotting. They emphasize sharpness of prints, color balance, value contrast and brilliance. They are also responsible for all supplies, materials and equipment.

Law Enforcement Photographer
(Police Photographer)
These photographers, who work in or for police departments, must have a combination of interests in law enforcement and photography. Some are free-lance photographers who are hired when needed; others are police officers who specialize in photography.

Larger crime labs employ several full-time photographic specialists who take pictures and operate specialized darkrooms and equipment. Areas of specialization include: evidence gathering, forensics, color techniques, processing and printing, motion picture work, photomicroscopy, radiography and the like. For more information, contact: Law Enforcement Training Division, Eastman Kodak Co., 343 State Street, Rochester, New York 14650.

Legal Photographer
Legal photographers work for lawyers. They take pictures of accidents, locations of crimes and other objects and events of which lawyers, prosecutors and detectives need a visual record. They are paid for their photographs and also for any time they spend in court, and are required to have a knowledge of legal procedures as well as of photography.

Medical Photographer
Every large hospital has one or more medical photographers on staff. They use still, motion picture and video cameras to record special cases, operations and events. Surgical procedures, hospital developments, public relations and special events are photographed for hospital records and for publicity. Surgeons, pathologists, the laboratory staff and public relations officers make use of medical photographers, who have a knowledge and understanding of medical procedures as well as strong capabilities in photography.

Microfilm Supervisor
These specialists supervise and coordinate the efforts and activities of people engaged in microfilm reproduction, laboratory processing, computer output microfilming, optical character recognition and microfiche duplicating. They are expert in using and repairing all microfilm equipment.

Museum Photographer
There are many places in art museums where photographers are needed. A photographic record is kept of every work in the collections. Conservators require photographs as they work on their projects. All museum publications use photographic work. The public relations staff requires photographs and transparencies for magazines and newspapers. Large museums will have one or more photographic specialists on staffs, but smaller museums with smaller budgets and fewer needs will use outside photographers for their work.

Photographer of Fine Art
Some photographers specialize in taking color or black and white pictures or color slides of art work for artists. The results may be used to make posters, in publicity releases, magazines or books or for an artist's personal records. Some photographers work only for museums, photographing their collections for records, for publications or for prints made available to the public. Some are free-lance photographers who work for artists and their agents, galleries, museums or publications. They must be knowledgeable about art, color and various art techniques in order to emphasize what the artists wish to express in their work.

Photofinishing Specialists
Photofinishing plants with fifty or more employees are quite common, and some hire over 100 workers. Production managers and supervisors are constantly needed, and must have management abilities as well as backgrounds in development and printing techniques and use of equipment. Both black and white and color capabilities are required in most laboratories.

Photofinishing specialists inspect and arrange negatives and transparencies, prepare positives and prints and dry, trim, mount and frame photographs for their clients. Some of this work is now mechanized, but at custom labs it is done by hand by experienced photography technicians.

Photographic Colorist (Tinter)
Usually working in portrait studios, these artists apply oil colors or other tinting media to photographs to produce lifelike tones. They use brushes, cotton swabs and airbrushes in their work, and are called on to enhance photographs to the specifications of customers or photographers.

Photographic Engineering
No guided missile or satellite goes into space without a detailed photographic record of its development and

function. Using photography to solve engineering and scientific problems employs many photographic specialists. Such specialists must have engineering backgrounds to accompany their expertise in photographic sciences. Most photographic engineering work is done for engineering firms (Rockwell or TRW, for example), for governmental agencies (NASA) or for production corporations (Lockheed Aircraft, Ford Motors, or RCA, for example).

Photographic Sales

An interest in all phases of photography may be combined with a desire to work with people and an ability in salesmanship, and may lead to positions in photographic sales at retail or wholesale levels. Operating a retail camera shop in the neighborhood, or selling photographic studio services to clients in commercial or industrial fields, are possible photographic sales careers.

Photography/Fine Arts Gallery

Photography is gradually coming to be considered fine art, and galleries which specialize in displaying and selling such photographs are gaining popularity. Gallery operators should have a thorough knowledge of photographic history, techniques and applications. They must understand the market for such products and be able to articulate their opinions on style, techniques, subject matter and quality.

Portrait Photographer

Portrait photographers outnumber all other kinds of photographic specialists. They record graduations, weddings, birthdays, family groups and special events. Using a variety of cameras, film and processes, portraits can be simple black and white pictures or dye-transfer work that rivals good portrait painting. Color processing work can either be done in the studio or sent out to specialized laboratories. Often established portrait photographers become essential parts of their communities because they may have photographed several generations of inhabitants, and recorded the historic continuity of the community.

Retoucher

Photographic retouchers use pencils, watercolors, brushes and airbrushes to retouch negatives or prints to comply with a photographer's wishes and ideas. In small laboratories, this work may be done by the owner or a lab worker; in large ones, there may be several retouchers who work full-time at their specialty.

School Photographer

There are many photographic careers in this specialized field, including photographers, developers, printers, detailers, spotters, croppers and salespeople. Work on your school yearbook will put you in personal contact with these people.

Slide Program or Slide Set Producer/Director

The availability of slides or slide sets is vital to good art teaching, especially in art appreciation and art history classes. There are several companies that provide such services to art educators. Tens of thousands of slides are available individually or in sets and programs.

Jobs in such slide producing companies include photographers, photocopiers, photo processors, art history consultants, program directors, and the staff members who work at slide cataloging, separating, numbering and classifying. Detailed catalogs must be designed and printed to present the available slides, strips and sets to art teachers who obtain them through mail order systems.

Teacher of Photography

Almost every university and college has a photography department, as do most community colleges and a great many high schools. Art schools and schools specializing in photography also require experienced photographers who are informed and skilled in such areas as visual design, photographic techniques, darkroom procedures, marketing and current trends, and who are able to communicate effectively with young people. Such photography teachers stimulate and encourage future photographers.

Television Careers (See Film and Television)

OST OF THE art careers outlined in this book deal with the practical application of art to fields such as advertising, construction, design photography, film and television. But there are artists who do not put in forty hours of work a week in offices or agencies, and whose creations are not simply utilitarian. Instead, they may sculpt or paint to enrich the lives of others, to make them aware and appreciative of certain facets of life. Some of these artists teach art; some devote themselves to careers in museums or galleries where art is exhibited or sold. Art careers can involve writing about art and artists, publishing art magazines and newsletters, doing police work, therapy or investment counseling.

Many of these art careers contribute to the development of contemporary society and the understanding of past cultures. They may be directed toward producing art or helping others appreciate it. Many other art careers are still developing, and some that will be common in the future are not yet even defined.

Probably the best known but least understood of these art career areas is fine art.

Leonard Baskin employs traditional woodcarving techniques but develops his sculpture, *Oppressed Man,* in his distinctive style. The painted pine work is 31 inches high. Photograph courtesy Collection of Whitney Museum of American Art

Watercolorist Lee Weiss discusses her technique with the sales staff of her gallery representative. After this briefing the staff will be able to describe the artist's working processes to prospective collectors. Photograph: Bruce Howell and the Louis Newman Galleries

Cultural Growth and Enrichment

Fine Art

The works of fine artists—painting, sculpture, prints, ceramics, photographs—are produced to be looked at and enjoyed. They enhance environments of all types and make life richer and more pleasant.

Most teenagers who are interested in art learn of fine art in school. They draw, paint, carve or work with clay to achieve aesthetic rather than practical results. Teenagers who maintain their interest in art, and realize that it is not easy to make a living as a fine artist, soon channel their interests toward more utilitarian art careers. It *is* possible to survive as a fine artist, but to survive requires flexibility, tenacity and dedication.

Income from the sale of paintings or sculptures cannot be predicted and is often sporadic. Most artists who produce fine art, therefore, have other jobs, often in other fields of art, that provide them with steady incomes and allow them time to pursue their favorite fine art media. Some artists supplement their income by private teaching, conducting workshops and seminars, doing demonstrations for art groups or judging shows and exhibitions. Some artists obtain grants in order to continue their work without distraction. And some do sell enough of their work to live comfortably.

In preparing for a possible career in fine art, students will take many undergraduate courses in painting, printmaking, sculpture, design and drawing. Although not many artists make a living at drawing, it is a skill common to most fine artists, and drawing classes are essential.

Some type of training is essential in almost every fine art career. Dealers and buyers do not ask about an artist's degrees or college classes, but the training, experience, instruction and associations gained in art school are vitally important to the development of fine artists. Some self-taught artists may exist, but the majority of successful artists have had excellent training from highly qualified and experienced teachers. Many successful fine artists have obtained advanced degrees such as the Master of Fine Arts (MFA) in their chosen specialty area.

The Role of Galleries in Fine Art Careers

How galleries operate is discussed in a later chapter, but because artists and galleries must work closely together to sell fine art, they are discussed here from the artist's point of view.

Some galleries, especially new or expanding ones, will take on new artists, but most have an established group with which their regular customers are familiar. They add new artists carefully and seldom. How then does an aspiring young artist get gallery representation?

Young artists must first establish a reputation by showing their work in group exhibitions, inviting friends and dealers to studio exhibits, showing at weekend parking lot shows or by joining local art associations. With even a small following and reputation and a few notices from local papers, a young artist can begin to think of looking for gallery representation.

Look for galleries that exhibit work similar to yours; such places will attract buyers looking for your kind of art. Take plenty of time and do your research carefully. After looking over all possible choices, you should be able to zero in on three or four likely galleries, not necessarily all in your own town or city. Write to the directors, ask for an appointment with each, and offer to send slides of your work for their inspection. If they like your slides, they will ask to see some of your work. Show the best pieces you have, those done in your strongest and surest style. Gallery directors who are attracted to your work will want to know about your training and your methods of working. They will also want to know how serious you are about your work, how long you work each day and how much work you produce.

Almost every gallery works on consignment, which means that you bring your work to the gallery, it is hung on the walls for a time, and no money is exchanged until a customer buys the work. The gallery then retains a set percentage of the selling price for their efforts and salesmanship, advertising and wall space, and to help cover overhead costs. Gallery staffs work diligently to sell their artists' work, and genuinely earn the percentages they retain.

The ultimate gallery experience for fine artists is to have a one-person show, complete with opening, press coverage and crowds of people. There are usually years of struggle and hard work before the first such invitation can be sent out, however. Many excellent fine artists must continue to work at related careers to earn their livings, and may never establish a wide enough reputation nor enough of their own work to have a solo show.

There are many opportunities to enter competitive exhibitions, and these are excellent chances to see how your work compares to that of your peers. Look for lists of these exhibitions in art magazines. Many national open exhibitions offer large prizes and contain the work of some of America's top artists. Being accepted in such shows, and perhaps winning awards, give you excellent credentials to show to gallery directors who might be interested in your work.

Museums sometimes exhibit the work of local young artists, and this is a good way to begin to develop a reputation. In the fine arts, the "name" or reputation of the artist is extremely important, and it takes many years to establish that reputation. People buy art because they like it, or because it may increase in value. The work of famous artists is easier to sell because it is familiar, attractive to own and valuable.

There is no effective way to determine whether or not a work of fine art will sell easily. Fine artists must strive to attain high quality and satisfy their own artistic requirements. What will sell for a short time and what will become classic cannot be predicted.

Although fine art is only a small fraction of the total body of art produced yearly in America, it is still considered the most glamorous, and making a living producing it is the goal of many young artists. However, that goal must be considered in the light of realistic facts and figures.

Painter

Fine art painters must work at their art diligently and constantly to produce enough high-quality work to insure their continued success as painters. Some artists begin their painting careers directly out of art school. Others may begin as illustrators and gradually develop a loyal following willing to purchase their paintings from galleries. Still others work at one art career (industrial design, for example) or some other job (such as teacher or real estate agent) and continue to work at their painting, exhibiting and selling what they can produce in their spare time. Although most require other jobs or activities to provide them with sufficient income, some very popular painters live comfortably from the sale of their work.

Fine art painters work in studios of various kinds. A separate, designated space is best, as it can be devoted entirely to art production and need not be cleaned up every day. Some studios are in buildings at the artists' homes, or in special rooms within their houses. Some artists prefer their studios to be away from home, and may rent space in office buildings, barns, garages, or large loft spaces. In addition to the space required for working, some special areas are needed for storage, working, keeping records and framing.

What painters do

Fine art painters work in many media: watercolors, acrylics, oils, egg tempera, casein, inks, collage and some exotic combinations.

Some painters require subject matter from which to work, and they may travel to paint on location, or sketch or take photographs from which to work in their studios. Some painters work with models, still lifes, animals or flowers as their subjects. Others make up the designs and subject matter as they work on their various surfaces.

They set aside regular hours to paint each day, and must produce work regularly in order to supply their customers or galleries, or to prepare for exhibitions. Galleries will not take on artists who cannot supply them regularly with new works.

Most painters choose their own subject matter and working processes. However, some artists take on commissions, which means they accept assignments from customers, clients and galleries to do certain kinds of work. Often they are partially paid in advance for these assignments, which are often requests for portraits.

When a painting is finished (on paper, canvas or boards) it must be framed to present to the public. Some galleries or agents provide the framing for work, but most artists do it themselves. Some make their own frames, some buy or order frames made to specifications and others have their work framed by professional framers (See Other Careers in the Fine Arts).

The price of an artist's work is established by supply and demand or by reputation. The work of beginning exhibitors will sell for less than that of more experienced painters or those with more impressive reputations. Established prices may be raised periodically as an artist's reputation becomes known and demand for his or her work increases. Gallery directors can help establish such price structures.

Artists must keep excellent records, both of their finances (income and expenses) and of their work (where paintings are and who sold or bought them). Because fine artists are self-employed, they must work directly with state and federal tax agencies. Artists must keep inventories of their work, insure it and provide for its shipment.

What qualities are helpful for a fine arts painter?

All of the above requirements call for self-discipline on the part of the artists. There is no one to tell them what to do or when to do it, and they must meet all their deadlines and obligations on their own.

They must be able to make themselves work, even when they do not feel like working. The stereotype of the artist who waits to be inspired is simply not practical. There are studio and bookkeeping jobs that can be done when artists are not in the mood to paint, but eventually gallery and customer needs must be satisfied.

Painters must be articulate and businesslike in their dealings with gallery directors, museum curators, the press and customers. They must continually strive to produce high quality work that will attract an expanding audience of buyers and admirers.

Painters must keep up with what is going on in the art world by reading books and magazines and attending gallery and museum openings. They join organizations and societies for exhibition opportunities and chances to talk with other artists.

What other careers require similar qualities?

The quality of self-motivation is required of all free-lance and fine artists. Free-lance designers and illustrators work as painters do, and often it is possible to combine these careers in one.

Editorial illustrators (See Editorial Design) work with similar techniques and products and work under the same conditions. Mural painters (See Other Careers in Architecture) and background painters in animation studios (See Film Animation) require similar training and employ similar techniques.

Art teachers at many levels are often trained as fine artists and teach techniques and methods of painting (See

Robert Motherwell uses abstract forms and powerful contrasts of shape and value to express his feelings and ideas. *Elegy to the Spanish Republic, 54* is one fine art painting of a series. Photograph: Daniel P. Duffy for The Museum of Modern Art, New York

Art Education). Art schools and colleges seek painting instructors who have established reputations as painters, because they contribute to the institution's prestige.

What can be done now?

High school students should take all the studio art and art history classes that are available, especially drawing, painting and design. You can never have too many drawing classes, and it is good to enroll in special Saturday drawing classes that some art schools or school districts provide. Get involved in as many art activities as your academic schedule will allow. Sketch, paint and draw on your own. Establish a mini-studio in a corner of your room. Always have a sketchbook handy and work in it constantly.

Read through fine art magazines to see what is being produced and how artists work. Libraries should have available such magazines as: *American Artist, Artforum, Art in America, Artnews* and *Art Week.*

Which colleges offer necessary programs?

Most colleges, universities and art schools offer courses leading to undergraduate degrees in fine arts. Those with very strong programs will also offer graduate degrees in painting, sculpture, printmaking or other specialized disciplines. Check the charts at the back of the book for schools that emphasize the fine arts, and obtain catalogs to determine whether or not they meet your individual needs.

Community colleges generally offer basic courses in

areas of fine art, and some colleges offer extension courses off campus. There are specialized schools and general art schools that may provide all the training and experience you need, and you should check the yellow pages for information on such schools or studios. Non-credit courses, workshops and seminars can provide excellent help in painting. Sources can be found in ads in *American Artist* and other art magazines.

Sculptor

Because all fine artists work in similar circumstances whether they paint, sculpt or print, the reader is encouraged to look through the previous section on painters to gain some understanding of the self-directed nature of the fine arts. Sculptors can either determine for themselves which direction they take with their art, or they may work with galleries, museums or agents to plot a strategy.

Sculptures are three-dimensional forms that vary in size from tiny to monumental. Traditional sculpture materials include such media as marble, wood, bronze and clay, each of which have different qualities and require different and specific techniques.

Contemporary sculpture, however, makes use of an incredibly wide range of materials and means of visual expression. Welding brought construction into the sculpture vocabulary, and electricity, motors and computers now provide opportunities for programming movement. Today's sculptors may work with light, sound, animation, cinematography, fibers, plastics, or such unconventional machines as chain saws and earth moving equipment. Some work only with concepts and no physical materials at all.

Sculpture today is exciting and highly imaginative, whether it is created from unfamiliar or traditional materials.

What sculptors do

The many sculptural processes vary drastically, and there is not sufficient space on these pages to describe all the possible techniques, materials and methods.

Some sculptors work as painters do, in that they execute their work in the desired medium and display the pieces for sale in galleries. Some works, especially those in clay, welded metal, wood or stone, are probably one-of-a-kind, while bronzes, cast metals and stone, some clay or fiberglass pieces and works using new reproductional techniques are produced in multiples from two to fifty or more. Such works, placed on consignment in galleries, shops or stores, are sold like paintings, with the gallery owners retaining a percentage of the sales.

Large welded metal sculptures often require more space than ordinary studios can provide. Here work is done outdoors. Photograph by Brill for Interlochen Center for the Arts

Large sculptural works are often commissioned by architects, builders or developers to be placed in front of buildings, in open courtyards or in other public places. In such cases the sculptors usually receive part of the cost of the work when the contract is signed; final payment is due on completion. Some large works of this type may take a year or more to complete, and can involve many workers besides the artists themselves. Advance payments keep the project running smoothly and prevent the sculptors from depleting their own funds. Artists who work on such large projects often need business managers or agents to handle their financial affairs while such work is in progress.

Sculptors usually receive commissions because of their reputations or as a result of open competitions. Artists are often invited to submit models of proposed sculptures, called maquettes, and a committee decides which sculptor is awarded the commission. The committee then provides funds for the duration of the project.

There are regional and national sculpture shows where artists compete with their peers. They often must submit slides of their work to be judged, so sculptors should be adept at photographing their sculptures. The problem of crating and shipping large works, for shows that require that the sculpture itself be sent, must be solved by each artist.

Like painters, not many sculptors can make comfortable livings by just selling their work and they must supplement their art income by holding down other jobs. Teaching sculpture in art schools or colleges is one way to work in sculpture and still be able to continue to sculpt creatively.

What qualities are helpful for a sculptor?

Like painters, sculptors must be self-disciplined and able to use their time efficiently. Because large works can take months to complete, they must be able to budget their finances to cover periods when no income is available. They must also be able to sustain interest in their work over such extended periods.

Of course, they must feel at ease working in three dimensions and in visualizing completed forms. They must study their art thoroughly, developing individual styles and techniques that make their work unique and attractive. They must be able to work with designers, contractors and architects if they are to produce sculptures suited to certain designed environments.

Sculptors must be constantly aware of developing trends and new techniques and materials so that their work stays competitive. They cannot be discouraged when commissions go to other artists, but must be able to overcome their feelings and stay optimistic and productive.

What other careers require similar qualities?

All fine artists (painters, printmakers and craftspeople) require similar qualities of self-discipline and self-motivation.

Model builders, set designers and architects require skills in three-dimensional construction and manipulation of materials. Puppeteers, jewelry designers and furniture designers must also work in three dimensions, although some of these careers may involve working for others rather than for oneself.

Some careers in industrial design require skills and abilities similar to those needed by sculptors.

What can be done now?

In high school, art classes of all types should be taken, especially sculpture and three-dimensional design. Design and drawing classes of all types are also important. Shop classes (metal, wood and plastics) can provide excellent background in working with these materials and developing working techniques.

Part-time work that involves any three-dimensional activity (welding, constructing, finishing and the like) can prove helpful. Visit museums and galleries to see what past and present sculptors have done. Take special sculpture classes if they are available at art schools, colleges or magnet schools that emphasize specific subjects.

Make drawings in your sketchbook, studying existing sculptures or inventing your own forms and ideas. Some magazines that include features on sculpture are: *American Artist, Art in America, Artforum, Artnews* and *National Sculpture Review*.

Which colleges offer necessary programs?

Schools with fine arts majors will generally offer sufficient courses in three-dimensional design and sculpture to satisfy most needs. However, if you have definite interests (such as bronze casting) be sure that foundry facilities and experienced faculty are available. Check the charts at the back of the book, and write for catalogs to see if your needs will be met.

Claire Falkenstein uses industrial tools as she works on *Leaping Fire,* a twenty-foot-high copper sculpture for a shopping mall in Fresno, California. All photographs courtesy Claire Falkenstein

American artist Claire Falkenstein's career spans more than five decades and half the globe. Her reputation as an artist and philosopher is well-known in both Europe and her native America. Falkenstein's contributions to art and to technical processes—the fusion of incompatible materials such as glass and metal, for example—have made her a sculptor of considerable stature.

Falkenstein was born in Coos Bay, Oregon. When she was seven her father, a lumber mill manager, allowed her to travel alone to San Francisco on a large schooner. Falkenstein now credits the sights and sounds of the San Francisco Bay as instrumental to her understanding of art and to her career as an artist. She maintains close ties with the bay area to this day.

Falkenstein's interest in art began early, and was encouraged by her family. She graduated from the University of California with a major in art and a minor in anthropology.

After a brief period as a teacher, Falkenstein began to develop her art. In San Francisco in the 1930's the environment for artists was very favorable. Falkenstein found stimulation and numerous opportu-

nities for creative discovery there. She and other artists felt that their work would be viewed critically but sympathetically, and that it would usually be exhibited under generally favorable conditions. Attention from respected critics was likely, and public response was often enthusiastic.

Falkenstein became a part of a vigorous art movement of bay area artists, and was prompted by them to expand her commitment to her art by moving to Paris, France. By this time her career was well-developed: her work was purchased by major museums in America and by private collectors.

Falkenstein spent thirteen years in Paris, living in a small apartment which served as both residence and studio. Often her large sculptures extended out windows and doors, and had to be dismantled and reassembled at selected sites.

Falkenstein has worked with metal, glass, wood, paper, water and air to create art for clients. Her art pieces are large welded fountains, stained glass windows, small kinetic sculptures receptive to light air currents, wooden sculptures, photography, mixed media collage, fused glass and jewelry.

Claire Falkenstein, Sculptor

Claire Falkenstein developed unique sculptural stained glass windows for St. Basil's Cathedral in Los Angeles. The commission included ten modules such as this, each 14 feet wide and 65 feet high.

Structure and Flow is a 20 × 20 × 14 foot sculptured fountain made of copper tubing, commissioned by the Long Beach Museum of Art. The lighting is carefully designed for maximum impact at night. Photograph: Bruce Howell

The best known examples of her work are *Montago Section* at the Eileen Norris Cinema Theater at the University of Southern California; the stained glass windows and doors of St. Basil's church in Los Angeles and a large fountain, *Structure and Flow No. 2*, also in Los Angeles.

Some of her best work is in Italy. She made the garden gates for the Foundation of Peggy Guggenheim at the Palazzo Venier dei Leoni, in Venice, and the Grotto Gates for the villa of Princess Pignatelli in Santa Marinella, Rome.

Falkenstein's words to young artists considering careers in the arts are simple. "You have to try without expecting success or failure. Sometimes it works, sometimes it doesn't, but you have to be willing to take risks."

Printmaker

The term "prints" is misunderstood by many people, especially those who are not familiar with art and art techniques. Part of the problem lies in the fact that "prints" can correctly refer to both *printed reproductions* (done photographically in a print shop on large machines) and *multiple originals* (done by individual artists in their studios). This second category fits into the fine arts area, and printmakers who produce these multiple originals are continuing production methods that are hundreds of years old.

Printmakers use several major techniques and many experimental methods and materials, but the work they produce is original, usually limited in number, printed by hand, numbered and signed. Major techniques and processes include: **intaglio** (etchings, engravings, drypoints), in which lines are printed from ink which settles in grooves below the surface of the metal plate; **relief** (woodcut, linocut, cardboard print), in which the inked, raised surfaces do the printing; **lithography**, which makes use of limestone or metal sheets, grease, water and ink; and **stencils** (serigraphy, stencils), where ink passes through cut or brushed-on stencils to create the images. There are also many experimental techniques, such as collagraphs and blind embossing, and combinations of several techniques that have expanded the boundaries of printmaking.

It is the processes of printmaking that determine the effectiveness of the final products. These processes may include engraving, cutting, carving, gluing, stencilling, scraping or burnishing before the plate or block is inked and printed. Some processes require large presses, and printmaking studios must comfortably accomodate tools, equipment, paper and prints.

What printmakers do

Like other fine artists, printmakers generally work on their own. They work in their studios, budgeting their own time and energy to create original finished prints, ready to exhibit or sell in galleries. Many galleries deal primarily in multiple-original creations, like prints, while some may handle both prints and paintings or sculpture.

Printmakers produce a certain number of each print, which they call one edition. The quality of these multiple units must be as equal as possible, and when a certain number (twenty, sixty-five or one hundred, for example) is completed, the source of the print, whether plate, stone, screen or woodblock, is destroyed or marked so that no further prints can be made from it. Thus the edition is limited. When completed, the prints are titled, numbered and signed, to assure gallery staff and buyers that there is only a limited number of the work available, thereby establishing the value of each one.

There are printmaking societies around the country that put on regional or national exhibitions of the work of printmakers. Artists may also exhibit their work in galleries, where the value of their work increases as their reputations spread. Like painters, printmakers must seek gallery representation with care, because sales generated in this way provide their basic income.

Sometimes corporations, galleries or individual patrons will commission an artist to produce an edition of prints. This means that the sale of all prints in the edition is guaranteed by the patron, and money will usually be advanced when the contract is signed.

Prints usually sell for more reasonable prices than one-of-a-kind paintings. Some painters and sculptors thus use printmaking to supplement their incomes and help make their work more visible to the buying public.

Many printmakers teach in art schools, colleges, universities and high schools. Often they are able to use institutional presses and other equipment to produce their own work.

Besides the numbered prints which are sold, printmakers keep several examples for themselves. These are called artist's proofs, and they usually remain in the printmakers' own collections, or go into the portfolios they show to gallery directors or clients.

Printmakers working in serigraphy must constantly check registrations to insure accurate multicolored images. Photograph: The Art Institute of Chicago

What qualities are helpful for a printmaker?

Printmakers must like to work with various methods and materials and must enjoy the entire printmaking processes with which they are involved. They spend much time preparing the plates or other surfaces from which the prints will be made, and they must be patient and careful in these early steps. They must be aware of textures, values and details, must understand the processes completely and must be able to anticipate the finished products.

Like other fine artists, they must be self-disciplined and self-motivated if they are to continue to be productive artists. They must satisfy the continuing requests of galleries and therefore must regularly develop new and exciting work.

They must monitor the printmaking field to keep track of current trends and developments, materials, and methods. They must enjoy the competition that exists in the fine art field.

Printmakers must be experimenters, looking for new and unique ways to use their equipment and their basic knowledge.

What other careers require similar qualities?

All successful fine artists must have similar qualities of self-motivation, attention to detail, interest in processes and the desire to compete.

Photography and careers in the printing industry may be of interest to printmakers because they make use of similar interests and strengths. Some areas of graphic design (See Graphic Design) would be attractive because of the processes required (silkscreen printing, for example) and the need for multiple products.

Many printmakers enjoy teaching the processes to students, and make excellent teachers at undergraduate and graduate levels.

What can be done now?

High school art classes should certainly include drawing, printmaking and design; art history and printing are also important. Get involved with the entire art program at school, but also take business classes, English, history and some humanities courses.

Check a local printmaking society to see if they accept students in their group, or join one in another city. Determine what kinds of print exhibitions, seminars, classes or demonstrations might be scheduled at local museums and galleries. Find out when student shows are scheduled at nearby art schools or colleges.

Part-time work in print shops, graphics studios or sign shops that may use silkscreen techniques are all helpful. Work in art supply stores would supply you with knowledge of available tools, equipment and supplies and may acquaint you with local artists working in print media.

Some magazines that often deal with fine art printmaking include: *Artnews, Art in America* and *American Artist.*

Which colleges offer necessary programs?

Most art schools and colleges offer majors in printmaking. Some are stronger in one area than another, and you are encouraged to write to several schools and ask for catalogs.

Some community colleges offer fine printmaking courses, especially if there are experienced printmakers on the faculties. Check the charts at the back of the book for fine art programs, and write for catalogs to determine the emphasis each school offers.

Fine Art Photographer

Fine art photography is personal work, done for the enjoyment of the process and the desire to produce beautiful, meaningful images. It differs from commercial photography in that it is not done on assignment nor for intentional mass reproduction, advertising or promotion.

Although there are many galleries that specialize in exhibition and selling photographic images, and many museums that provide photograph exhibition space, there are few artists who can make comfortable livings only by selling their prints in such ways.

Most photographers who produce museum or gallery quality prints, in color or black and white, work as professional commercial photographers or in other art positions, and work on personal fine art photography on their own time. A few fine art photographers such as Ansel Adams, Cole Weston and Wynn Bullock have achieved the reputations necessary to command high prices for their work. Such situations are the ultimate goal of many photographers, who work seriously at their skills and techniques while constantly developing their abilities and reputations.

Wynn Bullock's works feature close-ups of nature—things we do not usually notice. *Leaves and Cobwebs* is a 1968 silverprint. Photograph: The Detroit Institute of Arts; Purchase, Michigan State Council for the Arts Exhibition Fund

What fine art photographers do

The same processes are involved in both fine art photography and commercial work, except that fine art images are treated to insure longevity. The pictures are taken, developed and carefully sized. The finished prints are mounted and framed for protection and permanence.

The finished images must be seen by the public in order to be purchased, so shows and exhibitions must be arranged in galleries and museums. All costs involved in this process are the responsibility of the artists themselves.

Photographers establish their particular styles in a number of ways. Some photographers specialize in certain subject matter for their gallery work, and gain reputations for their specialties. For example, Diane Ensign-Caughey is well known for her nature and wildlife photography, and David Meunch for his landscape work. Other photographers prefer to work with a greater variety of subject matter. Some work only in black and white, others only in color. Some work in both areas or have developed hand coloring techniques to enhance their images. Some artists show their work only in galleries, while others rely on magazines and other publications to help them establish their reputations, hoping to exhibit in galleries later in their career development.

Working with galleries is an important aspect of fine art photography. Gallery directors choose their photographers with care and will scrutinize portfolios before they choose their artists. Slides and prints submitted as part of a portfolio must be only of the highest quality. Help in finding gallery and exhibition sites can be found in two publications: *Photographer's Market* and *Craftworker's Market*, both published by Writer's Digest Books. See the index of this book for references to portfolios, galleries and résumés.

Other outlets for fine art photography include posters, greeting cards, some types of magazines, calendars, book illustrations and post cards. The two sources listed above will also provide some contacts in these areas.

What qualities are helpful for a fine art photographer?

Besides the required photographic skills, fine art photographers must be sensitive and perceptive in choosing their subjects and printing their images. Personal styles make their images different from those of others who may be working with similar subjects. They must be businesslike in all their dealings with customers and galleries and must constantly strive to improve the quality of their work.

They must be able to budget their resources in order to stay within their irregular annual incomes. There are no weekly checks, necessarily, for a fine art photographer. Like other self-employed artists, fine art photographers must be motivated and capable of budgeting their time. Working schedules and deadlines must be self-imposed or based on gallery requirements.

Often, sporadic income from sales can be supplemented by private teaching, lecturing or overseeing seminars and workshops. In these cases, the ability to teach and to work with people is extremely important.

What other careers require similar qualities?

Other careers in photography require similar abilities and qualities. All self-employed and free-lance artists (designers, fine artists and craftspeople, for example) must be motivated and self-disciplined in order to produce their work at their own pace and yet meet all the deadlines and requirements imposed on them by galleries, magazines and customers.

What can be done now?

Art and photography classes in high school are very important, as they are for any photographic career. Involvement with school publications and camera clubs will provide excellent practical experience.

Attend photographic shows (check museums and galleries in your areas) and subscribe to good photo magazines such as *The Professional Photographer, Rangefinder, Studio Photography, Camera, Modern Photography, Infinity* and *Aperture*. Some major newspapers have sections on photographic news and reviews of exhibitions.

Enroll in seminars and special photography classes, if they are available, and check for local camera clubs that are part of community recreation or YMCA programs.

Part-time work in camera shops will familiarize you with all types of equipment; work in photo labs will help you understand developing and printing processes. Study design and composition, and use these principles when you take your own photographs. Check the library for books that might be of help in both the design and production processes of photography.

Which colleges offer necessary programs?

Any school that has a photography department will provide the necessary courses of instruction in processes and procedures. Fine art photographers must be aware of design principles and mood, so design classes are essential. Art schools, universities, colleges and community colleges can all offer the required subjects. See the charts at the back of the book.

If a school has a well-known fine art photographer on the staff, it would be an advantage to attend classes there, simply to learn about the attitudes, ideas and experience necessary for success in this career field where the rewards, although more often spiritual than financial, are nonetheless considerable.

Other Careers In The Fine Arts

Appraiser (See Other Careers in Art Services)

Art Critic (See Reporting and Writing About Art)

Art Dealer/Gallery Director (See Art Galleries)

Artists' Agent

Artists' agents work out of offices, warehouses or facilities in their homes. They represent artists to galleries, sales agencies, interior designers or directly to major clients by taking art work directly to possible sales locations around the country. They place advertisements for artists' work in art publications and show work to potential clients, both wholesale and retail. Artists' agents often schedule shows, workshops, seminars or demonstrations. They may also arrange for print editions to be made of their clients' work, if this is desirable. They often handle several artists, arranging their exhibition schedules and sales opportunities. For these services they receive either a predetermined compensation or a percentage of eventual sales.

Assemblage Artist

Assemblages are arrangements of three-dimensional materials—found objects or objects made by the artists—that are freestanding or arranged as relief sculptures. Assemblage artists gather a variety of three-dimensional materials (wood, metal, plastic, glass, paper, stone and the like) and adhere them to each other or to a backing or foundation. The finished works can be of any size; some are stationary while others have moving parts; some have themes and others are simply accumulations arranged to please the constructing artists.

Collage Artist

Collages are works of fine art composed of papers or fabrics adhered to supports such as cardboard, canvas, illustration board or heavy paper. Collagists gather a large variety of papers or fabrics in many colors, textures, sizes and shapes. They tear or cut them as needed, adhering pieces with appropriate glues, pastes, or other materials. Some works have additional painting or drawing added; others make use only of the collaged materials. The finished pieces are usually framed under glass or Plexiglas. They are exhibited in galleries, shops or shows for sale by the artists or their agents.

Conceptual Artist

Concept art is a style of expression in which the artists reveal their ideas (concepts) of proposed works of art in verbal or diagram form. The actual works may never be carried out. Conceptual artists work with galleries, museums or art publications to present their ideas in non-traditional ways, because their products (concepts) cannot be sold or displayed, since they are only ideas. They may have explanations printed or diagrammed, and these might be for sale or posted in galleries or other display areas. Some conceptual artists may rent space to make their presentations, or they may simply use space in a park or other public area.

Craftsperson (See Crafts)

Educator/Teacher/Instructor (See Art Education)

Environmental Artist/Earth Artist

Environmental art or earth works are large formations of moved earth, excavated by artists and best viewed from high vantage points. Artists use earth moving equipment to create their designs, often in deserts or other uninhabited places. The formations are not made to be permanent, but are intentionally allowed to erode and change. Photographs are taken of the construction processes and of the erosion or deterioration processes, and these can be sold to help cover the costs of production. Some environmental artists use plastic sheeting or other fabrics to wrap, drape or otherwise change the surfaces with which they work.

Foundary Worker

Foundry workers help prepare molds and cast sculptures in various molten metals. They may not be trained as artists or sculptors, but work with sculptors in developing three-dimensional products. Some foundry workers work only on sculptures; most spend the majority of their time on utilitarian casting. Some foundries specialize in casting art objects, and are set up by artists who employ other artists to do the mold making and casting for them.

Framer

Framing protects and preserves paintings and drawings, and makes them presentable for exhibition and sale. Framers work with artists, galleries and museums to design, construct and finish frames for them. They must know how to cut and join moldings, prepare liners, cut mats of all types and put together frames which enhance the works of art and preserve them properly. Some framers buy all their molding in finished condition, others finish their own and even prepare, stamp and finish elaborate relief decorations for the frames. Production framers and wholesale framers work on large orders for galleries, print sales representatives, photographers and frame suppliers and dealers, while custom framers give each painting individual attention.

Gallery Owner (See Art Galleries)

Kinetic Artist

Kinetic sculptures are three-dimensional constructions of varying sizes that have moving parts. Some kinetic artists use air currents or gravity to cause movement; others employ motors, solar cells, computers, electricity or other means to move segments of their pieces. Kinetic works are sold in galleries or are placed in museums or public places. Kinetic artists are sculptors whose main interest is movement.

Master Printer

Master printers are printmakers who are expert in certain printmaking techniques, and who produce images for other artists. They work in their own studios or for large printmaking studios, taking the prepared plates, blocks, stones or screens that other artist-printmakers have developed and executing the actual prints for them. They do not number or sign the works, but simply do the physical work of making the images.

Medalist

Medalists are sculptors who work in relief, and make the original sculptures from which medals of all types are cast. They carve in wax to prepare their master copies, from which molds are made and copies are cast. Their work is usually done to commemorate an historic event or the life of an important person. Medalists must be adept at making portraits, figures and lettering in shallow space, and in extremely fine detail and small size.

Mold Maker

Mold makers are craftspeople who make plaster, latex or other types of molds in which sculptures or medals are cast. They provide indispensible services for sculptors who work with bronze or other metals in their castings. If there are to be many copies of the original, the mold must be designed for repeated use. For limited editions, separate molds are often made from the original work for each casting. The complexity of the mold depends on the cuts, undercuts, surfaces and planes of the original model.

Muralist

Muralists are fine artists who produce frescoes or images on walls in oil, acrylics, latex paints or other media. They work by commission, which means that a corporation, individual patron, government agency or architect pays for the work to be done as assigned and required. The selected artist prepares a small-scale rendering of the proposed work, designed to fit a predetermined space. When the design is approved, contracts are signed, some advance payment is made and work begins on the site. Some murals are painted in artists' studios (on canvas or panels) and transported to the final location for installation, but most are painted directly on the wall.

Papermaker (See Other Careers in the Crafts)

Ansel Adams is known around the world for his dramatic landscape images, particularly of Yosemite. *Half Dome, Merced River, Winter Yosemite Valley* is a 1971 silverprint. Photograph: The Detroit Institute of Arts, Michigan State Council for the Arts Exhibition Fund

Photographer Of Fine Art (See Other Careers in Photography)

Portrait Artist

Portrait artists specialize in painting likenesses of the human form, whether full figure or facial. They expertly reproduce recognizable features and characteristic gestures, positions and attitudes. They attempt to capture the character of the sitter and express it in the finished work. Portrait painters are still in demand today, although photography has taken over the field to some extent.

Quick Sketch Artist

These artists use pencils, charcoal, pastels or other media to sketch quick portraits, often emphasizing the subject's best or most pleasing features. Quick sketch artists are often employed because of their novelty by theme parks, malls, recreation companies, circuses or fairs. Sometimes free-lancers set up easels in shopping malls or other areas with the consent of the managers.

Teacher/Instructor (See Art Education)

Teacher, Private

There are many fine artists who supplement their art income by giving private lessons. They may teach in their own studios, go to public locations to teach or conduct workshops while painting on location. Some teach individuals, others work with classes. These classes or lessons can be informally presented, or conducted just like those in art schools or colleges. Private teachers usually teach only their special interest, such as watercolor, oil, figures, portraits, landscapes, printmaking or sculpture.

Workshop Artist

Some artists supplement their regular gallery income by teaching in workshop situations. They travel from one location to another, teaching in studios or craft centers. For some artists, these workshops become their primary source of income. Some arrange their own workshops while others let workshop coordinators do all the publicity and preparation work. There are workshops that are centered around media (watercolor, collage, oils), subject matter (landscapes, portraits, figures, still life), design or location (Italy, New England, Carmel). Advertisements for such workshops can be found in *American Artist* magazine and other art publications.

Workshop Coordinator (See Art Program Director, Other Careers in Art Education)

The husband and wife team of Gertrud and Otto Natzler have long produced ceramic work of museum quality. Their glazes (such as this white matte glaze with copper reduction spots) are the envy of most professional potters. *Bowl*, gift of the Rose A. Sperry 1972 Revocable Trust. Photograph courtesy Los Angeles County Museum of Art

Cultural Growth and Enrichment

Crafts

Crafts are the original art of humanity. The baskets, bowls, weapons and beads of ancient peoples were the functional, utilitarian forerunners of today's product design. Craftspeople use their highly trained hands and eyes to produce aesthetically pleasing designs and objects—some practical, some of which are considered fine art. In Japan, such superb craftspeople are honored with the title *Living National Treasure.*

The crafts generally include work in ceramics, fibers, glass, metals, mosaics, wood, plastic and jewelry. As in the fine arts, there are wide ranges of abilities and skills in all these areas, and few crafspeople can make their livings by designing, producing and selling their own handmade crafts. Many teach crafts in schools, universities and craft centers, while others hold down other jobs and may work at their crafts in their spare time.

Art schools, craft centers and colleges with craft programs can provide the background and experience necessary to get a craft career started. The best practical experience is obtained through apprenticeships, during which developing artists study and work with master craftspeople. In such situations, business and creative skills are taught simultaneously. (Read *Apprenticeship in Craft,* by Gerry Williams, published by Daniel Clark Books, Box 65, Goffstown, NH 03045.)

Those interested in crafts careers should keep up-to-date on what is happening in their fields by reading such crafts magazines as *American Crafts, Ceramics Monthly, Fiberarts* and *Glass Magazine.* It is important to join craft organizations on local and state levels and visit crafts exhibitions, fairs and festivals. Craft magazines will list the times and places of such activities. Some books can also help acquaint students with career possibilities. (Check the bibliography for some available titles.)

A good art school, college or university art department expects artists to study more than their own specialized crafts. In early years students enrich their background with classes in drawing, painting, sculpture, art history and design. These classes encourage creativity and allow students to experience a wide range of aesthetic and practical problems and solutions. Craft students are also encouraged to work in other craft areas to gain an appreciation of the breadth of the field and to deal with form and texture in a variety of materials and techniques.

Craftspeople need not have college degrees; buyers are interested only in the quality of their products. But if craftspeople must supplement their craft income by teaching, they will need teaching credentials or a degree from an accredited school.

Artists can make livings at some crafts in commercial situations. Studios which specialize in ceramics, weaving, stained glass, mosaics and decorative wrought iron are several examples. There, craftspeople can improve their production techniques and make comfortable livings, but are not able, in most cases, to produce work of their own design. Instead, they must produce whatever goods the studio is making in production runs rather than one-of-a-kind, individual items. Such situations, however, allow artists to continue to work at their techniques and skills and create their own designs in their free time.

Craft shows, fairs, parking lot and studio sales are good places to sell individually crafted works. Regional and national competitive exhibitions often award prizes for the best work submitted. Being accepted into such shows or winning prizes awarded by nationally recognized artist-jurors helps establish a craftsperson's reputation and makes his or her work more valuable.

The work of top craftspeople is placed on a par with other fine art when it is recognized for its distinctive style and technique, and when it is in sufficient demand as to allow the craftsperson to make a living from its sale. Only a few craftspeople ever reach such stature in the art community.

Ceramist

Ceramists, also called potters or clayworkers, are artists who work with clay of various types. They may work as fine artists, producing one-of-a-kind pieces, or as production potters, turning out certain types of ware in quantity, and working for a large company or individual owner. Ceramists work with clays, terra cotta, stoneware or porcelain, and use such techniques as wheel throwing, coiling, slab construction or modeling. They may decorate their work with glazes, stains, engobes, surface reliefs, decals or by painting. Some artists make utilitarian objects, while others create sculptural forms which are aesthetic rather than practical.

While machinery now produces ceramic ware such as plates, cups and saucers in huge quantities in large factories, there are still many ceramists who work the clay with their hands, shaping it on a wheel and decorating their ware just as potters have done for centuries.

Nearly all art schools and colleges have ceramics departments which graduate clayworkers by the hundreds each year. These ceramists produce thousands of pots, bowls and other items for the highly competitive ceramics market. Galleries and shops of all sizes carry their work, and it is also sold at craft fairs, studio sales and sidewalk and mall exhibits. Such an abundance of work and opportunities to buy it keep prices low for most ceramic work. Better ceramists, with established reputations, some awards and a large clientele, may command higher prices for their work. There are several fine ceramists whose work sells in prestigious galleries and is considered fine art.

Excellent potters develop individual styles and decorate their ware with glazes they develop themselves. These characteristics add to the value and desirability of the work.

Ceramists need years of training in school to master the techniques of working with clay, formulating their own clay bodies, developing glazing and decorating techniques and creating new glazes. They can either work as an apprentice to a master potter, work in a production situation or start out on their own.

What ceramists do

Regardless of the style, size or use to be made of the clay piece, the basic procedures of all ceramists are much the same. They first conceive the idea, form and design of the piece, then build it or throw it on a wheel, decorate, glaze and fire it appropriately, and finally sell it.

The ideal of most ceramists is to have their own studio and kiln, and a ready market for all the work they produce. They are self-employed and must be disci-

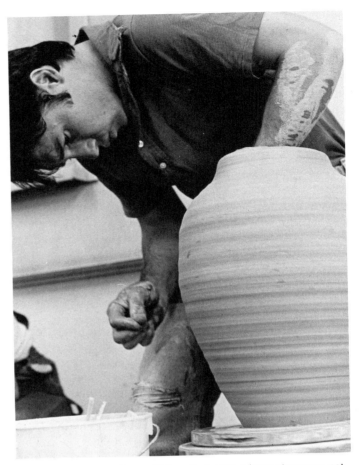

A student at Brigham Young University throws a large stoneware pot on his wheel. He first pulls the clay up, making the sides thinner and the form taller. He then shapes and trims the piece before putting it in the damp room for partial drying. Photograph: Mike Lee

Cultural Growth and Enrichment

plined enough to continue production and experimentation, and maintain gallery contacts and accurate records. Ceramists who have established their reputations usually have several outlets for their work (galleries, prestigious craft shops, department stores and the like).

The work of most successful ceramists has something unique about it. It may be size, form, use of glazes, type of clay, finish or overall appearance. These unique qualities make the pieces more valuable and more in demand by collectors and the public. There are hundreds of potters making similar objects; the challenge to any ceramist is to make his or her work stand out.

The top ceramists are fine artists who have followings for their work, gallery openings for their shows, invitations to be jurors and acceptance by the museum community.

What qualities are helpful for a ceramist?
They must enjoy working with their hands, and all the processes from concept development to opening and unloading the final kilns must be of vital interest to them. They must be self-motivated, not only to continue producing work, but to expand their ideas and range of expertise.

Ceramists must be constantly aware of their competition and any developments in their field. They must enjoy the chemistry of glazing, analysis of chemical formulas and the physical work of production. They must keep the commercial aspects of their craft in mind, and be creative and imaginative enough to make their work distinctive.

Ceramists must produce the required ceramic products and styles in time to meet outlet deadlines. Often this takes away from time for experimentation, but like artists who paint for galleries, they must satisfy such commitments before satisfying their own professional curiosity.

Ceramists therefore must work on schedules which are developed and refined over the years. Throwing, decorating and glazing are timed to meet kiln schedules and eventual shipping deadlines. Most ceramists have assistants (apprentices, husbands, wives or secretaries) who can handle the reams of time-consuming paperwork that most artists face.

New techniques such as photo imagery and decal experimentation should stimulate a ceramist's interest and motivate him or her to experiment. Learning to throw a pot on the wheel must be just the beginning of a long learning process for the successful ceramist.

What other careers require similar qualities?
The qualities of self-discipline and motivation are required of all fine artists and craftspeople who work in their own studios and set their own production pace. The enjoyment of working with one's hands and developing working processes and procedures is common to all the crafts and to model builders, toy designers, sculptors and other fine artists.

The ability to work with chemical formulas can be of use in careers in companies which produce ready-made glazes or paints for industry and craftspeople. Ceramics teachers are hired in junior high and high schools and through college and graduate school. Teaching also allows craftspeople to use institutional kilns and other equipment to produce their own work.

What can be done now?
Ceramics classes in high school are absolutely essential, as are design, drawing and painting courses and an art history class. Chemistry and physics are important to an understanding of glaze formulations and kiln construction and operation. Business and English classes can make a crafts career, especially an independent one, easier and more enjoyable.

Visit museums to study clay objects from past cultures, and the work of contemporary potters. Try to study the work of potters in the best galleries and notice what makes their work better than average. Visit craft fairs and festivals to see what is new every year.

Join crafts organizations if any are available. Take Saturday or scholarship ceramics classes whenever they are offered. Check local art schools or colleges for schedules. Ask your ceramics teacher about possible job openings, shows and exhibits. If there are production ceramics factories nearby, part-time work would help you understand their procedures and techniques. Magazines that can provide you with insights into claywork and new techniques include: *Ceramics Monthly, American Indian Art, American Craft, Studio Potter* and *Ceramics Review* (England). Sometimes useful articles on ceramics appear in *School Arts, American Artist* and *Art in America*.

Which colleges offer necessary programs?
Almost every college, university and art school has a ceramics department which will offer the courses necessary to prepare for a career in this craft. Those with an established or renowned ceramist on the staff, however, can offer considerable practical information, advice and personal insights into successful, productive careers.

Jewelry Designer

Human beings have considered the creation and ownership of jewelry a source of pleasure and a sign of wealth and status for thousands of years. In nomadic societies wealth was carried with the owner in the form of belts, buckles, fibulas, bracelets, necklaces, rings, earrings, pins and medallions since he or she had no permanent home where treasures might be kept. Stones and gems of high value were caged or mounted on rare, expensive metals and were crafted by designers who were honored for their abilities.

Today, jewelry and personal adornments of all types continue to be designed and constructed by jewelry experts. Some tools and techniques have changed over the years, but jewelry design remains primarily a hand-wrought craft.

Students who major in jewelry design in college will study, among other things, the design and drawing of jewelry; principles of casting, wax carving, and gemology (the study of gems and stones); chemistry; diamond grading; jewelry design trends; soft jewelry design and metalsmithing. This career area is very specialized and designers must make use of special equipment, techniques and materials.

A jewelry major may eventually become a self-employed jeweler or designer; a designer, casting technician, chemist or metalsmith in a jewelry manufacturing company; a costume jewelry designer, production worker or executive; or an employee of a company that manufactures such items as watches, belts, buttons, and class rings.

What jewelry designers do

After years of study and work, jewelry designers have mastered the many processes necessary to jewelry design. They know how to form and shape metals, treat and finish surfaces, cut and set gems and stones and work with plastics, wood, bone, ivory and found objects. They understand the hundreds of tools and the various materials and supplies needed to carry out their design ideas. They have studied design and are able to construct the jewelry as they have envisioned the design in their initial planning.

Jewelry designers generally follow a three-step process: design, construction and finish. Whether working on a single, unique piece or one that will be turned out by the thousands, the designer must first conceive the idea and draw it on paper, usually from several angles. When the idea is formulated and approved, the design is executed from the chosen materials, using the appropriate

Working at his bench, jewelry designer François Schneyder employs numerous tools and materials to create a unique bracelet design in silver. Photograph: Andrew Farie

tools. When completed, the surfaces of the materials are treated and textured according to the original design idea, and are finished to the desired luster.

Jewelry designers may carry out their own designs from concept to finish, or they may work on commissioned pieces. For example, a customer may ask the designer to make a man's ring using an Egyptian scarab and several pearls placed in a gold setting. Jewelry designers would usually rather create from their own designs, but they often take commissions to help establish their reputations and attract a steady following.

Workers in large jewelry manufacturing companies may only be involved in one or two of the processes, at which they become experts. Individual craftspeople are generally involved in all the processes, including the design.

What qualities are helpful for a jewelry designer?

Jewelry designers must be very organized, and able to work effectively with an incredible number of tools. Jewelry designers, like other craftspeople, must enjoy working with their hands, usually on very small pieces which involve great detail and extreme care.

The materials they use are usually quite expensive, and must therefore be handled carefully. Waste is almost unthinkable, although metals can be reused in most cases.

Jewelry designers must find and maintain excellent

and reliable sources for their materials and tools. They must keep abreast of current trends in body ornament and design while also making use of classic styles and adaptations.

They usually work on small pieces in a confined space and must feel comfortable in such situations. They must accept the fact that competition is fierce, and that there are many creative designers producing excellent work all over the country.

What other careers require similar qualities?

The process of design/construction/finish is typical of most of the crafts, although few besides jewelry involve work on such small pieces. The ability to carry out an idea or design is essential in working with metals of all types, as well as woods, fibers, plastics and ceramics.

Organization and attention to detail are required of industrial designers (See Industrial Design), woodworkers, some graphic designers (See Graphic Design), and in architecture.

Interest in jewelry may be transferred to careers in fashion design, consultation and sales, wholesale representation, showroom management, market assessment and the like.

Interest in gems and stones may lead to careers in selling, selecting, cutting and polishing them for industrial or individual clients. The ability to work with metals could provide career opportunities in industrial design, metal fabrication, model building, foundry work, sculpture or ornamental ironwork design or construction.

What can be done now?

High school students should take drawing and design classes, jewelry classes if available, and should add sculpture, ceramics and three-dimensional design courses when they are offered. Chemistry and physics will make process and materials easier to understand, and art history and history classes will provide historical contexts for jewelry and all the crafts. Classes and part-time work in which any types of tools are used will help students become aware of their abilities and aptitudes in these areas. Join jewelry clubs and find out about gem societies in your area.

Take high school scholarship classes in jewelry methods and production if they are offered in art schools and colleges. Go to museums to study ancient and contemporary jewelry design and techniques. Study jewelry in books and magazines and visit local crafts and jewelry shops and craft fairs to see what is being done.

Some magazines that are helpful to jewelry makers include: *American Indian Art, Ornament, Metalsmith* and *The Lapidary Journal.*

Helping teach crafts in summer schools, workshops and camps provides good experience in working with tools and teaching others what you know of your craft. Some museums may offer jewelry classes from time to time.

Which colleges offer necessary programs?

Some art schools and colleges have extensive jewelry programs and some craft centers will also have excellent departments with experienced teachers who can get you started on a career in jewelry design. Schools which feature strong crafts programs will generally have good jewelry departments and teachers. Check the charts at the back of the book and write to several schools, asking for catalogs that list all courses.

Jewelry design students also study drawing, painting, design and business, so the school you choose should have a good general program in art career preparation.

Like other craft areas, successful jewelry design careers do not depend upon a degree. A wide variety of art courses, however, will provide an extremely important foundation on which to develop your career.

Fibers, Textiles And Weaving

Interest in the design and handmade production of fabrics, textiles and fiber products has greatly increased in recent years. The revival of interest in handwoven materials, quilting, hand dyeing, screen printing, knotting and embroidery has also triggered renewed interest in textured, unusual machine-made fabrics. Although craftspeople are most interested in unique, hand-worked materials, knowledge of fabric and its production might also lead to careers in commerical textile industries.

Craftspeople are concerned with both traditional and innovative approaches to color, texture, design and processes. Pattern development, weave systems and drafting are processes that must be mastered. Contemporary artists work with mixed warps and wefts, eight harness rug and tapestry techniques, lace weaves, three-dimensional fiber forms, double warp weaves, appliqué, stitchery and quilting. Both loom and off-loom techniques are employed by many designers.

Besides actually weaving the fabrics, some designers decorate existing fabrics in unique ways, either producing textiles for themselves to use, exhibit or sell, or decorating it according to a customer's specifications.

Fiber art is not confined to utilitarian products. Uniquely crafted fabrics are exhibited in galleries, international art shows and museums in the form of wall hangings, sculptures and costumes.

Antonia Cosentino uses a two-harness tapestry floorloom and designs as she weaves, without a sketch or cartoon. She dyes her own yarns to get the exact colors she wants, and creates abstractions and pieces with landscape features. Photograph courtesy Antonia Cosentino

What textile and fabric designers do

Although all artists develop their own ways of working, the general fabric design process includes designing, making the pattern, setting up the loom, weaving or decorating the fabric and mounting the finished work for presentation. Some designers, like some oil painters, work without designs, sketches or patterns, but most establish some guidelines to follow.

Some artists do all the work that goes into fabric-making: they gather the wool, card, spin, dye and weave it. Others wish only to dye their yarns, and still others may prefer to use prepared and dyed yarns in their work.

Because of the broad range of individual expressions and techniques used by weavers and textile workers, no attempt will be made to relate how each one works. See the illustrations for several examples.

Stitchery, appliqué and other add-on techniques may be used to design fabric wall hangings and displays. Looms are often used for tapestries and creative treatments that require detailed drawings, called "cartoons," to insure correct placement of the illustration's colors, lines and textures.

When the fabrics or fiber designs are ready for sale, they are displayed in craft stores, galleries, museum shops, at craft fairs and sidewalk art shows. Boutiques, exclusive shops in malls and unique apparel stores often handle the work of respected craftspeople. Such work may be in fabric form, sold by the yard or piece, or may be finished clothing made from original fabrics.

Craft galleries, like painting galleries, often take work on consignment, and pay the designer an agreed-upon percentage of the sale after it has been made (See Art Galleries). Many craftspeople have sales in their own studios once or twice a year. Most weavers and fiber artists belong to associations or clubs which have sales and put on fairs, shows and exhibitions which become outlets for sales.

As in the case of fine arts painters, most weavers and fiber artists must supplement the income from their craft sales with income from another job. Many craftspeople teach their specialty in schools, workshops and craft centers, or give private lessons in their studios.

What qualities are helpful for fiber and textile artists?

They must have a good sense of design and color and enjoy working with yarns, threads and fibers of all types. Because most fiber crafts require a long time to complete, the artists must be patient and able to concentrate on their work for long periods.

Like other fine artists and craftspeople, fiber and textile artists must be self-motivated. They work alone in their studios, and must produce high quality work to sell.

Most of them must be satisfied to sell only a small amount of their work; they should be prepared to hold another job and work on their fibers in their spare time.

Fiber artists visit craft shows, exchange ideas, take or teach workshops and try to remain knowledgeable about their fields, because new innovations and materials are constantly coming into use. They must enjoy textile processes and must anticipate competition. There are many fine designers producing quality materials for sale.

What other careers require similar qualities?
Many of the crafts and fine arts careers require self-discipline, long concentration spans, alertness to developing trends in the field and the desire to maintain a creative atmosphere in the studio.

An interest in working with fabrics and textiles may lead to careers in fashion design or interior design, where fabrics are used for practical purposes. Wall covering designers often need custom-designed fabrics for specific areas, and must therefore have considerable knowledge of fabrics and their production.

What can be done now?
To obtain as broad an art background as possible, students should take all available art classes, especially drawing, painting, design and printmaking. If fabric or crafts classes are available, they should also be scheduled, as should art history, English, physics and history classes.

Check with local museums to see if they have collections of fabrics, fashion or stitchery for you to study. Check on the availability of classes on fabric or fibers at museums and recreation or craft centers.

Visit craft galleries to see what local artists are doing, and see if you might visit their studios to observe them at work. Perhaps you could get part-time work helping such artists with routine chores.

Public libraries usually have substantial collections of crafts books or books that specialize in fiber work or fabrics. Some magazines that are of interest include: *Fiberarts; The Flying Needle; Handwoven; Needle Arts; Quilter's Newsletter; Shuttle, Spindle & Dyepot; Surface Design Journal* and *The Textile Museum Journal.*

You may also join national organizations, such as the Handweavers Guild of America, the Embroiderer's Guild of America or the American Craft Council. See addresses in the appendix.

Which colleges offer necessary programs?
Schools with good crafts programs generally offer essential courses in fibers and weaving. Some craft centers (Worcester, Massachusetts and Brookfield, Connecticut, for example) have excellent programs. Get catalogs from colleges (See charts at the back of the book) and check on the fiber, weaving, fabrics or textile emphasis of each one.

You can design and produce exciting fabrics without a college degree. The tools, experiences, materials and breadth of courses available at art schools and universities will give you a well-rounded background, however, and will stimulate your creative development.

Other Careers In The Crafts

There are many thousands of craftspeople at work in their studios around the world. Some make comfortable livings by selling their work, but most work at other jobs and pursue their craft interests in their free time. There are hundreds of different craft techniques that vary only in detail. Several are briefly described here.

Appliqué Artist
Appliqué artists make decorative pieces by stitching shapes of colored cloth to cloth backgrounds, thus creating their designs. Appliqué can also be used in working with paper, (where it is called découpage), and with metals.

Basket Maker
Basket makers use cane, rushes and other fibers to make plaited or woven objects. They produce baskets, boxes, animals, masks and other three-dimensional forms.

Batik Artist
Batik artists use waxes, dyes and various tools, needles and brushes to create designs on fabrics. The applied wax acts as a stencil which prevents areas of the cloth from being dyed.

Bookbinder
Bookbinders assemble and produce handmade books. They cut, trim and stitch special papers, leathers and other materials to produce books that are unique, and possibly collector's items. They often bind new books, but also repair rare and valuable editions.

Candlemaker
Candlemakers use wax, colorants and textural materials to make both utilitarian and complex, decorative candles. Some are factory-made in quantity, while others are unique designs in wax.

Cloissoné Artist

Cloisonné work is a technique in which thin fillets of flattened wire are set on edge and attached to basic metal shapes. The cloissons (or cells) between the wires are filled with enamels, colored ceramic pastes, glass or stones which are fired, fused and then ground and polished smooth. Finished work may take the form of boxes, jewelry of various types, vases, napkin holders or other utilitarian or decorative products.

Commercial Potter (See Ceramist)

Découpage Artist

Découpage is the covering of an object's surfaces with cutout paper figures or designs. It might be considered collaging on three-dimensional surfaces.

Embroidery Worker

These craftspeople use needles and colored threads to embellish or decorate fabrics with raised designs. Usually the designs are placed on finished clothing or tableware, and the workers follow predetermined patterns and designs (See also Stitchery Artist, below).

Enamelist

Enamels are powdered colored glass, porcelain or ceramic glaze materials that are fused to metal bases or ceramic pieces by heating them in a kiln. Many enameling techniques (See Cloisonné, above) are used in the production of jewelry and art objects, but similar techniques can also be used in the creation of wall decorations and other crafted objects. Some enamelists also work on glass.

Furniture Maker

Furniture makers and designers work on individual pieces of furniture from concept to finished product. They design the piece, select the woods and metals of which it is made, form, finish and polish it. They are master artisans who make single, unique pieces, can duplicate antiques or make multiple sets (such as chairs) for their customers. They often work on commissions for special clients, interior designers or architects.

Gem Cutter (See Lapidarist, below)

Glass Artist

Glass artists are craftspeople who make one-of-a-kind pieces for exhibition and sale. They use such traditional glass techniques as blowing, forming, decorating, coloring and finishing, but produce unique work by varying the application of those techniques. The need for specialized kilns and tools has made this field less competitive than ceramics. Museums and galleries mount shows for glass artists in many parts of the country.

Glass Craftsperson

Commercial glassware companies need many specialists in various areas of glass production. Here is a partial list.

A glass blower removes a glass blob from the kiln and blows air into it through a long tube. The resulting hollow forms are made into vases, bottles, stemware, bowls and decorative art objects.

A glass decorator cuts or etches designs in all types of glassware. He or she uses acid solutions or sandblasting equipment to develop the patterns and designs of other artists.

Glass engravers use stone, copper and steel wheels to engrave designs, initials or pictures in glassware.

A glassware finisher finishes handblown or pressed glassware by forming and attaching pedestals, lips, decorative additions and handles. This task is usually the training ground for blowers, decorators, designers or glass artists.

Goldsmith

Goldsmiths work with gold, its alloys and other metals to form jewelry or art objects. They use specialized equipment and tools to form (pound, shape or cast), connect (solder and adhere) and finish (color, polish and add surface treatment) gold to make rings, bracelets, necklaces and art objects. Many goldsmiths are also jewelry designers.

Lace Maker

Most lace making is done on machines, but there are still artisans who create delicate, beautiful laces to decorate apparel. Creative lace making (known as knotting) may be used to form open tapestries or decorative wall pieces, and may be exhibited in museums and galleries.

Lacquerware Artist

Lacquer is a resin material that is colored and applied in many thin layers on a base form of wood, clay, cloth or basketry. Its hard surface may be carved into intricate designs. Carving lacquered surfaces is primarily an Asian craft.

Lapidarist

Lapidarists, or gem cutters, cut, polish and engrave gems or precious stones. Years of experience are needed to master the complex procedures related to gem cutting. These craftspeople must have precise, technical knowledge of gems and stones, their quality, various cuts and methods of polishing and setting.

Leather Worker

Leather artisans often handle the hides they use from selection, through tanning, treating, toning, graining, cutting, embossing, carving and decorating to finishing. They are familiar with the various grades of leather and know how to treat and decorate it appropriately for use in leather accessories, clothing and art objects.

Macramé Craftsperson

Macramé is a knotting craft that makes use of various tools, fibers and knots to create useful and decorative objects. Body ornamentation, clothing accessories, decorative wall hangings and plant hangers are several typical macramé products. By varying the type and weight of the fibers and the kinds of knots used, elaborate and complex works can be created. They are often exhibited and sold in galleries and craft shops.

Marquetry Artist

Marquetry is a method of decoration in which small pieces of wood veneer, mother of pearl, metal or ivory are inlaid in designs or patterns in a wood veneer or other surface. The work of these artisans is used for table tops, paneling and decorative surfaces on boxes, chests and other items.

Metalsmith

Metalsmiths work in many metals to create jewelry, body ornaments, chains and decorative and functional objects. They use hundreds of specialized tools and study for many years to master the myriad techniques associated with their craft. (See also Jewelry Designer, Crafts, and Goldsmith, above.)

Mosaicist

Mosaic artists work in one of the oldest forms of art in the world. Mosaic designs and pictures are made by setting tessarae (pieces of stone, glass, ceramics, etc.) in a mastic or plaster grout. Several basic methods are used to assemble the finished designs. Today, mosaicists work mostly on murals and wall designs for churches, civic buildings and public areas.

Musical Instrument Maker

Craftspeople who create violins, violas, guitars, lutes and other musical instruments from wood must be masters of their craft, with knowledge of the qualities of sound, tone and resonance. Most instruments are now made in factories, but many craftspeople still take great pride in designing and building quality instruments for important musicians.

Needleworker

Needleworkers employ many types of stitches in techniques such as patchwork, soft sculpture, appliqué, cloth collage, stitchery, embroidery, crochet, quilting, needlepoint, crewel, mola making, reverse appliqué and the like. Needleworkers may design their own work, but also may work on the designs of other artists.

Ornamental Iron Worker (See Other Careers in Industrial Design)

Papermaker

Papermaking is an ancient craft, first developed in China around 150 B.C. Today's papermakers, like those of the past, make paper from the fibers of plants. The fibers are cooked and beaten, and the pulp is formed into sheets, pressed and dried. There are a number of American hand mills in operation which produce custom book papers, stationery and two- and three-dimensional art work.

Potter (See Ceramist)

Puppeteer

Working with puppets of all types (marionettes, hand and rod puppets and the like) is really a form of theater arts, but the design and construction of the puppets themselves is a highly developed craft. Puppet designers, who are often also the puppeteers, use all available materials to make their "actors," but wood and papier mâché remain the most common materials. Puppeteers carve facial features, then build up and paint them; they design, cut out, sew and decorate their costumes. Puppet figures are used in live presentations, for television productions, children's theater and advertisements.

Quilter (See also Needleworker and Appliqué Artist, above)

Quilts are made both by hand and by sewing machine. Many are made using traditional designs and patterns, but contemporary quilters often use free-form designs and often develop their work into soft sculpture. Quilters use many types of stitches and fabrics, but the basic quilting system consists of a "quilt sandwich" with a backing fabric, a batting filler and a top layer on which the design is applied and stitched through the "sandwich."

Rug Maker

Handcrafted rugs are often made as hobby projects, but professional rug makers design and complete custom-designed rugs for clients, interior designers and for gallery exhibitions. The artist's fingers, various needles, latch-hooks and punch-needles are used to tie the many types of knots for different rug styles. Rugs are usually made for floor use, but highly textured designs also make distinctive wall hangings.

Silversmith (See Goldsmith and Metalsmith, above)

Stained Glass Designer

These craftspeople make the original sketches and working drawings (called cartoons) and prepare glass in chunks or sheets for fabrication into windows, art objects or decorative items. They try to make the glass picture or design compatible with the structure for which it is being made, and they work with architects and interior designers in this respect. They must develop techniques for cutting and placing the glass, leading, soldering, painting and finishing, and must understand glass stresses, symbolism, portraiture and ornamental styles. Individual craftspeople can carry out all these tasks in their studios, but in large stained glass studios, artisans may specialize in certain aspects of the total job.

Stitchery Artist (See Quilter, Appliqué Artist and Needleworker, above)

Tapestry Worker

Tapestries are colorful hand- or loom-woven wall hangings with pictures woven into them. Tapestry workers include designers, cartoon patternmakers, loom workers who set up the looms and supervise the weaving process, and the loom operators themselves.

Thrower

Throwers work on potter's wheels to form ware such as vases, bowls, plates, cups, urns and pitchers. They usually are employed by a ceramics studio to produce ware according to a designer's ideas and specifications. They work with pottery and porcelain, and might sometimes create their own designs to be produced as company products.

Tile Decorator

These artisans use silkscreen processes to print decorative designs or lettering on unglazed tile or bricks, which are then fired. The artists must be able to work with serigraph processes and make several types of stencils. The job may lead to design positions in various tile and ceramics companies.

Turner (Ceramics)

Turners shape unfired greenware on special lathes, following company designs and patterns. They work directly with leather-hard clay, before kiln firing.

Ware Decorator

In ceramics factories, ware decorators paint designs on bisque ware prior to final glaze firing. They apply some designs and colors with brushes but may also position decals in uniform patterns.

Ware Dresser

In the industrial ceramics process, ware dressers finish and polish glazed and decorated surfaces, separating the pieces into various grades as they work.

Weaver (Handweaver) (See Fibers, Textiles and Weaving)

Woodcrafter

Woodcrafters produce custom cabinetry, furniture, boxes, gun stocks and office or household items. They must master all techniques for cutting, forming, joining and finishing woods. They often work on entire projects from concept to finished work, although several artisans may often work together in larger studios. Woodcrafters do much of their work by hand (using hand tools) but also must know how to use lathes, all types of saws, joiners, drills, sanders and routers.

Art Education

At first glance, the relationship of art education to fine arts, crafts and cultural enrichment may not be as obvious as the work of sculptors, printmakers and museum directors. But school art programs establish the foundation for a lifelong enjoyment of the visual arts, and art education also encompasses the work of art historians and department heads responsible for entire art programs.

Art education begins in pre-school and kindergarten with painting, drawing and exposure to illustrations and the paintings of past artists. It continues through the grades and into high school, where it becomes more specialized, more concerned with processes and techniques and preparation for college or careers in art. Colleges and art schools help prepare students for the careers described in this book, and provide instruction in art appreciation and art history.

Art education is not an isolated study of certain skills. It gives young children a way to react creatively to their environment; as they grow older art teaches them to appreciate the skills and communicative abilities of others and to enjoy beautiful things. Art education helps art permeate all areas of school and of life. It is a language that enriches the school curriculum and enhances the lives of individuals around the world. The art teacher is the catalyst in this enrichment process and his or her art career can be one of the most rewarding of all.

Historically, art education has swung from one philosophical extreme to another. At some times art courses are slanted toward the practical skills needed to obtain jobs, rather than toward individual aesthetic growth. At other times, "art for art's sake" is education's guiding philosophy, and this generally separates the fine arts as a means of self-expression from the mechanical and industrial arts allied with jobs and business. John Dewey's early twentieth century child-centered education considered experience a major tool in learning, and art offered a variety of valuable experiences.

Students in a painting class learn by painting, but also by listening to an experienced painter and instructor like Richard L. Seyffert. Photograph: Art Students League, New York

Today, art teachers encourage their students to respond as individuals to their environments, and the goal of art teaching is to produce competent, expressive artists who have experience in a variety of artistic methods. Art teachers understand the inherent value of art in the total educational process, its importance to economic and social interaction and its capacity to enrich life.

The teaching of art in elementary and secondary schools can be carried out in several practical situations: the general classroom where all subjects are taught by a single teacher; the specialized classroom where drawing, painting and the like are taught by an artist-teacher; the magnet program, where art is the core upon which other studies in the school are built; the integrated program, where all parts of the school curriculum are infused with art concepts. Regardless of the type of program, the basic components of an art education program are activities which develop perceptual and expressive skills, help students understand their cultural heritage and develop their abilities to make aesthetic judgments.

How these important activities are designed and carried out becomes the responsibility of the art teacher. Much instruction is done in a class setting, but teacher and student may also work out ideas in one-on-one situations.

Art students entering colleges or art schools are faced with important decisions. Education at this level can lead either to an immediate teaching career or to advanced research and doctoral studies. Some students may be interested in art education outside the conventional school setting or may wish to work with special education groups. Some prefer administration, management or the development of art programs and curricula. Museum education, community services, college instruction, research and therapy are some other areas open to career-seeking students. Check the index for descriptions of these career areas as outlined in this book. Familiarity with the many opportunities available in the field of art education, as outlined on the following pages, will help students make these decisions.

Art Teacher (Elementary And Secondary)

Teachers of art open doors to visual communication. Creative teaching is a dynamic process that can change the lives of students, making them visually aware of their environment and the artistic expression of others.

Art teachers must be familiar with all forms of visual expression, have a working acquaintance with all media and a solid foundation in art history. Such a background helps them stimulate young people, sharpen their awareness and open their eyes.

Art can be the most exciting part of a school's curriculum. The magic that can happen in art rooms is both the responsibility and the reward of the art teacher.

What elementary art teachers do
It is not the task of elementary art teachers to make artists of all their students. To teach art is to give children opportunities and experiences that will enable them to understand, record and interpret new information creatively. Teachers help students learn to use a variety of media to express their ideas about the world around

them. Teachers are catalysts in the process whereby children learn to make aesthetic judgments.

Art teachers must develop courses that will satisfy such goals. Every school in the country has a unique physical and social environment; sensitive art teachers must be able to devise courses of study that will meet the individual requirements of each situation.

Once the requirements are clear, teachers arrange projects and lessons in a suitable sequence. These outlines become the art curricula for each school.

Teachers try to give their students as much experience with media and tools as resources and time will allow. How teachers meet this challenge depends on their individual feelings about teaching. Some wish to keep all members of their classes working on the same projects, while others are comfortable with many things going on in a room at the same time. The goals of both kinds of teachers may be the same, but they are reached by different routes.

The teaching of art to young students is a creative career. There are many ways to teach, just as there are many ways to create art. They all involve planning, demonstrating, providing materials, leading discussions, evaluating and displaying the work of the students.

What secondary art teachers do
Many of the activities of elementary art teachers are the same as those of secondary teachers. The profession does not require that teachers turn out a certain percentage of artists, but does call on them to explore with their students as many avenues of visual communication as possible. In addition, secondary teachers are concerned that talented young people who wish to pursue careers in art are given solid foundations and pointed in the right direction.

Secondary teachers also must structure their courses to fulfill certain requirements, usually determined by the school system, district or state. Within certain boundaries, the teachers select media, projects and subjects that will best satisfy those requirements. Secondary courses can be set up in several ways: to expose students to a wide range of art experiences; to specialize in one area in each course and concentrate on processes and media; or to combine the two techniques in some way.

Teachers are often asked to help seniors select work for their portfolios. A knowledge of current trends in art will help teachers keep students abreast of current art activities and choose appropriate material for their portfolios.

Secondary art teachers often stimulate young people to pursue careers in art. Their stimulation helps develop the next generation of commercial and fine artists.

Not all art teaching is carried on in regular school situations. Here, young pupils experiment with alternate ways of communicating visually in a museum's Young Artists Studio Class. Photograph: School of The Art Institute of Chicago

What qualities are helpful in teaching art?

Art teachers at either level must be enthusiastic about sharing their knowledge and skills. Some school districts require that teachers be practicing artists, especially at the secondary level. However, all art teachers should be able to demonstrate and explain a variety of techniques in many media.

Above all, art teachers must enjoy working with young people. Creativity flourishes neither in an atmosphere of restriction nor one of reckless abandon. Teachers must give their students a sense of freedom within certain structured situations. This helps prepare students for the structured situations they may encounter in their future art careers.

Art teachers must also believe that art is a very important part of living, and that it should not be restricted to art classes, but should permeate the school's entire program.

What other careers require similar qualities?

The ability to work with young people and to be able to organize vast amounts of material into relevant courses of study are required in all areas of art teaching: museum education, community workshops and adult programs, painting workshops, Saturday scholarship courses and the like. People who teach in colleges and art schools need similar qualifications and interests, but also need expertise in specialized fields.

Art specialists and consultants (See Other Careers in Art Education), children's book authors and illustrators and writers of student art materials, teachers' art magazines and books are often former school art teachers. Editors of art magazines and employers of publishing companies that deal with children's books would have similar interests.

What can be done now?

Future art teachers should be interested in all art courses available to them. Drawing, painting, printmaking, sculpture, crafts, design and art history will all help you establish a resource-rich background for teaching.

Often students can help at summer arts and crafts programs in recreation parks, camps or schools. Church schools often need summer volunteers and such experiences are excellent places to test your own suitability and interest in art teaching. Jobs in crafts programs for the elderly or for handicapped children are also excellent backgrounds for teaching.

One of the best ways to become aware of the scope of an art teacher's career is to watch your own teachers in class, and try to decide how you would do things under similar circumstances.

Helpful magazines you may wish to buy or check out at your libraries include: *School Arts, Art Education* and many of the crafts magazines listed in Crafts.

Which colleges offer necessary programs?

Most art schools do not stress teacher training in art education. Art teachers should work in two areas of study: education and art. Almost all teacher's colleges offer such programs, as do state colleges and universities that have education departments. Check with your state university, and consult the charts at the back of the book.

Joan Allemand, Art Supervisor of the Beverly Hills Unified School District, discusses the role of masks in various cultures as part of an in-service workshop. Two elementary school art teachers and an elementary school librarian are part of her study group. Photograph: Ken Gelms

Art Supervisor

Art supervisors, also called art specialists, consultants, coordinators or curriculum directors, are in charge of implementing art programs in school districts. Some districts may have two supervisors—one for elementary and another for secondary schools—or they may have single supervisors for all grades, kindergarten through twelve. One or more assistants may handle certain supervisory functions (such as museum-liaison, staffing, curricula, instruction, public relations or new trends), but in smaller districts a single person may take care of all these functions.

Supervisors must be attuned to the continual changes in education, but most particularly they must be aware of developments in art education. They must keep up with career development in all art areas and must be constantly aware of all area art activities, not only those in the schools.

Supervisors generally have been trained as teachers and have had classroom experience. They are interested in administration and the broad aspects of art education, and yet are concerned with the daily progress of the art program in district schools. They must work with supervisors in other subject areas to establish goals and directions for the entire school program. They work with school principals and teaching staff to devise programs to achieve those goals.

What art supervisors do

Art supervisors function at several levels. On the technical level, they are concerned with the administration of art programs: budgets, schedules, in-service training and the best use of personnel and time. These elements of the

career are vital to a smoothly running program and call on the supervisors' administrative skills and expertise.

The next level of supervision is most closely associated with art itself. The supervisors are concerned with classroom teaching, the relationships of teachers and students, the physical environment of the art rooms and the quality of instruction. This means observing teachers in class and making recommendations accordingly. Supervisors should be familiar with teaching methods, child psychology and current trends in art instruction. Their responsibility is to oversee *how* art is taught.

Supervisors also must be aware of *what* is being taught. A fine program contains a wide variety of media and art activities; supervisors must know whether or not such a program is in use. New ideas and media may be tried in pilot programs in one or two schools before introduction to the entire district. Supervisors must evaluate new trends and decide on their suitability for each district. This is the most creative of the many duties of supervisors.

The art supervisor is also responsible for the teaching personnel within the district. Some districts may be too small to have many art teachers; other systems may use general classroom teachers to teach art. Often, art specialists are hired to teach several days a week in each school, rotating from one classroom to another. The supervisors decide on or influence hirings and dismissals. They are in charge of teachers as well as course material.

In order to update teaching procedures, supervisors often organize in-service training programs, in which teachers learn of important changes in instructional methods or are shown new media or techniques. Supervisors may demonstrate such innovations themselves, or may bring in outside speakers from industry, graphic design studios, museums or colleges to demonstrate, motivate and discuss.

Supervisors are ultimately responsible to the school board for the development and implementation of art programs. They are also responsible, however, to the public, and are therefore engaged in public relations: informing parents and the public of the development of art programs in the schools. This is often done by arranging exhibits of student work for public viewing, or by arranging for newspaper or television coverage of special district or local school art events.

Cultural Growth and Enrichment

What qualities are helpful for an art supervisor?

The ability to organize vast amounts of information and to delegate responsibility is essential. Supervisors must be able to set goals and devise programs to achieve them. They must be able to assimilate, evaluate and communicate a wide variety of new ideas and information. They must be able to offer criticism and praise, and to maintain excellent morale among their assistants and teachers. They must be able to work with people at all levels of education, from students and principals to boards of education. They must be able to take charge and bear responsibility for their own decisions and for the work of their teachers.

What other careers require similar qualities?

Any career where supervision, training, organization and public relations are involved would need people with similar qualities. College teachers, department heads, coordinators of museum education programs, college art education instructors, directors of adult programs or recreational arts and crafts programs require similar backgrounds and have similar goals.

What can be done now?

Because most supervisors come from art teaching backgrounds (supplemented by studies in administration), people wishing to follow this career are encouraged to enter art education programs. They must be familiar with as many techniques and media as possible. High school students should take every art course available. Business, English and psychology courses are also important. Summer jobs helping with crafts and art activities in recreation programs, summer camps or church school programs are very helpful.

Some magazines that might give you further insights include *Art Education* and others that deal with media, art history and current trends. See the lists in the Fine Arts and in the Crafts sections of the book.

Which colleges offer necessary programs?

The best schools to attend are teachers' colleges and state colleges and universities with education programs. They will often have upper division courses in the administration of art programs. Studio courses are necessary for a working knowledge of media handling and techniques. Art theory, business administration and educational psychology courses will help prepare one for the multifaceted demands of an art supervision career.

College and Art School Teacher

When we realize that all manufactured goods, decorative work and fine arts are designed and often produced by artists, we begin to understand how great is the responsibility of the college art teacher. The art student's initial professional contact, growing awareness and increasing competence in any area of art are usually developed in college art rooms and studios.

It has not always been so. From ancient times until the seventeenth century, young people wishing to become artists apprenticed themselves to master artists from whom they learned the basics of drawing, color, design and technique. The first art academy was established in France in the seventeenth century. Its teachers, hired by the government, taught what government officials thought was the best kind of art. In the late nineteenth century, American colleges opened art divisions and teachers' colleges began programs to train future teachers in the instruction of art.

Today, college art departments give students a basic foundation in every phase of art. They also teach art appreciation, history and studio classes to students of other disciplines, helping them develop an awareness of the visual arts and their importance. Many schools include business classes in the art program, so students will be able to make intelligent financial decisions in their future careers.

What college art teachers do

College art teachers must have a basic understanding of the entire college art program and must be able to devise courses of instruction that will meet the goals of both the art departments and the schools. Following their own course outlines, they instruct, guide, encourage, critique and motivate their students to the highest possible degree of excellence. This is done both in classroom situations and with individual students. The teacher advises them on their art work, techniques, philosophies and career selections.

College art teachers are also specialists, and are often competent artists in their own fields. Architects, graphic designers, sculptors, stage designers and historians, for example, pass on to students the knowledge they have gained in their own professional careers. Through relationships with their instructors, students begin to choose their own careers according to their personal goals and abilities and the examples and skills of their teachers.

College teachers who are successful professional artists are often encouraged by school administrators and department heads to continue their professional activities. Painters, sculptors, printmakers and craftspeople con-

Drawing professor Edward Boccia gives individual attention to a student searching for the best possible solution to her illustration problem. Photograph: Washington University, St. Louis

tinue to produce work for exhibitions and sale, architects serve as consultants, graphic artists and designers might maintain their own commercial studios. These outside activities allow for personal professional growth and help keep teachers aware of trends in their own fields.

College teachers are often asked to serve on various committees: those that judge the portfolios of incoming freshmen, that decide on new courses or graduate programs, approve new faculty appointments or counsel students on careers. These are important responsibilities which lie beyond the boundaries of actual classroom teaching.

What qualities are helpful in college teaching?

The ability to work closely with students is as essential as the desire to communicate the importance of the arts. College art teachers must have excellent skills in their fields and be able to communicate verbally a variety of ideas and processes. Cooperation with other teachers is essential if the department is to function as a unit. Willingness to change and experiment is necessary in most areas of art, and teachers must be able to cope successfully with the excitement, dynamism and energy of an ever-changing art world.

What other careers require similar qualities?

All teaching and research situations require similar skills. Expertise in special areas is transferable to related art careers such as: counselor, elementary and high school art supervisor, curriculum specialist, government art program advisor, author or lecturer in art, museum researcher and art historian, art publishing consultant, museum docent, art project director and consultant and staff for historical societies or corporate art programs.

Check the index to locate descriptions of these career areas.

What can be done now?

High school students looking forward to college teaching would be wise to develop broad interests in all areas of art, taking all courses available and enrolling in Saturday courses or scholarship classes whenever they are available. Because a college art teacher must be proficient in a specialized area, this area should be carefully chosen. Reviewing the career requirements of any section of this book will help determine what can be done now in each area of interest.

Magazines that may provide more information on specialized areas and on teaching include: *Art News, School Arts, Art Teacher, The Art Bulletin, Craft Horizons, Art In America* and *American Artist*. Consult various sections of this book to obtain magazine titles in specialized career areas.

Which colleges offer necessary programs?

There are no schools which specifically train people to be college art teachers. Art professors come from professional art careers or from educational backgrounds. Some college teachers begin their teaching careers directly upon graduation from college or immediately after earning advanced degrees.

Review the various career areas that interest you. Then consult the charts at the back of the book for schools that specialize in these areas.

Cultural Growth and Enrichment

Using slides of the exterior and the floor plan of Monticello, this art history teacher explains some of Thomas Jefferson's architectural ideas. Photograph: Kent State University

Art Historian

Today, the work of an art historian covers a wide range of specialties and activities, including research, writing, teaching, film production, lecturing and library work in books, films and slides. All these specialties deal with the history of art and the impact art has had on the world's societies. Art historians are concerned with the reasons people have created art and the influences one generation of artists has had on another.

The first art historian was Pliny, a first century Greek scholar, who researched earlier sources to write his history of Greek art. The subject was not studied in depth again until Giorgio Vasari, a sixteenth century Italian, began to write about the painters, architects and sculptors who were his contemporaries. While Pliny thought of artists as craftspeople (like furniture makers), Vasari considered them professionals, the peers of philosophers and poets. With the establishment of the art academies in seventeenth century Europe, art history became a subject to be studied, and has since become an increasingly sophisticated discipline.

Some art history experts write only on early Renaissance art, or study only the art of eighteenth century Europe. Many specialize in the art of an area, a country or a period, while others may call architecture or sculpture their area of emphasis, and specialize within it.

What art historians do

There are hundreds of art books in stores today that are written by art historians to help shed light on art and artists of the past and present. To gain the knowledge required to write such books, these authors must do an enormous amount of research and travel internationally to view original art. Firsthand study provides the most accurate information; the authoritative writing of other historians is second best. Art historians who write must seek out the best sources of information.

The results of an art historian's painstaking research might be dispensed in book form, may provide information for other authors or the background for a film, or may lead to a better understanding of an artist or artistic period.

Many art historians wish to share their knowledge and experience with others, and become teachers. Most colleges have at least one art history teacher on their faculties. Some teach survey courses to the general student population, acquainting them with the major works of art and the principal art movements and styles. Others teach in specialized areas such as Baroque Art, Greek Art or the Art of the Sixties. In these teaching capacities, they are responsible for the transfer of knowledge about art to the next generation of artists and art historians. In smaller colleges or high schools, where faculties are small, art history teachers may also teach studio classes or courses in art appreciation.

A growing number of films based on the lives and works of artists are being made today. Film makers enjoy the challenge of using great visual resources such as art works to create visually exciting documentation, and the work of art historians plays a major role in such productions. The results are shown on art-oriented television stations, public television and in the nation's classrooms.

With the increased interest in art history at all levels of education, there is a growing need for more visual study aids such as slides and filmstrips. Those who produce and arrange these study aids must have art history backgrounds to do their jobs effectively. Slide sets have become the backbone of the art history teacher's instructional materials because they provide students with exposure to all types of art work.

What qualities are helpful for an art historian?

Art historians enjoy art (perhaps having begun as creative artists), and other types of history as well. Considerable study and research is required in this field, so it is helpful to be patient and a good note taker, with the ability to organize researched material into easy-to-understand blocks of facts. Art historians see the value of digging into the past to help understand the present. Because much of the resource material is in book form, and often original writings are in foreign languages, it is necessary to be able to read well, and comprehend what you read. Proficiency in several languages is an asset. Clear, concise speaking and writing will enable others to learn from your study and research.

What other careers require similar qualities?

Any type of historian needs similar abilities. People who work on museum staffs often have art history backgrounds, as do many writers for art magazines and other periodicals that have art features. Researchers, librarians, writers in other areas of the arts (music, dance, drama) need abilities that are similar, but require different technical backgrounds.

What can be done now?

If an art history class is available in your school, take it! General history classes will also give you valuable insights into political and social influences on art and artists. Some districts or schools offer Advanced Placement art history programs, while other districts have arrangements with local colleges whereby high school students can take college courses for credit. Visit museums and galleries of all types to see permanent collections and touring exhibits. Museums offer lectures and classes in various aspects of art history. Read books recommended by your art instructor or school librarian. Study another language.

Magazines that contain information of interest to art historians include: *Art News, Art In America, Artforum, Museum, Portfolio, Connoisseur* and *Arts of Asia*. Check with your own school library, the city library or a nearby college art department library.

Which colleges offer necessary programs?

Almost all schools have some courses in art history, but because the advanced study necessary to obtain degrees in art history is so specialized, only schools with extensive art programs will offer sufficient courses. Check the charts at the back of the book. If a career in art history interests you, it is wise to explore many areas, periods and types of art before specializing. Select a college that seems to fit your individual requirements by writing letters to department heads, asking what art history emphases are available.

Other Careers In Art Education

Art Center Education Director Or Staff Worker (See Art Program Director)

Art Consultant (See also Art Supervisor)
Consultants are school district personnel who suggest programs to teachers but are not responsible for implementation or for the hiring of personnel. Available for consultations at the district offices, they provide new ideas and programs, hold in-service workshops and demonstrate new techniques and teaching methods.

Art Coordinator (See Art Supervisor)

Art Curriculum Director (See Art Supervisor)

Art Program Director Or Instructor (Workshops)
The director makes all arrangements for obtaining students, getting facilities and hiring instructors. Programs may vary from a Saturday printmaking workshop at a downtown workspace to a painting trip to Greece or China. Directors should have a strong interest in art. Experience in the travel industry, and in coordinating schedules and arranging for facilities is an asset.

Directors hire workshop instructors to demonstrate, lecture and critique student work. Because many workshops are done on location (such as an outdoor painting site), the artists must be accustomed to working from nature or on location. Usually the instructors are hired because of their expertise, reputation and artistic specialty.

Workshops and art centers are excellent places for people of all ages to develop their interests in various kinds of art. Often they are sponsored by local art organizations, or are extensions of municipal or state museum or gallery complexes. Others are run by individuals who make all arrangements and advertise for students in art magazines or through the mail. Some centers provide space and personnel for student art competitions and exhibitions, and are thus directly involved with art education programs in the schools.

Art Specialist (See also Art Supervisor)
Art specialists usually have the same general job descriptions as art supervisors, but often specialize in one area, such as primary school art. Hired to teach elementary school art in a district, they may rotate from room to room or from school to school to work with students as their art teachers. Specialists may also be in charge of day to day contact with classroom teachers, helping them develop lessons to teach art to their own students. In this capacity, specialists work directly under the district art supervisor.

Artist-In-Residence
Some schools or school districts establish artist-in-residence programs in which successful and practicing artists are paid to set up studios in schools and work there, just as they would in their own home studios. Students visit the school studios and watch artists at work, to see how they create their works of art, and to ask them questions about careers, techniques and concepts. Discussions, seminars and lectures to students and faculty are usually part of the program, but the artists are often given the freedom of selecting media, subject and type of work to be done. Artist-in-residence programs run for varying lengths of time (from a few days to a year) and are temporary positions. Often the completed work, such as a mural or sculpture, will remain at the school.

Museum Art Education Programs (See Museums)

Photography Teacher (See Other Careers in Photography)

Private Art Instructor
Private art instructors teach one or several art techniques to children or adults in rented space or in their own studios. The teachers are completely responsible for obtaining students, arranging for fees, supplies, models and materials, and for instruction and critiquing. The career can be as simple as teaching two or three students in private studios, or as complex as arranging and teaching watercolor painting to thirty adults at a summer retreat.

Slide Program Or Slide Set Producer/Director (See Other Careers in Photography)

Teacher's Aide
Teachers' aides need not have advanced training in art, but must have a strong appreciation and a desire to help students and teachers in the art classroom. The aides help teachers carry out their work schedules and give individual help to students as they work. Aides prepare work areas, supervise the checking in and out of tools and materials, and help clean up. Often aides are volunteer positions, but in some districts they are paid by the district offices.

Art museums provide space for the display of works of art. Alexander Calder's gigantic mobile is exhibited in the courtyard space provided by architect I. M. Pei when he designed this new addition, the East Wing, to the National Gallery. Photograph: National Gallery of Art, Washington, DC

Museums

In the simplest terms, museums are the custodians of and repositories for art work. They make rare, valuable and famous works available for public study, enjoyment and appreciation.

There is no standard size for a museum. Some are small and may contain only the collections of a single family, as does the Frick Collection, in New York. Others are huge; the Louvre, in Paris, includes the art accumulations of the entire French nation. Some are the recipients of large individual collections such as the Kress and the Mellon Collections, now in the National Gallery in Washington, DC. Many museums start with single major collections and add to the total with museum purchases and the donations, gifts and loans of works from interested people.

Some museums contain collections from a single period, while others may display a cross section of art from all periods of history. Some may exhibit only work from their permanent collections while others allow space for traveling exhibits, exchange exhibitions from other museums or the work of local or contemporary artists.

Museum ownership varies according to the history and purpose of the museum. Some museums belong to nations, states, cities, universities or individual families; others are the property of trusts, corporations or cooperative societies.

The primary and most obvious function of art museums is to show the viewing public the works of various artists, past and contemporary. This, however, is not the sole reason for the existence of museums.

Education is a major concern of museum administrators. Groups of school children and adults can hear lectures, see films and view slide programs that help them understand art, its history and its contributions to world cultures. Some museums also send films and speakers out to schools, conduct museum workshops and classes for children and adults, maintain artist-in-residence programs, train docents (museum guides) and sponsor musical programs.

Restoration and the repair of works of art is another important part of most museum programs. Some institutions have large conservation departments where specialists use sophisticated equipment to detect deterioration in various kinds of work, to analyze present conditions and to repair all types of art work.

Art libraries are important adjuncts to most museums, and the collected books, catalogs and pamphlets are available to staff, members of museum associations, scholars, researchers, writers and, usually by special arrangement, the public.

Besides these activities, which are visible to an interested public, museums must maintain extensive libraries of slides, photographs and written descriptions of all the pieces in their collections. Storage and crating facilities are needed for works not on continuous display. Curators must make room for newly acquired works, and walls must be periodically redesigned. Museum bookshops have art books, slides, pictures, artifacts and original crafts for sale, and some museum programs include rental galleries where the work of contemporary artists may be rented or purchased. Museums also design and print many publications. The larger institutions have writers and graphic designers on staff to publish such catalogs, booklets, books, calendars and members' reports and bulletins. Staff photographers are available to take all the necessary pictures and slides for publications, publicity or reference purposes. Display artists are needed to design and build cabinets, display boxes and tables, podiums and walls, and to arrange lighting and design the displays of work.

Because of the tremendous public relations potential of museums, staffs are kept busy writing about and publicizing many scheduled activities. In addition, museums require security and maintenance crews to insure the safety and care of the works in the collections. Other types of museums, such as natural history and science, also require employees with art backgrounds.

Museum Director and Curator

The size of a museum determines the number of curators on its staff, but there is only one director in charge of each museum's operations. Directors for America's ten thousand museums of various types achieve their positions by climbing to the top of the curatorial ladder.

Curators are usually the most visible of museum personnel, after the director, since they put on shows, supervise installations, purchase new works of art and write essays for catalogs. In small museums, a single curator may be in charge of all exhibitions and the permanent collection. In large museums, there are senior curators, curators, associate and assistant curators for each department. For example, one position in a large museum could be associate curator of Islamic art.

Curators and directors have backgrounds in art history, with emphases on their areas of special interest (such as Islamic, American or European art, textiles, film or prints and drawings). Some may have been painters or sculptors at one time, but most are art historians, knowledgeable about lecturing, research and scholarly writing.

What museum directors do

As their titles imply, museum directors are in charge of the operation, growth and functioning of the entire museum. They have an understanding of all museum jobs and positions, because most have worked their way up through curatorial positions. They are knowledgeable about all areas of art history, although they can rely on the expertise of their curators whenever necessary.

Beside their scholarly achievements (many museum directors hold Ph.D. degrees) they must be skilled in dealing with budgets and finances, on which the public and the board of directors keep a sharp eye. They must encourage donors and patrons to make gifts of art or money to the museum. Directors must also be able to work with contemporary artists, and understand their philosophies, creative abilities and direction. They are often responsible to city or county governments. At the museum, they are completely responsible for the organization of the staff, which may range from a dozen people to many hundreds. Some have assistant or deputy directors to assist in their administrative work.

Museum directors seek donations of important art work to add to their collections or try to raise money to purchase such work. They arrange for financial grants and government assistance. They are the highly visible people who represent the cultural community as well as the museum itself.

What museum curators do

The visual presentations that the public sees are the work of curators. Curators in large museums may be in charge of a single, specialized area, such as Indian art, while in smaller institutions they may be in charge of everything that has to do with exhibitions and displays. Curators are generally art historians who are learning about administration. Their careers often begin in registrars' offices (See Other Careers in Museum Work) where they learn about research, collections, paperwork, insurance, cataloging and administrative details.

Curatorial careers include a variety of responsibilities. They purchase new works for collections, arrange for traveling exhibitions, install displays, work with budgets, write essays for exhibition catalogs, and search out sources such as galleries, auctions, other collections, artists' studios and catalogs of all types for further acquisitions.

They read specific and general art reference materials to stay abreast of developments in their special areas of expertise. Because of a particular specialty, they may be asked to be guest curators at other museums, and be in charge of all arrangements for gathering and mounting special exhibitions and preparing catalogs.

Cultural Growth and Enrichment

What qualities are helpful for museum directors and curators?

Directors and curators are basically involved with art history, and must enjoy the research, study and writing associated with it. The challenge of determining and working with budgets and their restrictions must attract them. They therefore must be able to organize their time, their resources, their physical environment and their schedules to get optimum results.

Because they work constantly with people at all levels of museum operation as well as with the public and civic officials, they must be patient, tolerant of other views and able to communicate effectively and tactfully. They must enjoy working with details, because the more specialized they become, the more detailed their work becomes.

The research and study aspects of their careers are constant. Directors and curators are expected to know all the latest findings and discoveries related to their areas of expertise.

Museum directors (and, to a lesser extent, curators) must be able to associate socially with wealthy patrons and political leaders. They must be especially oriented toward public relations, to enhance the reputation and importance of their museums.

What other careers require similar qualities?

All areas of museum work require people who are interested in art history and in the many tasks associated with operating art museums. Directors and curators of other types of museums require the same dedication to budgets, details, organization and communication.

Librarians (in museums, art schools, universities and private collections) require the same skills in organization, research, writing, study, display and attention to details. They also must know the available literature and how to assist researchers, curators and students in obtaining information.

Curators may wish to become art history teachers or directors of research because of their detailed knowledge in their specialized areas of study.

What can be done now?

In high school, students should take all the studio courses possible, and art history classes are essential. Advanced Placement art history is excellent, if available. Classes that broaden historical interest (European, American and Oriental history) and communicative skills (English, creative writing, and literature) are very important.

Part-time or volunteer work at museums would help develop a feeling for this career area. Such jobs might include working in the museum store, typing, filing and assisting in various departments, and so on.

Visit museums and galleries regularly, noting the way exhibits are arranged, how lighting is treated and how items are grouped and displayed. Take museum classes of all types. Study catalogs. Take out student memberships in several museums. Make yourself familiar with museum operations, because this will put you ahead of job candidates who have not had such experience.

Some magazines that might be of interest to future curators include: *Museum, Art News, Portfolio, Art In America, Museum News, Apollo* and *Connoisseur.*

Which colleges offer necessary programs?

A bachelor's degree is a minimal requirement for starting a curatorial career; a master's degree is preferable. A master's degree demonstrates a job applicant's familiarity with research, writing, study and content. Museum directors should have a Ph.D., although some do not. Experience at all levels of museum work is also very important.

An increasing number of universities offer professional training in museum administration, which includes art history, community relations, exhibition planning and installation, fund raising and business management. Check the charts at the back of the book for *Museum Work,* write for catalogs and look for courses in the areas listed above. Write to such schools for complete information on curatorial career courses of study.

Check also with local museum personnel (director, curators) for their advice on school selection. Some museums conduct schools for training museum workers.

ART CAREER PROFILE

Not all art careers involving museum work develop in *art* museums. There are art careers abounding in all museum work. Frank Ackerman is Chief of Museum Exhibition Services at the Los Angeles County Museum of Natural History, and as such is in charge of a group of artists who are experts in sculpture, illustration, graphic design, display design and construction, mural painting, scientific illustration and so on. Mr. Ackerman's own background is in graphic design, art direction and fine art. But the art realm over which he presides at the natural history museum is a fascinating blend of the arts and sciences.

The captions explain some of the art activities at this museum, but there are others: sign painting, lighting control, design and construction of display boxes and exhibits, facility planning, space analysis, publication design and graphic design, to name a few. Such a museum is a microcosm of the city in which it stands, and the required art services and skills are many and varied.

Frank Ackerman, chief of Museum Services at the Los Angeles County Museum of Natural History, works on a model of a new dinosaur hall, while designer Brian Weber looks on. The space arrangement and placement of exhibits in this remodeled museum area are planned by his staff. All photographs: Joseph Gatto

Illustrations of all kinds come out of the museum's graphic design and illustration studios. Scratchboard illustrations such as these by Mary Butler appear regularly in museum publications.

Museum Exhibition Services

Animals in museum exhibits are cast in fiberglass molds. Experts mount hides on the cast forms, and they are placed in a prepared environment designed to look as realistic as possible.

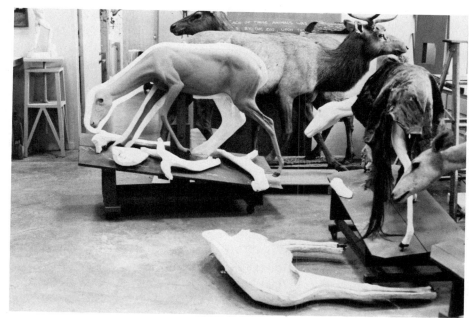

Fiberglass molds exactly duplicate the original clay sculptures.

Conservator And Restorer

Every major museum in the world has a conservation department, staffed with conservators, restorers, computer experts and artists with various specialties. In a private part of the museum these artists analyze, study, authenticate, restore, clean and touch up the works in the museum collections, those recently purchased or being considered for purchase.

These specialists have a deep concern for art history and understand art materials, techniques, media and styles. They use their knowledge of art and sophisticated, specialized equipment to carry out their analyses and their painstaking restorations and reconstructions.

Within the conservation field there are separate categories which require extensive special training, study and practice. For example, in one museum there may be separate laboratories, such as *analysis* (for identification, dating, determining materials), *objects* (for cleaning metal, wood, ceramics and sculpture), *paper* (for protection from insects, mold and fungus, and fumigating, mounting and cleaning), *textiles* (washing, cleaning, restoring, reweaving, redying) and *painting* (for study, restoration, determining media, repainting and reframing).

The conservation department is responsible for authenticating all museum pieces (determining their age, style, history and artists), and also for their care and protection. Each museum piece is scheduled for periodic evaluations to determine any deterioration, discoloring or mutilation. If any piece has suffered detrimental changes, corrective procedures are initiated before the work is returned to public viewing areas.

What conservators do

Museum conservation work is many-faceted. Each work, whether part of a collection or recently acquired, is treated in much the same way. It is recorded by the registrar (See Other Careers in Museum Work) and taken to an examining room, where it is photographed carefully and sent to an appropriate laboratory.

In the laboratory for analysis the work is dated and its materials are tested to determine the best and safest way to treat and clean it. Special equipment used here includes carbon-14 analyzers (to determine age), microscopy equipment and materials testing apparatus. Once the initial analysis is completed, the work is sent to a specific laboratory according to the material it is made of. Here it is handled by specialists who can clean, retouch, reweave, revarnish, repair, treat patinas, dry clean, fumigate and retard mold growth.

Conservators often determine that paintings have been badly retouched in the past, and must now have the

Rosso Fiorentino's work, *Virgin and Child with St. Anne and Young St. John* (1521) is painted in oils on a large wood panel. A museum restorer in-paints a tiny repaired section. Photograph: Los Angeles County Museum of Art

colors from certain sections removed and the entire work in-painted and retouched to bring back its original impact. Many months can be spent working on a single painting.

Besides their continuing processes of restoration and conservation, museum departments are constantly working on new ways to improve their abilities and skills. They now use X-ray radiographic images and computer image enhancement to separate images when two or more works exist on the same canvas or wood panel. Spacecraft photographic systems and image processing equipment are being used to analyze and study ancient works on paper.

Exciting techniques of preservation, such as Plexiglas encapsulation of works on paper may help maintain important paper documents, prints, drawings and notes. Studies are being made on the effects of ozone on art materials and the use of electrets and electrostatic charges to preserve works on paper and eliminate the need for fixatives.

What restorers do

Restoration work plays an important part in the overall conservation of works of art. Restorers become specialists in repairing and restoring works on canvas, paper and wood, works of ceramics, tile, porcelain, metal and wood, textiles, leathers, fabrics and costumes.

Restorers must know their materials well, and usually specialize in a single area, such as paintings. Some restorers are employed by museums but others work in their own studios, doing work for local museums without conservation departments, clients with extensive private collections and the public. They can reweave torn canvas, build up gesso grounds, eliminate worm holes, apply paint in the manner and style of the original artist, and varnish the work and refinish the frame to make it look almost new. This work can only be done after years of study and experience. It is time-consuming, demanding and important.

Restorers sometimes undertake massive projects, like the renovation of the paintings on the inside dome of a state capitol or the complete restoration of an important theater interior. They also are involved with the restoration and reconstruction of architectural masterpieces, temples and monuments.

In the museum conservation department, this polychromed carving from Romanesque Europe is studied with sophisticated viewing equipment before restoration work takes place. Photograph: Los Angeles County Museum of Art

What qualities are helpful for a conservation artist?

Artists who work in any type of conservation and restoration must have extensive backgrounds in art history and in another specialized area. The valuable objects on which they work cannot be entrusted to amateurs.

They must enjoy working in detail, and in spending time at research. They stay abreast of what is happening in conservation departments around the world and must have confidence in their own abilities and skills. A studio background (painting, drawing, ceramics and the like) is essential if they are to understand the techniques and media with which they work, yet they must subordinate their own creative ideas and desires (about painting, for example) and be able to concentrate on the style and technique of the work at hand.

What other careers require similar qualities?

The combination of skills in research, art history, laboratory work and a number of different art media are really unique to this career area. Each skill may lead into other directions, but the combination is not required elsewhere. Conservators and restorers may teach their skills in museum workshops or university classes. Similar abilities and qualities (patience, care, attention to detail, ability to work for long periods at a single project) are necessary in other types of museums, libraries and collections.

What can be done now?

High school students should take all the art history and studio art classes they can, and should include chemistry, physics, history and computer technology. Read art books and go regularly to museums to study styles, finishes, colors and techniques. Take scholarship classes at art schools and check with museums on what classes are available. Get part-time work at museums or galleries if possible.

Magazines that can help you understand this phase of museum work include: *Connoisseur, Museum, Museum News, The Art Bulletin, The Art Journal, Apollo, Antiques World, Technology and Conservation* and *Art and Antiques.*

Which colleges offer necessary programs?

Only a few universities offer programs in museum work (See the charts at the back of the book). Write to them and ask for catalogs which will show you the extent of their course offerings. Check with museum schools (Boston, for example) or ask at your museums about apprentice programs.

Study, research and degrees are essential in this highly specialized career area. Select your college with care. A prime requisite for success in this career is solid training.

Other Careers In Museum Work

All types of museums require the services of artists who are skilled in various design and production techniques. They also need interior designers, space planners, coordinators, teachers, docents, office workers and builders.

Archaeologist
Much of the art from ancient cultures that we see in the world's museums is there because of the work of archaeologists. They uncover and identify the objects that belonged to past cultures in order to reveal and preserve a record of their lifestyles and art.

Students interested in archaeology should concentrate on art and world history, social studies, geography, photography, drawing and ceramics classes.

Art Historian (See Art Education)

Bookstore Manager Or Salesperson
Most art museums have bookstores or museum shops where books, prints, artifacts, slides and craft objects are sold. In larger museums the manager will be on the staff, while in smaller institutions this position may be filled by a volunteer or part-time worker. Salespeople may either be on salary or may be volunteer docents who give their time to help run the stores. This is a career for sales-oriented people who are also knowledgeable in art.

Computer Operator/Programmer
Computers are used in several aspects of art museum operations, such as inventory control, filing, membership, mailings, data storage and retrieval, information on artists and on art work and the technical aspects of conservation and restoration. Those interested both in computer technology and art may find fascinating applications in art museum work. Many possible uses for computers in relation to art museums have not yet been fully explored.

Crate Builder (See Other Careers in the Art Services)

Deputy Director (See Museum Director)

Display Artist/Designer (See also Exhibit and Display Designer, Interior and Display Design)
Display artists or designers design and build the cabinets, boxes, stages, podiums and containers which are used to display various objects in museum collections. They are also responsible for the display lighting and environmental colors and textures. They are concerned both with security and aesthetics when they build, and must be familiar with opaque, translucent and transparent materials (natural woods, metals, glass and plastics). In large museums they work for the institutions, but in small museums the curator will hire outside artists to design and build the required displays. Industrial design or interior design backgrounds are extremely helpful.

Docent
Docents are generally volunteers who take classes in art, study the museum collections carefully and are trained to lecture on special aspects of items in the galleries. They lead tours and explain techniques, styles and periods of art that may be of interest to visitors. Experienced docents often instruct new docents in lecture techniques, painting and sculpture techniques and in the strengths of the museum collections.

Educational Services Coordinator
Educational services coordinators work with museum teachers (See below) in the planning and structuring of educational programs for children, teenagers and adults. This may involve classes, workshops, seminars, artist-in-residence programs, visiting lecturers, films, tours and other learning experiences.

Exhibitions And Publications Coordinator
These specialists coordinate the efforts of curators of special exhibits and the publications staff (writers, photographers, artists, historians, printers and publishers). Together these two departments develop meaningful literature and effective and attractive catalogs. Coordinators may publish definitive studies in cooperation with writers and other museums or work with other coordinators to develop catalogs for touring exhibitions which their museums may co-sponsor.

Film Program Coordinator
Many art museums have extensive film collections which emphasize art and artists or are historically important for the study of film. These specialists work with curators, teaching museum staffs to develop film schedules that are pertinent to current exhibits, classes, workshops or world affairs.

Graphic Designer (See also Graphic Design)
Art museums publish many catalogs, bulletins, newsletters, magazines and books, all of which require graphic design work. Posters are designed and printed to celebrate opening shows, and hundreds of signs and labels are required to guide visitors through the galleries. Large

museums will have their own graphic design studios with an art director and several designers.

Illustrator (See also Editorial Illustrator)
Illustrators provide the museum publications with necessary art work. Some of their work will be technical and scientific (when working with conservators, restorers, publishers) while others may be creative and free in style. They work with graphic designers to develop pamphlets, brochures, catalogs and promotional literature. They may also illustrate some of the display areas, furnishing paintings and drawings for use as backgrounds or explanatory graphics.

Librarian (See also Other Careers in the Art Services)
Large art museums have extensive libraries stocked with art books, catalogs, pamphlet files and specialized writings and materials. They are available to staff members, researchers, historians, graduate students, members of museum associations and occasionally to the public. Their librarians have broad backgrounds in art history and biographical materials as well as the necessary skills in library science. Their work is very specialized and extremely valuable to museum staff.

Liaison With Schools
Large museums usually have a liaison, or go-between, who works with public and private schools in the community, arranging visits and tour schedules for as many students as possible. Some programs may be arranged for special art history classes, while others may be for specific groups of community schoolchildren. The liaison is responsible for getting young people into the museum.

Museum Art Teacher (See also Art Teacher)
Museum art teachers hold classes in the museum's instructional areas. They may teach ceramics, painting, drawing, design, crafts, weaving or mask making to youngsters, teenagers or adults. Their classes are generally oriented toward more experimentation than is possible in the school classrooms, and their programs supplement what city art teachers are doing.

Museum Photographer (See Other Careers in Photography)

Public Relations Officer
People in this office prepare articles and releases for magazines and newspaper features. They work with local papers and national wire services in providing information to the media on museum activities, acquisitions, building programs, installations, exhibitions and the like. They arrange television interviews and press conferences

for directors, curators and administrators to keep the public informed on museum events and developments.

Registrar
Registrars' offices are the nerve centers of art museums. Registrars and assistants assemble and store vital information about every work in all the collections (history, conservation, insurance value, condition, previous history, publications, documentation and photographs). They also track each object's current history (movement from one museum to another, location in the museum, conservation and restoration reports and so on). In their files or in their computers are all the necessary and available information on thousands of pieces of art.

Researcher
These specialists are on call to all other museum staff. They dig into museum records and library holdings to find required bits of information on artists or their work. They may also carry out research for free-lance writers or other museums, using the facilities and materials available to them. Prior to important exhibitions they provide essential information for catalogs and other supportive writings.

Slide Librarian
Most museums have extensive slide collections of work in the museums and of other art subjects. These must be kept in meticulous order and should be available when needed for lectures, classes, seminars or personal study. Often slides of museum objects are available for purchase in the museum book stores.

Writer
Museum programs need writers of all types. Magazine and newspaper publicity is necessary, but more important are the writings for catalogs, bulletins, art magazines, scholarly works, books and other museum publications. Such writers need backgrounds in both art history and creative and technical writing so they will feel comfortable working on various types of museum publications.

Seven artists appear with their work in a group show in this university gallery. Openings for such exhibits bring many people into contact with both the artists and their work. Photograph: Texas A&I University

Art Galleries

While art museums display art work which they own or have on loan, galleries display art work that is for sale. Art galleries are the traditional places to display and sell art. The work of many fine artists will appear in galleries to be sold to collectors, decorators, and people interested in art.

Commercial sales galleries are the most familiar. There are many such galleries in the U.S. New York alone has over five hundred of them. Most commercial galleries are in large urban areas where there are more people likely to purchase fine art. Many are in resort areas, offering vacationers art work to remind them of their trip. Prestigious galleries tend to be located in prestigious parts of the cities, but there are also small galleries in small towns doing excellent business. Galleries tend to cluster together in certain sections of towns, or in certain towns, such as Santa Fe and Taos, New Mexico; Carmel, California; Rockport, Massachusetts or Miami Beach, Florida.

Auction galleries sell art work of all types (as well as other objects) to the highest bidders. Antique galleries often sell older art and craft work. Discount galleries sell prints, copies, imported work and paintings on velvet. Some frame shops have sections set aside to display and sell art, and some art museums operate rental galleries which may benefit certain museum programs or auxiliary groups. There are vanity galleries at which artists rent space to exhibit their work. There are cooperative galleries, operated by several artists who share in both profits and the responsibility for sales, management, staffing and overhead. Some dealers have private galleries which are open by appointment only.

Large galleries may be able to hang two hundred paintings and show additional sculpture or ceramic pieces. Small galleries may be able to hang only a few select pieces. Some galleries can have several one-person shows at one time, while others may have such exhibits one at a time or not at all.

Galleries tend to reflect the personalities and artistic preferences of the owners or directors, and may specialize in certain styles (such as abstract, realistic, experimental or traditional), media (watercolors, oils, printmaking or mixed media), periods (contemporary, twentieth century, art of the 60s or the like), or forms of expression (Surrealist, Impressionist, Expressionist, Minimal Art and so on).

Generally artists leave their work at the galleries *on consignment*. This means the artist is not paid until a sale is made. For all the expenses, experience and work of the gallery staff (overhead, sales force, advertising, brochures and exposure to the galleries' clientele) the galleries retain a percentage of every sale. This amount varies from twenty-five to sixty percent (depending on the artists, the locations and the circumstances) with forty to fifty percent being about average.

Galleries are in the business of selling art to the public. Production and sale of art is a cooperative experience, with the artist producing the work and the gallery making the contacts and sales. Neither could survive long without the other, and in ideal situations there is complete trust between them. Both are in business, however, and all transactions should be handled in businesslike ways. Records, contracts, receipts and checks change hands regularly. These should be done with care for both the galleries and the artists. They are partners in bringing fine art to the public's attention.

Gallery Owner/Director/Art Dealer

In most art galleries you will easily find the owner. Some large galleries have many salespeople, office workers, accountants and a director, but most galleries are small operations. In these the owner is the director and there might be only one or two people on the sales staff.

It is easy to get into the gallery business. All one needs is a rented space and a sales permit. It seems simple enough. Contact some artists and have them bring framed work to the new gallery space. Call on a few ceramists to bring in some work. Buy a few plants, send out the announcements, get a receipt book and wait for the crowds and the sales to begin.

It may be that easy to start up a gallery, but it is not easy to maintain the operation and produce revenue. If it were, there would be a gallery or two on every block. The gallery business is highly competitive and involves much more work than appears on the surface. And it requires enough initial funding to keep the business going for several years, until a steady clientele has been established.

What gallery directors, owners and art dealers do

Gallery directors and owners control all the operations involved in running galleries. They must develop a "stable" of exhibiting artists whose work is sufficiently varied to meet the diverse needs of purchasers, yet similar enough to appeal to most of the regular clientele. This is a continuing process. Artists may leave a gallery to exhibit their work elsewhere, or may cut their production down, while there are always many new artists who desire gallery representation. All are hoping to exhibit with a well-established gallery and gallery directors are always looking for artists who will supply appropriate art work for a long time.

The artists represented by each gallery generally want a one-person show every year or two. To accommodate this, the director must set an exhibition schedule to which both the gallery and the artists must adhere. Prior to the opening of each show, there are many things to be done. Art work is photographed. Brochures and announcements are produced and distributed. Food and beverages are arranged for the opening reception. The art work is delivered and the show is displayed.

There is more work at a show's opening. The director and the sales staff must provide information, make introductions and try to sell the featured art work. The work of well-known artists is sold more easily than that of newcomers. It might rain on opening day, discouraging attendance. The artist's style may have changed. There are countless possible problems.

After the reception the responsibilities continue. The

Hanging paintings and setting and adjusting lights are essential parts of preparing the gallery for an opening reception. Photograph: E. Bruce Howell for The Louis Newman Gallery

director must invite more people to see the work and encourage critical reviews by the newspapers and other media. The show usually will hang for three weeks or more. Sellout shows are infrequent, and most financially successful exhibits are the result of hard work by the director and staff.

While the one-person show is on display, the director must not disregard all the other artists who are represented by the gallery. Visitors may wish to see the work of a certain artist, or may not like the featured artist and may request to see other work. There is constant movement, activity and shifting of art work in a successful gallery.

Gallery directors must then accept and record payments, set up payment schedules, send bills, pay artists, keep inventories and ask for new art work. They must be aware of the latest work of their artists and the needs of their clients, and try to match these for successful sales.

What qualities are helpful for gallery directors and owners?

First of all gallery directors must be astute business people. They are in the business of selling art, not pleasing themselves. They must be very organized, able to schedule events and procedures months in advance. They must be able to operate their offices in efficient and productive ways.

Gallery directors must enjoy talking and working with customers as they purchase art work. Directors must be helpful and informative without being pushy. They must be tactful and sensitive to the needs and desires of the customers.

Gallery directors need knowledge of art and artists, both past and contemporary. They must be dedicated to finding good homes for the work of their artists.

What other careers require similar qualities?
Any sales-oriented careers require the qualities of organization, tact, sensitivity and interest in people. Sales work may include art books, art supplies and products, both retail and wholesale.

Traveling art representatives and agents place art work in galleries around the country. Mail order sales of prints and reproductions of all types may also be of interest. Students interested in gallery management might consider being an art consultant or selling art services to the art community.

What can be done now?
Successful operation of a gallery requires a businessperson who is interested in art. High school students should take all the art classes they can schedule (art history, especially) and should emphasize business courses of all types. Psychology, history, graphic design and English courses also are important. All will help make future gallery operation more enjoyable.

Part-time work in a gallery will help you understand the various tasks involved. Visit many galleries and attend openings. Notice the methods used by successful gallery directors. Collect gallery announcements, posters, brochures and pamphlets and file them for future reference. Attend seminars and workshops in artist/dealer relationships (listed in such art magazines as *American Artist*).

Which colleges offer necessary programs?
There are no formal courses in gallery ownership or directorship. Business courses are most important and most universities or business schools will provide what is needed. A business major and an art minor would be very useful. Some college extension programs have courses which include gallery visits. Seminars and workshops are given by gallery dealers' associations. Learning on the job is the best way to get information for running a gallery. A good business background is more essential than a complete art background.

Auction Galleries

When viewing an auction of art or craft work, the most noticeable person is the auctioneer. This is the person who takes the bids, wields the gavel and finally shouts, "Sold!" Before the auctioneers can do their work, however, staff members spend months gathering, classifying, appraising, authenticating, photographing and cataloging the merchandise.

These specialists come from a variety of backgrounds and interests. While no colleges offer courses in auctioneering, everyone brings to his or her career the personal interests and expertise essential to the operation.

What auction gallery staff do
The auction gallery business has many facets. In small companies, one person may handle several tasks, while in large operations (such as Christie's, Butterfield's Sotheby's) each person is a career specialist in a single specific area.

Auctioneers conduct the sales, announce the bid amounts and control the activities. They close the sales and direct the porters to the highest bidder.

Appraisers set the values on each piece according to current market values, recent sales, scarcity of the item and current trends in the public's interest. They work with the consignors (those selling the works) to establish worth and base bidding prices. Usually they have museum curatorial experience or have worked as insurance appraisers specializing in art.

Department heads secure art work to be auctioned, negotiate potential values and prices, have work photographed, authenticate the historical background, write catalog descriptions, have the catalog printed, and set up the displays. They may travel all over the world to find suitable articles for auction and sale. Most speak several languages so they can negotiate with various owners and potential buyers. Their backgrounds may be in art history, gemology, sales and management of jewelry operations, museum work, curatorship, appraising, insurance or commercial art galleries. There is no regular ladder to climb, but auction galleries obtain the best people to do the vital work for successful selling programs. Department heads preside over such areas as painting, sculpture, jewelry, crafts, silver, antiques and oriental carpets. Knowledge of various styles, media, periods, forms, languages and appraisal techniques is required for each of these areas.

Additionally, large auction systems need office workers, accountants, salespeople and security officers who enjoy art but are expert and efficient in their own work.

There are many specialized tasks involved in an auction. At Christie's East, François Curiel, director of Christie's in America, makes a jewelry sale. Delphine Espy, specialist for silver, holds the necklace while two porters watch. Photograph: Steve Friedman for Christie's New York

What qualities are helpful for auction gallery work?

The various careers require different skills and qualities, but all involved must be expert in their special areas. Because they are often dealing with merchandise of high value, they must be careful, organized, educated, considerate, cool-headed and skillful in handling the objects and the people involved. Check the index for the various career areas being considered, and notice the qualities necessary in each.

What other careers require similar qualities?

By looking over the discussion above, it can be seen that auction gallery careers closely parallel those in museum work, commercial galleries, jewelry sales and teaching. With skills in these areas, an individual might move from one career to another. Someone who does appraisals as part of auction gallery work might establish his or her own appraisal service, for example.

What can be done now?

High school students should take all the art courses and craft classes available, and all the art history they can schedule. Business courses, English, several languages, history and literature all are very important. Attend auctions to see how they are carried out, but remember that a lot of experience in basic areas (such as sales, research, management and museum curatorship) is required before positions in auction firms can be considered.

Some magazines that provide insights into the auction world include: *Art and Auction, The Butterfield Bulletin, Art and Antiques, Antiques World, Christie's Catalogs, Apollo* and *Connoisseur.*

Which colleges offer necessary programs?

There is no special training for a career in auction gallery work, but there is schooling available in all the specialized areas (art history, painting, crafts, museum work, and so on). Check the charts at the back of the book. If a career in auction work is a major goal, it is essential that you become as proficient as possible in a single specialized area.

Other Careers In Gallery Work

There are many specialized careers in gallery work that may be unique to individual businesses. Only general preparations can be made for such positions. The careers described below generally are associated with large gallery operations, or are carried out on a fairly large scale. In a small art gallery, the owner, manager or director probably would do all the required jobs.

Appraiser (See also Other Careers in the Art Services)
Appraisers evaluate works of art, crafts, jewelry and collectibles, placing a current value on them so galleries know how much to charge. Museums use appraisers to determine the insurance value of works in their collections.

Art Consultant (See also Other Careers
in the Art Services)
Art consultants work with clients and galleries. They are employed by clients to locate works of art in galleries or at auctions, and arrange for purchases or rental of such works. They are usually independent businesspeople, working out of their homes or private offices.

Art dealer (See Gallery Director)

Artist's Agent (See Sales Representative, below)

Corporate Sales Specialist
A corporate sales specialist is employed by a gallery to represent it to corporations wishing to purchase art. Corporations may seek art for their private collections or for their offices. Corporate sales specialists ascertain the needs and tastes of the corporation purchasers, gather possible art work and make presentations, usually at the corporate offices. They are salespeople with the special ability to work with corporate executives or their representatives. Specialists in corporate sales may carry out these responsibilities in addition to regular sales work in their galleries.

Exhibit Designer
These people are responsible for the arrangement of art work in the galleries. They analyze subjects, colors and sizes, and they group the pieces to show them to best advantage. In small galleries, the director does this work. In larger galleries, specialists on the staff will plan and carry out an exhibit design, usually arranging for shipment of art work to the gallery.

Exhibit Coordinator For Street Galleries
Coordinators organize and stage street gallery exhibits in shopping malls, parking lots, parks and other public spaces. They maintain files on available artists, arrange for the correct number and size of booths and displays, secure city permits, make all arrangements and send out publicity. For many artists, such exhibits are alternatives to conventional gallery shows.

Gallery Assistants
Many young artists begin careers in art as gallery assistants. They do not sell art, but are responsible for hanging and taking down shows, wrapping work for customers and maintaining the gallery itself.

Large galleries generally employ receptionists who meet the public, answer phones, schedule meetings and the like.

Free-lance gallery assistants may help the gallery plan and develop brochures, announcements or catalogs. They handle the gallery's graphic design needs.

Salesperson
At the heart of gallery operations is the sales staff. Salespeople study the art work in the galleries and learn as much as possible about the artists, so they can favorably represent both to the customers. At times they may be asked to deliver and install works of art in clients' homes or offices.

Sales Representative
Sales representatives (artists' agents) actually operate galleries out of their offices and trucks or vans. They act as wholesalers between artists and galleries far from where the artist works. They represent several artists as they travel to selected galleries around the country. Both the artist and the gallery give part of their usual commission to pay the agent a percentage commission. Such representation allows artists to have work in various and distant galleries without having to travel extensively to check on inventories and sales.

Reporting and Writing About Art

The activities of artists, craftspeople, museums and galleries are of great interest to all those involved with art. Such information is disseminated through magazines, newspapers and books. The people in the art community are avid readers of what is going on in their fields, and the most effective way of keeping up on art around the nation and the world is through written materials.

Writing About Art

There are more art books and magazines being published today than at any other time. Most artists' studios are jammed with things to read. Museums have extensive libraries, and publish bulletins and newsletters of their own. Gallery directors know who is showing in other galleries by reading newspapers and magazines. Art teachers get ideas from magazines and books. There are millions of words written about art and artists every month in most countries of the world, and art writers and authors are the active participants in this process.

Art books
Huge sections of bookstores are devoted to art books which run the gamut from research and analysis to how to draw cats. These books treat such areas as: biography (about artists and their lives), art history (general surveys and books on specific periods, movements, and works of art and architecture), theme books (flowers, landscapes or portraits, for example), textbooks (on techniques, history, drawing, painting and the like), so-called coffee table books (luxurious formats on artists, styles and themes), how-to-do-it books (texts, illustrative, informative, teaching) and how-I-do-it books (artists showing how they make their art).

These books are written by teachers, professional writers, artists, museum workers, researchers and compilers.

They are written for a wide variety of novices and professionals of all ages.

Some companies publish art books for a particular market: schools, for example, or artists, architects, photographers, or for documentation and historical research. The specialties are as varied as the purpose behind the writing.

Art magazines and papers
There are dozens of widely differing art magazines and art newspapers. Some treat all areas of arts and crafts, and are written for a broad market of artists and the public. Others deal with museum topics, antiques, photography, contemporary art movements and galleries, regional developments or themes such as western art, portraits, crafts or animal paintings.

Some art organizations put out monthly papers to inform their members about recent events or legislation. Often these art publications review exhibits, comment on current trends and keep artists abreast of developments in the art world.

All types of art magazines require writers and other staff to put them together.

Bulletins and catalogs
Major museums often produce elaborate local or national monthly bulletins which are sent to contributing members. They contain information on current shows, new exhibits and acquisitions, featured works or artists and museum events.

National art organizations, gallery associations, teachers' organizations, antique dealers and auction houses publish regular bulletins of interest to their members, possible members and subscribers. Local organizations and art clubs also publish bulletins and newsletters for their members. Some bulletins, also published by museums or art groups, feature the scholarly research of various staff members.

Most large museums also publish elaborate exhibition catalogs, which contain photographs, critical reviews, research pieces, documentation and descriptions of the exhibit's work. Such catalogs are often the size of substantial books, and are generally sold in bookstores and other museums. Writers include curators, researchers, museum personnel and recognized experts on the exhibition subject.

Magazine and newspaper features

Many general interest magazines and daily newspapers devote a section to art and feature artists, shows, book reviews, museum exhibitions, architecture or archeological discoveries. These are written to interest the general public in art activities around the world, or, in the case of newspapers, to inform the local art community about what is happening close to home. Some publications contain such features in each issue; others treat them as special features. Free-lance writers or staff art editors contribute to such publications.

There are many career opportunities for those who have studied journalism, who enjoy writing and who also understand and enjoy art. Working for art publications means helping readers understand the activities and the visual communication of artists.

M. Stephen Doherty is editor of *American Artist,* a magazine for students, teachers, amateurs and professional artists. At his New York desk he puts together material for the next issue. Photograph: Fredy Kaplan

Art or Architectural Critic

Betje Howell (right), an art critic and free-lance art essayist for local and national publications, interviews noted sculptor Jacques Lipchitz at a retrospective show of his work at the UCLA Galleries. Her critical essay on this exhibition was based on notes from this interview and her opinions of the works in the show. Photograph: E. Bruce Howell

Art criticism is talk and writing about art, and its chief goal is to promote understanding of the meaning and merits of art and architecture. Art critics are not so much interested in the history of art (although they have a solid background in it), but in the reasons for art's existence, the analysis of its importance, the effects it has on other art and artists and its value to the total scope and influence of art or architecture.

Art critics review works of art in museums and galleries and report their findings in newspaper columns or magazine sections devoted to art. Architectural critics study and analyze buildings and other structures and report in the same way. Through their writings and expressed judgements they set standards for artistic excellence. Their subjective opinions are based on their knowledge of art criticism, art history, the social implications of art and trends in collecting and dealing.

There are several types of art criticism, although we are most familiar with the journalistic criticism we read in magazines and newspapers.

Journalistic criticism is written to inform readers of shows and exhibitions. These are often reviews or summaries of shows, written to create interest and offer very brief critical analyses. Newspaper art critics usually visit many openings and galleries each week, and must work rapidly to meet deadlines. Architectural critics may only review one building every two weeks or so. Critics who write for magazines may go into more depth and can polish their work.

Pedagogical criticism occurs in colleges and universities when teachers of art, art history and art criticism express opinions about art and architecture. Studio teachers also act as critics when they express opinions about student work in progress or finished work.

Scholarly criticism is based on the research and analysis of college personnel or other experts, and usually places art work in an historical context. This writing is done for scholarly journals.

Popular criticism is carried on by the public, who are not experts in art or in criticism. They express their critical opinions by what they like, what they talk about and what they purchase for their homes and collections.

What art and architectural critics do

Critics look at art and architecture, and write their conclusions about artists or their work. The process of criticism may be divided into the following steps, which explain how critics evaluate a piece.

First, critics will describe the work, and perhaps how

they think the artist did it. Architectural critics will describe appearances, materials and processes of construction or finishing.

They then discuss design, format, use of color, draftsmanship, proportions and principles of organization according to their own standards.

Critics often attempt to interpret or express the meaning of the work. What impact does it have on viewers? The subjective opinions of critics are made known through their interpretations, which might describe why the art was done, what possibly influenced the artist and what are the principle and subordinate messages the artist communicates.

Finally, critics make a judgement of the work, a final evaluation based on the complete analyses outlined above. The art is given a sort of rating as it is compared to other works of similar type. Some judgements are based on historical models, some on predictions of future worth, some on craftsmanship, some on aesthetic appeal, some on utility and some on social significance. Most are based on some combination of these considerations.

What qualities are helpful for a critic?
Art and architecture critics must be extremely knowledgeable in their fields, and have excellent background and training. They must be inquisitive and able to communicate easily with others. They must enjoy writing and have excellent training in journalism.

They should be analytical and perceptive. They should also be as objective as possible in stating opinions, and flexible enough to change with time. They must, however, be convinced that their opinions are valid and should have confidence in them.

They in turn must be able to take the criticism that will come their way from artists, museum personnel, craftspeople and the public.

What other careers require similar qualities?
All art careers that involve writing would probably be enjoyable for critics. Art magazine writers, art feature writers, free-lance writers and authors must have the ability to communicate verbally about art. Criticism is also written about crafts, stage productions, dance, music, books and industrial and graphic design.

Other types of art writing (reports, biography, news and the like) also require facility with words and an intense interest in art, artists and artistic processes.

What can be done now?
Take studio art classes to help you understand art processes. Take art history, design and appreciation classes to develop a background in art and begin to investigate the opinions of others. Also necessary are English, journalism and creative writing classes as well as psychology, sociology and history.

Attend galleries and museums and read what critics say about what you see. Study writing techniques that appeal to you (not only in art criticism but also in music, architecture, dance, drama and film). Begin to write your own opinions and express your own feelings in words about the art you see. Write about art for school publications, newspapers and yearbooks.

Which colleges offer necessary programs?
Art criticism is not taught in every college, although some art schools and large fine arts departments offer courses in criticism and art writing. Check catalogs for such offerings; they change from time to time. Schools with offerings in art management, administration and large selections of art history courses sometimes provide art criticism classes. Check also on extension courses from universities and classes offered by museums, because they may engage art and architecture critics to offer seminars or courses in critical writing. Ask local critics where they obtained their scholastic background and which courses they found most helpful.

Art Magazine Editor and Staff

Art magazines of various types are primary sources of information for artists across the country. Beginning artists devour them to learn new techniques and broaden their knowledge and ideas about art. Professional artists look for new ideas or want to know what their colleagues are doing. Like most specialized magazines, art magazines make possible the exchange of information, innovation and ideas between people with common interests.

Putting together an art magazine requires the same technical staff as any other magazine (See Editorial Design). The difference is evident in the writers and editors, who are interested in writing about art and artists, and who wish to appeal to a specific audience.

Pick up an issue of any art magazine (*American Artist*, for example) and notice that all the feature articles, reviews, editorials, business articles and advertising are written about art and directed toward artists or art-oriented people. For those with an intense interest in both journalism and various forms of art, writing and editing art magazines and newspapers is an exciting career possibility.

Some of the most prominent art magazines are written for fine artists, but there are specialty magazines pub-

Editor M. Stephen Doherty discusses color separations for the cover and an interior page of *American Artist* with production editor Stanley Marcus. The color quality in art magazines is especially critical when paintings are being reproduced. Photograph: Fredy Kaplan

lished for every area of the visual arts (See the list of over sixty-five art magazines in the back of the book, or check the *What Can Be Done Now?* sections throughout the book).

Each of the sixty-five or so publications requires a complete staff of writers and production workers, and there are dozens more of these publications put out locally, internationally or by museums, art departments and other sources.

What art magazine editors do

Editors are responsible for everything in their magazines, from the front cover to the smallest advertisement. They delegate various responsibilities to their staffs, but the editors must oversee every part of the operation.

They plan the scope, theme and format of each issue many months in advance of its publication date. They assign editors, assistant editors, contributing editors and production staff to cover every aspect of preparation. They talk to free-lance writers and photographers and assign them to special projects. They follow every article from concept to final editing, and offer suggestions, change plans and pull the entire staff together to meet production deadlines. Often they will edit articles themselves to fit a designated space or emphasize a certain

point. They watch the preparation of color separations and the printing of color to assure artists of the best possible reproduction of their work.

They read letters that come to their magazines from readers, evaluate suggestions and accept any forthcoming praise. They must keep track of the content of other magazines and the work of prominent artists in order to provide the most complete and up-to-date editorial coverage in their specific areas of interest.

Editors with years of art publication experience are often considered experts and are asked to write, speak, make presentations and give lectures and seminars on their particular areas of expertise.

What qualities are helpful for an art magazine editor?

Usually, art magazine editors have been writers or members of production staffs of magazines or newspapers, and know production and publication processes from practical experience. Most also have art backgrounds and can write from experience. This combination of interests and knowledge makes them qualified to be editors.

They must read rapidly, spell correctly, understand grammar completely and speak articulately. They generally enjoy both art and editorial production, and are dedicated to helping artists understand their heritage and craft more completely.

What other careers require similar qualities?
All magazine production staff (See Editoral Design) require similar qualities. People interested in writing and editing for art magazines would also be comfortable writing essays, books, biographical material or working with museum publications.

Art criticism (See Art Critic) and art teaching (See Art Education) might also appeal to people interested in both the verbal and visual aspects of art. Copy editing (See Editorial Design) also requires similar background, qualities and interests. Experience in art and writing would also prepare people for careers in copywriting for advertising agencies, especially those with clients who produce art-related merchandise.

What can be done now?
Preparation for editorship must follow the normal paths to writing and journalism. High school classes should include all the art, design, English and writing classes available.

Check monthly art magazines (See list in back of the book) in school and public libraries, or go to art school or college libraries where the selection will be greater. Study the graphic design of such publications, read the articles, study the advertisements, look at the photographs and reproductions. Become familiar with all aspects of such magazines.

Part-time work in printing or publishing establishments will help you understand the technical aspects of printing and publication, while work in design studios will help you learn layout and production techniques.

Which colleges offer necessary programs?
Almost any college or university offers courses in art (art history, studio courses, survey courses, graphic design and so on) and writing (journalism, critical writing, English) which provide the proper background for art magazine work. Most art schools also have English and writing requirements. Because editors of art magazines have background in both art and journalism, you should make a decision on your major and minor fields as early as you can, and obtain catalogs from several appropriate schools.

Other Careers Writing About Art

Art Book Editor
These editors work for book companies and supervise the writing, obtaining of illustrations and the production of art books. They work with authors, photographers, photo archives, color specialists, production staff, book designers and printing houses to insure that desired quality and production standards are met. They work carefully with authors to develop styles and format, and may suggest changes, alternative approaches and the treatment of content.

Art Bulletin Editor
Museums, art organizations, national art clubs and art schools and colleges often publish bulletins that appear periodically. They may be very elaborate, as is the bulletin of the Metropolitan Museum of Art in New York, and include color, special articles and scholarly writing. The bulletins of smaller art organizations may be more modest. Editors must solicit articles and illustrations (or write and illustrate themselves) and get materials to the printers on schedule. Such bulletins are usually the primary communication link between organizations and their members.

Calendar Editor
Metropolitan gallery associations or smaller cities with large numbers of galleries often produce bulletins and calendars to let tourists, buyers, collectors and the public know what exhibits are being shown in the area. Museums also have calendars that list opening, continuing and coming exhibitions and special museum programs and tours. Calendar editors compile information, edit it to fit the desired format, have it set in type and approve the finished schedule. Newspaper art calendars include all the pertinent information on artists' names, galleries, dates, times and brief descriptions of the shows.

Copy Editor for Art Books
Copy editors are editorial specialists who read manuscripts from authors and make suggestions, alterations and changes that will improve the final book. They stress consistency of punctuation, spelling and writing style, and clarify content. They make authors' manuscripts more acceptable to book editors and publishers.

Researcher

There are people adept at investigating old books, original writings, letters, archives and collections and finding information pertinent to specific stories or articles. Researchers usually do not write for themselves, but are hired to gather the required information for authors working on books or articles. They gather data, verify authors' ideas and recollections and secure illustrations, permission and authentications necessary to document the author's works.

Who's Who in Art

There are a dozen or more biographical compilations and resource books (such as *Who's Who in American Art*) that list artists, architects and craftspeople of all types. Gathering names and pertinent information on these artists is an extensive task and many researchers, assistant editors and the like are needed to put the artist-supplied information together into a unified format.

Part Six | Services By and For Artists

Tressa Ruslander Miller is director of "Business & Art," a consulting service which helps corporations develop cultural programs and art collections. Here, she photographs gallery work which she will show to prospective corporate buyers. Photograph: Joseph Gatto

HUNDREDS OF ART careers have been discussed on the previous pages. Most have to do with producing and selling the work or the ideas of artists. This chapter explores careers that provide services by and for artists. Career predictions in fields unrelated to art indicate that in the coming years there will be dramatic increases in all service industries. Art fields will probably experience a similar expansion in service-related career opportunities.

Some services make use of the talents of artists (police and court artists, restorers of paintings and conceptualists for industry, for example); some have to do with artists and their work (art materials dealers, framers, shippers and photographers); and some address the business aspects of art careers (lawyers, accountants, show coordinators, agents, investment counselors).

Many of those employed in art service careers are not educated in art schools or colleges, but in college business, law, education, library and psychology departments. Some of these service careers are built around combinations of interests (education, psychology and therapy, for instance), while others are the result of strong interests in art and expertise in other areas (library science and art history, for example). Many of these service careers were not even in existence ten years ago, and are the result of the creative thinking of inventive and ambitious people. Here are some examples.

A successful accountant who is also a recognized expert in the construction industry has a deep interest in art and in collecting. He has devised bookkeeping and tax accounting procedures that help galleries simplify and regulate their business procedures. He has become the tax accountant for several major galleries in various parts of the country.

A woman who enjoys working with her home video equipment has developed a business that documents important art collection inventories for both individual and commercial clients. She videotapes the works of art in their customary positions for insurance purposes and inventory control.

An artist who formerly worked as a scenic designer in the film studios of Hollywood is now a conceptualizer for industrial and commercial businesses. He sits in on staff meetings when new products are being discussed, and by the time the meeting is over has dozens of sketches of possible products. His former career forced him to think quickly, sketch rapidly and visualize the ideas of movie directors. Now he transfers those skills to industrial design and planning.

Artists' agents abound, but one woman has put together a firm called "Business & Arts," which specializes in corporate cultural programs and activities. She works with corporations and consults officers, gallery directors and artists to arrange purchasing programs, corporate collections, commissions, corporate exhibitions and total cultural programs in a business setting. These programs might emphasize the cultural enrichment of the business environment or may be the beginnings of art-as-investment programs. The firm's founder works with both visual and performing artists. She helps set up necessary programs or takes over existing programs and administers them for interested corporations.

A lawyer in New York with an intense interest in the arts has become a specialist in representing visual and performing artists. He is expert in advising, prosecution and defense positions as regards contracts, copyright, resale royalties, health hazards, insurance, taxes and a number of other legal issues which concern artists. He and many other lawyers are becoming valuable to artists with increasingly complex financial affairs.

Several architects in Los Angeles have formed a non-profit consulting firm which provides advice and assistance to artists and architects. They maintain a staff which can help with technical services, arts management assistance, business referrals and legal information.

Creative people in many service areas can adapt their skills and knowledge to the needs of all types of artists, architects, design studios, collectors, gallery directors, craftspeople and designers. Artists and designers involved in big business require the expertise and organizational capabilities of professionals. Relying on experts to handle the business aspects of their careers frees their minds for creative work.

New service careers will probably develop rapidly as creative businesspeople see needs in the arts community and develop strategies and careers to meet them.

College students training to be art therapists must get involved in therapy processes to understand how they work. Photograph: John Kimpel

Art Therapist

Training for art therapy is a recent development, coming into importance only in the 1930's. The people who pioneered this important effort were independent practitioners, many of whom are still active today.

Art therapy is a human service profession that uses art to help people with certain physical and emotional problems. Art therapy can be used to diagnose and treat those problems by encouraging self-awareness and personal growth.

Some art therapists work in group situations in psychiatric hospitals, clinics, community centers, drug and alcohol treatment centers, schools and prisons, while others have practices built around individual or family counseling and therapy. Art therapists work with people of all ages and backgrounds.

What art therapists do

Art therapists use art as a vehicle for positive human change. They use drawing, painting and other forms of art work in diagnosis, treatment, rehabilitation and education.

Therapists base their methods on extensive studies, preparation and work. They encourage patients to draw certain things (houses, trees, people, for example). Through the drawings they are often able to interpret personal feelings and clarify and identify problems. Therapists then use art processes to strengthen their patients' self-images and help them relieve their emotional tensions. Extensive training and background prepares therapists to be sensitive to all types of responses and to use positive responses productively.

They keep the art work of their clients confidential, just as medical doctors keep such information from the public, but they share such information with colleagues when developing programs for rehabilitation. They often collaborate with social workers and psychologists in order to provide the best and most comprehensive treatment programs.

What qualities are helpful for an art therapist?

Any therapist must be interested in helping people solve their personal problems, and must be sensitive, inquisitive and thorough. Art therapists must understand art, psychology and psychiatry and must constantly refine and strengthen this understanding through study and experimentation.

Therapists must feel equally comfortable in both individual and group sessions. They must be willing to go through intensive study and preparation for their careers. Their work demands that they read and understand medical journals and books dealing with psychopathology, psychotherapy and clinical psychology.

A strong foundation and interest in all forms of art and visual expression is another important qualification. It is this unique combination that makes the work of art therapists so valuable.

What other careers require similar qualities?

Various areas of psychology and psychiatry require similar interests and background, the qualities of sensitivity and thoroughness and the desire to help others with personal problems.

Elementary and secondary art teachers should have a personal interest in using art to help others grow. College teachers who specialize in art education must be qualified in both art and psychology.

What can be done now?

High school students should take all the art classes possible (especially drawing, painting, three-dimensional design and ceramics) and also all the psychology, English and biology they can schedule. These are areas emphasized in art therapy training programs in college, and a strong start in high school is very beneficial.

Get involved in art activities in school. Help youngsters with special needs in crafts classes, summer camps, YMCA programs and so on. Teach at Sunday school, vacation schools and for recreation programs in parks, where you will be in contact with inquisitive young people. All these are positive experiences in your developmental background.

Check with such magazines as *American Journal of Art Therapy* and *Art Psychotherapy* for information on schools, projects, articles, bibliographies and current literature in the field.

Which colleges offer necessary programs?

Schools are developing new programs yearly, and you can get a current list of schools by writing to the American Art Therapy Association (AATA) (See "where to write" at the back of the book). Graduation from schools with AATA listing in the charts are preferred by those who are hiring career specialists in art therapy.

College programs require degrees in art, psychology or related fields, a strong foundation in drawing, painting and sculpture (maintain a good portfolio) and an emphasis on human psychology and the behavioral and social sciences. Check the charts at the back of the book.

Police and Court Artists

The work of police and court artists combines artistic talent with the ability to produce sketched representations of remembered or actual scenes. Police artists take verbal descriptions of a crime or criminal from eye witnesses and draw or model a recognizable approximation. Court artists are used by television stations and newspapers to make sketches of the figures involved in trials at which no television cameras are allowed.

Training for both of these art careers involves much drawing, especially of faces, and many hours of sketching. Police artists must be adept at portraiture and at listening carefully to witnesses' descriptions. Court artists must sketch quickly and accurately, using both line and color to give viewers an indication of what they saw. The figures they sketch are generally known to the public; their likenesses must be recognizable.

What police artists do

Police artists first talk patiently and carefully with eye witnesses to establish the identifying features of a suspect. Working with pastels, pencils or charcoal, they sketch and change their sketches according to the comments of the witness. They work on identifiable facial features such as shape of head, hairline, eyes, eyebrows, nose, mouth, mustache, chin, neck and ears, letting the witness select features from among numerous examples. The artist adjusts the features in the sketch to make it as close to the remembered face as possible.

Fernando Ponce listens to a witness describe a suspect, and sketches in pastels.

Adding a moustache changes a face considerably. Photographs: Joseph Gatto

What court artists do

With the permission of judges and attorneys, court artists take their drawing equipment directly into courtrooms or police offices and make quick sketches of the principle figures in certain cases. When cameras are not allowed to be present, these artists document the action taking place.

We see their work in newspapers, magazines and on television news programs. Their use of line (pencil, pen and ink, markers and the like) and color (watercolor washes and colored markers) conveys instant impressions of the scenes.

Court artists are sometimes free-lance artists who hold other art jobs and are hired for certain cases. Some are employed by television stations or newspapers, and have additional responsibilities when they are not sketching in court.

Bill Robles illustrates a court scene soon to appear on a television news program.

What qualities are helpful for these artists?

Police artists must produce accurate drawings and must be able to visualize features that are being described verbally. This takes patience, sensitivity and respect for the witnesses and their feelings.

Their work requires that they have excellent drawing ability and a flexible imagination to help witnesses with visualizations. Because they are involved with police work, they must also be committed to the apprehension of criminals.

Court artists must be able to draw or sketch quickly what they see. Because of the strict deadlines for television and newspaper work, they must be able to work under pressure and be able immediately to pick out characteristic features which will help the public identify those involved.

Both police and court artists work in circumstances far different from the traditional studio atmosphere, and they must be able to function efficiently in such situations.

What other careers require similar qualities?

Quick sketch artists, visualizers, conceptualists and illustrators must be able to make likenesses quickly, even though they often produce later, finished work from their sketches.

What can be done now?

High school students should be involved in all phases of art and photography in school, but especially in drawing and painting classes. Try to enroll in Saturday scholarship drawing classes at local art schools, museums or colleges. In preparation for police work, courses in psychology, history, English and biology should be taken.

Work constantly in your sketchbook. Fill book after book with sketches of friends, classmates, family and people on buses, trains, street corners—everywhere! Draw all the people you can.

Which colleges offer necessary programs?

There are no special courses or schools for either career. Both require many drawing and painting classes, in both portraiture and figure work, and hours of sketching. Most people who end up in these careers started their schooling as illustration majors and specialized after graduation in one particular area of interest.

Police artists are often trained in special schools, sponsored by police academies. Sometimes police artists teach courses in their specialty as part of a law enforcement program at community colleges. The sketching abilities of court artists usually spring from a love of and ability in drawing.

ART CAREER PROFILE

A witness tries to explain a change needed in the chin structure of a clay portrait modeled by police artist Fernando Ponce.

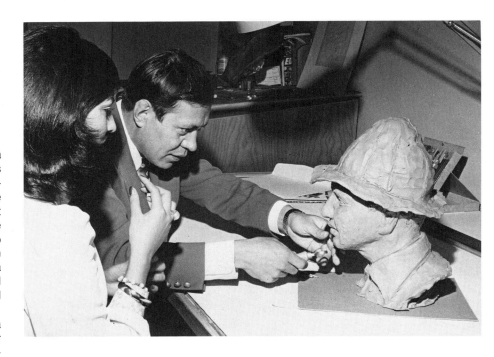

The room was a small cubicle, just off a larger and much busier room. Detectives rushed here and there with bits of information in hand or watched as a teletype rhythmically conveyed information about pending criminal cases. A drawing table with some oil pastels and a circular lamp was pushed up against the wall and on another table was a plaster bust of a man, staring into space. A disheveled wig gave the bust an almost comical appearance.

Hardly the working environment of a visual artist. No luxurious three or four week assignments with flexible deadlines. No well-stocked shelves of art supplies or crisp sheets of expensive paper. This is, however, the studio environment of Fernando Ponce, illustrator for the Los Angeles Police Department, and one of that department's leading figures in the apprehension of criminals. His tools are those of the visual artist, which he uses to translate verbal communication, often given under duress, into visual images that help witnesses and law enforcement officials to solve crimes.

Ponce is a competent illustrator, but illustration is not the only method available to him. He is also a fine sculptor, and when a witness responds more easily to three-dimensional forms, he uses his sculpture ability to manipulate large pieces of plasticine clay into likenesses of individuals.

Ponce must be able to put witnesses at ease with a gentle, patient voice and a reassuring attitude, but he must also recognize the limitation and breaking point of individual witnesses. Sometimes a witness will be placed under hypnosis to render a more accurate description from which the artist can work.

When it is impossible to bring certain kinds of physical evidence into a court room, Fernando Ponce has the ability to construct three-dimensional models as exhibits. Such models help show the trajectories of bullets, the physical characteristics of materials and construction, the positions of persons involved in a crime and so on. Models help juries visualize concepts and often make actual site visits unnecessary.

Fernando Ponce was born in Ecuador and was an accomplished painter and sculptor before joining the Los Angeles Police Department. He studied at the Art Center School of Design in Los Angeles.

Ponce works on approximately three cases a day and often over a hundred a month. Unlike police artists of the recent past, who used black and white sketches overlaid with acetate facial features in a variety of combinations, Ponce's illustrations are in color. He relies on his thorough knowledge of human anatomy to fill in the frequent information gaps of witnesses, and to determine when a face is anatomically impossible. He has done extensive studies in face reconstruction and has trained over seventy police artists throughout the United States in his police artist classes.

In one of the most intriguing cases Ponce has faced, a human skeleton was discovered and described to the artist. Ponce made a careful reproduction of the real skull and reconstructed the muscles of the face with plaster, paint and a wig. The result was John Doe #136—still unidentified. A similar sculpture of Ponce's was identified within two weeks after the bust was shown to the media.

Fernando Ponce, Police Artist

A model of the cashier's booth on a scale of 1″ = .5′. The trajectories of the bullets are reproduced with rods to help jurors understand the location and position of the murderer.

The cashier's booth in which a service station attendant was killed. Photographs: Los Angeles Police Department

Other Careers in the Art Services

Accountant For Artists

Some accountants become expert in setting up and handling the business affairs of artists, architects and galleries. They understand the variety of local, state and federal tax laws that affect artists and they advise their clients in regard to investments, tax schedules, studio operations, artist/dealer relationships and bookkeeping procedures.

Appraiser (Insurance/Public) (See also Other Careers in Gallery Work)

Appraisers fix a dollar value on works of art, and base their decisions on the history of the artist, current price trends, gallery selling price, inflation, supply and demand and the artist's potential. Appraisers are used to set insurance value, establish selling price or to determine the price to be asked for a work in an estate or collection or for resale in a gallery.

Art Consultant to Businesses (See Consultant, below)

Art Librarian

Art librarians are skilled specialists in library science. They have an intense interest in art and artists, and enjoy helping people use available resources. Their degrees are generally in library science, but most have studied art history, art theory and art production.

Librarians who specialize in art could find employment in several kinds of libraries. Large museums in every country of the world have extensive library holdings. (American librarians may also find work in the American Art sections of libraries in Europe and Asia.) Art librarians are also employed in large university libraries, special art libraries of large colleges or university art departments, art school libraries, the libraries of some individual art collections and in the extensive public library systems of large cities. Historical societies and civic or state art centers also require art library specialists.

If you are interested in both art and library work, this sort of career might interest you. Most universities that offer library science degrees also offer sufficient art courses for a double major or in-depth study.

Art Materials Merchandiser/Distributor

These salespeople operate or provide goods to art supply stores where artists buy their materials. They are in constant contact with artists of all types, and are often able to perform other services for artists, such as stretching canvases, cutting mats, suggesting new materials, media and books and referring artists to framers, accountants, galleries and agents.

Artist's Agent (See Sales Representative, Other Careers in Gallery Work)

Auctioneer (See Art Galleries)

Career Guidance Counselor

There are guidance counselors in art schools and colleges, but there are also some with city offices who became specialists in finding art jobs. They are usually closely associated with advertising agencies and graphic design studios and are able to put prospective designers in touch with studios and businesses who need artists.

Consultant

There are many kinds of consultants who work with artists and with industries and clients who need the services and work of artists. Most consultants know the work of many designers, architects, artists and photographers, for example, and when a corporation hires a consultant to help decorate a new building, he or she immediately begins the search for appropriate work. Consultants often arrange for artists to carry out large commissions for buildings. They match client needs to artists and designers who can satisfy them.

Some investment experts offer advice to individual collectors and corporations on purchasing art as an investment. The works of some artists appreciate, or gain value, over time. Investment counselors advise potential investors about artists whose work is most likely to appreciate, and help them choose the work.

There are also consultants who advise artists in various phases of their business, and help them choose appropriate galleries, write contracts or find lawyers or insurance agencies. They also advise artists on finances, investments, studio construction, markets and other important business considerations.

Crate Builder

Crate builders, often artists themselves, work with wood, fiberboard, cardboard and plastics to build crates and containers for shipping art work. People who require their services include painters, sculptors, antique dealers, collectors, museums, galleries, furniture builders and designers and craftspeople of all types. Crate builders build custom crates for each shipment, and usually pack and ship them for their clients.

Documentation Expert (See also Museum Conservator and Restorer)

Like appraisers, documentation experts are qualified by their experience and knowledge to verify that an artistic piece is the work of a certain artist. At an auction house or museum the potential buyer wants a work authenticated before making bids. Documentation experts make use of sophisticated laboratory equipment to help them determine the type of ink or paint used, age of the canvas or other material and composition of underpainting and pigments. They examine closely the style and execution of the work before making a definitive statement.

Document Restorer (See Museum Conservator and Restorer)

Framer (See Other Careers in the Fine Arts)

Insurance

There are special needs for insurance coverage that are unique to artists, and there are companies which help satisfy those needs. Artists must insure their work while it is in studios, in transit, at galleries or in museums. Because artists are often self-employed, they also need health, hospitalization and life insurance. Some companies organize blocks of artists or art associations (Artists Equity, for example) to offer lower-cost, group rates for particular and general needs.

Lawyers For Artists

There are lawyers in every major city who are familiar with local, state and federal laws as they affect artists of all types. These lawyers may have other types of clients, but offer important services to the art community through their special interests and expertise. For more information, write to Lawyers for the Arts Committee, Young Lawyers Section, Philadelphia Bar Association, 423 City Hall Annex, Philadelphia, PA 19107.

Mail Order Art Dealers

There are several mail order suppliers in North America who satisfy the needs of artists who do not live near good art supply stores. They perform all the services of art materials merchandisers (See above) but print and send out catalogs so artists can order through the mails. If artists live and work in isolated spots, this is a valuable and necessary service.

Manufacturer of Art Supplies

There are many companies (in America, Europe and the Orient) that make the supplies used by artists. Papers, inks, pencils, paints, boards, erasers, pens, plastics, glues, markers, pastels and media of all types are manufac-

tured. Drawing tables, easels, palettes, portfolios, lights and other equipment also must be made. These manufacturers supply what artists need. They often employ artists to use and test these materials and advise the manufacturer about their quality and performance.

Photographer for Artists (See Photographer of Fine Art, Other Careers in Photography)

Restorer/Cleaner (See also Museum Conservator and Restorer)

These specialists work for artists, galleries or owners, and restore damaged and faded paintings. They examine the surfaces, test the stability of canvas or paper, determine the media and correct processes to use, and reconstruct or retouch damaged areas. They use solvents to clean surfaces and can restore damaged works to their original condition.

Shipping and Storage

Both shipping and storage are services provided to artists, galleries, museums and owners alike. Usually the shipping company builds art crates (See above) and stores work for clients. The company ships the art work by any appropriate means within America or abroad. This is the way most art moves from galleries to customers, from artists to museums and so on. Some companies, however, move art in their own vans or trucks.

Television Inventory System Operators

The use of television taping equipment to simplify some art services is attracting an increasing number of artists and art owners. Television inventory system operators use their machinery to make visual inventories of houses, offices, galleries and studios, taping the art work. Verbal descriptions and notes, prices and costs are taped onto accompanying audio tracks. These are superb records for inventories, insurance purposes, collection appraisals and visual files.

Travel Exhibit Coordinator

These coordinators organize travel shows from certain geographical areas, with certain themes and media. Some shows include the work of a single artist or organization. The coordinators publish lists of their traveling shows, accept bookings, route the tours and make all crating and shipping arrangements. Some such operations are small in number of employees but have impressive lists of exhibition sites. Others work with larger museums and employ many people to keep the operation running smoothly.

An interested landlord makes space available at a nominal fee for printmakers. They work on their own and exhibit some of their prints there. Photograph: Janet Wolfe

Bibliography

Where to Write for More Information

Colleges and Art Schools

Out of print art books are valuable aids to researchers and art historians. Art librarians, such as this one at the Los Angeles County Museum of Art Library, make sure they remain in good condition. Photograph: Joseph Gatto

This art history teacher explains and demonstrates the filing procedure to students who
will make use of the slide collection in their
studies. Photograph: Joseph Gatto

Bibliography

There are not many books that treat a wide variety of art career opportunities in summary form. However, there are many books that describe in detail careers in certain areas. School, art school and college libraries are likely to have several of these on their shelves. Librarians can obtain the addresses of publishers if you are interested in finding out about others.

This bibliography lists books published within the past ten years or so and current magazines. Several are older, but contain valuable information and insights into certain career areas.

Alexander, Mary Jean. *Designing Interior Environments.* Harcourt Brace Jovanovich, New York, 1972.*

Allosso, Michael. *Your Career in Theatre, Radio, Television or Filmmaking.* Arco Publishing, New York, 1978.

American Film Institute. *Careers in Film and Television, Factfile #2.* Washington DC, 1977.

Anderson, Charles R. *Lettering.* Van Nostrand Reinhold, Co., New York.

Association of Collegiate Schools of Architecture (ACSA). *Architectural Schools in North America.* New York, 1982.

Benedict, Stephen and Linda C. Coe. *Arts Management: An Annotated Bibliography.* Center for Arts Information, New York, 1980.

Berger, Melvin. *Jobs in the Fine Arts and Humanities.* Lothrop, Lee and Shepard, New York, 1974.

Beverly Hills Bar Association, Los Angeles. *The Visual Artist's Manual.* Doubleday, 1982.

Berlyn, David. *Your Future in Television Careers.* Richards Rosen Press, New York, 1980.

Brown, Les. *Electric Media: Television.* Harcourt Brace Jovanovich, New York, 1974.*

Burcaw, G. Ellis. *Introduction to Museum Work.* American Association for State and Local History, Nashville, 1975.

Burns, William A. *Your Future in Museums.* Richards Rosen Press, New York, 1974.

Casewit, Curtis W. *Making a Living in the Fine Arts: Advice from the Pros.* Macmillan, New York, 1981.

Cataldo, John W. *Pen Calligraphy.* Davis Publications, Inc., Worcester, MA, 1978.

Colman, Hila. *City Planning: What It's All About.* World Publishing Co., New York, 1971.*

Cook, John W., and Heinrich Klotz (editors). *Conversations with Architects.* Praeger Publishers, New York, 1973.*

Coyne, John and Tom Hebert. *By Hand: A Guide to Schools and a Career in Crafts.* E. P. Dutton, New York, 1974.*

DeLong, Fred J. *Aim for a Job in Drafting.* Richards Rosen Press, New York, 1976.

Exploring Careers in the Humanities: A Student Guidebook. Superintendent of Documents, Washington DC, 1976 (S/N 017-080-01649-4).

Exploring Theatre and Media Careers: A Student Guidebook. Superintendent of Documents, Washington DC, 1976 (S/N 017-080-01640-1).

Exploring Visual Arts and Crafts Careers: A Student Guidebook. Superintendent of Documents, Washington DC, 1976 (S/N 017-080-01641-9).

Fixman, Adeline. *Aim for a Job in Cartooning.* Richards Rosen Press, New York, 1976.

Fixman, Adeline. *Your Future in Creative Careers.* Richards Rosen Press, New York, 1978.

Friedman, Arnold, et al. *Interior Design: An Introduction to Architectural Interiors.* American Elsevier Publ. Co., New York, 1970.*

Fujita, S. Neil. *Aim for a Job in Graphic Design and Art.* Richards Rosen Press, Inc., New York, 1979.

Genfan, Herb. *How to Start Your Own Craft Business.* Watson-Guptill, New York, 1974.

Gottschall, Edward M. (ed). *Typographic Directions.* Art Directions Book Co., New York, 1964.*

Great Lakes Arts Resource Directory: Conferences, Seminars and Workshops for Arts Managers. Great Lakes Arts Alliance, Cleveland, 1980.

Greer, Michael. *Your Future in Interior Design.* Richards Rosen Press, Inc., New York, 1980.

Haeberle, Billi. *Looking Forward to a Career: Radio and Television.* Dillon Press, Minneapolis, 1974.

*Titles followed by an asterisk are currently out of print.

Hawes, Carolyn, Margaret Johnson and Judith Nylen. *Your Career in Art and Design.* Arco Publishing, Inc., New York, 1977.

Hawkins, Arthur (ed). *Art Director at Work.* Hastings House Publishers, New York, 1959.*

Hayes, Colin. *The Artist's Manual.* Mayflower Books, New York, 1981.

Head, Edith. *Fashion as a Career.* Julian Messner, New York, 1966.*

Hellman, Hal. *The City in the World of the Future.* M. Evans & Co., New York, 1970.

Holden, Donald. *Art Career Guide.* Watson-Guptill Publications, New York, 1977.

Horton, Louise. *Art Careers.* Franklin Watts, New York, 1975*

Hymers, Robert P. *Professional Photographers in Practice.* International Publications Service, New York, 1973.

Jackson, Tom. *The Hidden Job Market for the Eighties.* Times Books, New York, 1981.

Jacques Cattell Press. *American Art Directory.* R. R. Bowker Co., New York, 1982.

Jameson, Robert. *The Professional Job Hunting System.* Performance Dynamics, Verona, NJ, 1972.*

Keppler, Victor. *Your Future in Photography.* Richards Rosen Press, New York, 1972.

Magnan, George. *Industrial Artist.* Reinhold Publishing Corp., New York, 1963.*

Magnan, George. *Visual Art for Industry.* Reinhold Publishing Corp., New York, 1961.*

Mauger, Emily M. *Modern Display Techniques.* Fairchild Publications, New York, 1964.

Meinhart, Carl and Carolyn and Alen E. Nourse. *So You Want To Be An Architect.* Harper & Row, New York, 1969.*

Muller-Brockmann, Josef. *A History of Visual Communication.* Hastings House Publishing Co., Inc., New York, 1980.

Muscutt, H. C. *Display Technique.* Taplinger Publishing Co., New York, 1964.*

Nakamura, Julia and Massy. *Your Future in Medical Illustrating: Art and Photography.* Richards Rosen Press, New York, 1971.

National Art Education Association. *Job Description in the Business World of Art and Design.* Washington, D.C., National Gallery of Art, 1978.

Nelson, Roy Paul and Byron Ferris. *Fell's Guide to Commercial Art.* Frederick Fell, Inc., New York, 1966.*

Piper, Robert J. *Opportunities in Architecture Today.* National Textbook Company, Skokie, IL, 1975.

Reiss, Alvin, (ed). *Arts Management Reader.* Marcel Dekker, New York, 1979.

Roth, Claire Jarrett and Adelle Weiss. *Art Careers.* Henry Z. Walck, Inc., New York, 1963.*

Roth, Richard. *Your Future in Architecture.* Richards Rosen Press, Inc., New York, 1979.

Schneider, Rita M. *Interior Design Careers.* Prentice-Hall, Englewood Cliffs, NJ, 1977.

Setzekorn, William D. *Looking Forward to a Career: Architecture.* Dillon Press, Inc., Minneapolis, 1974.

Shingleton, John. *Career Decision Making.* McGraw-Hill Co., New York, 1977.

Sommer, Elyse. *Career Opportunities in Crafts.* Crown Publishing Co., New York, 1977.

Stone, David K. *Art in Advertising.* Pitman Publishing Corp., New York, 1961.*

Wakin, Edward. *Jobs in Communications.* Lothrop, Lee and Shepard, New York, 1974.

Wettlaufer, George and Nancy. *Craftsman Survival Manual: Making a Full or Part-time Living from Your Crafts.* Prentice-Hall, Englewood Cliffs, NJ, 1974.*

Writer's Digest Books. *Photographer's Market.* Cincinnati, OH. Published annually.

Teachers may wish to make available to their students an excellent cassette/filmstrip series. The following titles are among the sets available from Son-A-Vision, Inc., 110 Washington Avenue, Pleasantville, NY 10570:

Your Portfolio Speaks for You
Advertising—Art at Work
Advertising—Layout Design
Designing with Type
How to Prepare a Mechanical

*Titles followed by an asterisk are currently out of print.

Art Magazines

This partial list includes magazines from many areas of interest and from a wide range of careers in art. Addresses can be obtained from *Reader's Guide to Periodical Literature* in your library.

American Artist
American Arts
American Cinematographer
American Craft
American Indian Art
Antiques World
Apollo
Architectural Digest
Architectural Record
Art and Antiques
Art Bulletin, The
Art Direction
Art Education
Artforum
Art in America
Artists of the Rockies and the Golden West
Art Journal
Art New England
Arts Canada
Arts Magazine
Arts of Asia
Camera
Ceramics Monthly
Christie's Catalog
Close Up
Communication Arts (CA)
Connoisseur
Contract
Crafts Report
Design
Design Drafting & ReproGraphics
Designers' Choice
Design for Art Education

Designers West
Fiber Arts
Glass Magazine
Graphic Design
Graphis (Switzerland)
Historic Preservation
Horizon
Images and Issues
Industrial Design (ID)
Interface Age
Interiors
Landscape Architect
Microcomputing
Modern Packaging
Modern Photography
Modo (Italy)
Museum
Nikon World
Obscura
Package Engineering
Packaging Design
Portfolio
Print
Print Letter (Switzerland)
Product Design and Development
Progressive Architecture
School Arts
Shuttle, Spindle and Dyepot
Sculpture
Southwest Arts
Studio International (London)
Studio Light
Tamarind Papers, The
Technical Photography
Technology and Conservation
Today's Art and Graphics
U & Lc
Up Date
Visual Merchandising
West Art

Some universities invite professional artists to spend time on campus as artists—in—residence, working on their own projects and meeting and talking with students. Here, visiting artist Tom Blackwell demonstrates his photo—realist process to a master class of undergraduate and graduate students. Photograph: University of Arizona, Tucson

Where to Write for More Information

The following are the addresses of organizations, associations, offices and boards which can supply brochures, lists, pamphlets and other important information to students interested in careers in art. Request information and help (in pursuing your career, choosing a good school or finding an apprentice program to aid in your career development) from those in your area of interest.

Advertising Typographers Association
461 Eighth Avenue
New York, New York 10001

American Art Therapy Association
428 East Preston Street
Baltimore, Maryland 21202

American Association of Museums
1055 Thomas Jefferson Street N.W.
Washington, D.C., 20007

American Association of Zoological Parks and Aquariums
Oglebay Park
Wheeling, West Virginia 26003

American Council for the Arts
570 Seventh Avenue
New York, New York 10018

American Crafts Council
44 West 53rd Street
New York, New York 10019

American Federation of Television and Radio Artists (AFTRA)
1350 Avenue of the Americas
New York, New York 10019

American Film Institute
Kennedy Center for the Performing Arts
Washington, D.C. 20566

American Institute of Architects (AIA)
1735 New York Avenue N.W.
Washington, D.C. 20006

American Institute of Graphic Arts (AIGA)
1059 Third Avenue
New York, New York 10021

American Society of Interior Designers (ASID)
1430 Broadway
New York, New York 10018

American Society of Landscape Architects (ASLA)
2013 I Street N.W.
Washington, D.C. 20006

Art Directors Club Inc.
488 Madison Avenue
New York, New York 10022

Artists Equity Association
3726 Albemarle Street N.W.
Washington, D.C. 20016

Association of College, University and Community Arts Administrators
Post Office Box 2137
Madison, Wisconsin 53701

Association of Collegiate Schools of Architecture (ACSA)
1735 New York Avenue N.W.
Washington, D.C. 20006

Association of Handicapped Artists
1735 New York Avenue N.W.
Washington D.C. 20006

Association of Medical Illustrators
5820 Wilshire Boulevard
Los Angeles, California 90036

Business Committee for the Arts, Inc.
Suite 2600. 1501 Broadway
New York, New York 10036

Center for Arts Information
625 Broadway
New York, New York 10012

College Art Association of America
16 East 52nd Street
New York, New York 10022

Education Council of the Graphic Arts Industry
4615 Forbes Avenue
Pittsburgh, Pennsylvania 15213

Foundation for Interior Design Education Research
  (FIDER)
242 West 27th Street
New York, New York 10001

Graphic Artists Guild
30 East 20th Street
New York, New York 10003

Industrial Design Society of America (IDSA)
6802 Poplar Place
McLean, Virginia 22101

International Alliance of Theatrical Stage Employees
1515 Broadway
New York, New York 10036

International Center of Photography
1130 Fifth Avenue
New York, New York 10028

National Academy of Design
1083 Fifth Avenue
New York, New York 10028

National Architecture Accrediting Board (NAAB)
1735 New York Avenue N.W.
Washington, D.C. 20006

National Art Education Association
1916 Association Drive
Reston, Virginia 22091

National Arts Job Bank
141 East Palace Avenue
Santa Fe, New Mexico 87505

National Assembly of State Arts Agencies
1010 Vermont Avenue N.W., Suite 316
Washington, D.C. 20005

National Association of Furniture Manufacturers
8401 Connecticut Avenue, Suite 911
Washington, D.C. 20019

National Association of Schools of Art (NASA)
11250 Roger Bacon Drive
Reston, Virginia 22090

National Council of Architectural Registration Boards
1735 New York Avenue N.W.
Washington, D.C. 20006

National Home Fashions League, Inc.
Post Office Box 58045
Dallas, Texas 75258

National Trust for Historic Preservation
1785 Massachusetts Avenue N.W.
Washington, D.C. 20036

Newspaper Guild
1125 15th Street N.W.
Washington, D.C. 20005

Opportunity Resources for the Arts
1501 Broadway
New York, New York 10036

Photographic Art and Science Foundation
111 Stratford Road
Des Plaines, Illinois 60016

Professional Photographers of America
1090 Executive Way
Des Plaines, Illinois 60018

Screen Cartoonists Guild
1616 West 9th Street
Los Angeles, California 90015

Society of Illustrators
128 East 63rd Street
New York, New York 10021

Union of Independent Colleges of Art (UICA)
4340 Oak Street
Kansas City, Missouri 64111

Women in Communications
Post Office Box 9561
Austin, Texas 78766

Colleges and Art Schools

The following schools in the USA and Canada offer programs with majors in art, most of which lead to undergraduate degrees (BA, BFA, etc.). Many of the universities listed offer graduate programs leading to MFA degrees. Write to schools that interest you, for catalogs, course listings and descriptions of degree programs in art. Address letters to: Art Department Chairman; Name of School; Department of Art; City, State and Zip Code.

Over 500 community colleges and local junior colleges are not listed here; nor are art schools with two- or three-year programs. Contact them directly. Names and addresses of these schools and colleges can be found at the nearest public library.

Because the information in this chart changes constantly, as departments add or drop programs from year to year, the authors cannot guarantee its accuracy, although it is as complete a list of course offerings as is available.

Some of the listed schools are accredited by, belong to, or have student chapters of national representational organizations. Such associations do not guarantee the quality of the programs offered, but do recommend their consideration. The initials in the chart refer to the following:

ASID *Student Chapter,* American Society of Interior Designers
AATA *Member:* American Art Therapy Association
ASLA *Accredited:* American Society of Landscape Architecture
AIGA *Recommended:* American Institute of Graphic Arts
FIDER *Accredited:* Foundation for Interior Design Education Research
NAAB *Accredited:* National Architectural Accrediting Board
NASA *Member:* National Association of Schools of Art
RAIC *Recognized:* Royal Architectural Institute of Canada
UICA *Member:* Union of Independent Colleges of Art

Because titles can be misleading or incomplete, some notes will help you understand the categories listed in the chart.

Administration/Management indicates areas of museum management, curatorship and directorship, but also refers to administration of art programs, art educational systems, management of galleries and art centers.

Architecture often includes landscape architecture and environmental and city planning. Schools with NAAB designations offer degrees, while others offer pre-architectural majors, which must be continued at NAAB schools.

Art History usually refers to professional training leading to advanced degrees for museum work or art history teaching; may also refer to survey courses for art majors or others.

Art Education usually refers to professional training to become an art teacher, with studio courses and practice teaching experiences. May mean introductory courses in art and design.

Art Therapy usually refers to programs that train professional career specialists in art therapy. Those schools with AATA listings offer degrees with art therapy majors.

Crafts/Fabrics can cover a wide range of skills and special interests, including bookbinding, woodcarving, ceramics, glassblowing, jewelry, enameling, metalsmithing, papermaking, stained glass and general crafts. The fabric area includes weaving and textile design.

Fashion Design/Illustration covers both areas of training (design and illustration) for careers in the fashion industry. Some schools have only one or the other, others have both.

Film/Television/Video covers all professional training in these areas. Some schools have entire film or video departments and include all aspects of film production; others offer only a course or two. Usually, film departments include animation.

Fine Arts includes all the fine arts—drawing, painting, printmaking and sculpture—although some schools emphasize one area more than others.

Graphic Design/Advertising includes courses in all areas of this field—book design, editorial graphics, advertising, packaging, TV graphics, calligraphy, lettering, typography, layout, paste-up, etc. Schools with AIGA designations usually have very complete programs.

Illustration refers to training for commercial illustration of magazines, record jackets, book jackets, books, advertising and other visual media. Cartooning is often included. Medical and Technical Illustration are separated in this chart and are listed under Medical Illustration.

Industrial Design refers to both general training in all types of product and package design, and such specialized areas as furniture, automotive or package design, or computer-assisted design.

Interior Design usually includes all general interior design courses, but can also include special emphases such as facility planning, interior environmental design, space use and so on. Schools with ASID designations have student chapters of this professional organization. Those with FIDER designations have programs accredited by that organization.

Landscape Architecture environmental and urban planning are emphasized along with landscape architecture in a number of schools, and those listed as ASLA schools are accredited by the American Society of Landscape Architects.

Museum Work/Conservation is difficult to categorize. Some schools specify this emphasis, but others do not mention it. Keep in mind the fact that many museums have apprentice programs to train people to fill specific career positions.

Photography refers generally to still photography, in black and white and in color. Some schools only have classes in taking pictures and designing an image, while others stress darkroom training and laboratory work.

Medical Illustration is a specialized area of technical illustration. Courses are available in a number of medical schools which are part of university campuses. Generally, these are graduate level courses.

Theater Arts/Stage refers to emphasis on stage and set design as well as costume design and make-up. Often these classes include construction and decoration of sets and sewing of costumes as well as making renderings and building models.

Table columns (headers, diagonal): Administration/Management · Architecture · Art History · Art Education · Art Therapy · Crafts/Fabrics · Fashion Design/Illustration · Film/Television/Video · Fine Arts · Graphic Design/Advertising · Illustration · Industrial Design · Interior Design · Landscape Architecture · Museum Work/Conservation · Photography · Medical Illustration · Theater Arts/Stage · Associations

School	Adm	Arch	ArtHist	ArtEd	ArtTher	Crafts	Fashion	Film/TV	FineArts	Graphic	Illus	IndDes	IntDes	LandArch	Museum	Photo	MedIll	Theater	Associations
ALABAMA																			
Alabama State U., Montgomery 36101			●	●		●			●	●	●					●			
Athens State College, Athens 35611			●	●		●		●	●	●						●			
Auburn U., Auburn 36830		●	●	●		●	●		●	●	●					●			
Auburn U. at Montgomery, 36117			●	●		●			●	●	●	●	●			●			NASA, NAAB, FIDER, ASID, AIGA
Birmingham Southern College, Birmingham 35204			●	●					●		●								
Huntingdon College, Montgomery 36106			●	●		●			●		●					●			
Jacksonville State U., Jacksonville 36265			●	●		●			●	●						●			AIGA
John C. Calhoun State, Decatur 35602	●		●	●		●	●	●	●	●	●	●	●		●	●			
Patrick Henry State Jr. College, Monroeville 35460									●										
Samford U., Birmingham 35209			●	●		●			●	●			●			●		●	ASID
Spring Hill College, Mobile 36608			●	●	●	●	●		●	●						●			AATA
Troy State U., Troy 36081			●	●		●		●	●	●	●					●		●	
Tuskegee Inst., Tuskegee 36088		●	●	●			●												NAAB
U. of Alabama, University 35486			●	●		●			●	●			●			●			FIDER, AIGA
—— Birmingham, Birmingham 35294			●	●		●			●	●						●			
—— Huntsville, Huntsville 35807			●	●				●	●	●	●		●			●			AIGA
U. of N. Alabama, Florence 35630			●	●		●			●	●	●	●				●		●	
U. of S. Alabama, Mobile 36688			●	●		●			●	●									AIGA
ALASKA																			
U. of Alaska Anchorage, Anchorage 99504			●	●		●			●							●		●	
—— Fairbanks, Fairbanks 99701			●			●			●										
ARIZONA																			
Arizona State U., Tempe 85281		●		●		●			●	●			●			●			NAAB, ASID
Grand Canyon College, Phoenix 85017			●	●		●			●		●					●		●	
Northern Arizona U., Flagstaff 86001				●		●	●		●	●	●		●			●			ASID, AIGA
U. of Arizona, Tucson 85721	●	●	●			●			●	●			●	●	●				ASLA, NAAB, ASID
ARKANSAS																			
Arkansas Arts Center, Little Rock 72203			●			●										●		●	
Arkansas State U., Jonesboro 72467				●		●			●	●	●					●			AIGA
Arkansas Tech U., Russellville 72801				●		●			●	●									AIGA
John Brown U., Siloam Springs 72761			●	●		●			●										
College of the Ozarks, Clarksville 72830			●			●			●										
Harding U., Searcy 72143			●			●			●	●	●								AIGA
Southern Arkansas U., Magnolia 71753			●	●		●			●	●						●			
Ouachita Baptist U., Arkadelphia 71923			●	●		●	●		●				●			●		●	AIGA
U. of Arkansas, Fayetteville 72701		●	●	●		●			●	●			●			●			NAAB, ASID, AIGA
—— at Little Rock, 72204			●	●		●			●	●	●					●			
—— at Monticello, 71655			●	●		●													
—— at Pine Bluff, 71601			●	●					●										
U. of Central Arkansas, Conway 72032				●		●			●										
CALIFORNIA																			
Academy of Art College, San Francisco 94102	●		●			●	●		●	●	●					●			
Art Center College of Design, Pasadena 91103			●				●		●	●	●	●	●			●			NASA, AIGA
Azusa Pacific College, Azusa 91702			●		●				●	●									
Biola College, La Mirada 90639			●		●				●	●									
California Baptist College, Riverside 92504			●		●				●				●						
California College of Arts & Crafts, Oakland 94618	●		●	●		●			●	●			●			●			NASA, FIDER, ASID, AIGA, UICA
California Inst. of the Arts, Valencia 91355			●						●	●						●			NASA, AIGA
California Lutheran College, Thousand Oaks 91360			●	●		●	●		●							●	●		
California Polytechnic State U., San Luis Obispo 93407	●	●	●			●			●	●			●			●			NAAB, ASID, AIGA
California State College at Bakersfield, 93309			●	●		●			●							●			
—— at San Bernardino, 92407			●	●		●			●		●					●			
—— Stanislaus, Turlock 95380	●		●			●			●	●	●					●		●	AIGA

Institution	Administration/Management	Architecture	Art History	Art Education	Art Therapy	Crafts/Fabrics	Fashion Design/Illustration	Film/Television/Video	Fine Arts	Graphic Design/Advertising	Illustration	Industrial Design	Interior Design	Landscape Architecture	Museum Work/Conservation	Photography	Medical Illustration	Theater Arts/Stage	Associations
CALIFORNIA																			
California State Polytechnic U., Pomona 91765		•	•	•		•			•	•			•			•			NAAB
California State U. Chico, Chico 95929	•		•	•		•		•								•		•	NASA
——— **Dominguez Hills**, Carson 90747			•	•		•			•	•						•			
——— **Fresno**, Fresno 93740			•	•		•			•				•			•			ASID
——— **Fullerton**, Fullerton 92634			•	•		•			•	•	•	•	•			•			NASA, ASID
——— **Hayward**, Hayward 94542	•	•				•			•	•						•			NASA
——— **Long Beach**, Long Beach 90840	•		•	•		•	•		•	•	•	•	•		•	•			NASA, FIDER, ASID
——— **Los Angeles**, Los Angeles 90032		•	•	•			•		•				•			•		•	NASA, ASID, AIGA
——— **Northridge**, Northridge 91321			•	•		•		•	•			•	•			•			ASID
——— **Sacramento**, Sacramento 95819	•		•	•	•	•		•	•							•		•	NASA, AATA
Chapman College, Orange 92666			•	•		•		•	•	•		•				•		•	
College of Notre Dame, Belmont 94022	•		•	•		•			•	•		•				•		•	
Dominican College of San Rafael, 94901	•		•	•		•			•	•						•		•	
Humboldt State U., Arcata 95521			•	•		•			•	•						•			NASA
Laguna Beach Sch. of Art, Laguna Beach 92651			•			•			•	•						•			
Loma Linda U., Riverside 92515			•	•		•			•	•		•				•			
Loyola Marymount U., Los Angeles 90045	•		•	•	•	•			•	•		•				•		•	AATA
Mills College, Oakland 94613			•	•		•		•	•							•			
Mount St. Mary's College, Los Angeles 90049			•	•		•		•	•							•		•	
Occidental College, Los Angeles 90041			•	•		•		•	•			•				•			
Otis Art Inst. of Parsons Sch. of Design, Los Angeles 90057		•				•	•		•	•		•				•			NASA
Pacific Union College, Angwin 94508		•	•			•			•	•	•		•			•			
Pepperdine U., Malibu 90265		•	•			•			•										
Pitzer College, Claremont 91711			•			•		•	•										
Pomona College, Claremont 91711			•			•			•							•			
San Diego State U., San Diego 92182	•	•	•	•		•	•		•	•			•			•			NASA, ASID, ALGA
San Francisco Art Inst., San Francisco 94133			•			•		•	•							•			NASA
San Francisco State U., San Francisco 94132			•	•		•		•	•			•			•	•	•		ASID
San Jose State U., San Jose 95192	•		•	•		•			•	•	•	•	•			•			NASA, ASID
Scripps College, Claremont 91711			•			•			•							•			
Sonoma State U., Rohnert Park 94928	•		•	•	•	•		•	•							•		•	AATA
Southern California Inst. Of Arch., Santa Monica 90404		•																	NAAB
Stanford U., Stanford 94305			•	•					•	•						•			AIGA
Stanislaus State College, Turlock 95380			•	•		•		•	•							•	•		
United State International U., San Diego 92131			•	•	•	•			•	•						•		•	AATA
U. of California at Berkeley, 94720		•	•	•					•					•		•			NAAB, ASLA
——— **at Davis**, 95616			•	•		•		•	•				•			•			ASID
——— **at Irvine**, 92717			•	•		•		•	•				•			•			ASID
——— **at Los Angeles**, 90024			•	•		•	•	•	•	•			•	•		•			NAAB, ASID, FIDER
——— **at Riverside**, 92521			•					•	•							•			
——— **at San Diego**, 92093			•					•	•							•			
——— **at San Francisco**, 94103															•				
——— **at Santa Barbara**, 93106			•			•			•							•			
——— **at Santa Cruz**, 95064	•	•	•			•		•	•							•	•		
U. of the Pacific, Stockton 95211			•	•		•			•	•	•					•			NASA
U. of Redlands, Redlands 92373			•	•		•			•							•			
U. of San Diego, San Diego 92110	•	•	•	•		•			•	•				•		•			NAAB, ASLA
U. of Santa Clara, Santa Clara 95053	•		•			•		•	•							•			
U. of Southern California, Los Angeles 90007	•	•	•	•		•			•							•			NAAB
Woodbury U., Los Angeles 90017			•			•	•		•	•	•	•	•			•		•	ASID
COLORADO																			
Adams State College, Alamosa 81102			•	•		•			•							•			
Colorado Inst. of Art, Denver 80203							•		•	•	•		•			•			ASID, AIGA
Colorado State U., Fort Collins 80523			•	•		•			•	•	•		•			•	•		ASID
Colorado Womens College, Denver 80220			•	•		•	•		•							•		•	
Fort Lewis College, Durango 81301			•	•		•			•							•			

Institution	Administration/Management	Architecture	Art History	Art Education	Art Therapy	Crafts/Fabrics	Fashion Design/Illustration	Film/Television/Video	Fine Arts	Graphic Design/Advertising	Illustration	Industrial Design	Interior Design	Landscape Architecture	Museum Work/Conservation	Photography	Medical Illustration	Theater Arts/Stage	Associations
COLORADO																			
Loretto Heights College, Denver 80236			●	●		●			●							●			
Metropolitan State College, Denver 80204			●	●		●			●	●	●	●				●			
Rocky Mountain Sch. of Art, Denver 80218			●			●	●		●	●	●					●			AIGA
U. of Colorado, Boulder 80309		●	●	●			●		●	●						●			NAAB
——, Denver 80202		●	●				●		●							●			
U. of Denver, Denver 80208	●		●	●		●			●	●	●					●			AIGA
U. of Northern Colorado, Greeley 80639	●		●	●		●			●	●						●			
U. of Southern Colorado, Pueblo 81001	●		●	●		●			●	●	●		●			●			
Western State College, Gunnison 81230			●	●		●			●										
CONNECTICUT																			
Albertus Magnus College, New Haven 06511			●	●	●	●			●							●		●	AATA
Brookfield Craft Center, Brookfield 06804						●			●										
Central Connecticut State College, New Britain 06050			●	●		●		●	●	●	●	●				●			AIGA
Connecticut College, New London 06320			●	●		●			●	●						●			
Fairfield U., Fairfield 06430			●						●							●			
Hartford Art Sch., West Hartford 06117				●		●		●	●	●						●			NASA
Paier Sch. of Art, Hamden 06511			●				●		●	●	●		●			●			ASID
Sacred Heart U., Bridgeport 06606			●				●	●	●							●			AIGA
Silvermine Guild Sch. of the Arts, New Canaan 06840			●			●			●	●	●					●			
Southern Connecticut State College, New Haven 06515			●	●		●			●	●						●			
Trinity College, Hartford 06106			●						●								●		
U. of Bridgeport, Bridgeport 06602			●	●		●		●	●	●	●	●				●	●		AIGA
U. of Connecticut, Storrs 06268		●	●	●					●	●	●		●			●			ASID, AIGA
U. of New Haven, New Haven 06505			●			●	●	●	●	●	●		●			●	●		AIGA
Wesleyan U., Middletown 06457	●	●	●	●					●	●				●		●			
Western Connecticut State College, Danbury 06810		●	●	●					●	●						●			
Yale U. Sch. of Art, New Haven 06520		●						●	●	●	●					●			NAAB, AIGA
DELAWARE																			
Delaware State College, Dover 19901			●	●		●			●	●			●			●			
U. of Delaware, Newark 19711			●		●	●	●	●	●				●			●			AIGA
FLORIDA																			
Art Inst. of Ft. Lauderdale, Ft. Lauderdale 33316	●	●				●	●	●	●	●			●			●			ASID
Barry College, Miami 33161			●	●		●			●	●						●			
College of Boca Raton, Boca Raton 33431			●		●	●			●	●			●			●	●		
Eckerd College, St. Petersburg 33733			●	●		●			●							●			
Flagler College, St. Augustine 32084			●	●		●			●	●						●			
Florida A & M U., Tallahassee 32307		●	●	●		●			●	●									NAAB
Florida Atlantic U., Boca Raton 33432			●	●		●	●	●							●				
Florida International U., Miami 33199			●	●		●			●							●			
Florida Southern College, Lakeland 33802			●	●		●			●	●						●			
Florida State U., Tallahassee 32306			●			●	●		●	●	●		●		●	●			FIDER, ASID
Jacksonville U., Jacksonville 32211	●		●	●		●			●	●						●			
Ringling School of Art, Sarasota 33580			●							●	●		●						ASID, AIGA
Rollins College, Winter Park 32789			●	●		●			●							●			
Stetson U., DeLand 32720			●	●		●			●										
U. of Central Florida, Orlando 32816			●			●		●	●	●	●			●		●			ASLA
U. of Florida, Gainesville 32611		●						●	●	●	●		●			●	●		NAAB, FIDER, ASID, AIGA
U. of Miami, Coral Gables 33124	●	●		●	●	●		●	●	●						●			NAAB, AATA
U. of S. Florida, Tampa 33620			●	●		●		●	●							●			
U. of Tampa, Tampa 33606	●		●	●		●			●							●			
U. of W. Florida, Pensacola 32504			●	●		●		●	●	●	●					●			AIGA

	Administration/Management	Architecture	Art History	Art Education	Art Therapy	Crafts/Fabrics	Fashion Design/Illustration	Film/Television/Video	Fine Arts	Graphic Design/Advertising	Illustration	Industrial Design	Interior Design	Landscape Architecture	Museum Work/Conservation	Photography	Medical Illustration	Theater Arts/Stage	Associations
GEORGIA																			
Art Inst. of Atlanta, Atlanta 30326		●	●			●			●	●	●		●			●			ASID
Atlanta College of Art, Atlanta 30309		●			●		●	●	●				●			●			NASA, ASID, AIGA, UICA
Augusta College, Augusta 30910		●	●	●					●	●						●			
Berry College, Mount Berry 30149		●	●	●			●	●	●							●			
Clark College, Atlanta 30314									●							●			
Columbus College, Columbus 31907		●	●	●				●	●							●	●		
Georgia College, Milledgeville 31061	●	●	●	●				●	●							●			
Georgia Inst. of Tech., Atlanta 30332		●																	NAAB
Georgia Southern College, Statesboro 30458		●	●	●				●					●			●			ASID
Georgia Southwestern College, Americus 31709		●	●	●	●	●	●		●							●			
Georgia State U., Atlanta 30303		●	●	●				●	●				●			●			ASID
La Grange College, Barnesville 30204		●	●	●					●			●				●			
Medical College of Georgia, Augusta 30912																	●		
Mercer U., Atlanta 30304		●	●	●					●										
N. Georgia College, Dahlonega 30597		●	●	●					●							●			
Piedmont College, Demorest 30535		●	●	●												●			
Agnes Scott College, Decatur 30030		●		●					●										
Shorter College, Rome 30161		●	●	●				●	●							●			
Tift College, Forsyth 31029		●	●				●	●	●							●			
U. of Georgia, Athens 30602		●	●	●				●	●				●	●		●			NASA, ASLA, FIDER, ASID
Valdosta State College, Valdosta 31698		●	●	●				●	●							●			AIGA
Wesleyan College, Macon 31297	●	●	●	●				●	●	●	●					●			
W. Georgia College, Carrollton 30117		●	●	●				●	●							●			
HAWAII																			
Brigham Young U., Laie 96762		●	●		●				●			●							
Honolulu Academy of Arts, Honolulu 96814									●										
U. of Hawaii, Honolulu 96822	●	●			●			●			●	●				●			NAAB, AIGA
IDAHO																			
Boise State U., Boise 83725		●	●	●		●	●	●	●	●	●		●			●			AIGA
College of Southern Idaho, Twin Falls 83301		●			●				●							●	●		
Idaho State U., Pocatello 83209		●	●		●				●							●			
Lewis-Clark State College, Lewiston 83501		●	●		●				●								●		
N. Idaho College, Coeur d'Alene 83814		●			●	●			●	●			●			●			
U. of Idaho, Moscow 83843	●	●	●	●			●	●	●	●	●		●	●		●			ASLA, NAAB, ASID, AIGA
ILLINOIS																			
Aurora College, Aurora 60507		●	●						●										
Barat College, Lake Forest 60045		●	●	●					●							●	●		
Bradley U., Peoria 61625		●	●	●			●	●	●	●						●			
Columbia College, Chicago 60605	●		●		●	●	●	●	●	●	●		●			●	●	●	ASID
DePaul U., Chicago 60614		●							●							●			
Eastern Illinois U., Charleston 61920		●	●		●			●	●							●			
Governors State U., Park Forest 60466		●			●		●	●								●			
Greenville College, Greenville 62246	●	●	●	●				●	●										
Harrington Inst. of Interior Design, Chicago 60605		●								●		●				●			FIDER, ASID
Illinois Inst. of Tech., Chicago 60616		●	●				●	●	●			●				●			NAAB
Illinois State U., Normal 61761	●	●	●	●		●		●	●	●	●					●		●	NASA, ASID, AIGA
Illinois Wesleyan U., Bloomington 61701	●		●	●		●			●	●	●					●			
Inst. of Design of Illinois Inst. of Tech., Chicago 60616		●	●					●		●	●	●				●			NASA, AIGA
Judson College, Elgin 60120		●	●	●					●								●		
Knox College, Galesburg 61401		●	●	●					●							●			
Loyola U., Chicago 60611		●	●	●			●	●	●							●			
Millikin U., Decatur 62522	●		●	●					●	●						●	●		
Morton College, Cicero 60650		●	●						●							●			
Northeastern Illinois U., Chicago 60625			●	●		●		●	●	●	●	●				●			AIGA

ILLINOIS

School	Administration/Management	Architecture	Art History	Art Education	Art Therapy	Crafts/Fabrics	Fashion Design/Illustration	Film/Television/Video	Fine Arts	Graphic Design/Advertising	Illustration	Industrial Design	Interior Design	Landscape Architecture	Museum Work/Conservation	Photography	Medical Illustration	Theater Arts/Stage	Associations
Northern Illinois U., DeKalb 60115	●		●	●		●		●	●	●		●			●	●		●	NASA, ASID
North Park College, Chicago 60625			●	●		●		●	●	●						●			
Northwestern U., Evanston 60201								●								●		●	
Olivet Nazarene College, Kankakee 60901			●	●		●		●	●	●						●			
Prairie State College, Chicago Heights 60411		●	●		●	●		●	●	●	●					●			
Quincy College, Quincy 62301			●	●		●		●	●	●						●			
Ray-Vogue Sch. of Design, Chicago 60611			●				●	●	●	●	●		●			●			AIGA
Rockford College, Rockford 61107	●		●	●		●		●	●							●	●		
Sangamon State U., Springfield 62708	●		●			●		●	●							●			
Sch. of the Art Inst. of Chicago, Chicago 60603			●	●	●	●	●	●	●	●	●		●			●	●		● NASA, VICA
Southern Illinois U. at Carbondale, 62901			●	●		●			●				●			●	●		NASA, ASID, FIDER
—— **at Edwardsville,** 62025			●	●		●			●							●		●	
U. of Chicago, Chicago 60637	●		●					●	●							●			
U. of Illinois at Chicago Circle, 60680		●		●				●	●	●	●					●		●	NAAB, AIGA
U. of Illinois at The Medical Center, Chicago 60612																	●		
U. of Illinois at Urbana-Champaign, Champaign 61820	●	●	●	●		●		●	●	●	●	●	●			●	●		NASA, ASID, NAAB
Western Illinois U., Macomb 61455	●	●	●	●	●	●		●	●		●		●						

INDIANA

School	Administration/Management	Architecture	Art History	Art Education	Art Therapy	Crafts/Fabrics	Fashion Design/Illustration	Film/Television/Video	Fine Arts	Graphic Design/Advertising	Illustration	Industrial Design	Interior Design	Landscape Architecture	Museum Work/Conservation	Photography	Medical Illustration	Theater Arts/Stage	Associations
Anderson College, Anderson 46011	●		●	●		●			●	●		●				●			AIGA
Ball State U., Muncie 47306		●	●	●		●			●	●	●		●			●			NAAB, ASID, AIGA
De Pauw U., Greencastle 46135			●	●		●	●		●	●	●					●			AIGA
Earlham College, Richmond 47374	●		●			●		●	●	●						●	●		
Franklin College, Franklin 46131			●	●		●			●							●			
Goshen College, Goshen 46526			●	●		●			●	●						●		●	
Grace College, Winona Lake 46590			●	●		●			●		●					●			
Hanover College, Hanover 47243			●	●		●		●	●							●			
Herron Sch. of Art (Indiana U.), Indianapolis 46202			●	●		●		●	●		●					●			NASA
Indiana State U., Terre Haute 47809			●	●		●			●	●			●			●			FIDER, ASID
Indiana U., Bloomington 47401			●			●				●						●			AIGA
Indiana U. at South Bend, 46615			●	●		●			●										
Indiana U.–Purdue U. at Fort Wayne, 46804			●	●		●			●							●			NASA
Indiana U. Southeast, New Albany 47150			●			●			●										
Marian College, Indianapolis 46226	●		●	●	●	●			●				●					●	AATA
Marion College, Marion 46952			●	●		●			●	●			●			●		●	
Purdue U., West LaFayette 47907			●	●		●		●	●	●			●	●					ASLA, FIDER, ASID, AIGA
Purdue U.–Calumet, Hammond 46323		●	●	●		●		●	●			●							
St. Francis College, Fort Wayne 46808			●	●		●	●		●	●	●					●			AIGA
St. Mary's College, Notre Dame 46556	●		●	●		●			●							●			NASA
Taylor U., Upland 46989			●	●		●		●	●	●						●			
U. of Evansville, Evansville 47702			●	●	●	●			●									●	AATA
U. of Notre Dame, Notre Dame 46556		●	●			●			●	●		●	●			●			NAAB
Valparaiso U., Valparaiso 46383			●	●		●			●	●						●			

IOWA

School	Administration/Management	Architecture	Art History	Art Education	Art Therapy	Crafts/Fabrics	Fashion Design/Illustration	Film/Television/Video	Fine Arts	Graphic Design/Advertising	Illustration	Industrial Design	Interior Design	Landscape Architecture	Museum Work/Conservation	Photography	Medical Illustration	Theater Arts/Stage	Associations
Clarke College, Dubuque 52001			●	●		●			●	●						●			
Coe College, Cedar Rapids 52402	●		●	●		●			●							●			
Cornell College, Mount Vernon 52314			●						●										
Des Moines Art Center, Des Moines 50312					●			●	●							●			
Drake U., Des Moines 50311			●	●	●	●			●	●	●		●			●		●	NASA, AATA, AIGA
Grand View College, Des Moines 50322			●	●					●	●						●	●		
Grinnel College, Grinnel 50112			●	●		●			●								●		
Iowa State U., Ames 50010		●	●	●		●	●		●	●	●		●						NAAB, ASID, AIGA
Iowa Wesleyan College, Mt. Pleasant 52641			●	●		●			●							●			
Loras College, Dubuque 52001			●	●					●							●			
Luther College, Decorah 52101		●	●	●		●			●	●			●	●		●			AIGA
Marycrest College, Davenport 52804			●	●		●	●	●	●	●			●			●			

Colleges and Art Schools

	Administration/Management	Architecture	Art History	Art Education	Art Therapy	Crafts/Fabrics	Fashion Design/Illustration	Film/Television/Video	Fine Arts	Graphic Design/Advertising	Illustration	Industrial Design	Interior Design	Landscape Architecture	Museum Work/Conservation	Photography	Medical Illustration	Theater Arts/Stage	Associations
IOWA																			
Morningside College, Sioux City 51106			●	●			●		●							●			
Mount Mercy College, Cedar Rapids 52402			●	●			●		●							●			
Northwestern College, Orange City 51041			●	●			●		●							●			
St. Ambrose College, Davenport 52803			●	●			●		●	●						●			
U. of Iowa, Iowa City 52242			●			●	●		●			●	●			●			ASID, AIGA
U. of Northern Iowa, Cedar Falls 50614			●	●			●	●	●	●			●			●			ASID
Wartburg College, Waverly 50677			●	●			●		●							●			
Westmar College, Le Mars 51031	●		●	●			●		●				●			●			
William Penn College, Oskaloosa 52577			●	●			●		●	●									
KANSAS																			
Baker U., Baldwin 66006			●	●			●		●										
Benedictine College, Atchison 66002			●	●			●		●							●			
Bethany College, Lindsborg 67456			●	●			●		●							●			
Bethel College, North Newton 67117			●	●			●		●										
Emporia State U., Emporia 66801			●	●	●	●			●		●		●			●		●	AATA
Fort Hays State U., Hays 67601			●	●	●	●		●	●	●						●		●	AATA
Friends U., Wichita 67213			●	●			●		●	●			●			●			
Kansas State U., Manhattan 66506		●	●	●		●	●		●	●	●		●			●			NAAB, FIDER, ASID, AIGA
Kansas Wesleyan, Salina 67401			●	●			●	●	●							●			
Marymount College, Salina 67401			●	●			●		●							●			
McPherson College, McPherson 67460			●	●			●		●				●			●	●		
Pittsburg State U., Pittsburg 66762			●	●	●	●	●		●	●		●	●			●		●	AATA
Sterling College, Sterling 67579			●	●			●		●	●			●			●	●		
U. of Kansas, Lawrence 66045		●	●	●		●	●		●	●	●	●	●			●		●	NAAB, NASA, ASID, AIGA
Washburn U., Topeka 66621			●			●			●	●						●			AIGA
Wichita State U., Wichita 67208			●	●		●	●	●	●	●	●					●			AIGA
KENTUCKY																			
Asbury College, Wilmore 40390			●	●			●		●							●			
Berea College, Berea 40404			●	●			●		●							●	●		
Brescia College, Owensboro 42301			●	●			●		●	●			●			●			
Campbellsville College, Campbellsville 42718			●	●			●		●	●			●			●	●		
Center College of Kentucky, Danville 40422			●	●			●	●	●				●						
Cumberland College, Williamsburg 40769			●	●			●		●							●			
Eastern Kentucky U., Richmond 40475			●	●			●		●	●			●			●			ASID
Georgetown College, Georgetown 40324			●	●			●		●							●			
Kentucky State College, Frankfort 40601			●	●			●		●	●									
Kentucky Wesleyan College, Owensboro 42301			●	●			●			●		●	●			●	●		
Louisville Sch. of Art, Anchorage 40223			●				●		●	●						●			NASA, AIGA
Morehead State U., Morehead 40351			●			●	●		●	●			●			●			ASID
Murray State U., Murray 42071			●	●			●	●	●	●	●					●			
Northern Kentucky U., Highland Heights 41076			●	●			●		●	●						●	●		
Spalding College, Louisville 40203			●				●		●										
Thomas More College, Crestview Hills 41017			●	●			●		●							●			
Transylvania U., Lexington 40508			●	●			●		●								●		
U. of Kentucky, Lexington 40506	●	●	●	●			●		●	●	●		●	●		●			FIDER, NAAB, ASID
U. of Louisville, Louisville 40292			●	●	●		●		●				●			●			ASID, AATA
Western Kentucky U., Bowling Green 42101			●	●			●		●	●						●			ASID
LOUISIANA																			
Grambling State U., Grambling 71245		●	●			●			●										
Louisiana College, Pineville 71360			●	●					●	●						●			
Louisiana State U., Baton Rouge 70803		●	●	●			●		●	●			●	●		●			NAAB, ASLA, FIDER, ASID
Louisiana State U. at Eunice, 70535			●	●			●		●					●					ASLA
Louisiana Tech. U., Ruston 71270		●	●	●			●	●	●	●	●		●			●			NAAB, ASID, AIGA
Loyola U. of the South, New Orleans 70118			●				●		●	●						●		●	

	Administration/Management	Architecture	Art History	Art Education	Art Therapy	Crafts/Fabrics	Fashion Design/Illustration	Film/Television/Video	Fine Arts	Graphic Design/Advertising	Illustration	Industrial Design	Interior Design	Landscape Architecture	Museum Work/Conservation	Photography	Medical Illustration	Theater Arts/Stage	Associations
LOUISIANA																			
McNeese State U., Lake Charles 70609		●	●	●					●							●			
New Orleans Art Inst., New Orleans 70119						●			●	●	●						●		
Nicholls State U., Thibodaux 70301			●	●		●			●	●						●			
Northeast Louisiana U., Monroe 71203			●	●		●			●	●						●			
Northwestern State U. of Louisiana, Natchitoches 71457			●	●		●	●		●	●			●			●			AIGA
Southeastern Louisiana U., Hammond 70402			●	●					●										
Southern U. A & M College, Baton Rouge 70813		●																	NAAB
Tulane U. (Newcomb College), New Orleans 70118		●	●	●		●			●		●					●	●		NASA, NAAB
U. of New Orleans, New Orleans 70122		●							●							●			
U. of Southwestern Louisiana, Lafayette 70501	●	●	●	●		●			●	●			●			●			NAAB
Xavier U. of Louisiana, New Orleans 70125		●	●	●	●			●	●	●	●					●	●		AATA
MAINE																			
Bates College, Lewiston 04240			●			●			●										
Bowdoin College, Brunswick 04011		●	●						●							●			
Portland Sch. of Art, Portland 04101			●			●			●	●	●					●			NASA, AIGA
Unity College, Unity 04988	●		●			●			●							●	●		
U. of Maine at Augusta, 04330		●	●	●		●		●	●	●	●					●		●	
— at Orono, 04469			●	●					●							●			NASA
U. of Southern Maine, Gorham 04038			●	●		●			●							●			NASA
MARYLAND																			
Bowie State College, Bowie 20715	●		●	●		●		●	●	●						●	●		
College of Notre Dame of Maryland, Baltimore 21210			●	●		●		●	●							●			
Coppin State College, Baltimore 21212		●	●	●		●		●	●		●	●	●			●			
Frostburg State College, Frostburg 21532			●	●		●			●	●						●	●		
Goucher College, Towson 21204			●	●	●			●	●							●	●		
Hood College, Frederick 21701	●		●	●	●	●	●		●	●			●			●	●		ASID
Johns Hopkins U., Baltimore 21205																	●		
Maryland College of Art & Design, Silver Spring 20902			●			●			●	●	●					●			NASA, AIGA
Maryland Inst. College of Art, Baltimore 21217			●	●		●	●	●	●	●			●			●			NASA, FIDER, ASID, UICA
Morgan State U., Baltimore 21239	●	●	●	●		●	●	●	●	●	●		●		●	●	●		NASA
Mount St. Marys College, Emmitsburg 21727			●	●					●								●		
St. Marys College of Maryland, St. Marys City 20686	●		●	●					●							●			
Salisbury State College, Salisbury 21801	●		●	●		●			●	●						●			
Towson State U., Towson 21204		●	●	●		●			●							●			
U. of Maryland, College Park 20742		●	●			●	●	●	●	●	●		●			●			NAAB, ASID, AIGA
— Eastern Shore, Princess Anne 21853			●	●		●			●							●			
Western Maryland College, Westminster 21157			●	●		●			●		●					●	●		
MASSACHUSETTS																			
Amherst College, Amherst 01002		●							●										
Anna Maria College, Paxton 01612			●	●	●	●			●	●			●			●		●	AIGA
Art Inst. of Boston, Boston 02215			●			●	●	●	●	●	●					●			AIGA
Assumption College, Worcester 01609			●	●		●			●								●		
Boston Arch. Center, Boston 02115		●											●			●			NAAB
Boston College, Newton 02159			●			●		●								●			
Boston U., Boston 02215			●	●		●		●	●	●	●					●			AIGA
Bradford College, Bradford 01830			●			●		●	●							●			
Brandeis U., Waltham 02154			●						●										
Butera Sch. of Art, Boston 02116			●						●	●	●					●			AIGA
Clark U., Worcester 01610	●	●	●	●	●	●			●	●	●	●				●			
College of the Holy Cross, Worcester 01610			●			●				●			●			●	●		
Emmanuel College, Boston 02115			●	●	●	●			●	●						●		●	
Framingham State College, Framingham 01701	●		●	●		●			●	●			●			●			
Harvard U. Graduate School of Design, Cambridge 02138		●	●					●	●	●	●			●		●			NAAB, ASLA, AIGA
Lesley College, Cambridge 02138			●	●	●	●			●							●			AATA

MASSACHUSETTS

Institution	Administration/Management	Architecture	Art History	Art Education	Art Therapy	Crafts/Fabrics	Fashion Design/Illustration	Film/Television/Video	Fine Arts	Graphic Design/Advertising	Illustration	Industrial Design	Interior Design	Landscape Architecture	Museum Work/Conservation	Photography	Medical Illustration	Theater Arts/Stage	Associations
Massachusetts College of Art, Boston 02215	•	•	•	•		•	•	•	•	•	•	•	•		•	•		•	NASA, AIGA
Massachusetts Inst. of Tech., Cambridge 02139		•						•		•						•			NAAB, AIGA
Mount Holyoke College, South Hadley 01075		•	•						•							•		•	
New England Sch. of Art and Design, Boston 02116			•			•		•	•	•			•			•			ASID, AIGA
Northeastern U., Boston 02115			•					•	•							•			
Regis College, Weston 02193			•	•		•		•	•							•			
Salem State College, Salem 01945			•	•		•		•	•							•			
Sch. of Fashion Design, Boston 02116			•				•				•								
Sch. of the Museum of Fine Arts, Boston 02115			•	•		•		•	•						•	•			
Smith College, Northampton 01063		•	•						•							•			
Southeastern Massachusetts U., North Dartmouth 02747	•		•	•		•	•	•	•	•	•				•	•	•		NASA
Springfield College, Springfield 01109	•		•		•	•			•						•	•	•	•	AATA
State College at Westfield, 01066			•	•		•			•		•					•			
Swain Sch. of Design, New Bedford 02740			•					•	•	•						•			NASA, AIGA
Tufts U., Medford 02155			•			•			•							•			
U. of Massachusetts, Amherst 01003	•		•	•					•				•			•			FIDER, ASID
Wellesley College, Wellesley 02181			•						•							•			
Wheaton College, Norton 02766			•						•							•			
Williams College, Williamstown 01267		•	•						•							•			
Worcester Art Museum Sch., Worcester 01608			•			•			•	•	•					•			NASA
Worcester Crafts Center, Worcester 01605						•										•			

MICHIGAN

Institution	Administration/Management	Architecture	Art History	Art Education	Art Therapy	Crafts/Fabrics	Fashion Design/Illustration	Film/Television/Video	Fine Arts	Graphic Design/Advertising	Illustration	Industrial Design	Interior Design	Landscape Architecture	Museum Work/Conservation	Photography	Medical Illustration	Theater Arts/Stage	Associations
Adrian College, Adrian 49221			•	•					•				•			•			
Alma College, Alma 48801	•		•	•		•	•	•	•	•	•	•			•	•			AIGA
Andrews U., Berrien Springs 49130			•	•					•			•	•			•			
Aquinas College, Grand Rapids 49506			•	•					•										
Calvin College, Grand Rapids 49506	•	•	•		•	•		•	•							•			AIGA
Center for Creative Studies, Detroit 48202			•			•	•	•	•	•	•	•			•	•	•	•	NASA, AIGA, UICA
Central Michigan U., Mount Pleasant 48859			•	•	•	•		•	•	•						•	•		
Cranbrook Academy of Art, Bloomfield Hills 48013		•				•	•		•	•	•	•				•			NASA, AIGA
Eastern Michigan U., Ypsilanti 48197	•		•	•		•		•	•	•			•			•			ASID
Grand Valley State College, Allendale 49401		•	•	•		•			•							•			NASA
Hillsdale College, Hillsdale 49242			•	•		•			•									•	
Hope College, Holland 49423			•	•		•			•							•			NASA
Kalamazoo College, Kalamazoo 49001			•	•		•			•									•	
Kendall Sch. of Design, Grand Rapids 49503		•	•					•	•	•	•		•			•		•	ASID, FIDER
Lawrence Inst. of Tech., Southfield 48075		•																	NAAB
Madonna College, Livonia 48150			•	•		•			•										
Marygrove College, Detroit 48221			•			•		•	•				•			•		•	
Mercy College, Detroit 48219				•		•			•										
Michigan State U., East Lansing 48824			•	•		•		•	•	•		•	•			•			FIDER, ASID, AIGA
Northern Michigan U., Marquette 49855			•	•		•		•	•	•	•	•	•			•			AIGA
Northwood Inst., Midland 48640			•			•	•		•				•			•			
Oakland U., Rochester 48063			•																
Olivet College, Olivet 49076			•	•				•	•										
Saginaw Valley State College, University Center, 48710			•	•		•		•	•	•						•			
Siena Heights College, Adrian 49221			•	•		•		•	•				•			•		•	AIGA
Spring Arbor College, Spring Arbor 49283			•	•		•	•	•	•	•	•					•			
U. of Detroit, Detroit 48221		•																	NAAB
U. of Michigan, Ann Arbor 48109		•	•	•		•		•	•	•	•			•		•	•		NAAB, NASA, ASLA, ASID, AIGA
Wayne State U., Detroit 48202			•			•		•	•	•	•	•	•			•			ASID
Western Michigan U., Kalamazoo 49012			•	•		•			•				•			•			NASA, ASID

MINNESOTA

Institution	Administration/Management	Architecture	Art History	Art Education	Art Therapy	Crafts/Fabrics	Fashion Design/Illustration	Film/Television/Video	Fine Arts	Graphic Design/Advertising	Illustration	Industrial Design	Interior Design	Landscape Architecture	Museum Work/Conservation	Photography	Medical Illustration	Theater Arts/Stage	Associations
Augsburg College, Minneapolis 55454			•	•		•		•	•	•						•			
Bemidji State U., Bemidji 56601			•	•		•		•	•	•			•			•			

	Administration/Management	Architecture	Art History	Art Education	Art Therapy	Crafts/Fabrics	Fashion Design/Illustration	Film/Television/Video	Fine Arts	Graphic Design/Advertising	Illustration	Industrial Design	Interior Design	Landscape Architecture	Museum Work/Conservation	Photography	Medical Illustration	Theater Arts/Stage	Associations
MINNESOTA																			
Bethel College, St. Paul 55112			•	•		•			•	•						•			
College of St. Benedict, St. Joseph 56374			•	•		•	•		•	•						•		•	
College of St. Catherine, St. Paul 55105		•	•	•		•			•	•						•			AIGA
College of St. Teresa, Winona 55987	•		•	•	•	•			•	•			•					•	AATA
Gustavus Adolphus College, St. Peter 56082		•	•	•		•		•	•							•		•	
Hamiline U., St. Paul 55104		•	•	•		•			•							•			
Mankato State U., Mankato 56001			•	•		•			•	•	•					•			NASA
Minneapolis College of Art & Design, Minneapolis 55404	•		•	•		•		•	•	•	•	•				•	•		NASA, AIGA, UICA
Moorhead State U., Moorhead 56560		•	•	•		•	•	•	•	•	•		•			•		•	
St. Cloud State U., St. Cloud 56301	•		•	•		•	•	•	•	•			•			•			
St. John's U., Collegeville 56321			•	•		•			•	•			•			•		•	
St. Mary's College, Winona 55987			•			•			•	•						•			
St. Olaf College, Northfield 55057		•	•	•		•		•	•	•						•			
Sch. of Associated Arts, St. Paul 55102		•							•	•	•					•			
U. of Minnesota at Duluth, 55812	•		•	•		•			•	•	•					•			AIGA
U. of Minnesota, Minneapolis 55455		•	•			•			•	•	•		•			•			NAAB, FIDER, ASID
———— **at Morris,** 56267			•	•		•			•							•			
MISSISSIPPI																			
Belhaven College, Jackson 39202			•	•					•							•			
Blue Mountain College, Blue Mountain 38610			•	•					•	•									
Delta State U., Cleveland 38733			•	•		•	•		•	•	•		•			•			ASID
Jackson State College, Jackson 39217			•	•		•			•	•						•			NASA
Mississippi College, Clinton 39058		•	•	•		•		•	•	•			•			•			ASID
Mississippi State U., Mississippi State 39762		•	•	•		•			•	•			•			•			NAAB, ASID
Mississippi U. for Women, South Columbia 39701		•			•	•			•	•	•		•			•			ASID, AIGA
Mississippi Museum of Art Sch., Jackson 39205		•							•						•	•			
U. of Mississippi, University 38677	•		•	•		•			•	•	•		•			•			ASID, AIGA
U. of Southern Mississippi, Hattiesburg 39401			•	•		•	•	•	•	•	•		•			•			ASID, AIGA
William Carey College, Hattiesburg 39401			•	•		•			•				•			•	•		
MISSOURI																			
Avila College, Kansas City 64145			•	•	•	•			•	•						•		•	AATA
Central Missouri State U., Warrensburg 64093			•	•		•		•	•	•	•	•	•						ASID, AIGA
Columbia College, Columbia 65201	•	•	•	•		•	•		•	•						•		•	AIGA
Culver-Stockton College, Canton 63435			•	•		•			•							•			
Drury College, Springfield 65802	•	•	•	•		•		•	•	•	•					•		•	
Fontbonne College, St. Louis 63105			•	•		•			•				•			•			
Kansas City Art Inst., Kansas City 64111		•			•	•	•	•	•	•	•	•	•			•			NASA, AIGA, UICA
Maryville College, St. Louis 63141		•	•	•	•	•			•	•			•			•		•	FIDER, ASID, AATA
Missouri Southern State College, Joplin 64801			•	•		•			•							•			
Missouri Western State College, St. Joseph 64507			•	•		•			•	•						•		•	
Northeast Missouri State U., Kirksville 63501			•	•	•	•			•	•						•		•	
Northwest Missouri State U., Maryville 64468			•	•		•			•							•			
St. Louis U., St. Louis 63701			•	•		•	•		•	•						•			
Sch. of the Ozarks, Point Lookout 65726			•	•		•			•	•	•					•			
Southeast Missouri State U., Cape Girardeau 63701			•	•		•	•	•	•	•			•			•			ASID
Southwest Baptist College, Bolivar 65613			•	•		•			•		•					•			
Southwest Missouri State U., Springfield 65802			•	•		•			•	•	•					•			
Stephens College, Columbia 65201		•	•	•		•	•		•	•	•		•			•		•	ASID, AIGA
U. of Missouri, Columbia 65211					•				•	•	•		•			•			FIDER, ASID
————, Kansas City 64110			•	•					•	•						•			AIGA
————, St. Louis 63121			•	•					•	•	•					•			
Washington U., St. Louis 63130		•	•	•		•	•	•	•	•	•				•	•	•		NAAB, NASA, AIGA
Webster College, St. Louis 63119	•		•	•		•		•	•							•		•	
William Jewell College, Liberty 64068			•	•		•			•							•			
William Woods College/Westminster College, Fulton 65251			•	•	•	•			•	•	•	•	•			•		•	ASID, AATA

	Administration/Management	Architecture	Art History	Art Education	Art Therapy	Crafts/Fabrics	Fashion Design/Illustration	Film/Television/Video	Fine Arts	Graphic Design/Advertising	Illustration	Industrial Design	Interior Design	Landscape Architecture	Museum Work/Conservation	Photography	Medical Illustration	Theater Arts/Stage	Associations
MONTANA																			
Eastern Montana College, Billings 59101			•	•		•		•	•							•			NASA
Montana State U., Bozeman 59717		•	•	•		•	•	•	•		•					•			NAAB, NASA, ASID, AIGA
Northern Montana College, Havre 59501			•	•		•			•							•			
Rocky Mountain College, Billings 59102			•	•		•		•	•	•			•			•			
U. of Montana, Missoula 59812			•	•		•			•							•			
Western Montana College, Dillon 59812			•	•		•			•							•			
NEBRASKA																			
Bellevue College, Bellevue 68005			•			•		•	•							•			
Chadron State College, Chadron 69337			•	•		•			•							•			
Concordia College, Seward 68434			•	•		•			•							•			
Creighton U., Omaha 68178		•	•			•		•	•							•			
Dana College, Blair 68008			•			•		•	•							•			
Hastings College, Hastings 68901			•	•		•			•							•			
Kearney State College, Kearney 68847			•	•		•		•	•	•						•	•		
Nebraska Wesleyan U., Lincoln 68504	•		•			•		•	•							•			AIGA
Nebraska Western College, Scottsbluff 69361			•	•		•			•							•			
Peru State College, Peru 68421			•	•		•			•									•	
U. of Nebraska, Lincoln 68588		•	•	•		•		•	•				•			•			NAAB, FIDER, ASID
—— **Omaha,** Omaha 68182			•	•		•			•				•			•			ASID
Wayne State College, Wayne 68787			•	•		•			•							•			
Nevada																			
U. of Nevada Las Vegas, Las Vegas 89154			•			•		•	•							•			
—— **Reno,** Reno 89557			•	•		•			•							•			
NEW HAMPSHIRE																			
Colby-Sawyer College, New London 03257			•			•			•							•			
Dartmouth College, Hanover 03755		•	•						•							•			
New England College, Henniker 03246			•			•		•	•							•			
Notre Dame College, Manchester 03104			•	•	•	•				•	•							•	
Plymouth State College, Plymouth 03264			•	•		•			•							•			
Rivier College, Nashua 03060			•	•	•	•		•	•	•	•					•	•	•	AIGA
U. of New Hampshire, Durham 03824	•	•	•	•					•							•		•	
NEW JERSEY																			
Caldwell College, Caldwell 07006			•	•	•	•	•		•	•	•					•		•	AIGA
Centenary College for Women, Hackettstown 07840			•	•		•	•		•	•						•		•	
Cook College, New Brunswick 08903									•					•		•			ASLA
Douglass College, New Brunswick 08903	•		•	•		•		•	•		•					•			
Drew U., Madison 07940			•			•			•							•			
duCret Sch. of the Arts, Plainfield 07060			•			•	•	•	•	•	•		•			•			
Farleigh Dickinson U., Rutherford 07070			•				•	•	•	•						•			
Georgian Court College, Lakewood 08701			•	•	•	•	•		•	•	•		•			•		•	AIGA
Glassboro State College, Glassboro 08028			•			•	•	•	•	•	•								AIGA
Jersey City State College, Jersey City 07305			•	•		•		•	•	•						•		•	NASA
Kean College of New Jersey, Union 07083	•		•	•		•	•	•	•	•			•		•	•			ASID, AIGA
Livingston College, New Brunswick 08903			•			•			•	•						•			
Monmouth College, West Long Branch 07764			•	•		•			•	•						•			
Montclair State College, Upper Montclair 07043	•			•	•	•		•	•	•	•					•		•	
Newark Sch. of Fine and Industrial Arts, Newark 07102			•			•			•	•	•	•	•			•			ASID
New Jersey Inst. of Tech., Newark 07102		•																	NAAB
Princeton U., Princeton 08540		•	•			•			•							•			NAAB
Rider College, Lawrenceville 08648			•			•			•									•	
Ridgewood Sch. of Art, Ridgewood 07450			•			•	•	•	•	•	•					•			AIGA
Rutgers, The State U. of New Jersey, Camden 08102	•		•	•	•	•			•	•	•					•			AIGA
——, Newark 07102	•			•		•		•	•	•						•	•		

	Administration/Management	Architecture	Art History	Art Education	Art Therapy	Crafts/Fabrics	Fashion Design/Illustration	Film/Television/Video	Fine Arts	Graphic Design/Advertising	Illustration	Industrial Design	Interior Design	Landscape Architecture	Museum Work/Conservation	Photography	Medical Illustration	Theater Arts/Stage	Associations
NEW JERSEY																			
——, New Brunswick 08903	•	•	•	•	•	•		•	•	•						•		•	
Rutgers College, New Brunswick 08903			•	•				•	•							•			
St. Peters College, Jersey City 07306			•	•		•		•	•										
Seton Hall U., South Orange 07079		•	•	•				•	•	•			•	•					
Trenton State College, Trenton 08625		•			•	•	•	•	•	•		•				•		•	ASID, AATA, AIGA
William Patterson College of New Jersey, Wayne 07470	•		•	•	•	•	•	•	•	•	•					•		•	AIGA
NEW MEXICO																			
American Classical College, Albuquerque 87106			•	•				•	•	•		•							
College of Santa Fe, Santa Fe 87501			•	•		•		•	•							•			
Eastern New Mexico U., Portales 88130			•	•		•		•	•		•					•		•	
New Mexico Highlands U., Las Vegas 07701	•		•	•		•			•							•			
New Mexico State U., Las Cruces 88003	•		•	•		•			•	•		•				•			
New Mexico State U., Farmington 87401			•		•			•	•							•			
U. of Albuquerque, Albuquerque 87112			•	•		•			•	•						•		•	
U. of New Mexico, Albuquerque 87131		•	•			•			•							•			NAAB
Western New Mexico U., Silver City 88061			•	•		•			•									•	
NEW YORK																			
Adelphi U., New York 10021	•		•			•	•		•	•			•			•			AIGA
Art Students League of New York, New York 10019									•	•	•								
Bernard Baruch College CUNY, New York 10010			•	•		•			•	•						•			
Brooklyn College CUNY, Brooklyn 11210		•	•			•			•	•									
C.W. Post Center of Long Island U., Greenvale 11948	•		•	•	•	•		•	•	•	•					•		•	AIGA
City College CUNY, New York 10031		•	•	•		•			•	•		•	•			•			NAAB, ASLA
City College of New York Graduate Center, New York 10036			•																
Colgate U., Hamilton 13346		•	•					•	•							•			
College of New Rochelle, New Rochelle 10801		•	•	•	•	•	•	•	•	•	•		•			•		•	AATA, AIGA
College of St. Rose, Albany 12203		•	•		•			•	•							•			
College of Staten Island SUNY, Staten Island 10301		•	•	•		•			•							•		•	
College of Staten Island CUNY, Staten Island 10301	•	•	•					•		•						•			
Columbia U., New York 10027		•	•						•										NAAB
Columbia U. Teachers College, New York 10021			•		•				•										
Cooper Union Sch. of Art and Arch., New York 10003		•	•			•		•	•	•			•			•			NAAB. NASA, AIGA
Cornell U., Ithaca 14853		•							•					•		•			NAAB, ASLA
Daemen College, Amherst 14226		•	•		•				•							•		•	
Dominican College of Blauvelt, Orangeburg 10962		•	•						•										
Eisenhower College, Seneca Falls 13148		•			•			•	•							•			
Elmira College, Elmira 14901		•	•		•				•							•			
Fashion Inst. of Tech., New York 10007		•				•	•	•	•	•	•		•			•			ASID, AIGA
Fordham U. at Lincoln Center, New York 10023		•							•							•		•	
Hartwick College, Oneonta 13820	•	•	•					•	•							•			
Hobart & William Smith Colleges, Geneva 14456		•	•						•										
Hofstra U., Hempstead 11550			•	•	•	•		•	•	•		•				•			AATA
Hunter College CUNY, New York 10021			•	•		•	•		•	•						•			
Ithaca College, Ithaca 14850			•					•	•							•			
Herbert H. Lehman College, Bronx 10468			•		•				•							•			
Long Island U. Brooklyn Center, Brooklyn 11201			•	•		•			•							•			
Manhattan College, Bronx 10471			•	•		•		•								•			
Manhattanville College, Purchase 10577			•	•		•		•	•	•						•	•		AIGA
Marymount College, Tarrytown 10591			•			•	•		•	•	•		•			•		•	ASID, AIGA
Malloy College, Rockville Center 11570			•	•		•			•	•						•			
Munson-Williams-Proctor Inst., Utica 13502			•			•			•							•			
Nazareth College of Rochester, Rochester 14610			•	•		•			•							•			
New York Inst. of Tech., Old Westbury 11568	•	•	•	•				•	•	•	•		•			•			NAAB, ASID, AIGA
New York Sch. of Interior Design, New York 10022		•							•				•			•			FIDER, ASID
New York State College of Ceramics, Alfred 14802			•	•		•		•	•							•	•		NASA

	Administration/Management	Architecture	Art History	Art Education	Art Therapy	Crafts/Fabrics	Fashion Design/Illustration	Film/Television/Video	Fine Arts	Graphic Design/Advertising	Illustration	Industrial Design	Interior Design	Landscape Architecture	Museum Work/Conservation	Photography	Medical Illustration	Theater Arts/Stage	Associations
NEW YORK																			
New York Inst. of Tech. Ctr. for Arch., Old Westbury 11568		•																	
New York U., New York 11208	•	•	•	•	•	•	•		•			•				•		•	AATA
Parsons Sch. of Design, New York 10011	•	•	•	•		•	•	•	•	•	•	•	•		•	•	•		NASA, AIGA
Pratt Inst., Brooklyn 11205	•	•	•	•	•	•	•		•	•	•	•	•			•	•		NAAB, NASA, ASID, AATA, AIGA
Pratt-New York Phoenix Sch. of Design, New York 10016		•				•		•	•	•						•			NASA, AIGA
Queens College, Flushing 11367		•	•	•	•	•			•	•						•	•		
Rensselaer Polytech. Inst., Troy 12181		•	•			•							•			•		•	NAAB
Roberts Wesleyan College, Rochester 14624		•			•				•							•			
Rochester Inst. of Tech., Rochester 14623		•	•		•		•	•	•	•	•	•					•		NASA, ASID, AIGA
St. Johns U., Jamaica 11432		•	•		•			•	•	•						•		•	
St. Lawrence U., Canton 13617		•	•		•				•							•			
St. Thomas Aquinas College, Sparkill 10976		•	•	•	•			•	•							•			AATA, AIGA
Sarah Lawrence College, Bronxville 10708		•	•		•			•	•							•			
Sch. of Visual Arts, New York 10010	•	•	•	•	•	•	•	•	•	•	•		•			•		•	AATA, AIGA
Skidmore College, Saratoga Springs 12866		•	•	•					•	•						•			NASA
Southhampton College of																			
Long Island U., Southhampton 11968	•		•	•	•	•			•	•	•					•	•	•	
State U. College at Brockport, 14420		•	•		•			•	•							•			
——— at Buffalo, 14222		•		•					•	•	•	•				•			NASA, AATA, AIGA
——— at Cortland, 13045		•		•				•	•							•			
——— at Fredonia, 14063	•	•		•	•			•	•	•	•					•	•	•	
——— at Geneseo, 14454		•		•				•	•							•			
——— at Oneonta, 13520		•	•		•				•					•		•			NAAB, ASLA
——— at Oswego, 13126	•	•		•					•					•	•	•			
——— at Plattsburg, 12901		•		•					•							•	•		
——— at Purchase, 10577		•						•	•	•						•		•	AIGA
——— at Potsdam, 13676	•	•		•					•							•			
State U. of New York at Albany, 12222		•						•	•					•	•				
——— at Alfred, 14802		•	•		•				•			•				•			
——— at Binghamton, 13901	•	•						•				•				•			NASA
——— at Brockport, 14420	•	•	•		•			•	•							•			
——— at Buffalo, 14214		•	•					•	•	•	•					•			NASA, NAAB, AIGA
——— at New Paltz, 12561	•	•	•		•			•	•							•			NASA
——— at Old Westbury, 11568		•		•					•							•			
——— at Stony Brook, 11794		•	•		•	•		•	•							•	•	•	
——— at Syracuse, 13210		•	•						•					•		•			
Syracuse U., Syracuse 13201		•	•	•		•	•	•	•	•	•	•	•		•	•			NAAB, NASA, FIDER, ASID, AIGA
Union College, Schenectady 12308		•							•							•	•		
U. of Rochester, Rochester 14627		•						•	•							•			
Utica College of Syracuse U., Utica 13502		•		•					•										
Vassar College, Poughkeepsie 12601	•	•						•	•								•		
Wells College, Aurora 13026	•	•	•		•				•							•			
NORTH CAROLINA																			
Atlantic Christian College, Wilson 27893	•		•	•		•			•	•						•			AIGA
Davidson College, Davidson 28036		•							•										
Duke U., Durham 27708		•	•		•				•							•			
E. Carolina U., Greenville 27834	•		•	•		•	•		•	•	•		•			•			NASA, ASID, AIGA
Elizabeth City State U., Elizabeth City 27909		•	•		•	•	•		•	•						•	•		
Greensboro College, Greensboro 27420		•	•		•				•							•			
Guilford College, Greensboro 27410		•	•		•				•							•			
Mars Hill College, Mars Hill 28754		•	•		•			•	•							•	•		
Meredith College, Raleigh 27611		•	•		•	•	•	•	•	•			•			•			
Methodist College, Fayetteville 28301		•	•		•				•							•	•		
N. Carolina A & T, Greensboro 27411		•	•		•				•										
N. Carolina Central U., Durham 27707	•		•	•		•	•		•	•						•			AIGA
Pembroke State U., Pembroke 28372		•	•	•		•			•					•		•			NAAB, ASLA

NORTH CAROLINA

Institution	Administration/Management	Architecture	Art History	Art Education	Art Therapy	Crafts/Fabrics	Fashion Design/Illustration	Film/Television/Video	Fine Arts	Graphic Design/Advertising	Illustration	Industrial Design	Interior Design	Landscape Architecture	Museum Work/Conservation	Photography	Medical Illustration	Theater Arts/Stage	Associations
Penland School of Crafts, Penland 28765						•			•							•			
St. Andrews Presbyterian College, Laurinburg 28352			•	•				•	•							•			
U. of N. Carolina at Asheville, 28814	•		•	•		•			•							•			
——— **at Chapel Hill**, 27514			•	•					•										
——— **at Charlotte**, 28223		•	•	•		•			•	•						•		•	NAAB
——— **at Greensboro**, 27412		•	•	•		•	•		•	•			•			•			ASID, AIGA
U. of N. Carolina State at Raleigh, 27650		•																	NAAB
U. of N. Carolina at Wilmington, 28406			•	•					•										
Wake Forest U., Winston-Salem 27109	•	•							•						•				
Western Carolina U., Cullowhee 28723,			•	•		•			•	•	•					•			AIGA
Winston-Salem State U., Winston-Salem 27102			•	•					•										

NORTH DAKOTA

Institution	Administration/Management	Architecture	Art History	Art Education	Art Therapy	Crafts/Fabrics	Fashion Design/Illustration	Film/Television/Video	Fine Arts	Graphic Design/Advertising	Illustration	Industrial Design	Interior Design	Landscape Architecture	Museum Work/Conservation	Photography	Medical Illustration	Theater Arts/Stage	Associations
Dickinson State College, Dickinson 58601			•		•				•	•						•			
Jamestown College, Jamestown 58401			•	•					•									•	
Minot State College, Minot 58701			•	•	•	•			•	•						•			
N. Dakota State U., Fargo 58102	•	•	•	•		•			•			•	•	•		•		•	NAAB, ASID
U. of N. Dakota, Grand Forks 58202			•	•	•				•							•			NASA
———, Williston 58801	•	•				•			•	•					•				
Valley City State College, Valley City 58072			•	•	•				•	•									

OHIO

Institution	Administration/Management	Architecture	Art History	Art Education	Art Therapy	Crafts/Fabrics	Fashion Design/Illustration	Film/Television/Video	Fine Arts	Graphic Design/Advertising	Illustration	Industrial Design	Interior Design	Landscape Architecture	Museum Work/Conservation	Photography	Medical Illustration	Theater Arts/Stage	Associations
Antioch College, Yellow Springs 45387			•	•	•		•		•							•		•	
Art Academy of Cincinnati, Cincinnati 45202			•						•	•	•					•			NASA, AIGA
Ashland College, Ashland 44805			•	•		•	•		•				•					•	
Baldwin Wallace College, Berea 44017			•	•	•				•							•			
Bowling Green State U., Bowling Green 43403			•	•	•	•	•		•	•	•					•		•	ASID, AATA
———, Huron 44839			•	•					•										
Capitol U., Columbus 43209			•	•	•				•	•						•		•	AATA
Case Western Reserve U., Cleveland 44106			•	•	•		•	•								•	•		
Central State U., Wilberforce 45384			•	•	•	•			•	•	•					•		•	AIGA
Cleveland Inst. of Art, Cleveland 44106			•	•		•	•		•	•	•	•				•	•	•	NASA, AIGA, UICA
Cleveland State U., Cleveland 44115			•	•	•				•							•			
College of Mt. St. Joseph, St. Joseph 45051	•		•	•	•	•			•	•	•					•			
College of Wooster, Wooster 44691		•	•	•					•							•			NASA
Columbus College of Art & Design, Columbus 43215		•		•	•	•			•	•	•		•		•	•		•	NASA, AATA, AIGA
Denison U., Granville 43023			•		•	•		•	•							•			
Edgecliff College, Cincinnati 45206			•	•	•				•		•		•					•	AATA
Findlay College, Findlay 45840			•	•	•				•		•					•		•	
Kent State U., Kent 44242		•	•	•	•	•	•	•	•	•	•	•	•			•		•	NASA, NAAB, ASID, AIGA
———, Canton 44720		•		•												•			NASA
———, Warren 43022		•							•							•			NASA
Kenyon College, Gambier 43022		•							•							•			
Malone College, Canton 44709			•	•		•			•	•						•			
Marietta College, Marrieta 45750			•	•		•			•	•						•	•		
Miami U., Oxford 45056	•	•	•	•	•	•	•		•				•	•		•			NAAB, ASID, AIGA
———, Middletown 45042			•	•	•				•	•		•				•			
Oberlin College, Oberlin 44074		•				•			•	•						•			NASA
Ohio Northern U., Ada 45810			•	•					•	•									
Ohio State U., Columbus 43210	•	•		•		•		•	•								•		NAAB, AIGA
Ohio U., Athens 45701			•	•	•				•	•	•		•			•			ASID
Ohio Wesleyan U., Delaware 43015			•	•	•	•			•	•						•		•	AATA
Toledo Museum of Art, Sch. of Design, Toledo 43697			•	•					•	•					•				
U. of Akron, Akron 44325			•	•	•	•			•	•	•					•			NASA
U. of Cincinnati, Cincinnati 45221	•	•	•		•	•	•	•	•	•	•	•	•			•			NAAB, NASA, FIDER, ASID, AIGA
U. of Dayton, Dayton 45469			•	•		•			•	•	•					•	•		
Wilberforce U., Wilberforce 45384			•			•			•	•	•					•	•		

School	Administration/Management	Architecture	Art History	Art Education	Art Therapy	Crafts/Fabrics	Fashion Design/Illustration	Film/Television/Video	Fine Arts	Graphic Design/Advertising	Illustration	Industrial Design	Interior Design	Landscape Architecture	Museum Work/Conservation	Photography	Medical Illustration	Theater Arts/Stage	Associations
OHIO																			
Wilmington College, Wilmington 45177		•	•	•					•							•		•	
Wittenberg U., Springfield 45501		•	•	•				•	•	•			•			•	•		
Wright State U., Dayton 45435	•		•	•	•	•	•		•	•	•					•		•	AATA
Youngstown State U., Youngstown 44555	•	•	•	•		•		•	•	•						•		•	
OKLAHOMA																			
Bethany Nazarene College, Bethany 73008			•	•					•										
Central State U., Edmond 73034		•	•	•		•		•	•	•			•						ASID
E. Central U., Ada 74820		•	•	•		•	•		•							•			
Langston U., Langston 73050		•	•	•					•							•			
Northeastern Oklahoma State U., Tahlequah 74464		•	•	•					•										
Northwestern Oklahoma State U., Alva 73717		•	•	•					•										
Oklahoma Baptist U., Shawnee 74801		•	•	•					•	•									
Oklahoma Christian College, Oklahoma City 73111		•	•	•					•							•		•	
Oklahoma City U., Oklahoma City 73106		•	•	•					•										
Oklahoma State U., Stillwater 74078		•	•	•				•	•	•		•				•			NAAB, ASID
Phillips U., Enid 73701		•	•	•					•							•			
Southwestern Oklahoma State U., Weatherford 73096		•	•	•		•		•	•	•	•					•			
U. of Oklahoma, Norman 73069		•	•		•	•	•	•	•	•	•	•	•			•			NAAB, ASID, AIGA
U. of Sci. and Arts of Oklahoma, Chickasha 73018		•	•	•					•							•			
U. of Tulsa, Tulsa 74104		•	•	•	•			•	•	•	•					•			AIGA
OREGON																			
Eastern Oregon State College, La Grande 97850		•	•	•					•							•		•	
Lewis and Clark College, Portland 97219		•		•					•	•	•					•			
Linfield College, McMinnville 97128		•	•	•					•	•						•			
Marylhurst Education Center, Marylhurst 97036		•		•					•	•						•			
Museum Art Sch., Portland 97205		•		•					•	•	•					•			NASA
Oregon College of Art, Ashland 97520								•	•	•	•	•				•			
Oregon College of Education, Monmouth 97361		•	•	•		•	•		•	•						•		•	AIGA
Oregon State U., Corvalis 97331		•	•	•					•	•	•					•			AIGA
Portland State U., Portland 97207	•	•		•					•	•	•			•					
Southern Oregon State College, Ashland 97520		•	•	•					•	•						•			
U. of Oregon, Eugene 97403	•	•	•	•				•	•	•	•		•	•		•			NAAB, ASLA, FIDER, AIGA
PENNSYLVANIA																			
Allegheny College, Meadville 16335		•		•					•							•			
Art Inst. of Philadelphia, Philadelphia 19103		•				•		•	•	•	•		•			•			ASID, AIGA
Art Inst. of Pittsburgh, Pittsburgh 15222		•				•	•	•	•	•	•		•			•	•		ASID
Beaver College, Glenside 19038		•	•	•					•	•						•	•		NASA
Bloomsburg State College, Bloomsburg 17815		•				•	•		•									•	
Bryn Mawr College, Bryn Mawr 19010		•							•						•				
Bucknell U., Lewisburg 17837		•		•					•										
California State College, California 15419		•		•					•										
Carnegie-Mellon U., Pittsburg 15235	•	•		•		•	•	•	•	•	•					•			NASA, NAAB, AIGA
Chatham College, Pittsburgh 15232		•	•	•					•							•			
Cheyney State College, Cheyney 19319		•		•					•	•						•			AIGA
Clarion State College, Clarion 16214	•	•	•	•					•	•							•		
College Misericordia, Dallas 18612		•	•	•	•				•	•	•					•	•		AATA
Dickinson College, Carlisle 17013		•		•					•							•			
Drexel U./Nesbitt College, Philadelphia 19104	•	•				•			•				•						NAAB, FIDER, ASID
Duquesne U., Pittsburgh 15219		•																	
E. Stroudsburg State College, East Stroudsburg 18301		•		•					•								•		
Edinboro State College, Edinboro 16444	•		•	•	•	•		•	•	•	•					•	•	•	AATA, AIGA
Franklin & Marshall College, Lancaster 17604		•							•										
Indiana U. of Pennsylvania, Indiana 15705		•	•	•	•				•		•								
Kutztown State College, Kutztown 19530		•	•		•		•	•	•	•						•		•	

	Administration/Management	Architecture	Art History	Art Education	Art Therapy	Crafts/Fabrics	Fashion Design/Illustration	Film/Television/Video	Fine Arts	Graphic Design/Advertising	Illustration	Industrial Design	Interior Design	Landscape Architecture	Museum Work/Conservation	Photography	Medical Illustration	Theater Arts/Stage	Associations
PENNSYLVANIA																			
LaRoche College, Pittsburgh 15237			•		•	•	•	•	•	•		•				•		•	ASID, AIGA
Lehigh U., Bethlehem 18015	•	•	•						•						•	•			
Lock Haven State College, Lock Haven 17745			•	•		•			•							•		•	AIGA
Lycoming College, Williamsport 17701			•		•			•	•							•		•	
Mansfield State College, Mansfield 16933			•	•		•			•	•	•					•		•	
Mercyhurst College, Erie 16546			•	•	•	•		•	•	•	•					•		•	
Millersville State College, Millersville 17064			•	•		•		•	•	•	•					•			
Moore College of Art, Philadelphia 19103		•	•	•		•	•		•	•	•		•	•		•	•		NASA, ASID
Pennsylvania Academy of Fine Arts, Philadelphia 19102		•							•						•				
Pennsylvania State U., University Park 16802	•	•	•	•		•		•	•	•						•			NAAB, AIGA
Philadelphia College of Art, Philadelphia 19102		•	•	•	•	•		•	•	•	•		•			•		•	NASA, AATA, AIGA
Philadelphia College of Textiles & Sci., Philadelphia 19104		•			•	•	•		•			•				•			
Point Park College, Pittsburgh 15222		•	•			•	•	•	•	•	•					•		•	
St. Francis College, Loretto 15940		•			•				•							•			
Seton Hall College, Greensburg 15601		•	•	•	•	•	•	•	•							•		•	
Shippensburg State College, Shippensburg 17257		•			•				•							•			
Slippery Rock State College, Slippery Rock 16057		•	•	•	•				•							•		•	
Temple U., Philadelphia 10122		•			•														NAAB, AATA
Thiel College, Greenville 16125	•		•		•	•			•							•	•	•	
Tyler Sch. of Art/Temple U., Philadelphia 19126		•	•	•		•		•	•	•	•					•			NASA, AIGA
U. of Pennsylvania, Philadelphia 19104		•	•			•			•							•			NAAB
U. of Pittsburgh, Pittsburgh 15260		•			•				•										
Villanova U., Villanova 19085		•	•		•				•							•		•	
Washington and Jefferson College, Washington 15311	•	•	•		•				•					•					
Waynesburg College, Waynesburg 15370	•	•	•		•				•					•					
W. Chester State College, West Chester 19380		•			•		•	•	•							•			
Westminster College, New Wilmington 16140		•	•		•				•										
Wilkes College, Wilkes-Barre 18766		•	•		•				•	•						•		•	
PUERTO RICO																			
Catholic U. of Puerto Rico, Ponce 00731		•	•		•				•	•									
Inter American U. of Puerto Rico, San German 00753		•	•		•				•							•			
U. of Puerto Rico, Mayaguez 00708	•	•			•				•							•			
——, Rio Piedras 00931	•	•			•				•	•									
——, San Juan 00931	•								•							•			NAAB
RHODE ISLAND																			
Brown U., Providence 02912		•			•				•										
Newport College—Salve Regina, Newport 02840		•	•		•				•							•			
Rhode Island College, Providence 02908	•	•	•		•		•			•						•			NASA
Rhode Island Sch. of Design, Providence 02903		•	•	•		•	•	•	•	•	•		•		•	•			NAAB, ASLA, FIDER, ASID, AIGA
Roger Williams College, Bristol 02809	•	•	•	•		•		•	•	•			•	•	•			•	
U. of Rhode Island, Kingston 02881		•			•			•	•							•			
SOUTH CAROLINA																			
Bob Jones U., Greenville 29614		•	•		•		•	•	•	•						•		•	AIGA
Claflin College, Orangeburg 29115		•	•		•			•	•	•									
Clemson U., Clemson 29631		•	•		•	•		•	•	•	•		•			•			NAAB
Coker College, Hartsville 29550		•	•		•		•	•	•							•			
College of Charleston, Charleston 29401		•	•		•				•										
Columbia College, Columbia 29203		•			•			•	•	•						•			
Converse College, Spartanburg 29301	•	•	•		•				•			•				•			
Francis Marion College, Florence 29501		•	•		•				•									•	
Furman U., Greenville 29613		•	•		•				•	•									
Newberry College, Newberry 29108	•		•		•				•									•	
Presbyterian College, Clinton 29325		•	•		•				•										
S. Carolina State College, Orangeburg 29117		•	•		•				•										

School	Administration/Management	Architecture	Art History	Art Education	Art Therapy	Crafts/Fabrics	Fashion Design/Illustration	Film/Television/Video	Fine Arts	Graphic Design/Advertising	Illustration	Industrial Design	Interior Design	Landscape Architecture	Museum Work/Conservation	Photography	Medical Illustration	Theater Arts/Stage	Associations
SOUTH CAROLINA																			
U. of S. Carolina, Columbia 29208	●	●	●	●	●		●	●	●	●			●		●	●	●	●	AIGA
Winthrop College, Rock Hill 29733		●	●		●	●			●	●	●		●			●		●	ASID, AIGA
SOUTH DAKOTA																			
Dakota State College, Madison 57042		●	●	●					●										
Mount Marty College, Yankton 57078		●	●	●		●	●		●							●		●	
Northern State College, Aberdeen 57401		●	●	●			●	●	●			●				●			
S. Dakota State U., Brookings 57006		●	●	●			●	●				●						●	ASID
U. of S. Dakota, Vermillion 57069	●	●	●	●					●							●			NASA
Yankton College, Yankton 57078		●	●	●		●	●		●							●		●	
TENNESSEE																			
Arrowmont Sch. of Arts & Crafts, Gatlinburg 37738				●					●										
Austin Peay State U., Clarksville 37040		●	●	●					●	●	●	●	●					●	AIGA
Carson-Newman College, Jefferson City 37760		●	●	●					●		●		●						
E. Tennessee State U., Johnson City 37601		●	●	●			●	●	●	●			●						
Fisk U., Nashville 37203		●	●	●					●				●						
George Peabody College, Nashville 37203		●	●	●		●			●				●						
Memphis Academy of Arts, Memphis 38112		●		●		●	●		●	●			●						NASA, AIGA
Memphis State U., Memphis 38152	●	●	●	●					●	●	●		●						ASID
Middle Tennessee State U., Murfreesboro 37132		●	●	●					●	●	●		●						ASID
O'More Sch. of Interior Design, Franklin 37064													●			●			FIDER, ASID
Southwestern College, Memphis 38112	●	●	●						●	●				●	●				
Tennessee State U., Nashville 37203	●			●	●				●	●	●	●	●			●	●		
Tusculum College, Greenville 37743		●	●	●					●				●						
Union U., Jackson 38301		●	●	●					●	●	●	●	●					●	AIGA
U. of Tennessee, Knoxville 37996		●	●	●			●	●	●	●			●				●		NAAB, ASID, FIDER, AIGA
Vanderbilt U., Nashville 37235			●						●							●			
TEXAS																			
Abilene Christian U., Abilene 79699		●	●	●					●	●									
Art Inst. of Houston, Houston 77002		●				●	●	●	●	●						●	●		AIGA
Austin College, Sherman 75090		●	●	●					●				●						
Baylor U., Waco 76703	●	●	●	●	●				●	●	●		●				●		
Corpus Christi State U., Corpus Christi 78404	●	●	●	●		●	●	●	●							●	●		
E. Texas State U., Commerce 75428		●	●	●	●	●	●	●	●	●	●	●	●			●		●	ASID, AIGA
Hardin-Simmons U., Abilene 79698		●	●	●					●							●			
Houston Baptist U., Houston 77036		●	●	●					●										
Incarnate Word College, San Antonio 78201	●	●	●	●					●				●			●		●	ASID
Lamar U., Beaumont 77710		●	●	●	●				●	●	●		●			●			ASID
Lubbock Christian College, Waco 76708		●	●	●					●	●									
McMurry College, Abilene 79697		●	●	●					●										
Midwestern State U., Wichita Falls 76308	●	●	●	●					●	●			●				●		
N. Texas State U., Denton 76203		●	●	●	●				●	●	●		●			●			FIDER, ASID, AIGA
Our.Lady of the Lake U., San Antonio 78285		●	●			●	●						●						
Pan American U., Edinburg 78539		●	●	●			●	●	●	●			●					●	AIGA
Rice U., Houston 77001	●	●		●					●	●						●			NAAB
Sam Houston State U., Huntsville 77340		●	●	●					●	●	●								AIGA
Southern Methodist U., Dallas 75275		●	●			●	●		●				●			●			
Southwest Texas State U., San Marcos 78666		●	●	●					●	●			●			●			ASID, AIGA
Stephen F. Austin State U., Nacagdoches 75962		●	●	●			●	●	●				●			●			ASID
Texas A and I U., Kingsville 78363		●	●	●	●				●	●	●		●						
Texas A and M U., College Station 77843	●													●					NAAB, ASLA
Texas Christian U., Fort Worth 76129		●	●	●		●	●		●	●	●		●			●			FIDER, ASID, AIGA
Texas Southern U., Houston 77004		●	●	●					●	●	●								
Texas Tech U., Lubbock 79409	●	●	●	●					●	●	●		●			●			NAAB, NASA, FIDER, ASID, AIGA
Texas Woman's U., Denton 76204		●	●	●		●	●		●	●	●			●		●	●	●	ASLA, FIDER, ASID

Information and Resources

TEXAS

	Administration/Management	Architecture	Art History	Art Education	Art Therapy	Crafts/Fabrics	Fashion Design/Illustration	Film/Television/Video	Fine Arts	Graphic Design/Advertising	Illustration	Industrial Design	Interior Design	Landscape Architecture	Museum Work/Conservation	Photography	Medical Illustration	Theater Arts/Stage	Associations
Trinity U., San Antonio 78284			●	●	●	●	●		●	●	●		●						
U. of Dallas, Irving 75061		●	●	●		●			●	●									
U. of Houston, Houston 77004	●	●	●		●	●		●	●	●	●		●			●			NAAB, ASID, AATA
U. of St. Thomas, Houston 77030			●	●	●		●	●						●		●	●	●	ASLA
U. of Texas at Arlington, 76019		●	●	●	●	●	●	●	●				●			●			NAAB, FIDER, ASID, AATA
——— **at Austin,** 78712		●	●	●	●	●	●	●	●							●	●	●	NAAB, FIDER, ASID, AIGA
——— **at El Paso,** 79968			●	●		●			●	●						●			
——— **of Permian Basin,** Odessa 79761				●		●			●	●						●			
——— **at San Antonio,** 78285		●	●			●			●							●			NASA
——— **at Tyler,** 75701	●		●	●		●		●	●	●			●			●		●	
——— **Health and Science Ctr.,** Dallas 75235																	●		
Wayland Baptist College, Plainview 79072			●		●			●		●	●					●		●	
W. Texas State U., Canyon 79016		●	●		●			●	●	●									

UTAH

	Administration/Management	Architecture	Art History	Art Education	Art Therapy	Crafts/Fabrics	Fashion Design/Illustration	Film/Television/Video	Fine Arts	Graphic Design/Advertising	Illustration	Industrial Design	Interior Design	Landscape Architecture	Museum Work/Conservation	Photography	Medical Illustration	Theater Arts/Stage	Associations
Brigham Young U., Provo 84602			●	●		●			●	●	●	●	●						ASID
Southern Utah State College, Cedar City 84720			●	●		●			●	●			●						
U. of Utah, Salt Lake City 84112		●	●		●		●	●	●	●			●			●			ASID, NAAB
Utah State U., Logan 84322			●	●		●	●		●	●	●			●		●			ASLA, ASID, AIGA
Weber State College, Ogden 84408			●	●		●			●	●	●					●			ASID
Westminster of Utah, Salt Lake City 84105			●	●		●			●							●			

VERMONT

	Administration/Management	Architecture	Art History	Art Education	Art Therapy	Crafts/Fabrics	Fashion Design/Illustration	Film/Television/Video	Fine Arts	Graphic Design/Advertising	Illustration	Industrial Design	Interior Design	Landscape Architecture	Museum Work/Conservation	Photography	Medical Illustration	Theater Arts/Stage	Associations
Bennington College, Bennington 05201		●	●			●			●										
Castleton State College, Castleton 05735			●	●		●		●	●	●	●					●		●	
Goddard College, Plainfield 05602		●	●	●	●	●		●	●			●	●			●		●	AATA
Norwich U., Montpelier 05602				●					●							●		●	
U. of Vermont, Burlington 05405		●	●	●		●			●							●			

VIRGINIA

	Administration/Management	Architecture	Art History	Art Education	Art Therapy	Crafts/Fabrics	Fashion Design/Illustration	Film/Television/Video	Fine Arts	Graphic Design/Advertising	Illustration	Industrial Design	Interior Design	Landscape Architecture	Museum Work/Conservation	Photography	Medical Illustration	Theater Arts/Stage	Associations
Bridgewater College, Bridgewater 22812			●			●			●										
Christopher Newport College, Newport News 23606			●	●		●			●							●		●	
College of William and Mary, Williamsburg 23189		●	●	●		●			●									●	
Hampton Inst., Hampton 23666		●	●	●		●	●	●	●	●	●					●	●		NAAB
George Mason U., Fairfax 22030			●			●			●										
James Madison U., Harrisonburg 22801			●	●		●		●	●	●		●	●			●		●	
Longwood College, Farmville 23901	●		●	●		●		●	●	●						●			AIGA
Mary Baldwin College, Staunton 24401	●	●	●	●	●	●			●	●		●	●			●		●	
Mary Washington College, Fredericksburg 22401	●	●	●	●		●			●	●					●	●			
Norfolk State U., Norfolk 23504			●	●		●			●	●	●					●			
Old Dominion U., Norfolk 23508			●	●		●			●	●						●			AIGA
Radford U., Radford 24142			●		●			●	●	●		●				●		●	ASID, AIGA
Randolph-Macon Woman's College, Lynchburg 24503			●	●		●		●	●										
Roanoke College, Salem 24153			●			●			●	●						●		●	
Sweet Briar College, Sweet Briar 24595	●		●	●		●			●	●						●			
U. of Richmond, Richmond 23173			●	●		●			●							●			
U. of Virginia, Charlottesville 22903	●	●	●						●							●			NAAB
Virginia Commonwealth U., Richmond 23284	●		●	●		●	●	●	●	●	●		●		●	●		●	NASA, FIDER, ASID, AIGA
Virginia Intermont College, Bristol 24201	●		●	●		●	●	●	●	●	●		●			●			
Virginia Polytechnic Inst., Blacksburg 24061		●	●	●		●		●	●			●	●	●		●			NAAB, ASLA, ASID
Virginia State U., Petersburg 23803			●	●		●			●	●									
Virginia Wesleyan College, Norfolk 23502			●	●		●			●									●	
Washington and Lee U., Lexington 24450	●	●	●						●							●		●	

WASHINGTON

	Administration/Management	Architecture	Art History	Art Education	Art Therapy	Crafts/Fabrics	Fashion Design/Illustration	Film/Television/Video	Fine Arts	Graphic Design/Advertising	Illustration	Industrial Design	Interior Design	Landscape Architecture	Museum Work/Conservation	Photography	Medical Illustration	Theater Arts/Stage	Associations
Burnley Sch. of Professional Art, Seattle 98122							●	●	●	●	●								AIGA
Central Washington U., Ellensburg 98926		●	●	●	●	●			●	●	●	●	●			●		●	

	Administration/Management	Architecture	Art History	Art Education	Art Therapy	Crafts/Fabrics	Fashion Design/Illustration	Film/Television/Video	Fine Arts	Graphic Design/Advertising	Illustration	Industrial Design	Interior Design	Landscape Architecture	Museum Work/Conservation	Photography	Medical Illustration	Theater Arts/Stage	Associations
WASHINGTON																			
Cornish Inst., Seattle 98102	•	•	•						•	•	•		•			•	•		ASID, AIGA
Eastern Washington U., Cheney 99004	•		•	•		•		•	•		•					•			
Fort Wright College, Spokane 99204			•	•		•			•										
Gonzaga U., Spokane 99258	•		•	•		•			•										
Pacific Lutheran U., Tacoma 98447			•	•		•		•	•	•	•		•			•			AIGA
St. Martin's College, Olympia 98503			•	•		•			•										
Seattle Pacific College, Seattle 98119			•		•	•	•	•	•			•	•	•					
Seattle U., Seattle 98122			•			•			•										
U. of Puget Sound, Tacoma 98416			•	•		•			•										
U. of Washington, Seattle 98195		•	•	•		•			•		•	•		•		•			NAAB, ASLA, NASA, ASID
Washington State U., Pullman 99164		•	•	•		•			•	•	•					•			NAAB, FIDER, ASID, AIGA
Western Washington State College, Bellingham 98225	•		•	•		•			•	•	•		•						ASID
Whitworth College, Spokane 99251			•	•		•			•							•			
WASHINGTON D.C.																			
American U., Washington D.C. 20016			•			•			•	•									
Catholic U., of America, Washington D.C. 20064	•	•	•			•			•										NAAB
Corcoran Sch. of Art, Washington D.C. 20006				•		•	•	•	•							•			NASA, AIGA
Georgetown U., Washington D.C. 20057			•			•	•	•	•							•			AIGA
George Washington U., Washington D.C. 20052	•		•	•	•	•	•	•	•	•			•			•			AATA
Howard U., Washington D.C. 20059			•	•		•			•	•	•		•			•			NASA, ASID
U. of the District of Columbia, Washington D.C. 20001			•	•		•			•		•		•			•			
WEST VIRGINIA																			
Bethany College, Bethany 26032			•	•		•		•	•	•									AIGA
Concord College, Athens 24712			•	•		•	•		•	•						•		•	
Davis & Elkins College, Elkins 26241			•	•		•			•									•	
Fairmont State College, Fairmont 26554			•	•		•		•	•		•	•	•			•		•	
Glenville State College, Glenville 26351			•	•		•			•							•			
Marshal U., Huntington 25701			•	•		•			•		•							•	
Morris Harvey College, Charleston 25304			•	•		•			•				•						
Salem College, Salem 26426	•		•	•	•	•			•	•	•			•	•	•	•	•	AATA
Shepherd College, Shepherdstown 25443			•	•	•	•			•	•	•					•		•	AIGA
W. Liberty State College, West Liberty 26074			•	•		•		•	•	•						•			
W. Virginia State College, Institute 25112		•	•	•		•		•	•	•	•					•		•	
W. Virginia U., Morgantown 26506			•	•		•			•	•						•			NASA, ASID
WISCONSIN																			
Beloit College, Beloit 53511	•		•	•		•			•					•	•		•		
Carroll College, Waukesha 53186			•	•		•		•	•	•						•	•	•	
Carthage College, Kenosha 53141			•	•		•			•	•						•			
Lawrence U., Appleton 54912	•		•	•		•								•	•	•			
Marian College, Fond du Lac 54935			•	•		•		•	•			•							
Milwaukee Inst. of Art, Milwaukee 53202						•		•	•	•	•	•	•			•			AIGA
Mount Mary College, Milwaukee 53222					•		•						•			•			ASID, AATA
Ripon College, Ripon 54971		•	•						•	•									
St. Norbert College, De Pere 54115			•	•					•	•	•					•		•	
Silver Lake College, Manitowoc 54220			•	•		•			•										
U. of Wisconsin at Eau Claire, 54701			•	•		•			•	•									
— at Green Bay, 54302			•	•		•			•	•						•		•	
— at La Crosse, 54601			•	•		•			•	•									
— at Madison, 53706				•	•	•	•	•	•	•	•		•	•		•		•	ASLA, ASID, AIGA
— at Milwaukee, 53201		•	•	•	•	•	•	•	•	•	•	•	•			•		•	NAAB, AIGA
— at Oshkosh, 54901	•		•	•		•			•	•	•		•			•			AIGA
— at Parkside, Kenosha 54141			•	•		•		•	•	•						•			
— at Platteville 53818			•	•		•		•	•	•									
— at River Falls, 54022			•	•		•		•	•	•					•	•	•		

	Administration/Management	Architecture	Art History	Art Education	Art Therapy	Crafts/Fabrics	Fashion Design/Illustration	Film/Television/Video	Fine Arts	Graphic Design/Advertising	Illustration	Industrial Design	Interior Design	Landscape Architecture	Museum Work/Conservation	Photography	Medical Illustration	Theater Arts/Stage	Associations
WISCONSIN																			
—— at Stevens Point, 54481			•	•	•				•				•						ASID
—— at Stout, Menomonie 54751			•	•	•	•			•	•	•		•						ASID
—— at Superior, 54880			•	•	•	•			•	•	•					•		•	AATA, AIGA
—— White Water, 53190			•	•	•	•	•	•	•				•			•		•	AIGA
Viterbo College, La Crosse 54601			•	•	•					•	•					•			AIGA
WYOMING																			
Central Wyoming College, Riverton 83501		•		•					•							•		•	
Teton Inst. of Art and Photography, Jackson 83001		•	•	•					•										
U. of Wyoming, Laramie 82071		•		•					•	•									AIGA
CANADA																			
ALBERTA																			
Alberta College of Art, Calgary T2M 0L4		•		•		•	•	•	•							•			AIGA
Banff Center, Sch. of Fine Arts, Banff T0L 0C0				•					•							•	•		
Mount Royal College, Calgary T3E 6K6		•	•	•					•		•		•			•			
U. of Alberta, Edmonton T6G 2C9		•							•	•		•				•			AIGA
U. of Calgary, Calgary T2N 1N4		•	•	•					•							•			RAIC
U. of Lethbridge, Lethbridge T1K 3M4		•	•	•					•							•			
BRITISH COLUMBIA																			
Kootenay Sch. of Art, Nelson V1L 3C7	•		•	•		•	•	•	•	•	•					•			
U. of British Columbia, Vancouver V6T 1W5		•	•	•				•	•							•			RAIC
U. of Victoria, Victoria V8W 2Y2		•							•							•			
MANITOBA																			
U. of Manitoba, Winnipeg R3T 2N2		•	•	•					•	•	•		•			•			FIDER, RAIC, AIGA
NEW BRUNSWICK																			
Mount Allison U., Sackville E0A 3C0		•							•							•			
U. de Moncton, Moncton E1A 3E9		•	•	•					•	•	•					•	•		
U. of New Brunswick, Fredericton E3B 5A3		•		•					•										
NOVA SCOTIA																			
U. of Nova Scotia College of Art & Design, Halifax B3J 3J6		•	•	•		•	•									•			
Nova Scotia Tech. College, Halifax B3J 2X4	•	•							•	•			•	•	•	•			RAIC
St. Francis Xavier U., Antigonish		•	•	•					•					•					
ONTARIO																			
Artists' Workshop, Toronto M5S 2M7		•				•	•	•	•	•	•					•			AIGA
Carleton U., Ottawa K1S 5B6	•	•																	RAIC
McMaster U., Hamilton L8S 4M2		•							•										
New Sch. of Art, Toronto M5S 2M7		•		•		•	•									•			
Ontario College of Art, Toronto M5T 1W1	•	•		•		•	•	•	•	•	•	•				•	•	•	
Queens U., Kingston K7L 3N6		•	•						•					•	•				
St. Lawrence College of Applied Art, Cornwall K6H 4Z1		•		•					•	•	•					•			
Toronto Sch. of Art, Toronto M5S 2M6		•	•	•					•		•					•			
U. of Guelph, Guelph N1G 2W1		•							•										
U. of Ottawa, Ottawa K1N 6N5	•	•		•				•	•							•			
U. of Toronto, Toronto	•	•	•						•										RAIC
U. of Waterloo, Waterloo N2L 3G1		•		•		•	•				•					•	•	•	
U of Western Ontario, London N6C 1E9		•							•							•			
U. of Windsor, Windsor N9B 3P4		•		•					•										
York U., Downsview M3J 1P3		•						•	•	•	•								AIGA
PRINCE EDWARD ISLAND																			
Holland College Sch. of Visual Arts, Charlottetown C1A 7N8		•	•	•		•			•	•	•		•			•		•	

	Administration/Management	Architecture	Art History	Art Education	Art Therapy	Crafts/Fabrics	Fashion Design/Illustration	Film/Television/Video	Fine Arts	Graphic Design/Advertising	Illustration	Industrial Design	Interior Design	Landscape Architecture	Museum Work/Conservation	Photography	Medical Illustration	Theater Arts/Stage	Associations
QUEBEC																			
Concordia U., Montreal H3G 1M8		•	•		•		•	•		•	•	•				•	•		
Loyola of Montreal, Montreal H4B 1R2		•	•					•		•	•					•			
McGill U., Montreal H3A 2T6	•	•	•																RAIC
Sir George Williams Campus, Montreal H3G 1M8		•	•		•		•	•		•						•	•		
U. de Montreal, Montreal H3C 3J7	•	•						•	•								•		RAIC
U. de Quebec, Trois Rivières G9A 5H7		•	•		•				•										NASA
U. Laval, Quebec G1K 7P4	•	•	•			•			•	•	•					•			RAIC, AIGA
SASKATCHEWAN																			
U. of Regina, Regina S4S 0A2		•	•		•		•	•											
U. of Saskatchewan, Saskatoon S7N 0W0		•	•		•			•											

Index

Today's students learn traditional sculpture techniques in classes such as this. Life-sized clay figures are built up over wood or metal armatures. Photograph: Kent State University

Acknowledgements

In the fourteen months it took to compile all the illustrations, photographs and interviews necessary to authenticate and complete this book, we contacted many dozens of people for help. Top designers, artists, architects, photographers, and craftspeople responded with the photographs and information we needed. We especially want to thank the following for their generous help and encouragement:

Frank Ackerman (Los Angeles County Museum of Natural History), Joan Allemand (Beverly Hills Unified School District), Roger Armstrong (Walt Disney Productions), Ed Benguiat (International Typeface Corporation), Terri Berkowitz (Professional Photographers of America), Stephen Bieck, Wesley Bloom, Commander William Booth (LAPD), Lisa Ott Bottom, Harold Burch, Christopher M. Carr, Richard Challis (Challis Galleries), Penny Darras-Maxwell, Beverly Jeanne Davis (NAEA), M. Stephen Doherty (Editor, *American Artist*), David Ellington (Editor, *Industrial Design*), Claire Falkenstein, Charles Ford (Ford Motor Co.), Jack Fox (Mattel Toys), Susanne Frantz (Curator, Tucson Museum of Art), Charles Gibilterra, Glenda Gilkey, Gretchen Goldie (Bright and Agate), William Gorman (Old Bergen Art Guild), Howard Green (Walt Disney Studios).

Also: Jason Hailey, Douglas Halbert (Honda of America), Michael Hager, Alice Hall, Corinne Hartley (Albert W. Hellenthal Advertising, Inc.), Joseph Henry (Director, Art Center College of Design), Neil Hoffman (Dean, Otis Art Institute of Parsons School of Design), Roger Hohendahl, George Horn, Robert Hopkins (American Yearbook Co.), Betje and E. Bruce Howell, Cheryl Hughes, Glen Johnson (Foster-Kleiser, Inc.), William J. Knight (General Motors Corp.), William Kovacs (Abel and Assoc.), Pat Kreamer, Dick Lloyd (Coca Cola, Los Angeles), Jacqueline Little (The Art Directors Club, Inc.), Mindy Machanic, George Magnan (Editor, *Design Drafting & ReproGraphics*), Said Mehrinfar, Tressa Miller, Gretta Moore, Deborah Morosini (ASID), Joseph Mugnaini, Eric Myer, Patrick Nagatani, Louis Newman (Louis Newman Galleries), Michael Novarese.

Also: Robert Peterson (Robert Peterson Design, Fernando Ponce (LAPD), Noel Quinn, Robert W. Read (Fitzhenry & Whiteside, Ltd.), Bill Robles, Gill Saben (Steve Chase Associates), Teri Sandison, Julius Schulman, Bill Singer (Josten's Inc.), Myrna Smoot (Los Angeles County Museum of Art), Jack Solomen (Solomen & Coart), Sony Corporation of America, Lorenzo Tedesco, Wayne Thom, Pat Topping, Gillian Tosky (Society of Illustrators), Linda Umgelter (Chaix & Johnson Architects), Rosalie Utterbach (Woodbury University), Emmet L. Wemple and Associates, Willardson and White Studios, and Natham Zackheim.